BUSINESS ETHICS
Concepts and Cases

Manuel G. Velasquez
The University of Santa Clara

Prentice-Hall, Inc., Englewood Cliffs, N.J. 07632

Library of Congress Cataloging in Publication Data
VELASQUEZ, MANUEL G.
   Business ethics.
   Includes bibliographical references and index.
     1. Business ethics.   2. Business ethics–Case studies.
I. Title.
HF5387.V44   174'.4   81-17690
ISBN   0-13-096008-X   AACR2

For My Father

Editorial production/supervision
by Peter Roberts
Cover design by Mark A. Binn
Manufacturing buyer: Harry P. Baisley

Printed in the United States of America
10   9   8

ISBN 0-13-096008-X

PRENTICE-HALL INTERNATIONAL, INC., *LONDON*
PRENTICE-HALL OF AUSTRALIA PTY. LIMITED, *SYDNEY*
PRENTICE-HALL OF CANADA, LTD., *TORONTO*
PRENTICE-HALL OF INDIA PRIVATE LIMITED, *NEW DELHI*
PRENTICE-HALL OF JAPAN, INC., *TOKYO*
PRENTICE-HALL OF SOUTHEAST ASIA PTE. LTD., *SINGAPORE*
WHITEHALL BOOKS LIMITED, *WELLINGTON, NEW ZEALAND*

CONTENTS

PREFACE

Authors of texts on business ethics are spared from beginning with the usual apologies for bringing another text into an overcrowded field. For in spite of a tremendous surge of interest in business ethics, remarkably few book-length discussions of ethical issues in business have appeared in print. This book and others like it, I hope, will begin to fill this unfortunate void. The primary aims of this text can be easily summarized. They are: (1) to introduce the reader to the ethical concepts that are relevant to resolving moral issues in business; (2) to impart the reasoning and analytical skills needed to apply ethical concepts to business decisions; (3) to identify the moral issues involved in the management of specific problem areas in business; (4) to provide an understanding of the social and natural environments within which moral issues in business arise; and (5) to supply case studies of actual moral dilemmas faced by businesses.

Although the author of a text on business ethics does not need to apologize for writing on this subject, he or she does owe readers at least some indication of the normative assumptions that underlie what he or she has written. In the hopes of partially discharging this debt and in order to outline the structure of this book, I will describe its major parts and the main assumptions underlying each part.

The text is divided into four parts, each containing two chapters. Part One provides an introduction to basic ethical theory. My central assumption here is that in the absence of any moral standards we humans would be in the kind of situation that the seventeenth century philosopher Thomas Hobbes called a "state of nature"; that is, a situation in which there is nothing to moderate the self-interested competition that Hobbes aptly called "a war of every man against every man." In order to advance one's aims in such normless situations each individual must strive to overcome every other individual. Yet the havoc this striving creates is itself destructive of those aims. Thus, by striving to protect their private interests in the absence of any moral standards, people are led to act collectively in ways that actually harm those interests. Moral standards allow us to break out of these kinds of dilemmas, because they alone provide the basis for the trust and cooperation on which social institutions can be erected.

The central idea in Part One, therefore, is that moral standards serve the function of lifting us out of the dilemmas posed by normlessness and thereby leave us all better off than we would be without them. I elaborate this idea in Chapter 1, where I also indicate how we come to accept these moral standards and how such standards govern our moral reasoning. Chapter 2 critically discusses three kinds of moral principles: utilitarian principles, principles based on moral rights, and principles of justice. These three kinds of moral principles each provide a partial solution to the dilemmas created by normlessness, and they lie at the basis of most of our own moral reasoning. They can therefore legitimately serve as the criteria for resolving the ethical dilemmas raised in our business world.

Having defined the social functions of moral standards and having identified three basic criteria for resolving moral issues in business, I then bring the resulting theory to bear on specific moral issues. Thus, Part Two examines the ethics of markets and prices; Part Three discusses environmental and consumer issues; and Part Four looks at employee issues. I assume in each part that in order to apply a moral theory to the real world we must have some information (and theory) about what that world is really like. Consequently, each chapter in these last three parts devotes several pages to laying out the empirical information that the decision-maker must have if he or she is to apply morality to reality. The chapter on market ethics, for example, provides a neoclassical analysis of market structure; the chapter on discrimination presents several statistical and institutional indicators of discrimination; the chapter on the individual in the organization relies on two models of organizational structure.

Each chapter of the text contains two kinds of materials. The main body of the chapter sets out the conceptual materials needed to understand some particular moral issue. This is followed by discussion cases that describe real business situations in which these moral issues are raised. I have provided these discussion cases on the assumption that a person's ability to reason about moral matters will improve if the person attempts to think through some concrete moral problems and allows himself or herself to be challenged by others who resolve the issue on the basis of different moral standards. These kinds of challenges force us to confront the adequacy of our moral norms and motivate us to search for more adequate principles when our own are shown to be inadequate. I hope that I have provided sufficient materials to allow the reader to develop a set of ethical norms that he or she can finally accept as adequate.

ACKNOWLEDGMENTS

I would like to acknowledge my gratitude to these publications for permission to reprint the following materials:

Excerpt on pages 313 and 314 is from *All the Livelong Day: The Meaning and Demeaning of Routine Work* by Barbara Garson. Copyright © 1973 by Barbara Garson. Reprinted by permission of Doubleday & Company, Inc.

Graphics on page 208 are from *The Limits to Growth: A Report for the Club of Rome's Project on the Predicament of Mankind,* by Donella H. Meadows, Dennis L. Meadows, Jorgen Randers, William W. Buhrens III. A Potomac Associates book published by Universe Books, N.Y., 1972. Graphics by Potomac Associates.

Excerpts on pages 136 and 137 are from *Newsweek,* August 13, 1979. Copyright © 1979 by Newsweek, Inc. All rights reserved. Reprinted by permission.

Excerpt on page 142 is from *The New York Times,* June 9, 1979. Copyright © 1979 by the New York Times Company. Reprinted by permission.

Excerpts on pages 99 and 100 are from Timothy Smith, "South Africa: The Churches vs. the Corporations." Reprinted by permission from *Business and Society Review,* Fall, 1975. Copyright © 1975 by Warren, Gorham and Lamont, Inc., 210 South Street, Boston, Mass. All rights reserved.

Excerpts on page 99 are from Timothy Smith, "Whitewash for Apartheid from Twelve U.S. Firms," *Business and Society Review,* Summer, 1977, pp. 59-60. Reprinted by permission from *Business and Society Review,* Fall 1975, Number 150. Copyright © 1975 by Warren, Gorham and Lamont, Inc., 210 South Street, Boston, Mass. All rights reserved.

Excerpts on pages 136, 142, 143 are from *The Wall Street Journal,* February 6, 1978, September 21, 1978, April 24, 1978, December 3, 1979, July 2, 1980, May 27, 1980. Reprinted by permission of *The Wall Street Journal,* copyright © Dow Jones & Company, Inc., 1978, 1979, 1980. All rights reserved.

Excerpt on page 36 is from "Why Should My Conscience Bother Me?" by Kermit Vandivier from *In the Name of Profit,* edited by Robert L. Heilbroner. Copyright © 1972 by Doubleday & Company, Inc. Reprinted by permission of Doubleday & Company, Inc. It is understood and agreed that there are no stated or implied warranties being extended from Doubleday with respect to this material.

Excerpts on pages 301, 302, 318, and 331 are from *Working: People Talk About What They Do All Day and How They Feel About What They Do,* by Studs Terkel. Copyright © 1974 by Studs Terkel. Reprinted by permission of Pantheon Books, a Division of Random House, Inc.

*   *   *

Like any other textbook author, I owe a large debt to the innumerable writers from whom I have shamelessly borrowed ideas and materials. I hope that I have redeemed myself sufficiently by giving due credit for my borrowings in the notes. I also owe special thanks to the many people who were kind enough to read through parts of the manuscript and to suggest helpful changes, including Gerald Cavanagh, William Frederick, Kirk Hanson, James Reites, Charles Phipps, Robert Senkewicz, Paul Locatelli, and Carol White.

My debts extend also to the hundreds of patient students who passed through my courses in business ethics during the last five years and who have been subjected to various manuscript versions of this text. I am especially thankful to those students whose own research uncovered materials that I subsequently incorporated into the case studies, including Blake Smith, Lynn Warren, and Sherrie Gong. My thanks also to Shiela Speciale, who for the past several years has patiently typed and retyped one revised version of the text after another. And, finally, my thanks to the Jesuit community at the University of Santa Clara who supported me throughout the writing of this book.

Manuel Velasquez
September, 1981

PART ONE
BASIC PRINCIPLES

Business ethics is applied ethics. It is the application of our understanding of what is good and right to that assortment of institutions, technologies, transactions, activities, and pursuits which we call "Business." A discussion of business ethics must begin by providing a framework of basic principles for understanding what is meant by the terms "good" and "right"; only then can one proceed to profitably discuss the implications these have for our business world. The first two chapters provide such a framework. Chapter One outlines some of the major moral issues that arise in business and describes what business ethics is in general. Chapter Two describes three approaches to ethical issues which together furnish a basis for analyzing ethical issues in business.

CHAPTER ONE
ETHICS
AND MORAL
REASONING

INTRODUCTION

Large-scale business organizations staffed by professional managers stand at the heart of today's Western societies. In capitalist countries they are called "corporations"; socialists refer to them as "enterprises." By whatever name, these modern organizations have created some of the central moral controversies of our age; controversies with which their professional managers must deal.[1]

First, there are the moral issues raised by the "external" effects that these organizations have had on the larger society. Because these organizations are large, their effects are large and the voices that protest them are loud. Consumer groups accuse businesses of immorally neglecting safety standards and of manipulating wants through advertising. Citizens' groups point to the foreign bribes and illegal campaign contributions by which various businesses have attempted to influence political processes around the world. And environmentalists claim that business growth policies have consumed our wild lands, forests, and natural resources while creating a major and potentially catastrophic pollution crisis.

Yet professional managers are often unsure how to deal with these moral issues. For example, during the 1940s Hooker Chemical Inc. used a trench called the

---

[1] A compact summary of many of these moral issues is contained in Clarence C. Walton, "The Executive Ethic," in *The Ethics of Corporate Conduct,* ed. Clarence Walton (Englewood Cliffs, N.J.: Prentice-Hall, Inc., 1977), pp. 173–211. A bibliography on these and other issues is Donald J. Jones, *A Bibliography of Business Ethics, 1971–1975* (Charlottesville, Va.: University Press of Virginia, 1977).

"Love Canal" outside the city of Niagara Falls, New York to dispose of 22,000 tons of chemical wastes, some of which were highly toxic and others of which were carcinogenic. Using the latest technology, the wastes were sealed within the trench and covered over. In 1952 the Love Canal property was sold to the city of Niagara Falls, since it was then thought that the wastes would remain safely underground indefinitely. The city used the property to build a school and a park, and sold the rest for residential housing. In 1958, Mr. Jerome Wilkenfeld, a technical manager for Hooker Chemical, learned that the chemical wastes might be migrating out of the trench. In his own words:

> On Monday, June 16, [1958], I received a call . . . that three or four children had been burned by material at the old Love Canal property which had been deeded to the school board several years ago. [Two of our employees] visited the area that afternoon and reported that road construction [was] being carried out . . . north of the area where we had been dumping. They did notice that in the northerly portion of the tract the ground had subsided and the ends of some drums which may have been thionyl residue drums were exposed and south of the school there is an area where benzene hexachloride spent cake was exposed. It [was] their feeling that if children had been burned it was probably by getting in contact with this material. . . . It was also noted that the entire area [was] being used by children as a playground even though not officially designed for that purpose. . . . However, we did not own the property. On the advice of counsel, we could not go in and do anything that the school board did not request us to do. [We managers had] discussions on many occasions about the problem. We always felt that it was necessary to work with the public authorities who had the title and ownership of it in developing the proper solutions. It was my understanding that the people who lived in the area knew that this was a former chemical dump and that these materials were hazardous and that the children should not get in there. . . . [But] we did not feel that we could [inform the people who lived adjacent to the Love Canal dump site of what the hazards to their health were] without incurring substantial liabilities for implying that the current owners of the property were doing inadequate care on the property.[2]

Caught in this dilemma, Hooker's managers decided to do nothing. Twenty-five years later they are now accused of immorally endangering the lives and health of children and residents who are alleged to have suffered a variety of birth defects, nerve diseases, respiratory illnesses, miscarriages, and possibly death from exposure to chemicals spilling out of the Love Canal trench. But in 1958 Jerome Wilkenfeld and his fellow managers were unsure where their ethical loyalties lay. Where did they lie?

A second kind of moral issue has been created by the "internal" conflicts that business organizations create among their own members. One set of problems

---

[2]U.S., Congress, House, *Hazardous Waste Disposal: Hearings before the Subcommittee on Oversight and Investigations of the Committee on Interstate and Foreign Commerce,* 96th Congress, 1st session, 21 and 22 March; 5 and 10 April; 16, 23, and 30 May; 1, 4, 5, 15, 18, and 19 June 1979, pp. 651, 653, and 665.

arises out of the competing demands made by business's internal constituencies. Stockholders, for example, sometimes complain that the officers and directors of corporations make unethical use of their funds. Employees accuse managers of being negligent in their moral duty to care for the safety of their employees and of recklessly exposing them to potentially lethal chemical substances. Civil rights groups declare that the hiring and promotion policies of many businesses discriminate against minorities and women, thereby violating their moral rights to equality.

But with the many demands being placed on them, managers sometimes see no fair way of balancing these conflicting interests. Jim Grimaldi, for example, is a projects manager in the Sunnyvale division of Universal Corporation.[3] He supervises several engineering groups, most of whose projects involve automotive brake design. These contracts have tight deadlines and allow only extremely narrow margins for error. As a consequence, his engineering groups often have to work at maximum speed and under great pressure. Each group is supervised by a "project engineer." Let Grimaldi speak in his own words:

> A couple of months ago I was sent a new engineer from our plant in Los Angeles, Joan Dreer, and told to put her to work right away as a project engineer. The company was making a push to move women into all company levels but had apparently run into a lot of problems with their engineers down in Los Angeles. They had decided that our place would have the fewest problems adjusting to women and they were pretty insistent that we find a way to work things out. When I first took Joan around our plant so she could get to know the men and the kind of work we do, several of the engineers took me aside and let me know in no uncertain terms that they didn't want a new woman to supervise their work. To make matters worse, Joan came on as a pushy and somewhat aggressive feminist. When one of the young engineers asked her if she was a "Miss" or a "Mrs." she retorted that her private life was her own affair and that he should get used to calling her "Ms."

Jim soon found that Joan had trouble with the project groups she supervised. The groups did not outrightly refuse to work, but dragged their feet in small ways so that they sometimes missed their deadlines. The other groups were also reluctant to cooperate with her group. Consequently, Jim became increasingly concerned about the impact Joan Dreer's presence would have on his ability to meet the deadlines he was given and what this would mean to his own career. He was also worried about the safety factor that brake design involved:

> I agree that it's important to move women into supervisory positions in the company, but I don't know whether we can really afford to do it just yet. I don't want to fire any of my engineers. That would be unfair since they have worked hard for us in the past under a lot of pressure. What should I do?

A third set of moral dilemmas arises out of conflicts between the employee's own aims and values on the one hand, and the objectives and policies of the organization on the other. The organization, for example, might insist on a production

---

[3]The statements in this case were pieced together from interviews with two engineers. There is no "Universal Corporation."

schedule that the manager is afraid will result in defective and perhaps dangerous products. Or the organization might ask the manager to investigate its employees in a way that the manager thinks is an invasion of their right to privacy. Or the employee may find himself or herself in an organization whose practices seem inimical to the best interests of the people the organization serves. Again, a real case may best illustrate the dilemma.

Kate Simpson had been working for the Atlanta branch of Lawton Medical Financing, Inc. (a small investment banking firm specializing in loans to medical groups) for one week.[4] Besides the two secretaries, the Atlanta branch consisted of three professionals: Kate Simpson, who planned on returning to graduate business school in six months and who was hired to help out in whatever capacity was needed; David Moore, an intelligent, affable, and energetic senior vice president who combined a pragmatic business streak with a strong moral sense; and Bill Hillman, a youngish vice president, who had been transferred from New York to the Atlanta branch four months before and who was outspoken about his intent to make Atlanta his permanent home. On Wednesday before leaving town, David had asked Kate to help him advise a hospital in Nashville that wanted to choose a consultant to study the purchase of a new facility. She was to review the proposals of the four consultants who were submitting bids. On Friday, when David returned, they were to meet with the hospital's board of directors to advise them on the proposals. Of the three bids she had received by Thursday noon, the one by Roberts and Company had emerged as the best study for the least amount of money:

> I happened to go into Bill Hillman's office and found him on the phone talking to Thomas Rice, the fourth consultant whose office was in the same building, and whose bid was due in a few hours. Bill was about to hang up as I entered: "Fine, Tom. You owe me one now," he was saying, "but don't worry about it. Good luck getting the thing cranked out by five." Bill looked up and saw me as he slid a copy of the Roberts and Company proposal into an envelope. "Tom Rice really likes to run it down to the wire," he said. "Tom's just finishing their hospital proposal. I told him we'd let him glance at Robert's version of the thing. Why don't you run it upstairs for him? You can wait and make sure we get it back." As I headed for the elevator I was furious with Bill for having placed me in the position of carrying a competitor's bid to Thomas Rice. But I had only a few moments to decide what I should do.

Thus, the ethical dilemmas that business organizations often present for their managers are not trivial. Nor are they avoidable. We cannot live without our business organizations because we cannot live without the large-scale production that these organizations make possible.[5] We have no choice but to face the ethical issues raised by our business institutions and attempt to deal with them.

---

[4] These materials are based on a case prepared by Cara F. Jonassen as a basis for class discussion rather than to illustrate either effective or ineffective handling of an administrative situation. The names of the individuals and the companies involved have been changed. With the permission of the author, Cara F. Jonassen.

[5] See Alfred D. Chandler, Jr., *The Visible Hand* (Cambridge: Harvard University Press, Belknap Press, 1977), pp. 6–12 and passim.

This text directly addresses the moral dilemmas that the managers of modern business organizations must face. This does not mean that it is designed to give moral advice to people in business nor that it is aimed at persuading people to act in certain "moral" ways. The main purpose of the text is to provide a deeper knowledge of the nature of ethical principles and concepts and an understanding of how these apply to the moral problems encountered in business. This type of knowledge and understanding should help managers like Wilkenfeld, Grimaldi, and Simpson see their way through the moral issues raised by their professions.

These first two chapters will begin by introducing the reader to some basic ethical principles, concepts, and methods of reasoning that can be used to analyze moral issues in business. The following chapters will then apply these principles and methods to the kinds of moral issues we have been discussing. Chapter Five, for example, analyzes the kinds of pollution issues with which Wilkenfeld had to deal; Chapter Seven deals with affirmative action issues such as the one Grimaldi faced; and Chapter Eight discusses the kinds of organizational dilemmas with which Simpson had to struggle. The reader may find it helpful to return to these "cases" when reading those chapters.

1.1 THE NATURE OF ETHICS

In 1968, Raymond Baumhart published a study of 100 businessmen who were asked, "What does *ethical* mean to you?" Typical of their replies were the following:[6]

—Before coming to the interview, to make sure that I knew what we would talk about, I looked up *ethics* in my dictionary. I read it and can't understand it. I don't know what the concept means. . . .

—*Ethical* is what my feelings tell me is right. But this is not a fixed standard, and that makes problems.

—*Ethical* means accepted standards in terms of your personal and social welfare; what you believe is right. But what confuses me . . . is the possibility that I have been misguided, or that somebody else has been poorly educated. Maybe each of us thinks he knows what is ethical, but we differ. How can you tell who is right then?

Fifty percent of the businessmen Baumhart interviewed defined "ethical" as "what my feelings tell me is right"; twenty-five percent defined it in religious terms as what is "in accord with my religious beliefs"; and eighteen percent defined "ethical" as what "conforms to 'the golden rule' ."[7] Yet feelings are a notoriously inadequate basis on which to make decisions of *any* sort and religious authority and

[6] Raymond Baumhart, *An Honest Profit; What Businessmen Say About Ethics in Business* (New York: Holt, Rinehart and Winston, 1968), pp. 11–12.

[7] *Ibid.,* p. 13.

the "golden rule" have been rather devastatingly criticized as inadequate foundations for ethical claims.[8] What then do "ethics" and "ethical" mean?

In popular usage the term "ethics" has a variety of different meanings. One of the meanings often given to it is: the principles of conduct governing an individual or a group.[9] We use the term "personal ethics," for example, to refer to the rules by which an individual lives his or her personal life, and use the term "accounting ethics" to refer to the code that guides the professional conduct of accountants.

Ethicians, however, use the term "ethics" to refer primarily to a theoretical study, just as chemists use the term "chemistry" to refer to a theoretical study of the properties of the elements and their compounds.[10]

The subject matter of ethics, however, differs in an important way from the subject matter of a natural science like chemistry. Whereas the natural sciences are concerned with the study of physical objects, ethics is concerned with the moral judgments involved in moral decisions. Suppose, for example, that I am trying to decide whether to lie on my income tax, and part of what makes me hesitant about lying is my belief that lying is wrong. Then my decision is a moral decision (that is, a decision that raises moral issues) and the judgment that lying is wrong is the moral judgment involved in this decision.

In order to understand what a moral judgment is we must begin by understanding what "normative judgments" are, since moral judgments are special kinds of normative judgments.

Normative Judgments

Normative judgments are claims that state or imply that something is good or bad, right or wrong, better or worse, ought to be or ought not to be.[11] Normative judgments, therefore, express values: They indicate a person's favorable or unfavorable attitude toward some state of affairs. The following are examples of normative judgments:

The Mona Lisa is a beautiful painting.
Your office is tastefully furnished.
These figures are mistaken.
You made the wrong investment.
Free enterprise is the best economic system.

---

[8] See, for example, Richard B. Brandt's criticism of religious authority in *Ethical Theory* (Englewood Cliffs, NJ: Prentice-Hall, Inc., 1959); Craig C. Lundberg criticizes the golden rule in "The Golden Rule and Business Management: Quo Vadas?," *Journal of Economics and Business* 20 (January 1968): 36–40; and on emotion see Kurt Baier, *The Moral Point of View*, abr. ed. (New York: Random House, Inc., 1965), pp. 83–90.

[9] "Ethic," *Webster's Seventh New Collegiate Dictionary* (Springfield, MA: G. & C. Merriam Company, 1974), p. 392. Similar definitions can be found in any popular dictionary.

[10] Fred Feldman, *Introductory Ethics* (Englewood Cliffs, NJ: Prentice-Hall, Inc., 1978), pp. 9–15.

[11] William K. Frankena, *Ethics*, 2nd ed. (Englewood Cliffs, NJ: Prentice-Hall, Inc., 1973), pp. 9–11.

Pornography should be illegal.
Price-fixing is unfair.
Labor unions violate management's rights.
You have an obligation to keep your word.
You should add eggs after the flour.

Because normative judgments express values, they usually carry some implications concerning the kind of conduct with which humans should respond to a situation. If I claim that a certain novel is "good," for example, I am implying that people should seek it, buy it, or read it. Normative judgments, therefore, are "action guiding": They usually are intended to influence human behavior in the present or in the future.

Nonnormative judgments, on the other hand, are value-neutral.[12] They describe, name, define, report, and make predictions concerning a certain state of affairs. They are not, however, intended to assert that the state of affairs is good or bad, right or wrong. Nonnormative judgments are not meant to imply a favorable or unfavorable attitude toward a given state of affairs, nor are they usually intended to guide human action with respect to that state of affairs. The following statements are examples of nonnormative judgments:

The Mona Lisa is an Italian painting.
Your office is furnished with a desk and a chair.
These figures do not match the auditor's.
Your investment lost money.
Free enterprise means different things to different people.
Pornography is illegal in certain states.
Many Americans believe that price-fixing is unfair.
Labor unions frequently disagree with management.
Most people believe a person should keep his or her word.
The recipe says the eggs should be added after the flour.

Of course, in certain contexts some of these "nonnormative statements" can be used to express normative judgments. When I say, for example, "Your investment lost money," I may intend this to mean, "You made the wrong investment." Some statements are ambiguous: They can be interpreted as either normative or nonnormative, depending on what the statement is taken to imply or is intended to imply in the context in which it is uttered. To determine whether a statement is normative or nonnormative one must determine whether it is merely meant to *describe* a certain state of affairs, or whether it is also meant to *prescribe* certain behavior vis-à-vis that state of affairs. Normative judgments are "prescriptive" whereas nonnormative judgments are simply "descriptive."

[12]*Ibid.*, p. 4.

Moral Judgments

Ethics does not study all normative judgments, only those that are concerned with what is *morally* right and wrong, or *morally* good and bad. To understand what this means, it may help to see that normative terms such as "right" and "wrong" or "good" and "bad" are generally applied on the basis of some explicit or implicit standards or criteria.[13] The standards may be *legal,* as when we judge that it is legally wrong to drive on the left side of a street because a state law prohibits this; or the standards may be *grammatical,* as when we judge that it is grammatically right to end sentences with prepositions because English grammar now permits this usage; or the standards may be *aesthetic,* as when we judge that *Moby Dick* is aesthetically good because it meets the aesthetic standards of art critics.

When something is judged to be *morally* right or wrong, or *morally* good or bad, the underlying standards on which the judgment is based are *moral* standards. Moral standards include both specific moral norms and more general moral principles. Moral norms are standards of behavior that require, prohibit, or allow certain specific kinds of behavior.[14] Prohibitions against lying, stealing, injuring, and so on, are all moral norms. Moral principles, on the other hand, are much more general standards that are used to evaluate the adequacy of our social policies and institutions as well as of individual behavior.[15] Examples of such principles would include principles of *rights,* which evaluate policies, institutions, and behavior in terms of the protection they provide for the interests and freedoms of individuals; principles of *justice,* which evaluate policies, institutions, and behavior in terms of how equitably they distribute benefits and burdens among the members of a group; and principles of *utility,* which evaluate policies, institutions, and behavior in terms of the net social benefits they produce. These three kinds of principles will be fully discussed in the next chapter.

When, then, does a decision raise ethical issues or when does it "involve" ethical issues? A decision raises (or involves) ethical issues when there is a question concerning whether or not the decision violates any moral standards. Analysis may show, of course, that the decision is perfectly consistent with all relevant moral standards: To say that a decision raises ethical issues does not mean that the decision is *immoral,* only that there is some reason to examine more closely whether it does or does not conform to some moral standard.

[13] This common view may be found in writers as diverse as Baier, *Moral Point of View,* pp. 8–26; and R. M. Hare, *The Language of Morals* (New York: Oxford University Press, 1964), pp. 111–26.

[14] On the nature and development of norms see Arnold Birenbaum and Edward Sagarin, *Norms and Human Behavior* (New York: Praeger Publishers, Inc., 1976), pp. 1–29; and Muzafer Sherif, *The Psychology of Social Norms* (New York: Octagon Books, Inc., 1965), pp. 89–112.

[15] Sometimes moral principles also seem to be used to evaluate the moral worth of *persons* and of *intentions.* We can safely ignore these uses, however, because the evaluation of actions seems to be more basic: a "morally good" person is one who regularly *does* what is morally right, and a "good intention" is an intention to *do* what is morally right.

Moral Standards

How, exactly, are moral standards different from other kinds of standards? Although there is some controversy concerning precisely what the distinguishing characteristics of moral standards are, the following features are most often pointed to as some of their more important distinguishing characteristics, and should thus give us a picture of moral standards clear enough for our purposes.

First, moral standards deal with matters that are (or are thought to be) of serious consequence to our human well-being.[16] That is, they are concerned with behavior that can seriously injure or seriously benefit human beings (or that is believed to be capable of having these consequences). The moral norm prohibiting price-fixing, for example, rests on the belief that price-fixing imposes serious injuries upon consumers; whereas the moral principle that employees have a moral right to collective bargaining rests on the belief that this right protects a critical interest of employees. The moral norms against lying, rape, enslavement, murder, theft, child-abuse, assault, slander, fraud, and so on, all plainly deal with forms of behavior that can cause serious injury to human beings. Thus the *seriousness* of moral standards sets them off from standards which deal with matters that are not as critically connected to our well-being, such as grammatical standards or rules of etiquette.

Secondly, moral standards cannot be established or changed by the decisions of particular authoritative bodies.[17] Laws and company codes for example, can be established and changed by the decisions of a legislature or of enfranchised voters and by the decisions of a company board of directors respectively. Moral standards are not made up by particular bodies, nor does their validity rest on the particular decisions of particular persons. The validity of moral standards rests, instead, on the adequacy of the reasons that are taken to support and justify them, and so long as these reasons are adequate the standards remain valid.

Thirdly, and perhaps most strikingly, moral standards are supposed to override self-interest.[18] That is, if a person has a moral obligation to do something, then the person is supposed to do it even if it is not in the person's own interests to do so. This is an obvious feature of the moral norms we commonly accept, such as the negative prohibitions on stealing, lying, and cheating, as well as the positive injunctions to be honest and to keep one's promises. We are supposed to adhere to these common moral norms even when (especially when?) contravening these norms would advance our own self-interest. A certified public accountant working for a corporation, for example, is commonly assumed to recognize that the accountant has an ethical duty to refrain from "knowingly misrepresent[ing] facts" (rule 102 of the AICPA Code of Professional Ethics) even when misrepresentation would make the boss look good and thereby lead to the accountant's career advancement.

[16] H.L.A. Hart, *The Concept of Law* (London: Oxford University Press, 1961), pp. 84–85. See also Charles Fried, *An Anatomy of Values* (Cambridge: Harvard University Press, 1970), pp. 91–142.

[17] See Baier, *Moral Point of View,* p. 88.

[18] The point is made in Michael Scriven, *Primary Philosophy* (New York: McGraw-Hill Book Company, 1966), p. 232–33.

(None of this means, obviously, that it is always unacceptable to act on self-interest, only that it is unacceptable when one's act is morally wrong.)

Fourthly, moral standards are based on impartial considerations.[19] The fact, for example, that my business will benefit from a bribe and that yours will lose from it, is irrelevant to whether or not bribery is morally wrong. Recent philosophers have expressed this point by saying that moral standards are based on "the moral point of view," that is, a point of view that does not evaluate standards according to whether or not they advance the interests of a particular individual or group, but that goes beyond personal interests to a "universal" standpoint in which everyone's interests are impartially counted as equal.[20] Other philosophers have made the same point by saying that moral standards are based on the kinds of impartial reasons that an "ideal observer" or an "impartial spectator" would accept, or that in deciding moral matters "each counts for one and none for more than one."[21]

Moral Standards and Society

We may gain a better understanding of moral standards if we note some of the important social functions they can serve. The members of a society typically adhere to a system of moral standards; a system, that is, of general ethical principles and related moral norms. The moral system of a society forbids certain behavior as wrong (such as, lying, stealing, and so on), and enjoins certain behavior as right (helping others, keeping one's promises). These moral standards serve several important functions, but two deserve special mention.[22]

First, a society's system of moral standards will identify situations in which each person must restrain his or her self-interest in order to secure a system of conduct that is mutually advantageous to everyone.[23] To more easily understand this function of moral standards, we can begin by noticing that it is not uncommon for a group of persons to find that self-interested (non-cooperative self-seeking) behavior is not always in each person's best interests. Take, for example, an army that is under attack. Suppose that if every soldier selflessly remains at his post, the army can easily turn back the attack; but if large numbers of soldiers desert, the attackers will slaughter the army and then catch and kill the deserters; and if only a few soldiers desert, the deserters will make it home safely while the rest will eventually be overcome. In such a situation, self-interest would tell every soldier that he should

---

[19] See, for example, Brandt, *Ethical Theory,* p. 250.

[20] Baier, *Moral Point of View,* p. 107.

[21] The point is made in Peter Singer, *Practical Ethics* (New York: Cambridge University Press, 1979), pp. 10–11.

[22] An important but perhaps obvious point should be made here: Neither of these functions is being offered as a *justification* of moral standards. They are simply intended to illustrate two important services that moral standards must be capable of performing.

[23] This, too, is a commonplace. See, J.L. Mackie, *Ethics: Inventing Right and Wrong* (New York: Penguin Books, 1977), pp. 105–24; Scriven, *Primary Philosophy,* pp. 238–59; Baier, *Moral Point of View,* pp. 155 and 106–9.

desert his post and be one of the few to escape safely to his home. But if every soldier tries to advance his private interests in this way, all of them will be killed. Thus, self-interested behavior is here not in every soldier's best interests. Paradoxically, the best interests of each soldier will be served only if each of them acts selflessly and remains at his post.

Although a society is not an army under attack (at least not usually), self-interested behavior within a society is, as with an army, not always in its members' best interests. In particular, a society whose members regularly cooperate in advancing socially beneficial goals even when this requires setting aside their immediate private interests, whose members leave each individual free to pursue his or her basic interests, and whose members share benefits and burdens in ways that are perceived as "fair" and "just," is a society that will have a much greater chance of surviving and flourishing than a society whose members act differently. In the first place, cooperation in advancing socially beneficial goals will produce a greater store of goods for all. In the second place, each individual will benefit from the respect shown for his or her interests when others leave the individual free to pursue those interests in peace and security. And in the third place, fairness and justice will provide the stability without which societies cannot long survive. The best interests of all members of a society will be served, therefore, if they do not always act out of self-interest. Just as the soldiers of an army under attack will survive only if each of them selflessly remains at his post, so will the members of a society also gain several major advantages (not the least of which is survival!) if each of its members selflessly restrains his or her self-interest and cooperates with others in the ways just described.

A major function of a society's moral standards is the prescription of specific ways in which the members of a society are to cooperate with each other, leave each other free, and deal fairly with each other. When everyone internalizes these moral standards and adheres to them in his or her conduct with others, the result is a productive, secure, and stable system of conduct that is in everyone's mutual best interests. Bankers, creditors, and consumers, for example, generally accept the moral norm of honesty in the business communications that pass between them millions of times each day, even when they have nothing to gain; and each of them in turn must depend upon everyone else's general acceptance of that norm. If dishonesty became a general practice in these daily business communications, our system of communication would collapse and our business system would fall with it. The norm of honesty is an internalized moral standard by which people generally restrain their self-interest and thereby cooperate to secure a system of communication that is in everyone's mutual best interests.

A second social function that moral standards serve is that they enable the resolution of social conflicts by providing publicly acceptable justifications for actions and policies.[24] To understand this second major function of moral standards,

---

[24] See John Rawls, *A Theory of Justice* (Cambridge: Harvard University Press, Belknap Press, 1971), pp. 4, 133, 582; see also Sir Patrick Devlin, *The Enforcement of Morals* (New York: Oxford University Press, 1965), pp. 6–10.

it will help if we begin by noting how *prudential claims* differ from *moral claims*. Prudential claims are based on self-interest: They take into account only the interests (desires, needs, aims) of the individual.[25] Moral claims, as we noted, are based on standards that go beyond a particular person's self-interests.

In any group of people, one or more persons often will want to do something beneficial to their self-interest but not to that of the others, that they will not be able to do unless they can persuade the others to let them do it or help them do it. As the owner of a factory, for example, I may want to burn coal that produces a high level of pollution. I will then have to find some way of persuading those other people upon whom the pollution will fall to allow me to do what I want. Or I may have to do a job that I cannot do alone and will have to find some way of persuading others to help me.

In situations of this sort, where a person must persuade others if he is to gain his end, prudential reasons will not be of much help. Other people will be persuaded only if I show them that the action is justified from a point of view that takes everyone's interests into account, not just my own. Moral standards provide such publicly acceptable considerations. By showing that I am morally entitled to carry out an action or that others are morally obligated to help me, I will be showing that my action is part of a system of conduct from which everyone benefits. As the owner of a pollution-generating factory, for example, I might claim that I have a moral right to generate pollution in my plant by virtue of the property rights I possess over that factory. And if it is clear that in the long run the individual's interests will best be protected by the recognition of people's property rights, then I will have succeeded in showing that my action is part of a system of conduct from which everyone benefits. By basing my position on moral standards I am, in effect, trying to justify my action from a point of view that impartially takes everyone's interests into account, and consequently from a point of view that is publicly acceptable.

It may be useful for us to summarize the discussion up to now. Ethics, we have been saying, is the study of a particular group of normative judgments: those judgments that are concerned with what is morally right and wrong, or morally good and bad. Judgments of moral right and wrong are based on standards that (1) deal with serious human injuries and benefits, (2) are not laid down by authoritative bodies, (3) override self-interest, and (4) are based on impartial considerations. Such standards can serve two important ends: When internalized they can help establish mutually beneficial systems of conduct, and they can provide publicly acceptable justifications for actions or policies.

Ethics differs from other inquiries such as the social sciences, which also study values.[26] Anthropologists and sociologists, for example, may study the moral beliefs of a particular village culture. In doing so, they attempt to develop accurate de-

[25] David P. Gauthier, *Practical Reasoning* (Oxford: The Clarendon Press, 1963), pp. 18–23; Marcus G. Singer, *Generalization in Ethics* (New York: Alfred A. Knopf, Inc., 1961), p. 220.
[26] See Frankena, *Ethics,* p. 4.

scriptions of the moral beliefs of that culture and perhaps even to formulate a descriptive theory about their structure. As anthropologists or sociologists, however, it is not their aim to determine whether or not these moral views are correct or incorrect. Ethics, on the other hand, is a study of moral standards whose explicit purpose is to determine as far as possible whether a given moral judgment is more or less correct. Whereas the sociologist asks, "Do Americans believe that bribery is wrong?," the ethician asks, "Is bribery wrong?" The ethician, then, is concerned with developing adequate *prescriptive* claims and theories, whereas an anthropological or sociological study of morality aims at being *descriptive*.

Business Ethics

This characterization of ethics has been intended to convey an idea of what the study of ethics encompasses. Our concern here, however, is not with ethics in general but with a particular field of ethics: *business* ethics.

Business ethics is a specialized study of moral right and wrong. It concentrates on how moral standards apply particularly to business policies, institutions, and behavior. A brief description of the nature of business institutions should make this clearer.

A society consists of people who have common ends and whose activities are organized by a system of institutions designed to achieve these ends. That men, women, and children have common ends is obvious. There is the common end of establishing, nurturing, and protecting family life; that of producing and distributing the materials on which human life depends; that of restraining and regularizing the use of force; that of organizing the means for making collective decisions; and that of creating and preserving cultural artifacts such as art, knowledge, and technology. The members of a society will achieve these ends by establishing the relatively fixed patterns of activity that we call "institutions": familial, economic, legal, political, and educational institutions.

The most significant institutions within contemporary societies are probably economic institutions. These are designed to achieve two ends: (1) production of the goods and services the members of society want and need, and (2) distribution of these goods and services to the various members of society. Thus, economic institutions determine who will carry out the work of production, how that work will be organized, what resources that work will consume, and how its products and benefits will be distributed among society's members.

Business enterprises are the primary economic institutions through which people in modern societies carry on the tasks of producing and distributing goods and services. They provide the fundamental structures within which the members of society combine their scarce resources—land, labor, capital, and technology—into usable goods, and they provide the channels through which these goods are distributed in the form of consumer products, employee salaries, investors' return, and government taxes. Mining, manufacturing, retailing, banking, marketing, transporting, insuring, constructing, and advertising are all different facets of the productive and distributive processes of our modern business institutions.

The most important kinds of modern business enterprises are corporations:

organizations that the law endows with special legal rights and powers. No one will deny that today large corporate organizations dominate our economies. In 1980 Exxon Corporation alone had sales of over $103 billion and held assets valued at $57 billion, while General Motors employed over 746,000 people. Of the world's 160 nations only eight have government budgets larger than Exxon's total sales revenues and only 30 have more workers engaged in manufacturing than General Motors does. About 50 percent of America's combined industrial profits and earnings are in the hands of about a hundred corporations, each of which has assets worth one billion dollars or more. The 195,000 smaller business firms that each have assets of less than $10 million control only about 10 per cent of the nation's assets and profits. As reported in *Fortune Magazine*'s annual summary, the 500 largest American industrial corporations in 1980 had combined sales of $1.65 trillion, combined profits of $81.2 billion, combined assets of $1.18 trillion, and a combined labor force of 15.9 million employees. These 500 corporations account for about 65 per cent of all industrial sales, 80 per cent of all industrial profits, 80 per cent of all industrial assets, and 75 per cent of all industrial employees.

The business corporation in its present form is a relatively new kind of institution (as institutions go): Although it developed from the sixteenth-century "joint stock company," most of its current characteristics were acquired during the nineteenth century. Modern corporations are organizations that the law treats as immortal fictitious "persons" who have the right to sue and be sued, own and sell property, and enter into contracts, all in their own name. As an organization the modern corporation consists of (1) stockholders who contribute capital and who own the corporation but whose liability for the acts of the corporation is limited to the money they contributed, (2) directors and officers who administer the corporation's assets and who run the corporation through various levels of "middle" managers," and (3) employees who provide labor and who do the basic work related directly to the production of goods and services. To cope with their complex coordination and control problems, the officers and managers of large corporations adopt formal bureaucratic systems of rules that link together the activities of the individual members of the organization so as to achieve certain outcomes or "objectives." So long as the individual follows these rules, the outcome will be achieved even if the individual does not know what it is and does not care about it.

Corporate organizations pose major problems for anyone who tries to apply moral standards to business activities: can we say that the acts of these organizations are "moral" or "immoral" in the same sense that the actions of human individuals are? And can we say that these organizations are "morally responsible" for their acts in the same sense that human individuals are? Or must we agree that it makes no sense to apply moral terms to organizations? Two views have emerged in response to these problems.[27] At one extreme is the view of philosophers who argue that since the rules that tie organizations together allow us to say that corporations "act"

---

[27]For the first view see Peter A. French, "The Corporation as a Moral Person," *American Philosophical Quarterly*, 16, no. 3 (July 1979): 207–215; for the second see John Ladd, "Morality and the Ideal of Rationality in Formal Organizations," *The Monist*, 54, no. 4 (1970): 488–516; the author's own view is based on David Copp, "Collective Actions and Secondary Actions," *American Philosophical Quarterly*, 16, no. 3 (July 1979): 177–86.

as individuals and that they have "intended objectives" for what they do, we can also say that they are "morally responsible" for their actions and that their actions are "moral" or "immoral" in exactly the same sense that a human being's are. The major problem with this view is that organizations do not seem to "act" or "intend" in the same sense that individual humans do and organizations differ from humans in morally important ways: organizations feel neither pain nor pleasure and they cannot act except through human beings. At the other extreme is the view of philosophers who hold that it makes no sense to hold business organizations "morally responsible" or to say that they have "moral" duties. These philosophers argue that business organizations are like machines whose members must blindly and undeviatingly conform to formal rules that have nothing to do with morality. Consequently it makes no more sense to hold organizations "morally responsible" for failing to follow moral standards than it makes to criticize a machine for failing to act morally. The major problem with this second view is that unlike machines at least some of the members of organizations usually know what they are doing and are free to choose whether to follow the organization's rules or even to change these rules. When an organization's members collectively, but freely and knowingly, pursue immoral objectives it ordinarily makes perfectly good sense to say that the actions they perform for the organization are "immoral" and that the organization is "morally responsible" for this immoral action.

Which of these two extreme views is correct? Perhaps neither. The underlying difficulty with which both views are trying to struggle is this: Although we say that corporate organizations "exist" and "act" like individuals, they obviously are not *human* individuals. Yet our moral categories are designed to deal primarily with individual humans who feel, reason, and deliberate, and who act on the basis of their own feelings, reasonings, and deliberations. So how can we apply these moral categories to corporate organizations and their "acts"? We can see our way through these difficulties only if we first see that corporate organizations and their acts depend on human individuals: Organizations are composed of human individuals and they act only when these individuals act. We can express this precisely in two somewhat technical claims:

I. *A corporate organization "exists" only if (1) there exist certain* human individuals *placed in certain circumstances and (2) our linguistic rules lay down that when those kinds of individuals exist in those kinds of circumstances, they shall count as a corporate organization.*

II. *A corporate organization "acts" only if (1) certain* human individuals *in the organization performed certain actions in certain circumstances and (2) our linguistic rules lay down that when those kinds of individuals perform those kinds of actions in those kinds of circumstances, this shall count as an act of their corporate organization.*

The rules of our own language say that a corporation exists, for example, when there exists a properly qualified group of individuals who have performed the necessary acts of incorporation. The rules of our language also say that a corporation acts when properly qualified members of the corporation carry out their assigned duties within the scope of their assigned authority.

Since corporate acts depend on human individuals it is these individuals who must be seen as the *primary* bearers of moral duties and moral responsibility: Human individuals are responsible for what the corporation does and if the corporation acts wrongly it is because of what some of these individuals did. Nonetheless it makes perfectly good sense to say that a corporate organization has "moral" duties and that it is "morally responsible" for its acts. But organizations have moral duties and are morally responsible in a *secondary* sense: A corporation has a moral duty to do something only if some of its members have a moral duty to make sure it is done, and a corporation is morally responsible for something only if some of its members are morally responsible for what happened (that is, they acted knowingly and freely). The central point that we must constantly keep before our eyes as we aim at analyzing the ethics of business activities and that we must not let the fiction of "the corporation" obscure, is that human individuals underlie the corporate organization and that, consequently, these human individuals are the primary carriers of moral duties and moral responsibilities. Below we will discuss how an organization's formal rules affect an individual's moral responsibility.

Business organizations are embedded in a larger society. They are, in the jargon of the social sciences, a "subsystem" which is part of a larger "social system." As such, business does not, cannot, exist without the tacit consent of that larger system. Through their laws the citizens of the larger system allow a business organization to exist by granting it the rights, powers, privileges, protections, and benefits which they believe the organization will need if it is to achieve the purpose for which it is created. Business organizations are part of the basic structure of society, and the moral standards that serve to ensure a stable, productive, and secure society by restraining the self-interest of its members in mutually beneficial ways must also apply to the members of business organizations.

Business ethics is a study of how these moral standards apply to the conduct of individuals involved in these organizations through which modern societies produce and distribute goods and services. Business ethics, in other words, is a form of applied ethics. It includes not only the analysis of moral principles and norms, but also attempts to apply the conclusions of this analysis to particular kinds of behavior: the behavior of people in business institutions.

Two Objections

Occasionally people object to the view that ethical standards should be applied to the behavior of people in business organizations. Persons involved in business, they claim, should single-mindedly pursue the financial interests of their firm and not sidetrack their energies or their firm's resources into "doing good works." Two different kinds of arguments are advanced in support of this view.

First, some have argued that in perfectly competitive free markets the pursuit of profit will by itself ensure that the members of society are served in the most socially beneficial ways.[28] For, in order to be profitable, each firm has to produce only what the members of society want and has to do this by the most efficient means available. The members of society will benefit most, then, if managers do not impose their own values on a business but instead devote themselves to the single-minded pursuit of profit, and thereby devote themselves to producing efficiently what the members of society themselves value.

Arguments of this sort conceal a number of assumptions that require a much lengthier discussion than we can provide at this stage. Since we will examine many of these claims in greater detail in the chapters that follow, we will here only note some of the more questionable assumptions on which the argument rests.[29] First, most industrial markets are not "perfectly competitive" as the argument assumes, and to the extent that firms do not have to compete they can maximize profits in spite of inefficient production. Secondly, the argument assumes that any steps taken to increase profits will necessarily be socially beneficial, when in fact several ways of increasing profits actually injure society: allowing harmful pollution to go uncontrolled, deceptive advertising, concealing product hazards, fraud, bribery, tax evasion, price-fixing, and so on. Thirdly, the argument assumes that by producing whatever the *buying* public wants (or values) firms are producing what all the members of society want, when in fact the wants of large segments of society (the poor and the disadvantaged) are not necessarily met because they cannot participate fully in the marketplace. Fourthly, the argument is essentially making a normative judgment ("managers *should* devote themselves to the single-minded pursuit of profits") on the basis of some assumed but unproved moral standards ("people *should* do whatever will benefit those who participate in markets"). Thus, although the argument tries to show that ethics does not matter, it can do this only by itself assuming an unproven moral standard that at least appears mistaken.

A second kind of argument sometimes advanced to show that business managers should single-mindedly pursue the interests of their firms and should ignore ethical considerations is embodied in what Alex C. Michalos calls the "loyal agent's argument."[30] The argument can be paraphrased as follows:

> As a loyal agent of his or her employer, the manager has a duty to serve his or her employer as the employer would want to be served (if the employer had the agent's expertise).
>
> An employer would want to be served in whatever ways will advance his or her self-interests.

[28] See, for example, H.B. Acton, *The Morals of Markets* (London: Longman Group Limited, 1971), pp. 14–18.

[29] For these and other criticisms see Alan H. Goldman, "Business Ethics: Profits, Utilities, and Moral Rights," *Philosophy and Public Affairs*, 9, no. 3 (Spring 1980): 260–86.

[30] Alex C. Michales, "The Loyal Agent's Argument," in *Ethical Theory and Business*, Tom L. Beauchamp and Norman E. Bowie, eds. (Englewood Cliffs, NJ: Prentice-Hall, Inc., 1979), pp. 338–48. See also Milton Friedman, "The Social Responsibility of Business is to Increase its Profits," *New York Times Magazine*, 13 (September 1970).

Therefore, as a loyal agent of his or her employer, the manager has a duty to serve his or her employer in whatever ways will advance the employer's self-interests.

The argument can be, and has often been, used to justify a manager's unethical or illegal conduct. The officer of a corporation, for example, may plead that although he engaged in certain illegal or unethical conduct (say, price-fixing), he should be excused because he did it not for himself but in order to protect the best interests of his company, or its shareholders, or its workers. The "loyal agent's argument" underlies this kind of excuse. More generally, if we replace "employer" with "government" and "manager" with "officer," we get the kind of argument that Nazi officers used after World War II to defend their involvement in Hitler's morally corrupt government.

The loyal agent's argument relies on several questionable assumptions. First, the argument tries to show, again, that ethics does not matter by assuming an unproven moral standard ("the manager *should* serve his or her employer in whatever way the employer wants to be served"). But there is no reason to assume that this moral standard is acceptable as it stands, and some reason to think that it would be acceptable only if it were suitably qualified (for example, "the manager should serve his or her employer in whatever *moral* way the employer wants to be served"). Secondly, the loyal agent's argument assumes that there are no limits to the manager's duties to serve the employer, when in fact such limits are an express part of the legal and social institutions from which these duties arise. An "agent's" duties are defined by what is called "the law of agency," that is, the law that specifies the duties of persons ("agents") who agree to act on behalf of another party and who are authorized by the agreement so to act. Lawyers, managers, engineers, stockbrokers, and so on, all act as "agents" for their employers in this sense. By freely entering an agreement to act as someone's agent, then, a person accepts a legal (and moral) duty to serve the client loyally, obediently, and in a confidential manner as specified in the law of agency.[31] But the law of agency states that "in determining whether or not the orders of the [client] to the agent are reasonable . . . business or professional ethics are to be considered," and "in no event would it be implied that an agent has a duty to perform acts which are illegal or unethical."[32] The manager's duties to serve his employer, then, are limited by the constraints of morality, since it is with this understanding that his duties as a loyal agent are defined. Thirdly, the loyal agent's argument assumes that if a manager agrees to serve a firm, then this agreement automatically justifies whatever the manager does on behalf of the firm. But this assumption is false: agreements to serve other people do not automatically justify doing wrong on their behalf. For example, it is clearly wrong for me to kill

[31] See Phillip I. Blumberg, "Corporate Responsibility and the Employee's Duty of Loyalty and Obedience: A Preliminary Inquiry," in *The Corporate Dilemma: Traditional Values Versus Contemporary Problems,* Dow Votaw and S. Prakash Sethi, eds. (Englewood Cliffs, NJ: Prentice-Hall, Inc., 1973), pp. 82–113.

[32] Quoted in *Ibid.,* p. 86.

an innocent person to advance my own interests. Suppose that one day I enter an agreement to serve your interests and that later it turns out that your interests require that I kill an innocent person for you. Does the agreement now justify my killing the innocent person? Obviously it does not since agreements do not change the moral character of wrongful acts. If it is morally wrong, then, for a manager to do something out of self-interest, it is also morally wrong for him to do it in the interests of his company even though he has agreed to serve the company. The assumptions of the loyal agent's argument, then, are mistaken.

1.2 MORAL REASONING

The last section defined ethics in terms of the moral standards on which moral judgments are based. We will turn in this section to examine the processes by which these moral standards are linked to moral judgments. We begin by describing how a person's ability to employ moral standards develops and then we turn to describing the reasoning processes in which these moral standards are employed.

Moral Development

Individuals are not born with an ability to understand and apply moral standards.[33] Just as there are stages of growth in physical development, so the ability to make reasoned moral judgments also develops in stages. As children we are simply told what is right and what is wrong, and we obey unthinkingly in order to avoid punishment: The child's adherence to moral standards is essentially based on self-interest. As we mature into adolescence, these moral instructions are gradually internalized. We begin to understand their implications more clearly, and we follow them because they advance the well-being of people we know and to whom we feel attached: Adherence to moral standards is now essentially based on loyalty to family, friends, and nation. It is only as rational and experienced adults that we finally acquire the ability to critically reflect upon the moral standards bequeathed to us by our families, peers, culture, or religion. We then begin to rationally evaluate these moral standards and their consequences, and to revise them where they are inadequate, inconsistent, or biased toward particular groups: Morality is now essentially based on universal principles that impartially take into account the interests of all persons.

The psychologist Lawrence Kohlberg has concluded on the basis of twenty years of research that there is a sequence of six stages in the development of a person's ability to reason about moral matters. Like many psychological theories Kohlberg's views have been called into question.[34] Nonetheless, there is a widespread consensus among psychologists that moral reasoning develops more or less in the way that Kohlberg claims it does. For our own purposes, we will accept

---

[33] Jean Piaget, *The Moral Judgment of the Child*, trans. Marjorie Grabain (New York: The Free Press, 1965), p. 398.

[34] For some of these criticisms see the papers collected in Thomas Lickona, ed., *Moral Development and Behavior: Theory, Research, and Social Issues* (New York: Holt, Rinehart and Winston, 1976).

Kohlberg's views, since they help us understand in detail how individuals may internalize moral standards and how they become more sophisticated and critical in their use and understanding of these standards.

Kohlberg groups his stages of moral development into three levels, each containing two stages, the second of which is the more advanced and organized form of the general perspective of each level. The sequence of six stages can be summarized as follows:[35]

LEVEL ONE: PRECONVENTIONAL STAGES

At these first two stages, the child is able to respond to rules and social expectations and can apply the labels, "good," "bad," "right," and "wrong." These rules, however, are seen as something external imposed on the self. Right and wrong are interpreted in terms of the pleasant or painful consequences of actions or in terms of the physical power of those who set the rules. The child sees situations only from his or her own point of view and, since the child does not yet have the ability to identify with others to any great extent, the primary motivation is self-interest.

Stage One: Punishment and obedience orientation.

At this stage the physical consequences of an act wholly determine the goodness or badness of that act. The child's reasons for doing the right thing are to avoid punishment or to defer to the superior physical power of authorities. There is little awareness that others have needs and desires similar to one's own.

Stage Two: Instrument and relativity orientation.

At this stage right actions are those that can serve as instruments for satisfying the child's own needs or the needs of those for whom the child cares. The child is now aware that others have needs and desires similar to his or her own and begins to defer to them in order to get them to do what he or she wants.

LEVEL TWO: CONVENTIONAL STAGES

Maintaining the expectations of one's own family, peer group, or nation is seen as valuable in its own right, regardless of the consequences. The person does not merely conform to expectations but exhibits loyalty to the group

---

[35] This summary is based on Lawrence Kohlberg, "Moral Stages and Moralization: The Cognitive-Developmental Approach," in *Moral Development,* ed. Lickona, pp. 31–53.

and its norms. The person is now able to see situations from the point of view of others in the group and assumes everyone is similar. The person is motivated to conform to the group's norms and subordinates the needs of the individual to those of the group.

Stage Three: Interpersonal concordance orientation.

Good behavior is living up to what is expected by those for whom one feels loyalty, affection, and trust, such as family and friends. Right action is conformity to what is generally expected in one's role as a good son, daughter, brother, friend, etc. Doing what is right is motivated by the need to be a "good person" in one's own eyes and in the eyes of others.

Stage Four: Law and order orientation.

Right and wrong are determined by loyalty to one's own nation. Laws are to be upheld except where they conflict with other fixed social duties. The person is now able to see other people as parts of a larger social system that defines individual roles and obligations, and he or she can separate the norms generated by this system from his or her interpersonal relationships and motives.

LEVEL THREE: POSTCONVENTIONAL, AUTONOMOUS, OR PRINCIPLED STAGES

At these stages the person no longer simply accepts the values and norms of the groups to which he or she belongs. Instead the person now tries to see situations from a point of view that impartially takes everyone's interests into account. The person questions the laws and values that society has adopted and redefines them in terms of self-chosen universal moral principles that can be justified to any rational individual. The proper laws and values are those to which any reasonable person would be motivated to commit himself or herself, whatever place the person holds in society and whatever society he or she belongs to.

Stage Five: Social contract orientation.

The person is aware that people hold a variety of conflicting personal views and opinions, and emphasizes fair ways of reaching consensus by agreement, contract, and due process. The person believes that all values and norms are relative and that, apart from this democratic consensus, all should be tolerated.

Stage Six: Universal ethical principles orientation.

Right action is defined in terms of universal principles chosen because of their logical comprehensiveness, their universality, and their consistency. These ethical principles are not concrete like the ten commandments but abstract universal principles dealing with justice, society's welfare, the equality of human rights, respect for the dignity of individual human beings, and with the idea that persons are ends in themselves and must be treated as such. The person's reasons for doing right are based on a commitment to these moral principles, and the person sees them as the criteria for evaluating all other moral rules and arrangements including democratic consensus.

According to Kohlberg, these six stages are sequential. That is, people do not enter a later stage until they have passed through each of the earlier ones. The stages, however, are not inevitable. A person may never reach the later stages but may remain stuck at one of the earlier stages throughout life. Kohlberg has argued, in fact, that much of the American population does not reach the later stages, but remains at stages three or four.

One of the purposes of studying ethics is to develop the individual's ability to reason about moral issues. In terms of Lawrence Kohlberg's developmental sequence, the study of ethics should enable the individual to acquire the more critical understanding of "right" and "wrong" that characterizes the later "autonomous" stages of moral development. One of the central aims of the study of ethics, therefore, is to develop the person's ability to move beyond a simple acceptance of the internalized moral standards of his or her family, peers, company, nation, or culture. By discussing, analyzing, and criticizing the moral judgments we and others make, we can acquire the intellectual skills needed to develop and determine for ourselves a set of moral principles to which we can rationally assent. We can get a clearer idea of these processes by looking more closely at the nature of moral reasoning.

Moral Reasoning

The terms "moral reasoning" and "ethical reasoning" refer to the reasoning process by which human behaviors, institutions, or policies are judged to be in accordance with or in violation of moral standards. Moral reasoning always involves two essential components: (1) an understanding of what moral standards require or prohibit and (2) evidence or information that shows that a particular policy, institution, or behavior has the kinds of features that these moral standards require or prohibit. Here is an illustration of moral reasoning whose author is offering us his reasons for claiming that American social institutions are unjust:

> The nonwhite . . . live in American society, fight for American society in disproportionate numbers and contribute cheap labor to American society, thereby enabling others to live disproportionately well. But the nonwhite . . . do not share in the benefits of the American society in which they live and for which they fight and to which they contribute. 41 percent of Negroes fall below the poverty line as compared with 12 percent of whites. Infant mortality is three times as high among nonwhite babies as among white. Whereas, Negroes make up 11 percent of the nation's work force, they have but 6 percent of the nation's technical and professional jobs, 3 percent of the managerial jobs and 6 percent of jobs in skilled trades. Discrimination which prevents people from getting out of their society what they contribute is unjust.[36]

In this example, the author has in mind a moral standard which he sets out at the end of the paragraph: "Discrimination which prevents people from getting out of their society what they contribute is unjust." The rest of the paragraph is devoted to citing evidence to show that American society exhibits the kind of discrimination proscribed by this moral principle. The author's moral judgment that American society is unjust, then, is based on a chain of reasoning that appeals to a moral standard and to evidence that American society has the features condemned by this standard. Schematically, then, moral or ethical reasoning usually has the kind of structure indicated in Figure 1.1.[37]

In many cases, one or more of the three components involved in a person's moral reasoning will not be expressed. More often than not in fact people will fail to make explicit the moral standards on which their moral judgments are based. A person might say, for example: "American society is unjust because it allows 41 per cent of Negroes to fall below the poverty line as compared with 12 per cent of whites." Here the unspoken moral standard on which the judgment "American society is unjust" is based is something like "a society is unjust if it does not treat minorities equal to the majority." And the disproportionate number of Negroes that fall below the poverty line is being cited as evidence that minorities in America are not treated equal to the white majority. The main reason that moral standards are often not made explicit is that they are generally presumed to be obvious. People put more of their efforts into producing evidence that a given policy, institution, or action conforms to, or violates, their unexpressed standards than they put into identifying or explaining the moral standards on which their judgments rely. Failure to make one's moral standards explicit leaves one vulnerable to all the problems created by basing critical decisions on unexamined assumptions: The assumptions may be inconsistent, they may have no rational basis, and they may lead the decision-maker into unwittingly making decisions with undesirable consequences. We saw at the end of the last section two arguments that tried to show that managers

---

[36] Edward J. Stevens, *Making Moral Decisions* (New York: Paulist Press, 1969), pp. 123-25.

[37] For a fuller discussion of this approach see Stephen Toulmin, Richard Rieke, and Allan Janik, *An Introduction to Reasoning* (New York: Macmillan Inc., 1979), pp. 309-37.

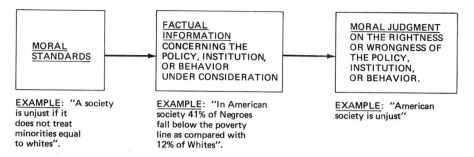

FIGURE 1-1

should not be ethical but both of which were based on assumed moral standards that were unacceptable once they were made explicit.

In order to uncover the implicit moral standards on which a person's moral judgments are based, one has to retrace the person's moral reasoning back to its bases. This involves asking (1) what factual information does the person accept as evidence for this moral judgment and (2) what moral standards are needed to relate this factual information (logically) to the moral judgment?[38] For example, suppose I judge that capital punishment is morally wrong. And suppose that I base my judgment on the factual evidence that capital punishment occasionally results in the death of innocent people. Then, in order to relate this factual information to my judgment, I must accept the general moral principle: Whatever occasionally results in the death of innocent people is morally wrong. This general moral principle is needed if there is to be a (logical) connection between the factual information ("capital punishment occasionally results in the death of innocent people") and the moral judgment that is based on this fact ("capital punishment is morally wrong"). Without the moral principle, the factual information would have no logical relation to the judgment and would therefore be irrelevant.

The moral standards on which adults base their moral judgments will usually be much more complex than this simple example suggests. Developed moral standards (as we will see) incorporate qualifications, exceptions, and restrictions that limit their scope. Also they may be combined in various ways with other important standards. But the general method of uncovering unexpressed moral standards remains roughly the same whatever their complexity: One asks what general standards relate a person's factual evidence to his or her moral judgments.

It is to be hoped that this account of ethical reasoning has not suggested to the reader that it is always easy to separate factual information from moral standards in a piece of moral reasoning; nothing could be farther from the truth. In practice, the two are sometimes intertwined in ways that are difficult to disentangle. And there are several theoretical difficulties in trying to draw a precise line separat-

[38]See Richard M. Hare, *Freedom and Reason* (New York: Oxford University Press, 1965), pp. 30–50; 86–111.

ing the two.[39] Although the difference between the two is usually clear enough for practical purposes, the reader should be aware that sometimes they cannot be clearly distinguished.

Analyzing Moral Reasoning

There are various criteria that ethicians use to evaluate the adequacy of moral reasoning. First and primarily, moral reasoning must be *logical.* The analysis of moral reasoning requires that the logic of the arguments used to establish a moral judgment be rigorously examined, that all the unspoken moral and factual assumptions be made explicit, and that both assumptions and premises be displayed and subjected to criticism.

Secondly, the factual evidence cited in support of a person's judgment must be *accurate,* it must be *relevant,* and it must be *complete.*[40] For example, the illustration of moral reasoning quoted above cites several statistics ("Whereas Negroes make up 11 percent of the nation's work force, they have but 6 percent of the nation's technical and professional jobs, 3 percent of . . . ") and relationships ("The nonwhite contribute cheap labor which enables others to live disproportionately well") that are claimed to exist in America. If the moral reasoning is to be adequate, these statistics and relationships must be *accurate:* They must rest on reliable statistical methods and on well-supported scientific theory. In addition, evidence must be *relevant:* It must show that the behavior, policy, or institution being judged has precisely those characteristics that are proscribed by the moral standards involved. The statistics and relationships in the illustration of moral reasoning given above, for instance, must show that some people are "prevented from getting out of [American] society what they contribute," the precise characteristic that is condemned by the moral standard cited in the illustration. And evidence must be *complete:* It must take into account all relevant information and must not selectively advert only to the evidence that tends to support a single point of view.

Thirdly, the moral standards involved in a person's moral reasonings must be *consistent.* They must be consistent with each other and with the other standards and beliefs the person holds.[41] Inconsistency between a person's moral standards can be uncovered and corrected by examining situations in which these moral standards require incompatible things. Suppose that I believe that (1) it is wrong to disobey an employer whom one has contractually agreed to obey, and I also believe that (2) it is wrong to help someone who is endangering innocent people's lives. Then suppose that one day my employer insists that I work on a project that might result in the deaths of several innocent people. The situation now reveals an incon-

---

[39] The difficulties are discussed in John R. Searle, *Speech Acts* (New York: Cambridge University Press, 1969), pp. 182–88.

[40] An excellent and compact account of these features may be found in Lawrence Habermehl; "The Susceptibility of Moral Claims to Reasoned Assessment," in *Morality in the Modern World,* ed. Lawrence Hebermehl (Belmont, CA.: Dickenson Publishing Co., Inc., 1976), pp. 18–32.

[41] *Ibid.*

sistency between these two moral standards: I can either obey my employer and avoid disloyalty, or I can disobey him and avoid helping endanger people's lives, but I cannot do both.

When inconsistencies between one's moral standards are uncovered in this way, one (or both) of the standards must be modified. In the example above I might decide, for instance, that orders of employers have to be obeyed *except* when they threaten human life. Notice that in order to determine what kinds of modifications are called for, one has to examine the *reasons* one has for accepting the inconsistent standards and weigh these reasons to see what is more important and worth retaining and what is less important and subject to modification. In the example above, for instance, I may have decided that the reason that employee loyalty is important is that it safeguards property but that the reason why the refusal to endanger people is important is that it safeguards human life. And human life, I then decide, is more important than property. This sort of criticism and adjustment of one's moral standards is an important part of the process through which moral development takes place.

There is another kind of consistency that is perhaps even more important in ethical reasoning. Consistency also refers to the requirement that one must be willing to accept the consequences of applying one's moral standards consistently to all persons in similar circumstances.[42] This "consistency requirement" can be phrased as follows:

If I judge that a certain person is morally justified (or unjustified) in doing A in circumstances C, then I must accept that it is morally justified (or unjustified) for any other person
(a) to perform any act relevantly similar to A
(b) in any circumstances relevantly similar to C.

I must, that is, apply the same moral standards to one situation that I applied to another one that was relevantly similar. (Two situations are "relevantly similar" when all those factors that have a bearing on the judgment that an action is right or wrong in one situation are also present in the other situation.) For example, suppose that I judge that it is morally permissible for me to fix prices because I want the high profits. Then if I am to be consistent, I must hold that it is morally permissible for my *suppliers* to fix prices when they want high profits. If I am not willing to consistently accept the consequences of applying to other similar persons the standard that price-fixing is morally justified for those who want high prices, then I cannot rationally hold that the standard is true in my own case.

The consistency requirement is the basis of an important method of showing that a given moral standard must be modified or rejected: the use of "counter-examples" or "hypotheticals." If a moral standard is inadequate or unacceptable, we

---

[42] See Marcus G. Singer, *Generalization in Ethics* (New York: Alfred A. Knopf, Inc., 1961), p. 5; Hare, *Freedom and Reason,* p. 15; Frankena, *Ethics,* p. 25.

can often show it is inadequate by showing that its implications in a certain hypothetical example are unacceptable. For instance, suppose someone should advance the claim that we ought always to do only what will benefit ourselves, that is, that we *ought* to act only egoistically. We might want to attack this view by proposing the hypothetical example of an individual who is made happy only when she does what will benefit *others* and *not* herself. According to the egoistic standard, this individual *ought* to do only what will make her unhappy! And this, we might want to hold, is clearly unacceptable. The egoist, of course, may want to modify his view (by saying "What I *really* meant by 'benefit ourselves' was . . . "), but that is another story. The point is that hypothetical "counter-examples" can be used effectively to show that a moral standard must be rejected or at least modified.

Moral Responsibility

The discussion up to now has focused on reasoning that is aimed at judging whether an action (or policy or institution) is morally right or wrong. Moral reasoning, however, is sometimes directed at a related but different kind of judgment: determining whether a person is *morally responsible,* or culpable, for having done something that was admittedly wrong. A person, for example, may have done something clearly wrong, such as kill an innocent human being. But if the person performed this wrongful action without knowing what he or she was doing, we do not hold the person morally responsible for the action. What the person did was wrong, but the person is *excused* by virtue of his or her ignorance. When, then, is a person morally responsible for having done something?

A person is morally responsible only for those actions and their consequences (1) that the person knowingly and freely performed and that it was morally wrong for the person to perform or (2) that the person knowingly and freely failed to perform and that it was morally wrong for the person to fail to perform.[43] Several manufacturers of asbestos, for example, were recently judged responsible for the lung diseases suffered by some of their workers. The judgment was based in part on the finding that the manufacturers had a duty to warn their workers of the known dangers of working with asbestos but they failed to perform this duty, and the lung diseases were a consequence of this failure.

There is wide agreement that two conditions diminish a person's responsibility for having done something wrong: *ignorance* and *inability*.[44] If a person did not know, or was not able to avoid, what he or she did, then that person cannot rightly be held morally responsible for it. Asbestos manufacturers, for example, have claimed that they did not know that conditions in their plants would cause lung cancer in their workers. If this is true, then it would be wrong to blame them for the diseases that have resulted. And recently, a group of managers accused of conspiring

---

[43] A person can also be morally responsible for good acts. But since we are concerned with determining when a person is excused from doing wrong, we will discuss moral responsibility only as it relates to wrongdoing and to being excused therefrom.

[44] This agreement goes back at least to Aristotle.

to fix prices pleaded that they were "forced into" the price-fixing conspiracy by being threatened with severe personal reprisals. Again, if this is true, then they were not fully responsible because they were not completely free to act otherwise.

It is important to understand exactly how "ignorance" and "inability" relate to a person's moral responsibility. For ignorance does not always diminish a person's moral responsibility for doing wrong. One exception is when a person deliberately keeps himself or herself ignorant of a certain matter precisely in order to escape responsibility. If an asbestos manufacturer, for example, told the company's doctors *not* to tell him the results of the medical examinations they carried out on his workers so that he would not be legally liable for leaving conditions in his factory unchanged, he would still be morally responsible if the tests turn out positive. A second exception is when a person negligently fails to take adequate steps to become informed about a matter that is of known importance. A manager in an asbestos company, for example, who has reason to suspect that asbestos may be dangerous, but who fails to inform himself on the matter out of laziness, cannot later plead ignorance as an excuse.

A person may be ignorant either of the relevant facts or the relevant moral standards. For example, I may be sure that bribery is wrong (a moral standard) but may not have realized that in tipping a customs official I was actually bribing him into cancelling certain import fees (a fact). On the other hand, I may be genuinely unsure whether bribing minor officials is wrong (a moral standard) although I know that in tipping the customs official I am bribing him (a fact).

Ignorance of *fact* generally diminishes responsibility for the simple reason that a person cannot be obligated to do something over which he or she has no control: moral obligation requires freedom.[45] Since people cannot control matters of which they are ignorant, they cannot have any moral obligations with respect to such matters, and their moral responsibility for such matters is correspondingly diminished. Negligently or deliberately created ignorance is an exception to this principle because such ignorance can be controlled. Insofar as we can control the extent of our ignorance, we become morally responsible for it and therefore also for its consequences. Ignorance of the relevant *moral standards* generally also diminishes responsibility because a person is not responsible for failing to meet obligations of whose existence he or she is genuinely ignorant or in doubt. However, to the extent that our ignorance of moral standards is the result of freely choosing not to ascertain what these standards are, to that extent we are responsible for our ignorance and for the wrong we do as a consequence.

Inability can be the result of either internal or external circumstances that render a person unable to do something or unable to keep from doing something: A person may lack sufficient power, skill, opportunity or resources to act, or the act may impose unreasonable costs or pain on the person, or the person may be physically constrained or subjected to threats or other forms of duress. Middle managers, for example, are sometimes intensely pressured or threatened by their superiors to

---

[45] See the discussion of this in Hare, *Freedom and Reason,* pp. 50–60.

reach certain production targets or to keep certain health information secret from workers or the public, although it is clearly unethical to do so.[46] If the pressures on managers are great enough, we generally hold, then their responsibility is correspondingly diminished.

Inability diminishes responsibility because, again, a person cannot have any moral obligation to do (or forbear from doing) something over which the person has no control. Insofar as circumstances diminish a person's ability to control his or her actions, responsibility for the actions also diminishes and it is wrong to blame the person.

Corporate Responsibility

Within the modern corporation, responsibility for a corporate act is often distributed among a number of cooperating participants. One team of managers, for example, may design a car, another team test it, and a third team build it; one person orders, advises or encourages something and another person acts on these orders, advice or encouragement; one person knowingly defrauds buyers and another group knowingly enjoys the resulting profits; one person contributes the means, and another person accomplishes the act; one group does the wrong, and another group conceals it. The variations on cooperation are endless. They reduce, however, to two main types: A person may offer his or her *positive* cooperation by doing something that helps bring about the corporate act, or the person may cooperate in a *negative* manner by simply refraining from doing anything to stop the corporate act.[47]

What is the individual's personal moral responsibility when cooperating with others positively or negatively in a corporate act that the individual believes is wrong? In discussing this question, traditional moralists have found it helpful to distinguish *formal* cooperation in wrongful activity from *material* cooperation.[48] A person formally cooperates in an evil corporate act with others if (1) the person *knowingly* and *freely* takes part in the evil corporate act or aids the others in its performance (negatively or positively) and (2) the person fully *approves* and wants the act to succeed. A person's cooperation in an evil corporate act with others is merely material if, although he or she does something which will help the others, the person does so unknowingly, unfreely, or without wanting to: the person cooperates, for example, because of the pressures placed upon him or her.

Formal cooperation, according to traditional moralists, does not differ in any significant way from any other deliberately immoral act: the person is fully responsi-

---

[46] "The Pressures to Compromise Personal Ethics," *Business Week,* 31 January 1977, p. 107.

[47] W. L. LaCroix, *Principles for Ethics in Business* (Washington, D.C.: University Press of America, 1976), pp. 106–7.

[48] *Ibid.;* see also Thomas M. Garrett, *Business Ethics* (Englewood Cliffs, NJ: Prentice-Hall, Inc., 1966), pp. 17–18, 77–80; and Henry J. Wirtenberger, S.J., *Morality and Business* (Chicago: Loyola University Press, 1962), pp. 109–14.

ble for the wrong even if this responsibility is shared with others.[49] If, for example, as a member of the board of directors of a corporation, I knowingly and freely act on insider's information to vote for some stock options that will benefit me but unfairly injure the other stockholders, then I am morally responsible for the wrongful corporate act of the board even if I share this responsibility with other members of the board.

Critics of this traditional view on formal cooperation have claimed that when an organized group, such as a corporation, acts together, their corporate act may be described as the act of the group and, consequently, the corporate group and not the individuals who make up the group must be held responsible for the act.[50] For example, we normally credit the manufacture of a defective car to the corporation that made it and not to the individual engineers involved in its manufacture; and the law typically attributes the acts of a corporation's managers to the corporation itself (so long as the managers act within their authority) and not to the managers as individuals. Traditionalists, however, can reply that, although we sometimes attribute acts to corporate groups, this linguistic and legal fact does not change the moral reality behind all such corporate acts: Individuals had to carry out the particular actions that in those circumstances counted as the act of the corporate group. Since individuals are morally responsible for the known and intended consequences of their free actions, any individual who knowingly, freely and approvingly cooperates in doing something that counts as a corporate act will be morally responsible for that act.

More often than not, however, employees of large corporations cannot be said to have "formally cooperated" in carrying out the corporation's acts or in pursuing its objectives. Employees of large-scale organizations follow bureaucratic rules that link their activities together to achieve corporate outcomes of which the employee may not even be aware. The engineers in one department may build a component with certain weaknesses, for example, not knowing that another department plans to use that component in a product that these weaknesses will render dangerous. Or the employees may feel pressured to conform to company rules with whose corporate outcomes they may not agree but which they are not in a position to change. A worker on an assembly line, for example, may feel he has no choice but to stay at his job even though he knows that the cars he and others help to build are dangerous. The bureaucratic structure of large organizations, therefore, can turn the cooperation of some of its members into material cooperation and then responsibility for their corporate acts falls mainly on those who are responsible for the corporation's bureaucratic structure (usually top managers) and for its faulty communications.

[49]*Ibid.;* see also Herbert Jone, *Moral Theology,* trans. Urban Adelman (Westminster, MD: The Newman Press, 1961), p. 236.

[50]Peter A. French, "Corporate Moral Agency", in *Ethical Theory and Business,* Tom L. Beauchamp and Norman E. Bowie, eds., (Englewood Cliffs, NJ: Prentice-Hall, Inc., 1979), pp. 175–86; see also Christopher D. Stone, *Where the Law Ends* (New York: Harper & Row, Publishers, Inc., 1975), pp. 58–69 for the legal basis of this view.

Material cooperation (unlike formal cooperation) is not necessarily something for which a person is morally responsible since a person's material cooperation may be based on ignorance or inability and these may be sufficient to rule out moral responsibility. Sometimes, however, people unwillingly cooperate in an evil corporate act although they know (to some extent) that it is evil and they have the ability (to some extent) to withdraw their cooperation: They cooperate because they are pressured or threatened into doing so. Traditional moralists have argued that four main factors generally affect a person's responsibility for cooperating under pressures or threats that impose serious personal costs on the person.[51]

1. The magnitude *of the evil.*   The more evil I know a corporate act is, the more wrong it is for me to cooperate in it and the less my responsibility is diminished by the personal costs involved. If my employer, for example, threatens to fire me unless I sell a used product that I know will kill someone, it would be seriously wrong for me to cooperate and the threat would not diminish my responsibility.

2. The nature *of the pressures of threats involved.*   In general, the less the personal costs of failing to cooperate, the greater my responsibility for cooperating. If, for example, I would merely suffer a relatively harmless reprimand for failing to cooperate with rules whose outcome I feel is wrong, my responsibility would be greater than it would be if the alternative to cooperating were loss of my life.

3. The certitude *of the evil.*   In general, the more certain I am that the corporate outcome of what I am doing is evil, the greater my responsibility if I cooperate with it and the less I am absolved by the personal costs involved. Suppose I am very doubtful, for example, that bribing minor officials is wrong or that tipping constitutes a bribe, and my boss threatens to fire me unless I stick to company rules that require me to give small tips to minor customs officials. Then I am less responsible for whatever wrong I do than I would be if I were completely free of these doubts (so long as I am not to blame for my own ignorance).

4. The extent *of one's contribution.*   In general, the more I do to ensure the success of a corporate act I know is evil, the more I am responsible for that act and the less my responsibility is diminished by a given pressure or threat. I may, for example, actually carry out the evil act (I pull the trigger), or I may provide a service to one of the agents (I buy him the gun), or I may merely refrain from interfering (I see the murder but do nothing to stop it).

Critics have contested the extent to which these four factors affect a person's responsibility. Some have claimed that evil may never be done no matter what the

---

[51]See, for example, Wirtenberger, *Morality and Business,* p. 111, and Garrett, *Business Ethics,* p. 10.

personal consequences.[52] Other critics have claimed that I am as responsible when I refrain from interfering with evil as I am when I perform the evil myself, since knowingly *allowing* something to happen is morally no different from knowingly *making* it happen.[53] Neither of these criticisms seems to be correct, but the reader should make up his or her own mind on the matter. Discussing all the issues the criticisms raise would take us too far afield.

1.3 SUMMARY

This chapter has developed the idea that ethics is the study of judgments concerned with moral right and wrong, that is, with judgments based on moral standards. The first section of the chapter clarified this idea by explaining what moral standards are and by describing the kinds of social functions they serve. The second section turned to explaining in detail how moral standards form the basis of moral judgments, that is, to explaining what moral reasoning is. We first described how a person's capacity to engage in moral reasoning develops and then outlined the general structure that moral reasoning usually has. We ended by describing several methods by which moral reasoning can be analyzed and corrected and by explaining how moral responsibility is determined.

The discussion, however, has not yet developed any specific standards for distinguishing right from wrong. That is the burden of the next chapter, which will describe three kinds of standards that are commonly employed in moral reasoning: utilitarian moral standards, standards concerned with moral rights, and standards of justice.

QUESTIONS FOR REVIEW AND DISCUSSION

1. Define the following concepts: ethics, normative judgment, moral judgment, moral norm, moral principle, moral standard, prudential claim, business ethics, preconventional morality, conventional morality, autonomous morality, moral reasoning, consistency requirement, moral responsibility, formal cooperation, material cooperation.
2. "Ethics is a purely private matter." Discuss this statement.
3. "Ethics has no place in business." Discuss.
4. "Kohlberg's views on moral development show that the more morally mature a person becomes, the more likely he is to obey the moral norms of his society." Comment.

[52] Alan Donagan, *The Theory of Morality* (Chicago: University of Chicago Press, 1977), pp. 154–57, 206–7.
[53] Singer, *Practical Ethics,* p. 152.

CASES FOR DISCUSSION

The Air Force Brake

On June 28, 1967, Ling-Temco-Vought (LTV) Aerospace Corporation contracted to purchase 202 aircraft brakes from B.F. Goodrich for the A7D, a new plane that Ling-Temco-Vought was constructing for the Air Force. B.F. Goodrich, a tire manufacturer, agreed to supply the brakes for less than $70,000. According to Mr. Vandivier, a Goodrich employee who worked on this project, Goodrich had submitted this "absurdly low" bid to LTV because it badly wanted the contract.[1] Even if Goodrich lost money on this initial contract, the Air Force afterwards would be committed to buying all future brakes for the A7D from B.F. Goodrich.

Besides a low price, the Goodrich bid carried a second attractive feature: The brake described in its bid was small; it contained only four disks (or "rotors") and would weigh only 106 pounds. Weight was of course an important factor for Ling-Temco-Vought, since the lighter the Air Force plane turned out to be, the heavier the payload it could carry.[2]

The four-rotor brake was designed primarily by John Warren, an engineer who had been with Goodrich for seven years. As senior project engineer, Warren was directly in charge of the brake. Working under him was Searle Lawson, a young man of twenty-six who had graduated from engineering school only one year earlier. Warren made the original computations for the brake and drew up the preliminary design.

Using Warren's design, Lawson was to build a prototype of the four-rotor brake and test it in the Goodrich laboratories. By simulating the weight of the A7D plane and its landing speed, Lawson was to ensure that the brake could "stop" the plane fifty-one consecutive times without any changes in the brake lining. If the brake "qualified" under this indoor laboratory test, it would then be mounted on airplanes and tested by pilots in flight. Kermit Vandivier, though not an engineer, was to write up the results of these laboratory qualifying tests and submit them as the laboratory report prior to the test flights.

Upon testing the prototype of Warren's four-rotor brake in simulated "landings" in the laboratory, Lawson found that high temperatures built up in the brake and the linings "disintegrated" before they made the required fifty-one consecutive "stops."[3]

> Ignoring Warren's original computations, Lawson made his own, and it didn't take him long to discover where the trouble lay—the brake was too small. There simply was not enough surface area on the disks to stop the aircraft without generating the excessive heat that caused the linings to fail. . . . Despite the evidence of the abortive tests and Lawson's careful computations,

[1] Kermit Vandivier, "Why Should My Conscience Bother Me?," *In the Name of Profit* (Garden City, NY: Doubleday & Co., Inc., 1972), p. 4.

[2] *Ibid.*

[3] *Ibid.*

Warren rejected the suggestion that the four-disk brake was too light for the job. Warren knew that his superior had already told LTV, in rather glowing terms, that the preliminary tests on the A7D brake were very successful. . . . It would [also] have been difficult for Warren to admit not only that he had made a serious error in his calculations and original design but that his mistake had been caught by a green kid, barely out of college. (Statement of Mr. Vandivier)[4]

Lawson decided to go over Warren's head to Warren's supervisor, Robert Sink. The supervisor, however, deciding to rely on the judgment of Warren who was known to be an experienced engineer, told Lawson to continue with the tests as Warren had directed.

Dejected, Lawson returned to the laboratory and over the next few months tried twelve separate times to get the brake to pass the "fifty-one-stop" qualifying tests, using various different lining materials for the brakes. To no avail: the heat inevitably burnt up the linings. By April 1968, Lawson was engaged in a thirteenth attempt to qualify the brakes.

On the morning of April 11, Richard Gloor, who was the test engineer assigned to the A7D project, came to me and told me he had discovered that sometime during the previous twenty-four hours instrumentation used to record brake pressure had *deliberately* been miscalibrated so that while the instrumentation showed that a pressure of 1,000 pounds per square inch had been used to conduct brake stops numbers forty-six and forty-seven . . . , 1,100 pounds per square inch had actually been applied to the brakes. Maximum pressure available on the A7D is 1,000 pounds per square inch. Mr. Gloor further told me he had questioned instrumentation personnel about the miscalibration and had been told they were asked to do so by Searle Lawson. (Statement of Mr. Vandivier)[5]

The thirteenth series of tests also ended in failure and the results could not be used to qualify the brake. Mr. Vandivier, however, was anxious to ascertain why Lawson had asked to have the instruments miscalibrated:

I subsequently questioned Lawson who admitted he had ordered the instruments miscalibrated at the direction of a superior. . . . Mr. Lawson told me that he had been informed by . . . Mr. Robert Sink, project manager at Goodrich, . . . and Mr. Russell Van Horn, project manager at Goodrich that "Regardless of what the brake does on test, we're going to qualify it." (Statement of Mr. Vandivier)[6]

Lawson then undertook the fourteenth and final attempt to qualify the brake. To ensure that the four-rotor brake passed the fifty-one-stop tests, Mr. Vandivier

[4] *Ibid.*, pp. 8–9.

[5] U.S., Congress, *Air Force A-7D Brake Problem: Hearing before the Subcommittee on Economy in Government of the Joint Economic Committee,* 91st Congress, 1st session, 13 August 1969, p. 2. Hereafter cited as "Brake Hearing."

[6] *Ibid.*, p. 3.

later testified, several procedures were used that violated military performance criteria.

> After each stop, the wheel was removed from the brake, and the accumulated dust was blown out. During each stop, pressure was released when the brake had decelerated to 10 miles per hour [and allowed to coast to a stop]. By these and other irregular procedures, the brake was nursed along. (Statement of Mr. Vandivier)[7]

When the fourteenth series of test stops was completed, Lawson asked Vandivier to help him write up a report on the brake indicating the brake had been qualified.

> I explained to Lawson that . . . the only way such a report could be written was to falsify test data. Mr. Lawson said he was well aware of what was required, but that he had been ordered to get a report written regardless of how or what had to be done . . . [He] asked if I would help him gather the test data and draw up the various engineering curves and graphic displays that are normally included in a report. (Statement of Mr. Vandivier)[8]

Kermit Vandivier had to make up his mind whether to participate in writing up the false report.

> [My] job paid well, it was pleasant and challenging, and the future looked reasonably bright. My wife and I had bought a home . . . If I refused to take part in the A7D fraud, I would have to either resign or be fired. The report would be written by someone anyway, but I would have the satisfaction of knowing I had had no part in the matter. But bills aren't paid with personal satisfaction, nor house payments with ethical principles. I made my decision. The next morning I telephoned Lawson and told him I was ready to begin the qualification report. (Statement of Mr. Vandivier)[9]

Mr. Lawson and Mr. Vandivier worked on the curves, charts, and logs for the report for about a month, "tailoring" the pressures, values, distances, and times "to fit the occasion." During that time, Mr. Vandivier frequently discussed the tests with Mr. Russell Line, the senior executive for his section, a respected and well-liked individual.

> Mr. Line . . . advised me that it would be wise to just do my work and keep quiet. I told him of the extensive irregularities during testing and suggested that the brake was actually dangerous and if allowed to be installed on an aircraft, might cause an accident. Mr. Line said he thought I was worrying too much about things which did not really concern me. . . . I asked Mr. Line if his conscience would hurt him if such a thing caused the death of a pilot,

---

[7]*Ibid.*, p. 4.

[8]*Ibid.*, p. 5.

[9]Vandivier, "Why Should My Conscience Bother Me?," p. 4.

and this is when he replied I was worrying about too many things that did not concern me and advised me to "do what you're told." (Statement of Mr. Vandivier)[10]

Eventually, Mr. Vandivier's superiors also insisted that he write up the entire report and not just the graphs and charts. Mr. Vandivier complied and on June 5, 1968 the qualifying report was finally issued.

1. Were any moral issues involved in Mr. Vandivier's decision to write up the final qualifying report? Explain.

2. In your judgment, is it morally right or morally wrong for a person in Mr. Vandivier's situation to write up a false report as he did? Formulate the moral standards on which your judgment is based. Do your standards meet the consistency requirement (that is, would you be willing to apply the same standards in other similar situations)?

3. At which of Kohlberg's levels would you place Mr. Vandivier? Mr. Lawson? Mr. Warren? Mr. Line? Yourself? Explain each of your answers.

4. In your opinion, would Mr. Vandivier be morally responsible for any "accidents" that resulted when pilots tested the brake? Explain your answer. Would this responsibility be shared with any others? Explain.

Asbestos in Industry

Clarence Borel began working as an installer of industrial insulation in 1936, a job that necessarily exposed him to heavy concentrations of asbestos dust. Among the insulating materials with which he worked were asbestos products manufactured by Johns-Manville Corporation and other asbestos companies. At the end of a day working with asbestos materials, Borel's clothes would be covered with the dangerous dust:

> You just move them just a little and there is going to be dust, and I blowed this dust out of my nostrils by handfuls at the end of the day, trying to use water too, I even used Mentholatum in my nostrils to keep some of the dust from going down in my throat, but it is impossible to get rid of all of it. Even your clothes just stay dusty continually unless you blow it off with an air hose . . . I knew the dust was bad, but we used to talk [about] it among the insulators, [about] how bad was this dust, could it give you TB, could it give you this, and everyone was saying no, that dust don't hurt you, it dissolves as it hits your lungs . . . There was always a question, you just never knew how dangerous it was. I never did know really. If I had known, I would have gotten out of it. (Statement of Clarence Borel)[1]

But Borel did not "get out of it." Shortly after making the statement above, Borel died of a form of lung cancer known as mesothelioma that had been caused by asbestosis.

[10]*Brake Hearing,* pp. 5 and 6.

[1]Borel v. Fiberboard Paper Products Corporation, et. al., 493 F. 2d 1076 (1973), p. 1082.

Asbestosis is a scarring of the lung tissue that has been associated with 10 percent of the deaths among asbestos workers. The onset of asbestosis is usually gradual, becoming noticeable only when a period of ten to thirty years elapses after the initial exposure. During this period the worker will feel, and will be diagnosed as, healthy. Once inhaled, however, asbestos fibers can remain permanently in the lungs, causing a tissue reaction that progresses slowly and apparently irreversibly. By the time the disease is diagnosable, a decade or more has elapsed since the date of the injurious exposure; each exposure to asbestos dust can cause additional tissue changes. The disease gradually makes breathing so difficult that victims become pulmonary cripples incapable of any exertion, even climbing stairs. Ten percent of all asbestosis victims die as a result of secondary lung complications. Mesothelioma is a highly malignant and particularly painful cancer of the chest linings that is associated exclusively with asbestos exposure and is usually fatal within a year after symptoms appear. People with such lung cancers become suddenly emaciated, after having been vigorous productive individuals. Like asbestosis, mesotheliomas take two or more decades to appear, and during these years the future victim will feel and be diagnosed as normal. Many cancers caused by current work with asbestos will not appear until the year 2000. Studies have shown that cigarette smoking and earlier lung disease can substantially increase a person's risk of contracting lung cancer from asbestos exposure.

Asbestos is a grayish-white fibrous mineral that is heat resistant and possesses remarkable strength and flexibility. These qualities have rendered it virtually irreplaceable in our society as an electrical and heat insulator. Over three thousand products commonly found in homes and factories contain asbestos, including electrical insulation, fireproofing, brakedrums, filters, acoustical tiles, potholders, and so on. As a result, about 4 million workers (and innumerable consumers) have been exposed to heavy concentrations of asbestos in the United States alone since the 1940s. Today between 1.5 and 2.5 million U.S. workers are employed in environments with significant asbestos exposure. Since about 35 percent of heavily exposed asbestos workers are killed by asbestos-related diseases, about 1.5 million of these workers will die as victims of asbestos exposure over the next three decades.[2]

Johns-Manville is the largest producer of asbestos fiber in the United States. In 1979 it had sales of $168.2 million worth of asbestos fibers, plus sales of several million more dollars worth of asbestos paper and textiles, asbestos cement, and asbestos cement products. The company conducts mining and manufacturing operations in the United States, Canada, and twelve other countries. Johns-Manville was incorporated in New York in 1926 and has been dealing in asbestos products since the 1920s. Net sales in 1979 were $2.28 billion, up from $.58 billion in 1970. Total (pretax) profits in 1979 were $217.8 million, up from $55.6 million in 1970. Today Johns-Manville employs about 32,500 workers.

[2]U.S., Congress, House, *Asbestos-related Occupational Diseases: Hearings before the Subcommittee on Compensation, Health, and Safety of the Committee on Education and Labor,* 94th Congress, 2nd session, 23 and 24 October; 13 and 14 November 1978, pp. 132–135. Hereafter cited as "Asbestos Hearings."

It is difficult to say when Johns-Manville first became aware of the danger of asbestosis. The first medical reference to asbestos-related diseases among American workers appeared in 1918, in a monograph published by the U.S. Bureau of Labor Statistics. This paper noted that insurance company records showed increased mortality among asbestos workers and commented that these companies were now reluctant to insure them. During the period 1924–1929 a series of medical studies of asbestosis among textile factory workers appeared in British journals. These reports stimulated Johns-Manville to commission two studies on the effects of asbestos. The first of these studies, which Dr. Leroy V. Gardner carried out at the Saranac Laboratory in New York, was part of a series of experiments on animals that continued for several years. On November 20, 1936, Mr. Brown, head of the legal department of Johns-Manville, wrote to Dr. Gardner clarifying the terms of their agreement to sponsor these animal studies:

> It is our further understanding that the results obtained will be considered the property of those who are advancing the required funds, who will determine to what extent and in what manner they shall be made public. In the event it is deemed desirable that the results be made public, the manuscript of your study will be submitted to us for approval prior to publication.[3]

Eventually, Dr. Gardner dropped from the study.

The second study, a health survey of asbestos workers that Dr. A. J. Lanza carried out for the asbestos industry, was ready for publication in 1934. Mr. Hobart, a private attorney, was asked to review Lanza's article for the industry before it was published. On December 15, Mr. Hobart wrote to Mr. Brown (head of Johns-Manville's legal department) saying that the Lanza report should be changed before publication. In particular, any comparisons between asbestosis and silicosis (a recognized occupational disease) should be eliminated. The letter read, in part, as follows:

> And if it is the policy of Johns-Manville to oppose any [legislative] bill that attempted to include asbestos as compensable, it would be very helpful to have an official report to show that there is a substantial difference between asbestosis and silicosis, and, by the same token, it would be troublesome if an official report should appear from which the conclusion might be drawn that there is very little, if any, difference between the two diseases.[4]

On December 21, Mr. Brown sent these and other requests for changes to Dr. Lanza in a letter that read, in part, as follows:

> I trust that you will give his [Hobart's] comments and suggestions, as well as those mentioned in my letter of December 10th, your most serious consideration. I am sure that you understand fully that no one in our organization is suggesting for a moment that you alter by one dot or title any scientific facts

[3]*Ibid.*, p. 31.
[4]*Ibid.*, pp. 28–29.

or inevitable conclusions revealed or justified by your preliminary survey. All we ask is that all of the favorable aspects of the survey be included and that none of the unfavorable be unintentionally pictured in darker tones than the circumstances justify. I feel confident we can depend upon you and Dr. McConnell to give us this "break."[5]

The Lanza report was published in 1935, with a few (but not all) of the changes for which Johns-Manville had asked.[6] The essence of the article was not changed: of 126 randomly sampled asbestos workers employed three years or more, 106 had abnormal lung findings.[7]

The number of employees who were beginning to succumb to asbestosis had started to pose a problem for asbestos manufacturers, since some of these employees or their survivors were now suing for compensation. A 1935 memorandum from Mr. Brown (of Johns-Manville) reported on an industry meeting held on January 15, 1935 at which the participants had discussed their emerging problems with asbestosis-afflicted workers and had also discussed strategies for dealing with these problems. The memo read in part:

> It appeared that among the problems common to all industry were the following:
>
> 1. The menace of ambulance-chasing lawyers in combination with unscrupulous doctors. The uncertainties surrounding diagnosis of any of the various forms of pneumoconiosis are so many that a question of fact is presented in every case. Expert testimony can be produced by both plaintiff and defendant, and . . . the jury is not likely to favor the opinion of the experts produced by the employers. . . .
> 2. One of the speakers stated that "the strongest bulwark against future disaster for industry is the enactment of properly drawn occupational disease legislation." Such legislation would (a) eliminate the jury and empower a medical board to pass upon the existence of the disease and the extent of the disability; (b) eliminate the shyster lawyer and the quack doctor, since fees would be strictly limited by law.[8]

By the latter 1930s, several dozen articles had been published suggesting that, although asbestosis was caused by inhaling asbestos dust, the danger might be controlled by maintaining a low level of exposure. An extensive study by the U.S. Public Health Service published in 1938, in fact, suggested that daily exposure to asbestos dust concentrations of up to 5 million particles per cubic foot of air would be safe as a "tentative standard."[9] The first large-scale survey of asbestos insulation applicators (as opposed to workers in asbestos mines and factories) was published by Dr. Fleisher and others in 1946. The authors examined large numbers of insu-

---

[5]*Ibid.*, pp. 29 and 643.

[6]*Ibid.*, p. 643.

[7]A. J. Lanza et. al., "Effects of the Inhalation of Asbestos on the Lungs of Asbestos Workers," *Public Health Reports*, 4. January 1935, pp. 1–12.

[8]*Asbestos Hearings*, pp. 94–95.

[9]W. C. Dressen, et. al., "A Study of Asbestosis in the Asbestos Textile Industry," *Public Health Bulletin*, no. 241 (1938).

lation applicators, 95 percent of whom had worked in eastern Navy shipyards for less than ten years, and found only three cases of asbestosis. They concluded that "asbestos covering of naval vessels is a relatively safe operation," especially since the measured exposures to asbestos dust for the insulation workers were with one exception below what the 1938 U.S. Public Health Service study had proposed as a tentative standard of safety.[10]

In 1947, the American Conference of Governmental Industrial Hygienists recommended that employers use the 1938 proposed standard and limit the work environment to no more than 5 million particles of asbestos dust per cubic foot of air. Nearly all workers, it suggested, could be repeatedly exposed to these concentrations day after day without adverse effect. Except for this recommendation, the government did very little about asbestosis during the next several years: Regulations were few and government inspections and supervision were infrequent. Johns-Manville itself did not conduct any more major tests to determine the hazards of its products.

By the early 1960s, several more reports had been published indicating that the incidence of asbestos-related disease was now climbing at an alarming rate. Then, in 1965, I.J. Selikoff and his colleagues published a definitive study on asbestosis entitled "The Occurrence of Asbestosis Among Insulation Workers in the United States."[11] The authors examined 1,522 members of an insulation workers union and found that 44 percent of those who had been exposed to asbestos for ten to nineteen years had asbestosis; 73 percent of those who had been exposed twenty to twenty-nine years had it; 87 percent of those who had been exposed thirty to thirty-nine years had it; and 94 percent of those exposed more than 40 years had the disease. The authors concluded that "asbestosis and its complications are significant hazards among insulation workers."

Two years before Dr. Selikoff's study was officially published the substance of his findings had been announced at asbestos industry meetings.[12] Johns-Manville became concerned and, in 1964, for the first time, the company fixed the following warning labels on its asbestos products:

> This product contains asbestos fiber. Inhalation of asbestos in excessive quantities over long periods of time may be harmful. If dust is created when this product is handled, avoid breathing the dust. If adequate ventilation control is not possible, wear respirators approved by the U.S. Bureau of Mines for pneumoconiosis-producing dusts.[13]

Johns-Manville did not feel that more warning than this was necessary. According to Dr. Paul Kotin, senior vice-president for health, safety, and environment for Johns-Manville Corporation:

[10]W. E. Fleisher, et. al., "A Health Survey of Pipe Covering Operations in Constructing Naval Vessels," *Journal of Industrial Hygiene and Toxicology,* January 1946.

[11]I. J. Selikoff, et. al., "The Occurrence of Asbestosis among Insulation Workers in the United States, *Annals of the New York Academy of Science,* 132 (1965); 139–55.

[12]*Asbestos Hearings,* pp. 50 and 51.

[13]Borel v. Fiberboard Paper Products, p. 1104.

Johns-Manville was aware of the fact [that] asbestos exposure was potentially a hazard, and Johns-Manville certainly made no secret of the fact it was a hazard. . . . Johns-Manville had the responsibility of informing the people [to whom] it was selling the material [and] . . . it did this. . . . Now, whether Johns-Manville had the responsibility for going to the work site of the insulation manufacturers anymore than the Bayer Corporation has for going into my home when I take an aspirin [is another matter]. Rather, it suffices [to say] . . . in its ads, "avoid excessive use" or, now, "use only as directed." (Statement of Dr. Kotin in 1977)[14]

Clarence Borel never worked for Johns-Manville. Instead, Borel worked for a building contractor who employed him to install asbestos insulation that Johns-Manville (and other firms) had manufactured. Shortly before he died, however, Borel argued that Johns-Manville should be held responsible for his sickness and should pay him compensation. He claimed that the manufacturer knew that asbestos was dangerous and had a duty to inform the final users of its asbestos products that inhaling the dust could be fatal. Johns-Manville also had had a duty, he claimed, to test asbestos products more thoroughly in order to ascertain the dangers involved in their use.[15]

Johns-Manville, however, held that Clarence Borel's own employer should have warned him of the dangers of asbestos, or that Borel should have protected himself against the asbestos dust by wearing a mask (or by asking his employer to furnish ventilating blowers), since, in his own words, he "knew the dust was bad."[16] Johns-Manville also claimed that the manufacturers of the asbestos products that Borel handled were not responsible for Borel's disease and death because manufacturers did not know enough about asbestosis during the period at which Borel probably contracted the disease. And lastly, Johns-Manville claimed, there was no way of knowing whether Borel's disease had been caused by Johns-Manville's products or by asbestos from the products of other manufacturers that Borel had also handled.

Before he died, Borel was asked about the use of respirators. He replied that they were not furnished by his employers during his early work years. Although respirators were later made available on some jobs, insulation workers were not required to wear them and had to make a special request if they wanted one. According to Borel, when respirators were furnished, they were uncomfortable, could not be worn in hot weather, and "you can't breathe with the respirator." Borel further claimed that no respirator in use during his working life could prevent the inhalation of asbestos dust.

1. Identify the moral issues that you think are involved in this case. Explain your answers.

[14] *Asbestos Hearings*, p. 116.
[15] Borel v. Fiberboard Paper Products, p. 1086.
[16] *Ibid.*, p. 1091.

2. In your opinion, was Johns-Manville morally responsible for Clarence Borel's condition? Identify the factors that in your opinion are decisive in making Johns-Manville morally responsible or that were decisive in absolving Johns-Manville from the responsibility. Explain why these factors are decisive. Was the moral responsibility for Clarence Borel's condition shared by any other parties in the case? Explain.

3. In your view, what moral duties, if any, did Johns-Manville (or other parties in the case) have that should have been carried out? Formulate the moral standards on which your view is based. Do your standards meet the consistency requirement?

CHAPTER TWO
ETHICAL PRINCIPLES
IN BUSINESS

INTRODUCTION

Recently, several members of Congress proposed that the federal government should be granted sole power to confer corporate status on businesses. Such "federal chartering" of businesses, they claimed, would strengthen the government's ability to regulate corporate activities and to eliminate corporate abuses. During a congressional hearing called to examine this proposal, the following exchange took place between Senator Durkin who favored the proposal, and a witness who was testifying against the proposal:[1]

Senator Durkin:

Good morning, ladies and gentlemen. We are beginning an inquiry that, in my opinion, is crucial to the well-being of our people and the country. How do we control and hold accountable huge institutions? To what extent do we profit from these organizations, and to what extent is each of us limited or harmed by their actions? DuPont allegedly [suppressed] price competition among retailers of its Lucite brand paint. I wonder how much more it cost somebody to paint his house because of DuPont's alleged price-fixing! We have, over the last few years, begun to appreciate the real costs of some industrial activities of the past [that] affect our health and environment. The federal response to these problems has been to look at one problem at a time. [But] why not consolidate the hundreds of federal laws and regulations into concise constitutional principles in a single document [on federal chartering]?

[1]U.S., Congress, Senate, *Hearings Before the Committee on Commerce on Corporate Rights and Responsibilities,* 94th Congress, 2nd session, June 1976, pp. 1, 4, 6, 9, 11, 14.

44

Witness:

Mr. Chairman, I am here today to present for your consideration my views on why the proposal for federal chartering of corporations should be rejected. A corporation is created by a voluntary contractual agreement between individuals seeking to promote their own financial self-interest. Corporations are created and sustained by freedom of association and contract, and the source of these freedoms is individual rights. As long as you are not wronging anybody else, you have the right to combine with others for any purpose, and the state has no right to monitor, or restrict, or [define] the form of [a] contractual arrangement. I have rights as an individual, and I delegate them to the Congress to make laws in accordance with standards of justice and for the protection of individual rights.

The conclusions of Senator Durkin and the witness were essentially moral judgments. They were not debating whether the law allows federal chartering nor were they debating whether federal chartering is constitutional. Instead, they were judging whether it would be right to *create* a federal chartering law. Their judgments appealed to three basic kinds of moral standards by which we evaluate the moral adequacy of our laws, institutions, and activities: utilitarianism, rights, and justice.

Senator Durkin, for example, argued in favor of federal chartering of businesses by claiming that it would diminish the social costs associated with certain corporate abuses. His argument was an implicit appeal to what is called a "utilitarian" standard of morality; a moral principle, that is, that claims that something is right to the extent that it diminishes social costs and increases social benefits. The witness, on the other hand, argued against federal chartering by claiming that it would violate the "rights of individuals" and be contrary to "standards of justice." These arguments were also appeals to moral standards. Individual rights are based on moral principles that indicate the areas in which the freedom of individuals must be respected, while justice is based on moral principles that identify equitable ways of distributing benefits and burdens among the members of a society.

These three kinds of moral principles constitute three of the most important types of ethical standards studied by moral philosophers. Each kind of principle employs distinctive moral concepts, and each one emphasizes aspects of moral behavior that are neglected or at least not emphasized by the others. The purpose of this chapter is to explain each of these three approaches to moral judgments by describing the kinds of concepts and information that each standard employs.

2.1 UTILITARIANISM: SOCIAL COSTS AND BENEFITS

Several years ago, the Council on Environmental Quality put forth the following claims in a report entitled *Environmental Quality:*

When the expected gains are large relative to the costs it is clearly in our interests to move forward in cleaning up the environment. And such improvement should, of course, continue as long as the perceived added gains of attaining each higher level of environmental quality exceed the expected costs.[2]

Basing its recommendations on these standards, the Council on Environmental Quality recommended that we ought to institute certain pollution abatement measures in the Delaware estuary that were estimated to cost between $85 million and $155 million but whose benefits to society would range between $130 million to $310 million. The Council recommended rejection of measures that would cost $215 million to $315 million but result in social benefits of only $140 million to $320 million. The former, less costly measures were preferred because they were expected to produce greater net benefits for society than any of the other available alternatives.

The standards on which the Council on Environmental Quality based its recommendations are a version of what has traditionally been called "utilitarianism." "Utilitarianism" is a general term for any view that holds that actions and practices should be evaluated on the basis of the aggregate social benefits and the aggregate social costs associated with the actions or practices. In any given situation, the proper, or "right," action or practice is the one that will produce the greatest net benefits (or the lowest net costs) for society as a whole.

In the recommendation of the Council on Economic Quality, "costs" and "benefits" were restricted to economic costs and benefits and were measured in monetary terms. But this need not be the case. The "benefits" of an action may include any desirable goods (pleasures, health, life, satisfactions, knowledge, happiness) produced by the action, and "costs" may include any of its undesirable evils (pain, sickness, death, dissatisfaction, ignorance, unhappiness). The inclusive term used to refer to the net benefits of any sort produced by an action is "utility," hence the name "utilitarianism" for a theory that advocates selection of those actions that maximize benefits and minimize costs.

It is often assumed that the best way of evaluating the propriety of a business decision is by relying on utilitarian cost-benefit analysis.[3] The socially responsible action for a business to take is the one that will produce the greatest net benefits for society (or impose the lowest net costs). This section examines this widespread ethical standard.

Traditional Utilitarianism

Jeremy Bentham (1748-1832) is generally considered the founder of traditional utilitarianism.[4] Bentham sought an objective basis for making value judg-

---

[2] Council on Environmental Quality, *Environmental Quality* (Washington, D.C.: U.S. Government Printing Office, 1971), p. 118.

[3] Thomas A. Klein, *Social Costs and Benefits of Business* (Englewood Cliffs, NJ: Prentice-Hall, Inc., 1977).

[4] Jeremy Bentham, *The Principles of Morals and Legislation* (Oxford, 1789); Henry Sidgwick, *Outlines of the History of Ethics,* 5th ed. (London, 1902), traces the history of utili-

ments that would provide a common and publicly acceptable norm for determining social policy and social legislation. The most promising way of reaching such an objective ground of agreement, he believed, is by looking at the various policies a legislature could enact and comparing the beneficial and harmful consequences of each. The right course of action from an ethical point of view would be to choose the policy that would produce the greatest amount of utility. Summarized, the utilitarian principle holds that:

> *An action is right from an ethical point of view if and only if the sum total of utilities produced by that act is greater than the sum total of utilities produced by any other act the agent could have performed in its place.*

The utilitarian principle assumes that we can somehow measure and add the quantities of benefits produced by an action and subtract from them the measured quantities of harm the action will have, and thereby determine which action produces the greatest total benefits or the lowest total costs. That is, the principle assumes that all the benefits and costs of an action can be measured on a common numerical scale and then added or subtracted from each other.[5] The satisfactions that an improved work environment imparts to workers, for example, might be equivalent to five hundred positive units of utility, while the resulting bills that arrive the next month might be equivalent to seven hundred negative units of utility. So the total combined utility of this act (improving the work environment) would be two hundred units of *negative* utility: That is, its costs would outweigh its benefits.

When the utilitarian principle says that the right action for a particular occasion is the one that produces more utility than any other possible action, it does not mean that the right action is the one that produces the most utility for the person performing the action but rather, the one that produces the most utility for *all* persons affected by the action (including the person performing the action).[6] That is, to ascertain what I ought to do on a particular occasion I must first determine what alternative actions are available to me on that occasion. Secondly, for each alternative action I must estimate the benefits and costs that the action would produce for *each* and *every* person affected by the action. Thirdly, the alternative that produces the greatest sum total of utility must be chosen as the ethically right action. The immediate and long-range costs and benefits each alternative will provide for each individual must be taken into account as well as any indirect effects each action will have on the behavior of those influenced by the action.

---

tarian thought to Bentham's predecessors. Some modern expositions of utilitarian thought may be found in Michael D. Bayles, ed. *Contemporary Utilitarianism* (Garden City, NY: Doubleday & Co., Inc., 1968); and J.J.C. Smart and Bernard Williams, *Utilitarianism: For and Against* (London: Cambridge University Press, 1973).

[5] Henry Sidgwick, *Methods of Ethics,* 7th ed. (Chicago: University of Chicago Press, 1962), p. 413.

[6] John Stuart Mill, *Utilitarianism* (Indianapolis: The Bobbs-Merrill Co., Inc., 1957), p. 22.

Utilitarianism is in many respects an attractive theory. For one thing, it matches fairly nicely the views that we tend to advocate when discussing the choice of government policies and public goods. Most people will agree, for example, that when the government is trying to determine on which public projects it should spend tax monies, the proper course of action would be for it to adopt those projects that objective studies show will provide the greatest benefits for the members of society at the least cost. And this, of course, is just another way of saying that the proper government policies are those that would have the greatest measurable utility for people or, in the words of a famous slogan, those that will produce "the greatest good for the greatest number."

Utilitarianism also seems to fit in rather neatly with the intuitive criteria that people employ when discussing moral conduct.[7] When people explain, for example, why they have a moral obligation to perform some action, they will often proceed by pointing to the benefits or harms the action will impose upon human beings. Moreover, morality requires that one impartially take everyone's interests equally into account. Utilitarianism meets this requirement insofar as it takes into account the effects actions have on everyone and insofar as it requires one to impartially choose the action with the greatest net utility regardless of who gets the benefits.

Utilitarianism also has the advantage of being able to explain why we hold that certain types of activities are generally morally wrong (lying, adultery, killing), while others are generally morally right (telling the truth, fidelity, keeping one's promises). The utilitarian can say that lying is generally wrong because of the costly effects lying has on our human welfare. When people lie to each other, they are less apt to trust each other and to cooperate with each other. And the less trust and cooperation, the more our welfare declines. On the other hand, telling the truth is generally right because it strengthens cooperation and trust, and thereby improves everyone's well-being. In general, then, it is a good rule of thumb to tell the truth and to refrain from lying. Traditional utilitarians would deny, however, that any kinds of actions are always right or always wrong. They would deny, for example, that dishonesty or theft is necessarily always wrong. If in a certain situation more good consequences would flow from being dishonest than from any other act a person could perform in that situation, then, according to traditional utilitarian theory, dishonesty would be morally right in that particular situation.

Utilitarian views have also been highly influential in economics.[8] A long line of economists, beginning in the nineteenth century, argued that economic behavior could be explained by assuming that human beings always attempt to maximize their utility and that the utilities of commodities can be measured by the prices people are willing to pay for them. With these and a few other simplifying assumptions (such as the use of indifference curves), economists were able to derive the familiar supply and demand curves of sellers and buyers in markets and explain

[7]Richard Brandt, *Ethical Theory* (Englewood Cliffs, NJ: Prentice-Hall, Inc., 1959), p. 386.
[8]For example, William Stanley Javons, *Theory of Political Economy* (1871); Alfred Marshall, *Principles of Economics* (1890); Cecil Arthur Pigou, *Wealth and Welfare* (1912).

why prices in a perfectly competitive market gravitate toward an equilibrium. More importantly, economists were also able to demonstrate that a system of perfectly competitive markets would lead to a use of resources and to price variations that would enable consumers to maximize their utility (defined in terms of Pareto optimality) through their purchases.[9] On utilitarian grounds, therefore, these economists concluded that such a system of markets is better than any other alternative.

As we noted in the introduction, utilitarianism is also the basis of the techniques of economic cost-benefit analysis.[10] This type of analysis is used to determine the desirability of investing in a project (like a dam, a factory, or a public park) by figuring whether its present and future economic benefits outweigh its present and future economic costs. To calculate these costs and benefits discounted monetary prices are estimated for all the effects the project will have on the present and future environment and on present and future populations. Carrying out these sorts of calculations is not always an easy matter, but various methods have been devised for determining the monetary prices of even such intangible benefits as the beauty of a forest (for instance, we might ask how much people pay to see the beauty of a similar privately owned park). If the monetary benefits of a certain public project exceed the monetary costs and if the excess is greater than the excess produced by any other feasible project, then the project should be undertaken. In this form of utilitarianism the concept of utility is restricted to monetarily measurable economic costs and benefits.

Problems of Measurement

One major set of problems with utilitarianism is centered around the difficulties encountered when trying to measure "utility."[11] One problem is this: How can the utilities different actions have for different people be measured and compared as utilitarianism requires? Suppose you and I would both enjoy getting a certain job: How can we figure out whether the utility you would get out of having the job is more or less than the utility I would get out of having it? Each of us may be sure that he or she would benefit most from the job, but since we cannot get into each other's skin, this judgment has no objective basis. Since comparative measures of the values things have for different people cannot be made, the critics argue, there is no way of knowing whether utility would be maximized by giving me the job or giving you the job. And if we cannot know which actions will produce the greatest amounts of utility, then we cannot apply the utilitarian principle.

[9] See Paul Samuelson, *Foundations of Economic Analysis* (Cambridge: Harvard University Press, 1947). A system is "Pareto optimal" if no one in the system can be made better off without making some other person worse off; an "indifference curve" indicates the quantities of one good a person would willingly trade for given quantities of another good.

[10] E.J. Mishan, *Economics for Social Decisions: Elements of Cost-Benefit Analysis* (New York: Praeger Publishers, Inc., 1973), pp. 14–17.

[11] See, for example, Wesley C. Mitchell, "Bentham's Felicific Calculus" in *The Backward Art of Spending Money and Other Essays* (New York: Augustus M. Kelley, Inc., 1950), pp. 177–202.

A second problem is that some benefits and costs seem intractible to measurement. How, for example, can one measure the value of health or life?[12] Suppose that installing an expensive exhaust system in a workshop will eliminate a large portion of certain carcinogenic particles that workers might otherwise inhale. And suppose that as a result some of the workers probably will live five years longer. How is one to calculate the value of those years of added life, and how is this value to be quantitatively balanced against the costs of installing the exhaust system?

A third problem is that because many of the benefits and costs of an action cannot be reliably predicted, they also cannot be adequately measured.[13] The beneficial or costly consequences of basic scientific knowledge, for example, are notoriously difficult to predict. Yet suppose that one has to decide how much to invest in a research program that will probably uncover some highly theoretical, but not immediately usable, information about the universe. How is the future value of that information to be measured, and how can it be weighed against either the present costs of funding the research or the more certain benefits that would result from putting the funds to an alternative use, such as adding a new wing to the local hospital or building housing for the poor?

Yet a fourth problem is that it is unclear exactly what is to count as a "benefit" and what is to count as a "cost."[14] This lack of clarity is especially problematic with respect to social issues that are given significantly different evaluations by different cultural groups. Suppose a bank must decide, for example, whether to extend a loan to the manager of a local pornographic theater or to the manager of a bar that caters to homosexuals. One group of people may see the increased enjoyment of pornography connoisseurs or the increased enjoyment of homosexuals as *benefits* accruing to society. Another group, however, may see these as harmful and hence as *costs*.

The critics of utilitarianism contend that these measurement problems undercut whatever claims utilitarian theory makes to providing an objective basis for determining normative issues. These problems have become especially obvious in debates over the feasibility of corporate social audits.[15] Although business firms have

---

[12] For a discussion of this problem see Michael D. Bayles, "The Price of Life," *Ethics,* 89, no. 1 (October 1978): 20–34; Jonathan Glover, *Causing Death and Saving Lives* (New York: Penguin Books, 1977); Peter S. Albin, "Economic Values and the Value of Human Life," in *Human Values and Economic Policy,* ed. Sidney Hook (New York: New York University Press, 1967).

[13] G.E. Moore, *Principia Ethica,* 5th ed. (Cambridge: Cambridge University Press, 1956), p. 149.

[14] Alastair MacIntyre, "Utilitarianism and Cost-Benefit Analysis: An Essay on the Relevance of Moral Philosophy to Bureaucratic Theory," in *Values in the Electric Power Industry,* ed. Kenneth Syre (Notre Dame, IN: University of Notre Dame Press, 1977).

[15] David H. Blake, William C. Frederick, and Mildred S. Myers, "Measurement Problems in the Social Audit," in *Ethical Theory and Business,* eds. Tom L. Beauchamp and Norman E. Bowie (Englewood Cliffs, NJ: Prentice-Hall, Inc., 1979), pp. 246–252; for a review of the literature see Task Force on Corporate Social Performance, *Corporate Social Reporting in the United States and Western Europe* (Washington, DC: U.S. Government Printing Office, 1979), pp. 2–36.

been increasingly pressured to produce an "audit" or report measuring the social costs and benefits resulting from their business activities,[16] their efforts have been stymied by their inability to place quantitative measures on their various programs,[17] and by differences of opinion over what should be counted as a benefit. The only way of resolving these problems is by arbitrarily accepting the valuations of one social group or another. But this in effect bases utilitarian cost-benefit analysis on the subjective biases and tastes of that group.

Utilitarian Replies to
Measurement Objections

The defender of utilitarianism has an array of replies ready to counter the measurement objections enumerated above.

First, the utilitarian may argue that, although utilitarianism ideally requires accurate quantifiable measurements of all costs and benefits, this requirement can be relaxed when such measurements are impossible.[18] Utilitarianism merely insists that the consequences of any projected act be expressly stated with as much clarity and accuracy as is humanly possible, and that all relevant information concerning these consequences be presented in a form that will allow them to be systematically compared and impartially weighed against each other. Expressing this information in quantitative terms will facilitate such comparisons and weighings. But where quantitative data are unavailable, one may legitimately rely on shared and common-sense judgments of the comparative values things have for most people. We know, for example, that by and large cancer is a greater injury than a cold, no matter who has the cancer and who has the cold; similarly, a steak has a greater value as food than a peanut, no matter whose hunger is involved.

The utilitarian can also point to several common-sense criteria that can be used to determine the relative values that should be given to various categories of goods. One criterion, for example, depends on the distinction between "intrinsic" and "instrumental" goods.[19] Instrumental goods are things that are considered valuable only because they lead to other good things. A painful visit to the dentist, for example, is only an instrumental good (unless I happen to be a masochist): It is desired only as a means to health. Intrinsic goods, however, are things that are desirable independently of any other benefits they may produce. Thus, health is an intrinsic good: It is desired for its own sake. (Many things, of course, have both intrinsic and

---

[16] Raymond A. Bauer and Dan H. Fenn, Jr., *The Corporate Social Audit* (New York: Sage Publications, Inc., 1972), pp. 3–14.

[17] John J. Corson and George A. Steiner, *Measuring Business's Social Performance: The Corporate Social Audit* (New York: Committee for Economic Development, 1974), p. 41.

[18] Tom L. Beauchamp, "Utilitarianism and Cost-Benefit Analysis: A Reply to MacIntyre," in *Ethical Theory*, eds. Beauchamp and Bowie, pp. 276–82.

[19] See Amitai Etzioni and Edward W. Lehman, "Dangers in 'Valid' Social Measurements," *Annals of the American Academy of Political and Social Sciences*, 373 (September 1967): 6; also William K. Frankena, *Ethics*, 2nd ed. (Englewood Cliffs, NJ: Prentice-Hall, Inc., 1973), pp. 80–83.

instrumental value. I may go skiing, for example, both because skiing is a means to health and because I enjoy skiing for itself.) Now it is clear that intrinsic goods take priority over instrumental goods. Under most circumstances, for example, money, which is an instrumental good, must not take priority over life and health, which have intrinsic values.

A second common-sense criterion that can be used to weigh goods turns on the distinction between needs and wants.[20] To say that someone *needs* something is to say that without it he or she will be harmed in some way. People's "basic" needs consist of their needs for things without which they will suffer some fundamental harm such as injury, illness, or death. Among a person's basic needs are the food, clothing, and housing required to stay alive; the medical care and hygienic environment required to remain healthy; and the security and safety required to remain free from injury. On the other hand, to say that a person *wants* to do something is to say that the person desires it: The person believes it will advance his or her interests in some way. A need, of course, may also be a want: If I know I need something then I may also want it. Many wants, however, are not needs but simply desires for things without which the individual would not suffer any fundamental harm. I may want something simply because I enjoy it, even though it is a luxury I could as well do without. Desires of this sort that are not also needs are called "mere wants." In general, satisfying a person's basic needs is more valuable than satisfying his or her mere wants. If people do not get something for which they have a basic need, they may be injured in a way that makes it impossible for them to enjoy the satisfaction of any number of mere wants. Since the satisfaction of a person's basic needs makes possible not only the intrinsic values of life and health but also the enjoyment of most other intrinsic values, satisfaction of the basic needs has a value that is greater than that of satisfying mere wants.

But these common-sense methods of weighing goods are only intended to aid us in situations where quantitative methods fail. In actual fact the consequences of many decisions are relatively amenable to quantification, the convinced utilitarian will claim. This constitutes the utilitarian's second major reply to the measurement objections outlined above.

The most flexible method of providing a common quantitative measure for the benefits and costs associated with a decision, the utilitarian may hold, is in terms of their monetary equivalents.[21] Basically this implies that the value a thing has for a person can be measured by the price the person is willing to pay for it. If a person will pay twice as much for one thing as for another, then that thing has exactly twice the value of the other for that person. In order to determine the average values items have for a group of people, then, one need merely look at the average prices given to those items when everyone is allowed to bid for them on open markets. In

[20]See Kenneth Arrow, *Social Choice and Individual Values,* 2nd ed. (New York: John Wiley & Sons, Inc., 1951), p. 87; and Norman E. Bowie, *Towards a New Theory of Distributive Justice* (Amherst: The University of Massachusetts Press, 1971), pp. 86–87.

[21]See, for example, the techniques enumerated in Mishan, *Economics for Social Decisions.*

short, market prices can serve to provide a common quantitative measure of the various benefits and costs associated with a decision. In general, to determine the value of a thing one need merely ask what it sells for on an open market. If the item does not sell on an open market, then one can ask what similar items are selling for.

The use of monetary values also has the advantage of allowing one to take into account the effects of the passage of time and the impact of uncertainty.[22] If the known monetary costs or benefits lie in the future, then their present values can be determined by discounting them at the appropriate rate of interest. If the monetary costs or benefits are only probable and not certain, then their expected values can be computed by multiplying the monetary costs or benefits by the appropriate probability factor.

A standard objection against using monetary values to measure all costs and benefits is that some goods, in particular health and life, cannot be priced. The utilitarian may argue, however, that not only is it possible to put a price on health and life but that we do so almost daily. Anytime people place a limit on the amount of money they are willing to pay to reduce the risk that some object poses to their lives, they have set an implicit price on their own lives. For example, suppose that people are willing to pay $5.00 for a piece of safety equipment that will reduce the probability of their being killed in an auto accident from .00005 to .00004, but they are unwilling to pay any more than that. Then, in effect, they have implicitly decided that .00001 of a life is worth $5, or in other words, that a life is worth $500,000. Such pricing is inevitable and necessary, the utilitarian may hold, so long as we live in an environment in which risks to health and life can be lowered only by giving up (trading off) other things that we may want and on which we set a clear price.

Finally, the utilitarian may say, where market prices are incapable of providing quantitative data for comparing the costs and benefits of various decisions, other sorts of quantitative measures are available.[23] Should people disagree, for example, as they often do, over the harmful or beneficial aspects of various sexual activities, then sociological surveys or political votes can be used to measure the intensity and extensiveness of people's attitudes. Economic experts can also provide informed judgments of the relative quantitative values of various costs and benefits. Thus the utilitarian will grant that the problems of measurement encountered by utilitarianism are real enough. But they are at least partially soluble by the various methods enumerated above. There are, however, other criticisms of utilitarianism.

Problems with Rights and Justice

The major difficulty with utilitarianism, according to some critics, is that it is unable to deal with two kinds of moral issues: those relating to *rights*[24] and those

---

[22]*Ibid.*, pp. 118–24 and 141–44.

[23]E. Bruce Frederickson, "Noneconomic Criteria and the Decision Process," *Decision Sciences*, 2, no. 1 (January 1971): 25–52.

[24]Bowie, *Towards a New Theory of Distributive Justice*, pp. 20–22.

relating to *justice.*[25] That is, the utilitarian principle implies that certain actions are morally right when in fact they are unjust or they violate people's rights. Some examples may serve to indicate the sort of difficult "counter-examples" critics pose for utilitarianism.

First, suppose that your uncle had an incurable and painful disease, so that as a result he was quite unhappy but does not choose to die. Although he is hospitalized and will die within a year, he continues to run his chemical plant. Because of his own misery he deliberately makes life miserable for his workers and has insisted on not installing safety devices in his chemical plant, although he knows that as a result one worker will certainly lose his life over the next year. You, his only living relative, know that on your uncle's death you will inherit his business and will not only be wealthy and immensely happy, but also intend to prevent any future loss of life by installing the needed safety devices. You are cold-blooded, and correctly judge that you could secretly murder your uncle without being caught and without your happiness being in any way affected by it afterwards. If it is possible for you to murder your uncle without in any way diminishing anyone else's happiness, then according to utilitarianism you have a moral obligation to do so. By murdering your uncle, you are trading his life for the life of the worker, and you are gaining your happiness while doing away with his unhappiness and pain: The gain is obviously on the side of utility. However, the critics of utilitarianism claim, it seems quite clear that the murder of your uncle would be a gross violation of his right to life. Utilitarianism has led us to approve an act of murder that is an obvious violation of an individual's most important right.

Secondly, utilitarianism can also go wrong, according to the critics, when it is applied to situations that involve social justice. Suppose, for example, that the fact that they are paid subsistence wages forces a small group of migrant workers to continue doing the most undesirable agricultural jobs in an economy but produces immense amounts of satisfaction for the vast majority of society's members, since they enjoy cheap vegetables and savings that allow them to indulge other wants. Suppose also that the amounts of satisfaction thereby produced, when balanced against the unhappiness and pain imposed upon the small group of farm workers, results in a greater net utility than would exist if everyone had to share the burdens of farm work. Then, according to the utilitarian criterion, it would be morally right to continue this system of subsistence wages for farm workers. Yet to the critics of utilitarianism, a social system that imposes such unequal sharing of burdens is clearly immoral and offends against justice. The great benefits the system may have for the majority does not justify the extreme burdens that it imposes on a small group. The shortcoming this counter-example reveals is that utilitarianism allows benefits and burdens to be distributed among the members of society in any way whatsoever, so long as the total amount of benefits is maximized. But in fact, some ways of distributing benefits and burdens (like the extremely unequal distributions involved in the counter-example) are unjust, regardless of how great the store of benefits such

[25]*Ibid.,* pp. 22–24.

distributions produce. Utilitarianism looks only at how much utility is produced in a society and fails to take into account how that utility is distributed among the members of society.

Utilitarian Replies to Objections on Rights and Justice

In order to deal with the sorts of counter-examples that critics of traditional utilitarianism have offered, utilitarians have recently proposed an important and influential alternative version of utilitarianism called "rule-utilitarianism."[26] The basic strategy of the rule-utilitarian is to limit utilitarian analysis to the evaluations of moral rules. According to the rule-utilitarian, when trying to determine whether a particular *action* is ethical, one is never supposed to ask whether that particular action will produce the greatest amount of utility. Instead, one is supposed to ask whether the action is required by the correct moral rules that everyone should follow. If the action is required by such rules, then one should carry out the action. But what are the "correct" moral rules? It is only this second question, according to the rule-utilitarian, that is supposed to be answered by reference to maximizing utility. The correct moral rules are those that would produce the greatest amount of utility if everyone were to follow them. An example may make this clear.

Suppose I am trying to decide whether or not it is ethical for me to fix prices with a competitor. Then, according to the rule-utilitarian, I should not ask whether this particular instance of price-fixing will produce more utility than anything else I can do. Instead, I should first ask myself: What are the correct moral rules with respect to price-fixing? Perhaps I might conclude, after some thought, that the following list of rules includes all the candidates:

1. Managers are never to meet with competitors for the purpose of fixing prices.
2. Managers may always meet with competitors for the purpose of fixing prices.
3. Managers may meet with competitors for the purpose of fixing prices when they are losing money.

Which of these three is the correct moral rule? According to the rule-utilitarian, the correct moral rule is the one that would produce the greatest amount of utility for everyone affected. Let us suppose that after analyzing the economic effects of price-fixing, I conclude that within our economic and social circumstances people would benefit much more if everyone followed rule 1 than if everyone followed rule 2 or 3. If this is so, then rule 1 is the correct moral rule concerning price-fixing. Now that I know what the correct moral rule on price-fixing is, I can go on to ask a second question: Should I engage in this particular act of fixing prices? To answer this second question I only have to ask: What is required by the correct moral rules?

[26]S.E. Toulmin, *An Examination of the Place of Reason in Ethics* (Cambridge: Cambridge University Press, 1950), ch. 11; J. Rawls, "Two Concepts of Rules," *Philosophical Review*, 64 (1955): 3–32; J. O. Ormson, "The Interpretation of the Philosophy of J.S. Mill," *Philosophical Quarterly*, 3 (1953): 33–40.

As we have already noted, the correct rule is to never fix prices. Consequently, even if on this particular occasion, fixing prices actually would produce more utility than not doing so, I am, nonetheless, ethically obligated to refrain from fixing prices because this is required by the rules from which everyone in my society would most benefit.

The theory of the rule-utilitarian, then, has two parts, which we can summarize in the following two principles:

I. *An action is right from an ethical point of view if and only if the action would be required by those moral rules that are correct.*

II. *A moral rule is correct if and only if the sum total of utilities produced if everyone were to follow that rule is greater than the sum total of utilities produced if everyone were to follow some alternative rule.*

Thus, according to the rule-utilitarian, the fact that a certain action would maximize utility on one particular occasion does not show that it is right from an ethical point of view.

For the rule-utilitarian, the flaw in the counter-examples that the critics of traditional utilitarianism offer is that in each case the utilitarian criterion is applied to particular actions and not to rules. Instead, the rule-utilitarian would urge, we must use the utilitarian criterion to find out what the correct moral *rule* is for each counter-example, and then evaluate the particular actions involved in the counter-example only in terms of this rule. Doing this will allow utilitarianism to escape the counter-examples undamaged.

The counter-example involving the rich uncle and the murderous heir, for example, is a situation that deals with killing a sick person. In such situations, the rule-utilitarian might argue, it is clear that a moral rule that forbids killing without the due process of law will, in the long run, have greater utility for society than other kinds of rules. Such a rule, therefore, is the correct one to apply to the case. It would be wrong for the heir to kill his uncle because doing so would violate a correct moral rule and the fact that murder would on this particular occasion maximize utility is irrelevant.

The case dealing with subsistence wages, the rule-utilitarian would argue, should be treated similarly. It is clear that a rule that forbade unnecessary subsistence wages in societies would in the long run result in more utility than a rule which allowed them. Such a rule would therefore be the correct rule to invoke when asking whether practicing "wage slavery" is morally permissible, and the practice would then be rejected as ethically wrong even if it would maximize utility on a particular occasion.

The ploy of the rule-utilitarian, however, has not satisfied the critics of utilitarianism, who have pointed out an important difficulty in the rule-utilitarian position: According to its critics, rule-utilitarianism is traditional utilitarianism in disguise.[27] These critics argue that rules that allow (beneficial) exceptions will produce more utility than rules that do not allow any exceptions. But once a rule allows these exceptions, the critics claim, it will allow the same injustices and violations of rights that traditional utilitarianism allows. Some examples may help us see more clearly what these critics mean. The critics claim that if a rule allows people to make an exception whenever an exception will maximize utility, then it will produce more utility than it would if it allowed no exceptions. For example, more utility would be produced by a rule which says "People are not to be killed without due process *except when doing so will produce more utility than not doing so,*" than would be produced by a rule that simply says "People are not to be killed without due process." The first rule will *always* maximize utility, while the second rule will maximize utility only *most* of the time (because the second rule rigidly requires due process even when it would be more beneficial to dispense with due process). Since the rule-utilitarian holds that the "correct" moral rule is the one that produces more utility, he must hold that the correct moral rule is the one which allows exceptions when exceptions will maximize utility. But once the exception clause is made part of the rule, the critics point out, then applying the rule to an action will have exactly the same consequences as applying the traditional utilitarian criterion directly to the action since the utilitarian criterion is now part of the rule. In the case of the sick uncle and murderous heir, for example, the rule that "People are not to be killed without due process except when doing so will produce more utility than not doing so," will now allow the heir to murder his uncle exactly as traditional utilitarianism did before. Similarly, more utility would be produced by a rule which says "Subsistence wages are prohibited *except in those situations where they will maximize utility,*" than would be produced by a rule that simply says, "Subsistence wages are prohibited." So the rule that allows exceptions will be the "correct" one. But this "correct" rule will now allow the society we described earlier to institute wage slavery, exactly as traditional utilitarianism did. Rule-utilitarianism, then, is a disguised form of traditional utilitarianism and the counter-examples that set difficulties for one seem to set similar difficulties for the other.

Many rule utilitarians do not admit that rules produce more utility when they allow exceptions. Since human nature is weak and self-interested, they claim, humans would take advantage of any allowable exceptions and this would leave everyone worse off. Other utilitarians refuse to admit that the counter-examples of the critics are correct. They claim that if killing a person without due process really would produce more utility than all other feasible alternatives, then all other alternatives must have greater evils attached to them. And if this is so, then killing the person without due process really would be morally right. Similarly, if in certain

---

[27]See David Lyons, *Forms and Limits of Utilitarianism* (Oxford: Oxford University Press, 1965).

circumstances subsistence wages really are the least (socially) injurious means to employ in getting a job done, then in those circumstances subsistence wages are morally right exactly as utilitarianism implies.

There are two main limits to utilitarian methods of moral reasoning, therefore, although the precise extent of these limits is controversial. First, utilitarian methods are difficult to use when dealing with values that are difficult and perhaps impossible to measure quantitatively. Secondly, utilitarianism by itself seems to deal inadequately with situations that involve rights and justice, although some have tried to remedy this deficiency by restricting utilitarianism to the evaluation of rules. To clarify our ideas on these issues, the next two sections will examine methods of moral reasoning that explicitly deal with the two moral issues on which utilitarianism seems to fall short: rights and justice.

2.2 RIGHTS

In 1977 several shareholders of General Electric, Ford, General Motors, Standard Oil of California, and Texaco advised these corporations that they intended to present the following proposal for action at the next stockholders' meeting:

> Whereas South Africa's apartheid system legalizes racial discrimination in all aspects of life and deprives the black population of their most basic human rights, . . .
> Whereas black opposition to apartheid and black demands for full political, legal, and social rights in their country has risen dramatically within the last year, . . .
> Whereas Prime Minister Vorster has openly declared his intention to . . . deny political rights to South African blacks,
> Therefore be it resolved that [this corporation] shall cease further investment in the Republic of South Africa.[28]

The concept of a "right" obviously appears in many of the moral arguments and moral claims invoked in business discussions. Employees, for example, argue that they have a "right to equal pay for equal work"; managers assert that unions violate their "right to manage"; investors complain that taxation violates their "property rights"; consumers claim that they have a "right to know." Moreover, public documents often employ the notion of a right. The American Constitution itself enshrines a long "Bill of Rights," defined largely in terms of the duties the federal government has to not interfere in certain areas of its citizens' lives. The Declaration of Independence was based on the idea that "all men . . . are endowed by their Creator with certain unalienable rights . . . among these are life, liberty,

---

[28]Excerpt from 1977 proxy statements of General Electric, Ford, General Motors, Standard Oil of California, and Texaco. A fuller discussion of these proposals can be found in the cases at the end of this chapter.

and the pursuit of happiness." In 1948 the United Nations adopted a "Universal Declaration of Human Rights," which claimed that "all human beings" are entitled, among other things, to:

> the right to own property alone as well as in association with others . . .
>
> the right to work, to free choice of employment, to just and favorable conditions of work, and to protection against unemployment . . .
>
> the right to just and favorable renumeration ensuring for [the worker] and his family an existence worthy of human dignity . . .
>
> the right to form and to join trade unions . . .
>
> the right to rest and leisure, including reasonable limitation of working hours and periodic holidays with pay . . .

The concept of a right and the correlative notion of duty, then, lie at the heart of much of our moral discourse. This section is intended to provide an understanding of these concepts and of some of the major kinds of ethical principles and methods of analysis that underlie their use.

The Concept of a Right

In general, a right is an individual's entitlement to something.[29] A person has a right when that person is entitled to act in a certain way or is entitled to have others act in a certain way toward him or her. The entitlement may derive from a *legal* system that permits or empowers the person to act in a specified way or that requires others to act in certain ways toward that person; the entitlement is then called a "legal right."[30] The American Constitution, for example, guarantees all citizens the "right to freedom of conscience" and commercial statutes specify that each party to a valid contract has a "right" to whatever performance the contract requires from the other person. Legal rights are limited, of course, to the particular jurisdiction within which the legal system is in force.

Entitlements can also derive from a system of *moral* standards independently of any particular legal system. The "right to work," for example, is not guaranteed by the American Constitution, but many argue that this is a right that all human beings possess. Such rights, which are called "moral rights" or "human rights," are based on moral norms and principles that specify that all human beings are permitted or empowered to do something or are entitled to have something done for them.[31] Moral rights, unlike legal rights, are usually thought of as being universal insofar as they are rights that all human beings of every nationality possess to an equal extent

---

[29] H.J. McCloskey, "Rights," *The Philosophical Quarterly*, 15 (1965): 115–127; for a review of the literature on rights see R. Martin and J.W. Nickel, "Recent Work on the Concept of Rights," *American Philosophical Quarterly*, 17, no. 3 (July 1980): 165–80.

[30] Joel Feinberg, *Social Philosophy* (Englewood Cliffs, NJ: Prentice-Hall, 1973), pp. 55–67.

[31] *Ibid.*, pp. 84–97.

simply by virtue of being human beings. Unlike legal rights, moral rights are not limited to a particular jurisdiction. If humans have a moral right not to be tortured, for example, then this is a right that human beings of every nationality have regardless of the legal system under which they live.

Rights are powerful devices whose main purpose is that of enabling the individual to pursue certain interests or activities and of protecting these pursuits. Sometimes we use the term "right" to indicate the mere *absence of prohibitions* against doing something. In this weak sense of the term (where the enabling and protective aspects are minimal), for example, I have a "right" to do whatever the law or morality does not positively forbid me to do. Other times we use the term "right" to indicate that a person is authorized or empowered to do something that secures the *interests of others*. An army officer, for example, acquires legal rights of command which empower him to secure the interests of society. However, the most important moral rights, and those that will concern us in this chapter, are rights which *impose prohibitions or requirements* on others and which enable individuals to pursue *their own interests*. These moral rights (we will mean these kinds of rights when we use the term "moral rights") identify those activities or interests that the individual is empowered to pursue, or must be left free to pursue, or must be helped to pursue; and they protect the individual's pursuit of those interests and activities within the boundaries specified by the rights. Moral rights have three important features that define these enabling and protective functions.

First, moral rights are tightly correlated with duties.[32] This is because one person's moral right can generally be defined in terms of the moral duties other people have toward that person. My moral right to worship as I choose, for example, can be defined in terms of the moral duties other people have to not interfere in my chosen form of worship. And the moral right to a suitable standard of living can be defined in terms of the duty that governments (or some other agents of society) have to ensure a suitable standard of living for their citizens. Duties, then, are generally the other side of moral rights: If I have a moral right to do something, then other people have a moral duty not to interfere with me when I do it; and if I have a moral right to have someone do something for me, then that other person (or group of persons) has a moral duty to do it for me. Thus, moral rights impose correlative duties on others, either duties of non-interference or duties of positive performance.

In some cases, the correlative duties imposed by a right may fall not on any specific individual but on all the members of a group. If a person, for example, has the "right to work" (a right mentioned in the United Nations' Universal Declaration of Human Rights), this does not necessarily mean that any specific employer has a duty to provide that person with a job. Rather, it means that all the members of society, through their public agencies, have the duty of ensuring that jobs are available to workers.

---

[32] *Ibid.*, p. 62.

Secondly, moral rights provide individuals with autonomy and equality in the free pursuit of their interests.[33] That is, a right identifies activities or interests which people must be left free to pursue or not pursue as they themselves choose (or must be helped to pursue as they freely choose) and whose pursuit must not be subordinated to the interests of others except for special and exceptionally weighty reasons. If I have a right to worship as I choose, for example, then this implies that I am free to worship if and as I personally choose, and that I am not dependent on anyone's permission in order to worship. It also implies that I cannot generally be forced to stop worshipping on the grounds that society will gain more benefits if I am kept from worshipping: The gains of others do not generally justify interference with a person's pursuit of an interest or an activity when that pursuit is protected by a moral right. To acknowledge a person's moral right, then, is to acknowledge that there is an area in which the person is not subject to my wishes and in which the person's interests are not subordinate to mine. There is an area, in short, within which we stand as autonomous equals.

Thirdly, moral rights provide a basis for justifying one's actions and for invoking the protection or aid of others.[34] If I have a moral right to do something, then I have a moral justification for doing it. Moreover, if I have a right to do something, then others have no justification for interfering with me. On the contrary, others are justified in restraining any persons who try to prevent me from exercising my right or others may have a duty to aid me in exercising my right. When a stronger person helps a weaker one defend his or her rights, for example, we generally acknowledge that the act of the stronger person was justified.

Because moral rights have these three features, they provide bases for making moral judgments that differ substantially from utilitarian standards.[35] First, moral rights express the requirements of morality from the point of view of the *individual* while utilitarianism expresses the requirements of morality from the point of view of *society as a whole.* Moral standards concerned with rights indicate what is due to the individual from others and they promote the individual's welfare and protect the individual's choices against encroachment by society. Utilitarian standards promote society's aggregate utility, and they are indifferent to the individual's welfare except insofar as it affects this social aggregate. Second, rights limit the validity of appeals to social benefits and to numbers. That is, if a person has a right to do something, then it is wrong for anyone to interfere, even though a large number of people might gain much more utility from such interference. If I have a right to life, for example, then it is morally wrong for someone to kill me, even if many others would gain much more from my death than I will ever gain from living. And if the members of a minority group have a right to free speech then the majority must

---

[33] See Richard Wasserstrom, "Rights, Human Rights, and Racial Discrimination," *The Journal of Philosophy,* 61 (29 October 1964): 628–41.

[34] *Ibid.,* p. 62.

[35] See Ronald Dworkin, "Taking Rights Seriously," in *Taking Rights Seriously,* ed. Ronald Dworkin (Cambridge: Harvard University Press, 1978), pp. 184–205.

leave the minority free to speak, even if the majority is much more numerous and intensely opposed to what the minority will say.

Although rights generally override utilitarian standards, they are not immune from all utilitarian considerations: If the utilitarian benefits or losses imposed on society become great enough, they might be sufficient to breach the protective walls the right sets up around a person's freedom to pursue his or her interests. In times of war or major public emergencies, for example, it is generally acknowledged that civil rights may legitimately be restricted for the sake of "the public welfare." And the property rights of factory owners may be restricted in order to prevent pollution that is imposing major damages on the health of others. The more important is the interest protected by a right, the larger the utilitarian trade-offs must be: Rights erect higher walls around more important interests, and so the level of social benefits or costs needed to breach the walls must be greater.

Negative and Positive Rights

A large group of rights called "negative rights" is distinguished by the fact that its members can be defined wholly in terms of the duties others have to *not* interfere in certain activities of the person who holds a given right.[36] For example, if I have a right to privacy, this means that every other person, including my employer, has the duty not to intervene in my private affairs. And if I have a right to use, sell, or destroy my personal business assets, this means that every other person has the duty not to prevent me from using, selling, or destroying my business property as I choose.

On the other hand, "positive rights" do more than impose negative duties. They also imply that some other agents (it is not always clear who) have the *positive* duty of providing the holder of the right with whatever he or she needs to freely pursue his or her interests.[37] For example, if I have a right to an adequate standard of living, this does not mean merely that others must not interfere: It also means that if I am unable to provide myself with an adequate income, then I must be provided with such an income (perhaps by the government). Similarly, the right to work, the right to an education, the right to adequate health care, and the right to social security are all rights that go beyond noninterference to also impose a positive duty of providing people with something when they are unable to provide it for themselves.

Positive rights were not emphasized until the twentieth century. Negative rights were often employed in the seventeenth and eighteenth centuries by writers of manifestos (like the Declaration of Independence and the Bill of Rights), who were anxious to protect individuals against the encroachments of monarchical governments. Positive rights became important in the twentieth century when society increasingly took it upon itself to provide its members with the necessities of life that they were unable to provide for themselves. The United Nations decla-

---

[36] Feinberg, *Social Philosophy,* pp. 59–61.
[37] *Ibid.*

ration, for example, is influenced by this trend when it provides for the rights "to food, clothing, housing, and medical care." The change in the meaning of the phrase "the right to life" is another indication of the rising importance of positive rights. Whereas the eighteenth century interpreted the "right to life" as the negative right to not be killed (this is the meaning the phrase has in the Declaration of Independence), the twentieth century has reinterpreted the phrase to refer to the positive right to be provided with the minimum necessities of life.

Much of the debate over moral rights has concentrated on whether negative or positive rights should be given priority. So-called "conservative" writers, for example, have claimed that government efforts should be limited to enforcing negative rights and not expended on providing positive rights.[38] This is the crux of the debate over whether government efforts should be restricted to protecting property and securing law and order (that is, protecting people's negative rights) or whether government should in addition provide the needy with jobs, job training, housing, medical care, and other welfare benefits (that is, provide for people's positive rights). So-called "liberal" authors, on the other hand, hold that positive rights have as strong a claim to being honored as negative rights and that, consequently, government has a duty to provide for both.[39]

Contractual Rights and Duties

Contractual rights and duties (sometimes called "special" rights and duties or "special obligations") are the limited rights and correlative duties that arise when one person enters an agreement with another person.[40] For example, if I contract to do something for you, then you are entitled to my performance: You acquire a contractual *right* to whatever I promised, and I have a contractual *duty* to perform as I promised.

Contractual rights and duties are distinguished, first, by the fact that they attach to *specific* individuals and the correlative duties are imposed only on other *specific* individuals. If I agree to do something for you, everyone else does not thereby acquire new rights over me, nor do I acquire any new duties toward them. Secondly, contractual rights arise out of a specific transaction between particular individuals. Unless I actually make a promise or enter some other similar arrangement with you, you do not acquire any contractual rights over me.

Thirdly, contractual rights and duties depend on a publicly accepted system of rules that define the transactions that give rise to those rights and duties.[41] Contracts, for example, create special rights and duties between people only if these

---

[38] See, for example, Milton Friedman, *Capitalism and Freedom* (Chicago: The University of Chicago Press, 1962), p. 22–36; Friedrich Hayek, *The Road to Serfdom* (Chicago: The University of Chicago Press, 1944), pp. 25–26.

[39] Peter Singer, "Rights and the Market," in *Justice and Economic Distribution,* eds. John Arthur and William Shaw, (Englewood Cliffs, NJ: Prentice-Hall, Inc., 1978), pp. 207–21.

[40] H.L.A. Hart, "Are There Any Natural Rights," *Philosophical Review,* 64 (April 1955): 185.

[41] J.R. Searle, *Speech Acts* (Cambridge: The University Press, 1969), pp. 57–62.

people recognize and accept a system of conventions that specifies that by doing certain things (such as signing a paper) a person undertakes an obligation to do what he or she agrees to do. When a person goes through the appropriate actions, other people know that person is putting himself or herself under an obligation because the publicly recognized system of rules specifies that such actions count as a contractual agreement. And because the publicly recognized system obligates or requires the person to do what he or she says, or suffer the appropriate penalties, everyone understands that the person can be relied on to keep the contract and that others can act in accordance with this understanding.

Without the institution of contract and the rights and duties it can create, modern business societies could not operate. Virtually every business transaction at some point requires one of the parties to rely on the word of the other party to the effect that the other party will pay later, will deliver certain services later, or will transfer goods of a certain quality and quantity. Without the social institution of contract, individuals in such situations would be unwilling to rely on the word of the other party, and the transactions would never take place. The institution of contracts provides a way of ensuring that individuals keep their word, and this in turn makes it possible for business society to operate. Employers, for example, acquire contractual rights to the services of their employees in virtue of the work contract that employees enter, and sellers acquire contractual rights to the future cash that credit buyers agree to give them.

Contractual rights and duties also provide a basis for the special duties or obligations that people acquire when they accept a position or a role within a legitimate social institution or an organization. Married parents, for example, have a special duty to care for the upbringing of their children; doctors have a special duty to care for the health of their patients; and managers have a special duty to care for the organization they administer. In each of these cases, there is a publicly accepted institution (such as a familial, medical, or corporate institution) that defines a certain position or role (such as parent, doctor, or manager) upon which the welfare of certain vulnerable persons (such as the parent's children, the doctor's patients, the manager's corporate constituencies) depends. Society attaches to these institutional roles special duties of caring for these vulnerable dependents and of protecting them from injury, duties that the person who enters the role knows he or she is expected to fulfill. When a person freely enters the role knowing what duties society attaches to the acceptance of the role, that person in effect enters an agreement to fulfill those duties. The existence of a system of contractual obligations ensures that individuals fulfill these agreements by laying on them the public obligations that all agreements carry. As a result, these familial, medical, and corporate institutions can continue to exist and their vulnerable members are protected against harm. We should recall here that a person's institutional duties are not unlimited. In the first chapter we noted that as a "loyal agent," the manager's duties to care for the corporation are limited by the ethical principles that govern any person. Similarly, a doctor cannot murder other people in order to obtain vital organs for the patients whom he or she has a duty to care for.

What kind of ethical rules govern contracts? The system of rules that underlies contractual rights and duties has traditionally been interpreted as including several moral constraints:[42]

1. Both of the parties to a contract must have full knowledge of the nature of the agreement they are entering.
2. Neither party to a contract must intentionally misrepresent the facts of the contractual situation to the other party.
3. Neither party to the contract must be forced to enter the contract under duress or coercion.
4. The contract must not bind the parties to an immoral act.

Contracts that violate one or more of these four conditions have traditionally been considered void.[43] Below we shall discuss the basis of these sorts of conditions.

A BASIS FOR MORAL RIGHTS: KANT

How do we know that people have rights? This question can be answered in a fairly straightforward way when it is asked about legal rights: A person has certain legal rights because the person lives within a legal system that guarantees those rights. But what is the basis of moral rights?

Utilitarians have suggested that utilitarian principles can provide a satisfactory basis for moral rights: People have moral rights because the possession of moral rights maximizes utility. It is doubtful, however, that utilitarianism can serve as an adequate basis for moral rights. To say that someone has a moral right to do something is to say that he or she is entitled to do it regardless of the utilitarian benefits it provides for others. Utilitarianism cannot easily support such a nonutilitarian concept.

A more satisfactory foundation for moral rights is provided by the ethical theory developed by Immanuel Kant (1724–1804). Kant in fact attempts to show that there are certain moral rights and duties that all human beings possess, regardless of any utilitarian benefits that the exercise of those rights and duties may provide for others.

Kant's theory is based on a moral principle that he calls the "categorical imperative" and that requires that everyone should be treated as a free person equal to everyone else. That is, everyone has a moral right to such treatment, and everyone has the correlative duty to treat others in this way. Kant provides at least two

---

[42]Thomas M. Garrett, *Business Ethics* (Englewood Cliffs, NJ: Prentice-Hall, Inc., 1966), pp. 119–24.

[43]*Ibid.,* p. 75. See also, John Rawls, *A Theory of Justice* (Cambridge: Harvard University Press, The Belknap Press, 1971), pp. 342–50.

ways of formulating this basic moral principle; each formulation serves as an explanation of the meaning of this basic moral right and correlative duty.

The First Formulation of Kant's
Categorical Imperative

Kant's first formulation of the categorical imperative goes like this: "I ought
never to act except in such a way that I can also will that my maxim should become
a universal law."[44] A "maxim" for Kant is the reason a person in a certain situation
has for doing what he or she plans to do. And a maxim would "become a universal
law" if every person in a similar situation chose to do the same thing for the same
reason. Kant's first version of the categorical imperative, then, comes down to the
following principle:

> *An action is morally right for a person in a certain situation if and only if the
> person's reason for carrying out the action is a reason that he or she would be
> willing to have every person act on, in any similar situation.*

An example may help to clarify the meaning of Kant's principle. Suppose that I am
trying to decide whether to fire an employee because I do not like the employee's
race. According to Kant's principle, I must ask myself whether I would be willing
to have an employer fire any employee whenever the employer does not like the
race of his or her employee. In particular, I must ask myself whether I would be
willing to be fired myself should my employer not like my race. If I am not willing
to have everyone act in this way, even toward me, then it is morally wrong for me
to act in this way toward others. A person's reasons for acting, then, must be "re-
versible": One must be willing to have all others use those reasons even against oneself. There is an obvious similarity, then, between the categorical imperative and the
so-called "golden rule": "Do unto others as you would have them do unto you."

Kant points out that sometimes it is not even possible to *conceive* of having
everyone act on a certain reason, much less be *willing* to have everyone act on that
reason.[45] For example, suppose that I am considering breaking a contract because it
has committed me to do something I do not want to do. Then I must ask whether I
would be willing to have everyone break any contract that one did not want to
keep. But it is impossible to even conceive of everyone making and then breaking
contracts in this way since if everyone knew that any contract could be broken,
then people would cease making contracts altogether (what possible purpose would
they serve?) and contracts would no longer exist. Consequently, since it is impossible to conceive of everyone making and breaking contracts in this way, it is also
impossible for me to be willing to have everyone act like this (how can I want something I cannot even conceive?). It would be wrong, therefore, for me to break a

---

[44] Immanuel Kant, *Groundwork of the Metaphysics of Morals*, trans. H.J. Paton (New
York: Harper & Row, Publishers, Inc., 1964), p. 70.
[45] *Ibid.*, p. 91.

contract simply because I do not want to keep it. A person's reasons for acting, then, must also be universalizable: It must be possible, at least in principle, for everyone to act on those reasons.

The first formulation of the categorical imperative, then, incorporates two criteria for determining moral right and wrong: universalizability and reversibility.

Universalizability: The person's reasons for acting must be reasons that everyone *could* act on at least in principle.

Reversibility: The person's reasons for acting must be reasons that he or she would be *willing* to have all others use, even as a basis of how they treat him or her.

This formulation of Kant's categorical imperative is attractive for a number of reasons, not the least of which is that it seems to capture some fundamental aspects of our moral views. Frequently, for example, we say to a person who has done something wrong or who is about to do something wrong: How would you like it if he did that to you? or How would you like it if you were in her place?, thereby invoking something like reversibility. Or we may ask, What if everybody did that? and thereby invoke universalizability.

Unlike the principle of utilitarianism, Kant's categorical imperative focuses on a person's interior motivations and not on the consequences of one's external actions. Moral right and wrong, according to Kantian theory, are distinguished not by what a person accomplishes, but by the reasons the person has for what he tries to do.[46] Kant argues that to the extent that a person performs an action merely because it will advance the person's own future interests or merely because the person finds the action pleasurable, the action "has no moral worth." A person's action has "moral worth" only to the degree that it is *also* motivated by a sense of "duty," that is, a belief that it is the right way for people to behave. And, Kant claims, to be motivated by a sense of "duty" is to be motivated by reasons that I wish everyone would act upon. Consequently, my action has "moral worth" (that is, it is morally right) only to the extent that it is motivated by reasons that I would be willing to have every person act on. Hence the categorical imperative.[47]

The Second Formulation of Kant's Categorical Imperative

The second formulation Kant gives of the categorical imperative is this: "Act in such a way that you always treat humanity, whether in your own person or in the person of any other, never simply as a means, but always at the same time as an end."[48] Or, never treat people *only* as means, but always also as ends.

[46] *Ibid.*, p. 62.
[47] *Ibid.*, pp. 64–70.
[48] *Ibid.*, p. 96.

What Kant means by "treating humanity as an end" is that I should treat each human being as a being whose existence as a free rational person should be promoted. For Kant this means two things: (1) respecting each person's freedom by treating people only as they have freely consented to be treated beforehand and (2) developing each person's capacity to freely choose for him or herself the aims he or she will pursue.[49] On the other hand, to treat a person only as a means is to use the person only as an instrument for advancing my own interests and involves neither respect for, nor development of, the person's capacity to choose freely. Kant's second version of the categorical imperative can be expressed in the following principle:

> *An action is morally right for a person if and only if in performing the action, the person does not use others merely as a means for advancing his or her own interests, but also both respects and develops their capacity to choose freely for themselves.*

This version of the categorical imperative implies that human beings each have an equal dignity that sets them apart from things like tools or machines and that is incompatible with their being manipulated, deceived, or otherwise unwillingly exploited to satisfy the self-interests of another. The principle in effect says that people should not be treated as objects incapable of free choice. By this principle, an employee may legitimately be asked to perform the unpleasant (or even dangerous) tasks involved in a job if the employee freely consented to take the job knowing that it would involve these tasks. But it would be wrong to subject an employee to health risks *without the employee's knowledge.* In general, deception, force, and coercion fail to respect people's freedom to choose and are therefore immoral (unless, perhaps, a person first freely consented to have force used against himself or herself).

Kant argues that making fraudulent contracts by deceiving others is wrong and that deliberately refraining from giving others help when they need it is also wrong. By deceiving a person into making a contract that that person would not otherwise freely choose to make, I fail to respect that person's freedom to choose and merely use the person to advance my own interests. And by failing to lend needed and easily extended help to another person, I limit what that person is free to choose to do.

The second formulation of the categorical imperative, according to Kant, is really equivalent to the first.[50] The first version says that what is morally right for me must be morally right for others: Everyone is of equal value. If this is so, then no person's freedom should be subordinated to that of others so that the person is used merely to advance the interests of others. And since I myself am of value, I cannot sacrifice myself to mere self-interest. And this, of course, is what the second

---

[49] See Fred Feldman, *Introductory Ethics* (Englewood Cliffs, NJ: Prentice-Hall, Inc., 1978), pp. 119-28; and Rawls, *A Theory of Justice,* pp. 179-180.

[50] Kant, *Groundwork,* p. 105.

version of the categorical imperative requires. Both formulations come down to the same thing: People are to treat each other as free and equal in the pursuit of their interests.

Kantian Rights

A large number of authors have held that the categorical imperative (in one or the other of its formulations) explains why people have moral rights.[51] As we have seen, moral rights identify interests that individuals must be left free to pursue as they autonomously choose (or which we must help them pursue as they choose) and whose free pursuit must not be subordinated to our own interests. And that is precisely what both formulations of Kant's categorical imperative require in holding that people must be respected as free and equal in the pursuit of their interests. In short, moral rights identify the specific major areas in which persons must deal with each other as free equals, and Kant's categorical imperative implies that persons should deal with each other in precisely this way. The categorical imperative, however, cannot by itself tell us what particular moral rights human beings have. In order to know what particular rights human beings have, one first must know what interests humans have and must know whether there are good reasons for giving the free pursuit of one interest, rather than another, the protected status of a right (clearly, not all interests can be turned into rights, since interests can conflict with each other). For example, to establish that humans have a right to free speech, one has to show that freedom to say what one chooses is critically important to human beings and that it is more important than the free pursuit of other conflicting interests that humans may have (such as an interest in repressing ideas that we find distasteful, offensive, or disturbing). Insofar as free speech is critically important, humans must leave each other equally free to speak as they choose: Everyone has a moral right to freedom of speech. But insofar as free speech conflicts with another human interest that can be shown to be of equal or greater importance (such as our interest in not being libeled or defamed), the right to freedom of speech must be limited.

Although later chapters will present various arguments in support of several particular rights, it might be helpful here to give a rough sketch of how some rights have been plausibly defended on the basis of Kant's two formulations of the categorical imperative. First, human beings have a clear interest in being helped by being provided with the work, food, clothing, housing, and medical care they need to live on when they cannot provide these for themselves. Suppose we agree that we would not be willing to have everyone (especially ourselves) deprived of such help when it is needed, and that such help is necessary if a person's capacity to choose

[51] See, for example, A.K. Bierman, *Life and Morals: An Introduction to Ethics* (New York: Harcourt Brace Jovanovich, Inc., 1980), pp. 300–301; Charles Fried, *Right and Wrong* (Cambridge: Harvard University Press, 1978), p. 129; Dworkin, *Taking Rights Seriously*, p. 198; Thomas E. Hill, Jr., "Servility and Self-Respect," *The Monist*, 57, no. 1 (January 1973): 87–104; Feinberg, *Social Philosophy*, p. 93; Gregory Vlastos, "Justice and Equality," p. 48 in *Social Justice*, ed. Richard Brandt (Englewood Cliffs, NJ: Prentice-Hall, Inc., 1964), pp. 31–72.

freely is to develop and even survive.[52] If so, then no individual ought to be deprived of such help. That is, human beings have *positive rights* to the work, food, clothing, housing, and medical care they need to live on when they cannot provide these for themselves and when these are available.

Secondly, human beings also have a clear interest in being free from injury or fraud and in being free to think, associate, speak, and live privately as they choose. Suppose we agree that we would be willing to have everyone be free of the interference of others in these areas, and that interference in these areas fails to respect a person's freedom to choose for him or herself.[53] If so, then everyone ought to be free of the interference of others in these areas. That is, human beings have these *negative rights:* the right to freedom from injury or fraud, the right to freedom of thought, freedom of association and freedom of speech, and the right to privacy.

Thirdly, as we have seen, human beings have a clear interest in preserving the institution of contracts. Suppose we agree that we would end up dropping the institution of contracts (which we are unwilling to do) if everyone stopped honoring their contracts or if everyone had to honor even contracts that were made under duress or without full information; and suppose we agree that we show respect for people's freedom by honoring the contracts they freely make with us and by leaving them free and fully informed about any contracts they make with us.[54] If so, then everyone ought to honor his or her contracts and everyone ought to be fully informed and free when making contracts. That is, human beings have a *contractual right* to what they have been promised in contracts, and everyone also has a right to be left free and fully informed when contracts are made.

Each of the rights just described has been sketched in barest outline, and each one requires a great deal more in the way of qualifications, adjustments with other (conflicting) interests, and full supporting arguments. Crude as it is, however, the list provides some idea of how Kant's categorical imperative might be used in establishing positive rights, negative rights, and contractual rights.

Problems with Kant

In spite of the attractiveness of Kant's theory, critics have argued that, like utilitarianism, it has its limitations and inadequacies. A first problem that critics

[52] For a similar argument based on Kant's first formulation of the categorical imperative see Marcus Singer, *Generalization in Ethics* (New York: Alfred A. Knopf, Inc., 1961), pp. 267–74; for one based on Kant's second formulation see Alan Donagan, *The Theory of Morality* (Chicago: The University of Chicago Press, 1977), p. 85; also see I. Kant, *Metaphysical Elements of Justice* (New York: Bobbs-Merrill Co., Inc., 1965), pp. 91–99.

[53] See Alan Gewirth, *Reason and Morality* (Chicago: The University of Chicago Press, 1978), who argues for these rights (p. 256) on the basis of a principle that, although different from Kant's first formulation in some important respects, is nonetheless very much like it: "Every agent must claim that he has rights to freedom and well-being for the reason that he is a prospective purposive agent . . . it follows, by the principle of universalizability, that all prospective purposive agents have rights to freedom and well-being" (p. 133); Donagan, *The Theory of Morality*, pp. 81–90, argues for these on the basis of Kant's second formulation.

[54] See Singer, *Generalization in Ethics*, pp. 255–57, for a discussion of how Kant's first formulation provides a basis for the obligation to keep one's promises and for truthfulness in the making of promises; see Donagan, *Theory of Morality*, pp. 90–94, for a discussion of the same subject in terms of the second formulation.

have traditionally pointed out is that Kant's theory is not precise enough to always be useful. One difficulty lies in trying to determine whether or not one would (as the first formulation requires) "be willing to have everyone follow" a certain policy. Although the general thrust of this requirement is usually clear, it sometimes leads to problems. For example, suppose I am a murderer: Would I then be willing to have everyone follow the policy that all murderers should be punished? In a sense I would be willing to, since I would want to be protected from other murderers, but in another sense I would not be willing, since I do not want to be punished myself; which sense is correct?[55] It is also sometimes difficult to determine whether or not (as the second formulation states) one person is using another "merely as a means." Suppose, for example, that an employer pays only minimum wages to her employees and refuses to install the safety equipment they want, yet she says she is "respecting their capacity to freely choose for themselves" because she is willing to let them work elsewhere if they choose. Is she then treating them merely as means or also as ends? Critics complain that they cannot answer such questions because Kant's theory is too vague.[56] There are cases, then, where the requirements of Kant's theory are unclear.

Second, some critics claim that, although we might be able to agree on the kinds of interests that have the status of moral rights, there is substantial disagreement concerning what the *limits* of each of these rights are and concerning how each of these rights should be balanced against other conflicting rights.[57] And Kant's theory does not help us resolve these disagreements. For example, we all agree that everyone should have a right to associate with whomever one wants, as well as a right not to be injured by others. But how should these rights be balanced against each other when a certain association of people begins to injure others? Suppose the loud music of a group of trombone players, for example, disturbs others; or suppose a corporation (which is an association of people) pollutes the air and water on which the health of others depends. Kant's categorical imperative does not tell us how the conflicting rights of these persons should be adjusted to each other: Which right should be limited in favor of the other?

A defender of Kant, however, can counter this second kind of criticism by holding that Kant's categorical imperative is not intended to tell us how conflicting rights should be limited and adjusted to each other. To decide whether one right should be curtailed in favor of a second right one has to examine the relative importance of the *interests* that each right protects. What arguments can be given to show, for example, that a corporation's interest in financial gains is more or less important than the health of its neighbors? The answer to this question will determine whether or not a corporation's right to use its property for financial gains should be

---

[55] See Jonathan Harrison, "Kant's Examples of the First Formulation of the Categorical Imperative," in *Kant, A Collection of Critical Essays*, ed. Robert Paul Wolff (Garden City, NY: Doubleday & Co., Inc., 1967), pp. 228–45; see also in the same work, the reply by J. Kemp and the counter-reply by J. Harrison, both of which focus on the meaning of "is willing."

[56] Fred Feldman, *Introductory Ethics*, pp. 123–28; Robert Paul Wolff, *The Autonomy of Reason* (New York: Harper Torch Books, 1973), p. 175.

[57] For example, J.B. Mabbott, *The State and the Citizen* (London: Arrow, 1958), p. 57–58.

limited in favor of its neighbors' right not to have their health injured. All that Kant's categorical imperative is meant to tell us is that everyone must have equal moral rights and that everyone must show as much respect for the protected interests of others as he or she wants others to show for his or her own. It does not tell us what interests people have, nor what their relative importance is.

A third group of criticisms that have been made of Kant's theory is that there are counter-examples which show that the theory sometimes goes wrong. Most counter-examples to Kant's theory focus on the criteria of universalizability and reversibility.[58] Suppose that an employer can get away with discriminating against blacks by paying them lower wages than whites for the same work. And suppose also that he is so fanatical in his dislike of blacks that he is willing to accept the proposition that if his own skin were black, employers should also discriminate against him. Then, according to Kant's theory, the employer would be acting morally. But this, according to the critics, is wrong, since discrimination is obviously immoral.

Defenders of a Kantian approach to ethics, of course, would reply that it is the critics, not Kant, who are mistaken. If the employer genuinely and conscientiously would be willing to universalize the principles on which he is acting, then the action is in fact morally right for him.[59] For us, who would be unwilling to universalize the same principle, the action would be immoral. We may also find that it would be morally right for us to impose sanctions on the employer to make him stop discriminating. But, insofar as the employer is trying to remain true to his own universal principles, he is acting conscientiously and, therefore, in a moral manner.

THE LIBERTARIAN OBJECTION:
NOZICK

Some important views on rights that are different from the ones we just sketched have been proposed recently by several "libertarian philosophers."

Libertarian philosophers go beyond the general presumption that freedom from human constraint is usually good, to claim that such freedom is necessarily good and that all constraints imposed by others are necessarily evil except when needed to prevent the imposition of greater human constraints. The American philosopher Robert Nozick, for example, claims that the only basic right that every individual possesses is the negative right to be free from the coercion of other human beings.[60] This negative right to freedom from coercion, according to Nozick, must

---

[58] Feldman, *Introductory Ethics,* pp. 116-17.

[59] For example, Richard M. Hare, *Freedom and Reason* (New York: Oxford University Press, 1965), who uses Kant's first formulation (p. 34), defends himself against the example of the "fanatic" in this way.

[60] Robert Nozick, *Anarchy, State, and Utopia* (New York: Basic Books, Inc., Publishers, 1974), p. ix.

be recognized if individuals are to be treated as distinct persons with separate lives, each of whom has an equal moral weight that may not be sacrificed for the sake of others. The only circumstances under which coercion may be exerted upon a person is when it is necessary to keep him or her from coercing others.

According to Nozick, prohibiting people from coercing others constitutes a legitimate "moral" constraint that rests on "the underlying Kantian principle that individuals are ends and not merely means; they may not be sacrificed or used for achieving of other ends without their consent."[61] Thus Nozick seems to hold that Kant's theory supports his own views on freedom.

Nozick goes on to argue that the negative right to freedom from the coercion of others implies that people must be left free to do what they want with their own labor and with whatever products they manufacture by their labor.[62] And this in turn implies that people must be left free to acquire property, to use it in whatever way they wish, and to exchange it with others in free markets (so long as the situation of others is not thereby harmed or "worsened"). Thus, the libertarian view that coercive restrictions on freedom are immoral (except when needed to restrain coercion itself) is also supposed to justify the free use of property, freedom of contract, the institution of free markets in which individuals can exchange goods as they choose without government restrictions, and the elimination of taxes for social welfare programs. But there is no basis for any *positive* rights nor for the social programs they might require.

Nozick and other libertarians, however, pass too quickly over the fact that the freedom of one person necessarily imposes constraints upon other persons. Such constraints are inevitable, since when one person is granted freedom, other persons must be constrained from interfering with that person. If I am to be free to do what I want with my property, for example, other people must be constrained from trespassing on it and from taking it from me. Even the "free market system" that Nozick advocates depends on an underlying system of coercion: for I can "sell" something only if I first "own" it, and ownership depends essentially on an enforced (coercive) system of property laws. Consequently, since granting a freedom to one person necessarily imposes constraints on others, it follows that if constraints require justification, then freedom will likewise always require justification.

The same point can be made in a different way. Because there are many different kinds of freedoms, the freedom one group of agents is given to pursue some of its interests will usually restrict the freedom other agents have to pursue other conflicting interests. For example, the freedom of corporations to use their property to pollute the environment as they want can restrict the freedom of individuals to breathe clean air whenever they want. And the freedom of employees to unionize as they want can conflict with the freedom of employers to hire whatever nonunion workers they want. Consequently, allowing one kind of freedom to one group entails restricting some other kind of freedom for some other group: A decision in

[61]*Ibid.*, pp. 30–31.
[62]*Ibid.*, p. 160; see also pp. 160–62.

favor of the freedom to pursue one interest implies a decision against the freedom to pursue another kind of interest. This means that we cannot argue in favor of a certain kind of freedom by simply claiming that constraints are always evil and must always be replaced by freedom. Instead, an argument for a specific freedom must show that the interests that can be satisfied by that kind of freedom are somehow better or more worth satisfying than the interests that other opposing kinds of freedoms could satisfy. Neither Nozick nor other libertarians supply such arguments.

Moreover, it is not obvious that Kantian principles can support libertarian views like that of Nozick. Kant holds, as we saw, that the dignity of each person should be respected and that each person's capacity to choose freely should be developed. Because we have these duties to each other, government coercion is legitimate whenever it is needed to ensure that the dignity of citizens is being respected or when it is needed to secure the full development of people's capacity to choose. And this, as Kant argues, means that government may legitimately place limits on the use of property and on the making of contracts and impose market restrictions and compulsory taxes when these are needed to care for the welfare or development of persons "who are not able to support themselves."[63] We have no reason to think that only negative rights exist. People can also have positive rights and Kant's theory supports these as much as it supports negative rights.

2.3 JUSTICE AND FAIRNESS

On Friday, December 9, 1977, a Senate subcommittee heard the testimony of several workers who had contracted "brown lung" disease by breathing cotton dust while working cotton mills in the south.[64] Brown lung is a chronic disabling respiratory disease with symptoms similar to asthma and emphysema and is a cause of premature death. The disabled workers were seeking a federal law that would facilitate the process of getting disability compensation from the cotton mills, similar to federal laws covering "black lung" disease contracted in coal mines.

Senator Strom Thurmond:

A number of people have talked to me about this and they feel that if the federal government enters the field of black lung, it should enter the field of brown lung; and if those who have suffered from black lung are to receive federal consideration, then it seems fair that those who have suffered from brown lung receive federal consideration. . . . If our [state's cotton mill] workers have been injured and have not been properly compensated, then steps should be taken to see that is done. We want to see them treated fairly and squarely and properly, and so we look forward to . . . the testimony here today.

[63] Kant, *The Metaphysical Elements of Justice,* p. 93.

[64] U.S. Congress, Senate, *Brown Lung: Hearing Before a Subcommittee of the Committee on Appropriations,* 95th Congress, 1st Session. 9 December, 1977, pp. 3, 52, 53, 54, 59, and 60.

Mrs. Beatrice Norton:

I started in the mill when I was fourteen years old and I had to get out in 1968 . . . I worked in the dust year after year, just like my mother. I got sicker and sicker . . . [In 1968 I] suddenly had no job, no money, and I was sick, too sick to ever work in my life again . . . State legislators have proven in two successive sessions that they are not going to do anything to help the brown lung victims, so now we come to you in Washington and ask for help. We've waited a long time, and many of us have died waiting. I don't want to die of injustice.

Mrs. Vinnie Ellison:

My husband worked for twenty-one years [in the mill] in Spartanburg, and he worked in the dustiest parts of the mill, the opening room, the cardroom, and cleaning the air-conditioning ducts . . . In the early sixties he started having trouble keeping up his job because of his breathing. In 1963 his bossman told him that he had been a good worker, but wasn't worth a damn anymore, and fired him . . . He had no pension and nothing to live on and we had to go on welfare to live . . . My husband worked long and hard and lost his health and many years of pay because of the dust. It isn't fair that [the mill] threw him away like so much human garbage after he couldn't keep up his job because he was sick from the dust. We are not asking for handouts; we want what is owed to my husband for twenty-five years of hard work.

Disputes among individuals in business are often interlaced with references to "justice" or to "fairness." This is the case, for example, when one person accuses another of "unjustly" discriminating against him or her, or of showing "unjust" favoritism toward someone else, or of not taking up a "fair" share of the burdens involved in some cooperative venture. Resolving disputes like these requires that we compare and weigh the conflicting claims of each of the parties and strike a balance between them. Justice and fairness are essentially comparative. They are concerned with the comparative treatment given to the members of a group when benefits and burdens are distributed, when rules and laws are administered, when members of a group cooperate or compete with each other, and when people are punished for the wrongs they have done or compensated for the wrongs they have suffered. Although the terms "justice" and "fairness" are used almost interchangeably, we tend to reserve the word "justice" for matters that are especially serious, although some authors have held that the concept of fairness is more fundamental.[65]

Standards of justice are generally taken to be more important than utilitarian considerations.[66] If a society is unjust to some of its members, then we normally condemn that society, even if the injustices secure more utilitarian benefits for everyone. If we think that slavery is unjust, for example, then we condemn a so-

---

[65] John Rawls, "Justice as Fairness," *The Philosophical Review,* 67 (1958); 164–194; R.M. Hare, "Justice and Equality," in *Justice and Economic Distribution,* eds. Arthur and Shaw, p. 119.

[66] Rawls, *A Theory of Justice,* pp. 3–4.

ciety that uses slavery, even if slavery makes that society more productive. Greater benefits for some cannot justify injustices for others. Nonetheless, we also seem to hold that if the social gains are sufficiently large, a certain level of injustice may legitimately be tolerated.[67] In countries with extreme deprivation and poverty, for example, we seem to hold that some degree of equality may be traded off for major economic gains that leave everyone better off.

But standards of justice do not generally override the moral rights of individuals. Part of the reason for this is that, to some extent, justice is based on individual moral rights. The moral right to be treated as a free and equal person, for example, is part of what lies behind the idea that benefits and burdens should be distributed equally.[68] More important, however, is the fact that, as we saw, a moral right identifies interests people have, the free pursuit of which may not be subordinated to the interests of others except where there are special and exceptionally weighty reasons. This means that, for the most part, the moral rights of some individuals cannot be sacrificed merely in order to secure a somewhat better distribution of benefits for others. Yet correcting extreme injustices may justify restricting some individuals' rights. Property rights, for example, might be legitimately redistributed for the sake of justice. We will discuss trade-offs of this sort more fully after we have a better idea of what justice means.

Issues involving questions of justice and fairness are usually divided into three categories. *Distributive justice,* the first and basic category, is concerned with the fair distribution of society's benefits and burdens. In the 1977 brown lung hearings, for example, Senator Thurmond pointed out that if federal law helped workers afflicted by black lung, then it was only "fair" that it also help workers afflicted by brown lung. *Retributive justice,* the second category, refers to the just imposition of punishments and penalties upon those who do wrong: A "just" penalty is one that in some sense is deserved by the person who does wrong. Retributive justice would be at issue, for example, if we were to ask whether it would be fair to penalize cotton mills for causing brown lung disease among their workers. *Compensatory justice,* the third category, concerns the just way of compensating people for what they lost when they were wronged by others: A just compensation is one that in some sense is proportional to the loss suffered by the person being compensated (such as loss of livelihood). During the brown lung hearings, for example, both Mrs. Norton and Mrs. Ellison claimed that, in justice, they were owed compensation from the cotton mills because of injuries inflicted by the mills.

This section examines each of these three kinds of justice separately. The section begins with a discussion of a basic principle of distributive justice (equals should be treated as equals) and then examines several views on the criteria relevant to determining whether or not two persons are "equal." The section then turns to a

---

[67]See, for example, Rawls, *A Theory of Justice,* p. 542; and Joel Feinberg, "Rawls and Intuitionism," pp. 114–16 in *Reading Rawls,* ed. Norman Daniels (New York: Basic Books, Inc., Publishers, n.d.), pp. 108–24; and T.M. Scanlon, "Rawls' Theory of Justice," pp. 185–91 in *ibid.,* pp. 160–205.

[68]See, for example, Vlastos, "Justice and Equality."

brief discussion of retributive justice and ends with a discussion of compensatory justice.

Distributive Justice

Questions of distributive justice arise when different people put forth conflicting claims on society's benefits and burdens and all the claims cannot be satisfied.[69] The central cases are those where there is a scarcity of benefits—such as jobs, food, housing, medical care, income, and wealth—as compared to the numbers and the desires of the people who want these goods. Or (the other side of the coin) there may be too many burdens—unpleasant work, drudgery, substandard housing, health injuries of various sorts—and not enough people willing to shoulder them. If there were enough goods to satisfy everyone's desires and enough people willing to share society's burdens, then conflicts between people would not arise and distributive justice would not be needed.

When people's desires and aversions exceed the adequacy of their resources, they are forced to develop principles for allocating scarce benefits and undesirable burdens in ways that are just and that resolve the conflicts in a fair way. The development of such principles is the concern of distributive justice.

The fundamental principle of distributive justice is that equals should be treated equally and unequals, unequally.[70] More precisely, the fundamental principle of distributive justice may be expressed as follows:

Individuals who are similar in all respects relevant to the kind of treatment in question should be given similar benefits and burdens, even if they are dissimilar in other irrelevant respects; and individuals who are dissimilar in a relevant respect ought to be treated dissimilarly, in proportion to their dissimilarity.

If, for example, Susan and Bill are both doing the same work for me and there are no relevant differences between them or the work they are doing, then in justice I should pay them equal wages. But if Susan is working twice as long as Bill and if length of working time is the relevant basis for determining wages on the sort of work they are doing, then, to be just, I should pay Susan twice as much as Bill. Or, to return to our earlier example, if the federal government rightly helps workers who have suffered from black lung and there are no relevant differences between such workers and workers who have suffered from brown lung, then, as Senator Thurmond said, it is "fair that those who have suffered from brown lung [also] receive federal consideration."

This fundamental principle of distributive justice, however, is purely formal.[71] It is based on the purely logical idea that we must be consistent in the way

[69] Rawls, *A Theory of Justice*, pp. 126–30.

[70] William K. Frankena, "The Concept of Social Justice," in *Social Justice*, ed. Brandt, pp. 1–29; C. Perelman, *The Idea of Justice and the Problem of Argument* (New York: Humanities Press, Inc., 1963), p. 16.

[71] Feinberg, *Social Philosophy*, pp. 100–102; Perelman, *Idea of Justice*, p. 16.

we treat similar situations. And the principle does not specify the "relevant respects" that may legitimately provide the basis for similarity or dissimilarity of treatment. Is race, for example, relevant when determining who should get what jobs? Most of us would say no, but then what characteristics are relevant when determining what benefits and burdens people should receive? We will turn now to examine different views on the kinds of characteristics that may be relevant when determining who should get what. Each of these views provides a "material" principle of justice, that is, a principle that gives specific content to the fundamental principle of distributive justice.

Justice as Equality: Egalitarianism

Egalitarians hold that there are no relevant differences among people that can justify unequal treatment.[72] According to the egalitarian, all benefits and burdens should be distributed according to the following formula:

Every person should be given exactly equal shares of society's benefits and burdens.

Egalitarians base their view on the proposition that all human beings are equal in some fundamental respect and that, in virtue of this equality, each person has an equal claim to society's goods.[73] And this, according to the egalitarian, implies that goods should be allocated to people in equal portions.

Equality has, of course, appeared to many as an attractive social ideal and inequality, as a defect. "All men are created equal," says our Declaration of Independence, and the ideal of equality has been the driving force behind the emancipation of slaves, the prohibition of indentured servitude, the elimination of racial, sexual, and property requirements on voting and holding public office, and the institution of free public education. Americans have long prided themselves on the lack of overt status consciousness in their social relations.

In spite of their popularity, however, egalitarian views have been subjected to heavy criticisms. One line of attack has focused on the egalitarian claim that all human beings are equal in some fundamental respect.[74] Critics claim that there is *no* quality that all human beings possess in precisely the same degree: Human beings differ in their abilities, intelligence, virtues, needs, desires, and in all their other physical and mental characteristics. If this is so, then human beings are unequal in all respects.

---

[72] Christopher Ake, "Justice as Equality," *Philosophy and Public Affairs,* 5, no. 1 (Fall 1975): 69–89.

[73] Kai Nielsen, "Class and Justice" in *Justice and Economic Distribution,* eds., Arthur and Shaw, pp. 225–45; see also Gregory Vlastos, *Justice and Equality.* Vlastos interprets "equality" in a much different sense than I do here.

[74] Bernard Williams, "The Idea of Equality," in *Philosophy and Society,* 2nd series, ed. Laslett and Runciman (London: Blackwell, 1962), pp. 110–31.

A second set of criticisms argues that the egalitarian ignores some characteristics that should be taken into account in distributing society's goods: need, ability, and effort.[75] If everyone is given exactly the same things, critics point out, then the lazy person will get as much as the industrious one, even though the lazy one does not deserve as much. If everyone is given exactly the same, then the sick person will get only as much as healthy ones, even though the sick person needs more. If everyone is given exactly the same, the handicapped person will have to do as much as talented persons, even though the handicapped person has less ability. And if everyone is given exactly the same, then individuals will have no incentives to exert greater efforts in their work; as a result, society's productivity and efficiency will decline. Since the egalitarian formula ignores all these facts, and since it is clear that they should be taken into account, critics allege, egalitarianism must be mistaken.

Some egalitarians have tried to strengthen their position by distinguishing two different kinds of equality: political equality and economic equality.[76] *Political equality* refers to an equal participation in, and treatment by, the means of controlling and directing the political system. This includes equal rights to participate in the legislative process, equal civil liberties, and equal rights to due process. *Economic equality,* on the other hand, refers to equality of income and wealth and equality of opportunity. The criticisms leveled against equality, according to some egalitarians, apply only to economic equality and not to political equality. Although everyone will concede that differences of need, ability, and effort may justify some inequalities in the distribution of income and wealth, everyone will also agree that political rights and liberties should not be unequally distributed. Thus, the egalitarian position may be correct with respect to political equality, even if it is mistaken with respect to economic equality.

Other egalitarians have claimed that even economic equality is defensible if it is suitably limited. Thus, they have argued that every person has a right to a minimum standard of living and that income and wealth should be distributed equally until this standard is achieved for everyone.[77] The economic surplus that remains after everyone has achieved the minimum standard of living can then be distributed unequally according to need, effort, etc. A major difficulty that this limited type of economic egalitarianism must face, however, is specifying what it means by "minimum standard of living." Different societies and different cultures have different views as to what constitutes the necessary minimum to live on. A relatively primitive economy will place the minimum at a lower point than a relatively affluent one. Nonetheless, most people would agree that justice requires that affluent societies satisfy at least the basic needs of their members and not let them die of starvation, exposure, or disease.

[75] Feinberg, *Social Philosophy,* 109–11.

[76] See Bowie, *A New Theory of Distributive Justice,* pp. 60–64.

[77] See D.D. Raphael, "Equality and Equity," *Philosophy,* 21 (1946): 118–32. See also, Bowie, *A New Theory of Distributive Justice,* pp. 64–65.

Justice Based on Contribution:
Capitalist Justice

Some writers assume that society's benefits should be distributed according to the contributions people make to society. The more people contribute through their work, for example, the more they should get; the less their contribution, the less they should get. Quite simply:

Benefits should be distributed according to the contribution each individual makes to achieving the aims of his or her group (the firm, society, humanity, etc.).

The main question raised by this view of distributive justice is how the "contribution" of each individual is to be measured.

One long-lived tradition has held that contributions should be measured in terms of *work effort.* The more effort people put forth in their work, the greater the share of benefits to which they are entitled. This is the assumption behind the "Puritan ethic," which held that every individual had a religious obligation to work hard at his "calling" (the career to which God summons each individual) and that God justly rewards hard work with wealth and success, while He justly punishes laziness with poverty and failure.[78] In the United States this Puritan ethic has evolved into a secularized "work ethic" which places a high value on individual effort and which assumes that, whereas hard work does and should lead to success, loafing is and should be punished.[79]

But there are many problems with using effort as the basis of distribution.[80] First, to reward a person's efforts without any reference to whether the person produces anything worthwhile through these efforts is to reward incompetence and inefficiency. Secondly, if we reward people solely for their efforts and ignore their abilities and relative productivity, then talented and highly productive people will be given little incentive to invest their talent and productivity in producing goods for society. As a result, society's welfare will decline.

A second important tradition has held that contributions should be measured in terms of *productivity:* The better the quality of a person's contributed product, the more he or she should receive. ("Product" here should be interpreted broadly

---

[78] See Francis X. Sutton, Seymour E. Harris, Carl Kaysen, and James Tobin, *The American Business Creed* (Cambridge: Harvard University Press, 1956), pp. 276–78; the classic source is Max Weber, *The Protestant Ethic and the Spirit of Capitalism,* trans. Talcott Parsons (London: 1930); see also, Perry Miller, *The New England Mind: From Colony to Province* (Cambridge: Harvard University Press, 1953), p. 40–52.

[79] See A. Whitner Griswold, "Three Puritans on Prosperity," *The New England Quarterly,* 7 (September 1934): 475–88; see also Daniel T. Rodgers, *The Work Ethic in Industrial America* (Chicago: The University of Chicago Press, 1978).

[80] John A. Ryan, *Distributive Justice,* 3rd edition (New York: The Macmillan Co., 1941), pp. 182–83; Nicholas Rescher, *Distributive Justice* (New York: The Bobbs-Merrill Co., Inc., 1966), pp. 77–78.

to include services rendered, capital invested, commodities manufactured, and any type of literary, scientific, or aesthetic works produced.)[81] A major problem with this second proposal is that it ignores people's needs. Handicapped, ill, untrained, and immature persons may be unable to produce anything worthwhile; if people are rewarded on the basis of their productivity, the needs of these disadvantaged groups will not be met. But the main problem with this second proposal is that it is difficult to place any objective measure on the value of a person's product, especially in fields like the sciences, the arts, entertainment, athletics, education, theology, and health care. And who would want to have their products priced on the basis of someone else's subjective estimates?

In order to deal with the last difficulty above, some authors have assumed that the value of a person's product should be determined by the market forces of supply and demand.[82] The value of a product would then depend not on its intrinsic value but upon the extent to which it is both relatively scarce and is viewed by consumers as desirable. Unfortunately, this method of measuring the value of a person's product still ignores people's needs. Moreover, to many people market prices are an unjust method of evaluating the value of a person's product precisely because markets ignore the intrinsic values of things. Markets, for example, reward entertainers more than doctors. Also, markets often reward a person who through pure chance has ended up with something (an inheritance, for example) that is scarce and that people happen to want. This, to many, seems the height of injustice.

Justice Based on Needs and Abilities: Socialism

Since there are probably as many kinds of socialism as there are socialists, it is somewhat inaccurate to speak of "the" socialist position on distributive justice. Nonetheless, the dictum proposed first by Louis Blanc (1811-1882) and then by Karl Marx (1818-1883) and Nikolai Lenin (1870-1924) is traditionally taken to represent the "socialist" view on distribution: "From each according to his ability, to each according to his needs."[83] The socialist principle, then, can be paraphrased as follows:

Work burdens should be distributed according to people's abilities, and benefits should be distributed according to people's needs.

[81] Rescher, *Distributive Justice*, pp. 78–79; Ryan, *Distributive Justice*, pp. 183–85.

[82] Rescher, *Distributive Justice*, pp. 80–81; Ryan, *Distributive Justice*, pp. 186–87.

[83] Karl Marx, *Critique of the Gotha Program* (London: Lawrence and Wishart, Ltd., 1938), pp. 14 and 107; Louis Blanc, *L'Organization du Travail* (Paris; 1850) cited in D.O. Wagner, *Social Reformers* (New York: The Macmillan Co., 1946), p. 218; Nikolai Lenin, "Marxism on the State," pp. 76–77; on the question whether Marx had a theory of distributive justice, see Ziyad I. Husami, "Marx on Distributive Justice," in *Marx, Justice, and History,* Marshall Cohen, Thomas Nagel, and Thomas Scanlon, eds. (Princeton: Princeton University Press, 1980), pp. 42–79.

This "socialist" principle is based first on the idea that people realize their human potential by exercising their abilities in productive work.[84] Since the realization of one's full potentiality is a value, work should be distributed in such a way that a person can be as productive as possible, and this implies distributing work according to ability. Secondly, the benefits produced through work should be used to promote human happiness and well-being. And this means distributing them so that people's basic biological and health needs are met, and then using what is left over to meet people's other nonbasic needs. But perhaps most fundamental to the socialist view is the notion that societies should be communities in which benefits and burdens are distributed on the model of a family. Just as able family members willingly support the family, and just as needy family members are willingly supported by the family, so also the able members of a society should contribute their abilities to society by taking up its burdens while the needy should be allowed to share in its benefits.

There is something to be said for the socialist principle: Needs and abilities certainly should be taken into account when determining how society's benefits and burdens should be distributed. Most people would agree, for example, that we should make a greater contribution to the lives of cotton mill workers with brown lung disease who have greater needs than to the lives of healthy persons who have all they need. Most people would also agree that individuals should be employed in occupations for which they are fitted and that this means matching each person's abilities to his or her job as far as possible. Vocational tests in high school and college, for example, are supposed to help students find careers that match their abilities.

However, the socialist principle has also had its critics. First, opponents have pointed out that under the socialist principle there would be no relation between the amount of effort a worker puts forth and the amount of remuneration she receives (since remuneration depends on need not on effort). Consequently, opponents conclude, workers would not be motivated to put forth any work efforts at all, knowing that they will receive the same whether they work hard or not. The result will be a stagnating economy with a declining productivity.[85] Underlying this criticism is a deeper objection, namely that it is unrealistic to think that entire societies could be modeled on familial relationships. Human nature is essentially self-interested and competitive, the critics of socialism hold; and so, outside the family, people cannot be motivated by the fraternal willingness to share and help that is characteristic of families. Socialists have usually replied to this charge by arguing that human beings are taught to be self-interested and competitive by modern social and economic institutions that inculcate and encourage competitive and self-interested behavior, but that they are not that way by nature. By nature, humans are born into families where they instinctively value helping each other. If these in-

---

[84] Marx, *Critique of the Gotha Program;* see also John McMurtry, *The Structure of Marx's World View* (Princeton: Princeton University Press, 1978), Ch. I.

[85] Bowie, *A New Theory of Distributive Justice,* pp. 92–93. See also Norman Daniels, "Meritocracy," in *Justice and Economic Distribution,* Arthur and Shaw, eds., pp. 164–78.

stinctive and "natural" attitudes continued to be nurtured instead of being eradicated, humans would continue to value helping others even outside the family. The debate on what kinds of motivations human nature is subject to is still largely unsettled.

A second objection that opponents of the socialist principle have urged is that if the socialist principle were enforced, it would obliterate individual freedom.[86] Under the socialist principle, the occupation each person entered would be determined by the person's abilities and not by his or her free choice. If a person has the ability to be a university teacher but wants to be a ditch-digger, the person will have to become a teacher. Similarly, under the socialist principle, the goods a person gets will be determined by the person's needs and not by his or her free choice. If a person needs a loaf of bread but wants a bottle of beer, he or she will have to take the loaf of bread. The sacrifice of freedom is even greater, the critics claim, when one considers that in a socialist society some central government agency has to decide what tasks should be matched to each person's abilities and what goods should be allotted to each person's needs. The decisions of this central agency will then have to be imposed on other persons at the expense of their freedom to choose for themselves. The socialist principle substitutes paternalism for freedom.

Justice as Freedom: Libertarianism

The last section discussed libertarian views on moral rights; libertarians also have some clear and related views on the nature of justice. The libertarian holds that no particular way of distributing goods can be said to be just or unjust apart from the free choices individuals make. Any distribution of benefits and burdens is just if it is the result of individuals freely choosing to exchange with each other the goods each person already owns. Robert Nozick, a leading libertarian, suggests this principle as the basic principle of distributive justice:

> *From each according to what he chooses to do, to each according to what he makes for himself (perhaps with the contracted aid of others) and what others choose to do for him and choose to give him of what they've been given previously (under this maxim) and haven't yet expended or transferred.*[87]

Or, quite simply, "From each as they choose, to each as they are chosen." For example, if I choose to write a novel or choose to carve a statue out of a piece of driftwood, then I should be allowed to keep the novel or the statue if I choose to keep it. Or, if I choose, I should be allowed to give them away to someone else or to exchange them for other objects with whomever I choose. In general, people should be allowed to keep everything they make and everything they are freely given. Obviously, this means it would be wrong to tax one person (that is, take the person's money) in order to provide welfare benefits for someone else's needs.

[86] Bowie, *ibid.*, pp. 96–98.
[87] Robert Nozick, *Anarchy, State, and Utopia*, p. 160.

Nozick's principle is based on the claim (which we have already discussed) that every person has a right to freedom from coercion that takes priority over all other rights and values. The only distribution that is just, according to Nozick, is one that results from free individual choices. Any distribution that results from an attempt to impose a certain pattern on society (for instance, imposing equality on everyone or taking from the have's and giving to the have-not's) will therefore be unjust.

We have already noted some of the problems associated with the libertarian position. The major difficulty is that the libertarian enshrines a certain value—freedom from the coercion of others—and sacrifices all other rights and values to it, without giving any persuasive reasons why this should be done. Opponents of the libertarian view argue that other forms of freedom must also be secured, such as freedom from ignorance and freedom from hunger. These other forms of freedom in many cases override freedom from coercion. If a man is starving, for example, his right to be free from the constraints imposed by hunger is more important than the right of a satisfied man to be free of the constraint of being forced to share his surplus food. In order to secure these more important rights, society may impose a certain pattern of distribution, even if this means that in some cases some people will have to be coerced into conforming to the distribution. Those with surplus money, for example, may have to be taxed to provide for those who are starving.

A second related criticism of libertarianism claims that the libertarian principle of distributive justice will generate unjust treatment of the disadvantaged.[88] Under the libertarian principle, a person's share of goods will depend wholly on what the person can produce through his or her own efforts or what others choose to give the person out of charity (or some other motive). But both of these sources may be unavailable to a person through no fault of the person. A person may be ill, handicapped, unable to obtain the tools or land needed to produce goods, too old or too young to work, or otherwise incapable of producing anything through his or her own efforts. And other people (perhaps out of greed) may refuse to provide that person with what he or she needs. According to the libertarian principle, such a person should get nothing. But this, say the critics of libertarianism, is surely mistaken. If people through no fault of their own happen to be unable to care for themselves, their survival should not depend on the outside chance that others will provide them with what they need. Each person's life is of value and consequently each person should be cared for, even if this means coercing others into distributing some of their surplus to the person.

Justice as Fairness: Rawls

The discussions above have suggested several different considerations that should be taken into account in the distribution of society's benefits and burdens: political and economic equality, a minimum standard of living, needs, ability, ef-

---

[88] Rawls, *A Theory of Justice,* pp. 65–75.

fort, and freedom. What is needed, however, is a comprehensive theory capable of drawing these considerations together and fitting them together into a logical whole. John Rawls provides one approach to distributive justice that at least approximates this ideal of a comprehensive theory.[89]

John Rawls's theory is based on the assumption that conflicts involving justice should be settled by first devising a fair method for choosing the principles by which the conflicts will be resolved. Once a fair method of choosing principles is devised, the principles we choose by using that method should serve us as our own principles of distributive justice.

Rawls proposes two basic principles that, he argues, we would select if we were to use a fair method of choosing principles to resolve our social conflicts.[90] The principles of distributive justice that Rawls proposes can be paraphrased by saying that the distribution of benefits and burdens in a society is just if and only if:

1. *each person has an equal right to the most extensive basic liberties compatible with similar liberties for all, and*
2. *social and economic inequalities are arranged so that they are both*
   a. *to the greatest benefit of the least advantaged persons, and*
   b. *attached to offices and positions open to all under conditions of fair equality of opportunity.*

Rawls tells us that principle 1 is supposed to take priority over principle 2 should the two of them ever come into conflict. And within principle 2, part b is supposed to take priority over part a.

Principle 1 is called the "principle of equal liberty." Essentially it says that each citizen's liberties must be protected from invasion by others and must be equal to those of others. These basic liberties include the right to vote, freedom of speech and conscience and the other civil liberties, freedom to hold personal property, and freedom from arbitrary arrest.[91] If the principle of equal liberty is correct, then it implies that it is unjust for business institutions to invade the privacy of employees, to pressure managers to vote in certain ways, to exert undue influence on political processes by the use of bribes, or to otherwise violate the equal political liberties of society's members. According to Rawls, moreover, since our freedom to make contracts would diminish if we were afraid of being defrauded or were afraid that contracts would not be honored, the principle of equal liberty also prohibits the use of force, fraud, or deception in contractual transactions and requires that just contracts should be honored.[92] If this is true, then contractual transactions with customers (including advertising) ought morally to be free of fraud, and employees have a moral obligation to render the services they have justly contracted to their employer.

[89]*Ibid.*, pp. 577–87.
[90]*Ibid.*, pp. 298–303.
[91]*Ibid.*, p. 61.
[92]*Ibid.*, pp. 108–14 and 342–50.

Part a of principle 2 is the "difference principle." It assumes that a productive society will incorporate inequalities, but it then asserts that steps must be taken to improve as far as possible the position of the most needy members of society, such as the sick and the disabled.[93] Rawls claims that the more productive a society is, the more benefits it will be able to provide for its least advantaged members. Since the difference principle obliges us to maximize benefits for the least advantaged, this means that business institutions should be as efficient in their use of resources as possible. If we assume that a market system like ours is most efficient when it is most competitive, then the difference principle will in effect imply that markets should be competitive and that anticompetitive practices like price-fixing and monopolies are unjust. In addition, since pollution and other environmentally damaging "external effects" consume resources inefficiently, the difference principle also implies that it is wrong for firms to pollute.

Part b of principle 2 is the "principle of fair equality of opportunity." It says that everyone should be given an equal opportunity to qualify for the more privileged positions in society's institutions.[94] This means not only that job qualifications should be related to the requirements of the job (thereby prohibiting racial and sexual discrimination), but that each person must have access to the training and education needed to qualify for the desirable jobs. A person's efforts, abilities and contribution would then determine his or her remuneration.

The principles that Rawls proposes are quite comprehensive and bring together the main considerations stressed by the other approaches to justice that we have examined. But Rawls not only provides us with a set of principles of justice, he also proposes a general method for evaluating in a fair way the adequacy of any moral principles. The method he proposes consists of determining what principles a group of rational self-interested persons would choose to live by if they knew they would live in a society governed by those principles but they did not yet know what each of them would turn out to be like in that society.[95] We might ask, for example, whether such a group of rational self-interested persons would choose to live in a society governed by a principle that discriminates against blacks when none of them knows whether he himself or she herself will turn out to be a black person in that society. The answer, clearly, is that such a racist principle would be rejected and consequently, according to Rawls, the racist principle would be unjust. Thus, Rawls claims that a principle is a morally justified principle of justice if and only if the principle would be acceptable to a group of rational self-interested persons who know they will live in a society governed by the principles they accept but who do not yet know what sex, race, abilities, religion, interests, social position, income, or other particular characteristics each of them will possess in that future society.

Rawls refers to the situation of such an imaginary group of rational persons as the "original position," and he refers to their ignorance of any particulars about

[93] *Ibid.*, pp. 75–83 and 274–84.
[94] *Ibid.*, p. 83–90.
[95] *Ibid.*, pp. 17–22.

themselves as the "veil of ignorance."[96] The purpose and effect of decreeing that the parties to the original position do not know what particular characteristics each of them will possess is to ensure that none of them can protect his or her own special interests. Because they are ignorant of their particular qualities, the parties to the original position are forced to be fair and impartial and to show no favoritism toward any special group: They must look after the good of all.

According to Rawls, the principles that the imaginary parties to the original position accept will *ipso facto* turn out to be morally justified.[97] They will be morally justified because the original position incorporates the Kantian moral ideas of reversibility (the parties choose principles that will apply to themselves), of universalizability (the principles must apply equally to everyone), and of treating people as ends (each party has an equal say in the choice of principles). The principles are further justified, according to Rawls, because they are consistent with our deepest considered intuitions about justice. The principles chosen by the parties to the original position match most of the moral convictions we already have and where they do not, according to Rawls, we would be willing to change them to fit Rawls's principles once we reflect on his arguments.

Rawls goes on to claim that the parties to the original position would in fact choose his (Rawls's) principles of justice, that is, the principle of equal liberty, the difference principle, and the principle of fair equality of opportunity.[98] The principle of equal liberty would be chosen because the parties will want to be free to pursue their major special interests whatever these might be. Since in the original position each person is ignorant of what special interests he or she will have, everyone will want to secure a maximum amount of freedom so that he or she can pursue whatever interests he or she has upon entering society. The difference principle will be chosen because all parties will want to protect themselves against the possibility of ending up in the worst position in society. By adopting the difference principle, the parties will ensure that even the position of the most needy is cared for. And the principle of fair equality of opportunity will be chosen, according to Rawls, because all parties to the original position will want to protect their interests should they turn out to be among the talented. The principle of fair equality of opportunity ensures that everyone has an equal opportunity to advance through the use of his or her own abilities, efforts, and contributions.

If Rawls is correct in claiming that the principles chosen by the parties to the original position are morally justified, and if he is correct in arguing that his own principles would be chosen by the parties to the original position, then it follows that his principles are in fact morally justified to serve as our own principles of justice. These principles would then constitute the proper principles of distributive justice.

[96] *Ibid.*, pp. 136–42.

[97] *Ibid.*, pp. 46–53.

[98] The core of the argument is at *ibid.*, pp. 175–83, but parts may also be found at pp. 205–9; 325–32; 333–50; 541–48.

Critics, however, have objected to various parts of Rawls's theory.[99] Some have argued that the original position is not an adequate method for choosing moral principles. According to these critics, the mere fact that a set of principles is chosen by the hypothetical parties to the original position tells us nothing about whether the principles are morally justified. Other critics have argued that the parties to the original position would not choose Rawls's principles at all. Utilitarians, for example, have argued that the hypothetical parties to the original position would choose utilitarianism and not Rawls's principles. Still other critics have claimed that Rawls's principles are themselves mistaken. Rawls's principles, according to these critics, are opposed to our basic convictions concerning what justice is.

In spite of the many objections that have been raised against Rawls's theory, his defenders still claim that the advantages of the theory outweigh its defects. For one thing, they claim, the theory preserves the basic values that have become embedded in our moral beliefs: freedom, equality of opportunity, and a concern for the disadvantaged. Secondly, the theory fits easily into the basic economic institutions of Western societies: It does not reject the market system, work incentives, nor the inequalities consequent on a division of labor. Instead, by requiring that inequalities work for the benefit of the least advantaged and by requiring equality of opportunity, the theory shows how the inequalities that attend the division of labor and free markets can be compensated for and thereby made just. Thirdly, the theory incorporates both the communitarian and the individualistic strains that are intertwined in Western culture. The difference principle encourages the more talented to use their skills in ways that will rebound to the benefit of fellow citizens who are less well off, thereby encouraging a type of communitarian or "fraternal" concern.[100] Yet the principle of equal liberty leaves the individual free to pursue whatever special interests the individual may have. Fourthly, Rawls's theory takes into account the criteria of need, ability, effort, and contribution. The difference principle distributes benefits in accordance with need, while the principle of fair equality of opportunity in effect distributes benefits and burdens according to ability and contribution.[101] And fifthly, the defenders of Rawls argue, there is the moral justification that the original position provides. The original position is defined so that its parties choose impartial principles that take into account the equal interests of everyone, and this, they claim, is the essence of morality.

Retributive Justice

Retributive justice concerns the justice of blaming or punishing persons for doing wrong. Philosophers have long debated the justification of blame and punishment, but we need not enter these debates here. More relevant to our purposes is the question of the conditions under which it is just to punish a person for doing wrong.

[99] See the articles collected in *Reading Rawls,* ed. Daniels; see also Brian Barry, *The Liberal Theory of Justice* (Oxford: Clarendon Press, 1973); Robert Paul Wolff, *Understanding Rawls* (Princeton: Princeton University Press, 1977).

[100] Rawls, *A Theory of Justice,* pp. 105-8.

[101] *Ibid.,* p. 276.

The first chapter discussed two major conditions under which a person could not be held morally responsible for what he or she did: ignorance and inability. These two conditions are also relevant to determining the justice of punishing or blaming someone for doing wrong: If people do not know or freely choose what they are doing, then they cannot justly be punished or blamed for it. For example, if the cotton mill owners mentioned at the beginning of this section did not know that the conditions in their mills would cause brown lung disease, then it would be unjust to punish them when it turns out that their mills caused this disease.

A second condition of just punishments is certitude that the person being punished actually did wrong. Many firms, for example, use more or less complex systems of "due process" that are intended to ascertain whether the conduct of employees was really such as to merit dismissal or some other penalty.[102] Penalizing an employee on the basis of flimsy or incomplete evidence is rightly considered an injustice.

Thirdly, just punishments must be consistent and proportioned to the wrong. Punishment is consistent only when everyone is given the same penalty for the same infraction; punishment is proportioned to the wrong when the penalty is no greater in magnitude than the harm that the wrongdoer inflicted.[103] It is unjust, for example, for a manager to impose harsh penalties for minor infractions of rules, or to be lenient toward favorites but harsh toward all others. If the purpose of a punishment is to deter others from committing the same wrong or to prevent the wrongdoer from repeating the wrong, then punishment should not be greater than what is consistently necessary to achieve these aims.

Compensatory Justice

Compensatory justice concerns the justice of restoring to a person what the person lost when he or she was wronged by someone else. We generally hold that when one person wrongfully harms the interests of another person, the wrongdoer has a moral duty to provide some form of restitution to the person he or she wronged. If, for example, I destroy someone's property or injure him bodily, I will be held morally responsible for paying him damages.

There are no hard and fast rules for determining how much compensation a wrongdoer owes the victim. Justice seems to require that the wrongdoer as far as possible should restore whatever he or she took and this would usually mean that the amount of restitution should be equal to the loss the wrongdoer knowingly inflicted on the victim. Yet some losses are impossible to measure. If I maliciously in-

---

[102] On the relation between justice and due process see David Resnick, "Due Process and Procedural Justice," in *Due Process*, eds. J. Roland Pennock and John W. Chapman (New York: New York University Press, 1977), pp. 302–310; employee due process procedures are discussed in Maurice S. Trotta and Harry R. Gudenberg, "Resolving Personnel Problems in Nonunion Plants," in *Individual Rights in the Corporation*, eds. Alan F. Westin and Stephen Salisbury (New York: Pantheon Books, Inc., 1980), pp. 302–10.

[103] On the relation between justice and consistency in the application of rules see Perelman, *The Idea of Justice*, pp. 36–45; proportionality in punishment is discussed in John Kleinig, *Punishment and Desert* (The Hague: Martinus Nijoff, 1973), pp. 110–33; and C.W.K. Mundle, "Punishment and Desert," *Philosophical Quarterly*, IV (1954): 216–28.

jure someone's reputation, for example, how much restitution should I make? Some losses, moreover, cannot be restored at all: For can the loss of life or the loss of sight be compensated? In cases of this sort, where the injury is such that full restoration of the loss is not possible, we seem to hold that the wrongdoer should at least pay for the material damages the loss inflicts upon the injured person and his or her immediate family.

Traditional moralists have argued that a person has a moral obligation to compensate an injured party only if three conditions are present:[104]

1. The action that inflicted the injury was wrong or negligent. For example, if by efficiently managing my firm I undersell my competitor and run her out of business, I am not morally bound to compensate her since such competition is neither wrongful nor negligent; but if I steal from my employer, then I owe him compensation, or if I fail to exercise due care in my driving, then I owe compensation to those whom I injure.
2. The person's action was the real cause of the injury. For example, if a banker loans a person money and the borrower then uses it to cheat others, the banker is not morally obligated to compensate the victims; but if the banker defrauds a customer, the customer must be compensated.
3. The person inflicted the injury voluntarily. For example, if I injure someone's property accidentally and without negligence, I am not morally obligated to compensate the person. (I may, however, be *legally* bound to do so depending on how the law chooses to distribute the social costs of injury.)

The most controversial forms of compensation undoubtedly are the "preferential treatment" programs that attempt to remedy past injustices against groups. If a racial group, for example, has been unjustly discriminated against for an extended period of time in the past and its members consequently now hold the lowest economic and social positions in society, does justice require that members of that group be compensated by being given special preference in hiring, training, and promotion procedures? Or would such special treatment itself be a violation of justice by violating the principle of equal treatment? Does justice legitimize quotas even if this requires turning down more highly qualified nonminorities? These are complex and involved questions that we will not be able to answer at this point. We will return to them in a later chapter.

2.4 SUMMARY: UTILITY, RIGHTS, AND JUSTICE

The last three sections have described the three main kinds of moral standards that today lie at the basis of most of our moral judgments and that force us to bring distinctive kinds of considerations into our moral reasonings. Utilitarian standards

---

[104] Henry J. Wirtenberger, S.J., *Morality and Business* (Chicago: Loyola University Press, 1962), pp. 109–19; see also Herbert Jone, *Moral Theology,* trans. Urban Adelman (Westminster, MD: The Newman Press, 1961), pp. 225–47.

must be used when we do not have the resources for attaining everyone's objectives, so we are forced to consider the net social benefits and social costs consequent on the actions (or policies or institutions) by which we can attain these objectives. When these utilitarian considerations are employed, the person must bring into his or her moral reasoning measurements, estimates, and comparisons of the relevant benefits and costs. Such measurements, estimates, and comparisons constitute the information on which the utilitarian moral judgment is based.

Our moral judgments are also partially based on standards that specify how individuals must be treated or respected. These sorts of standards must be employed when our actions and policies will substantially affect the welfare and freedom of specifiable individuals. Moral reasoning of this type forces consideration of whether the behavior respects the basic rights of the individuals involved and whether the behavior is consistent with one's agreements and special duties. These sorts of considerations require information concerning how the behavior affects the basic needs of the humans involved, the freedom they have to choose, the information available to them, the extent to which force, coercion, manipulation, or deception are used upon them, and the tacit and explicit understandings with which they entered various roles and agreements.

And thirdly, our moral judgments are also in part based on standards of justice that indicate how benefits and burdens should be distributed among the members of a group. These sorts of standards must be employed when evaluating actions whose distributive effects differ in important ways. The moral reasoning on which such judgments are based will incorporate considerations concerning whether the behavior distributes benefits and burdens equally or in accordance with the needs, abilities, contributions, and free choices of people as well as with the extent of their wrongdoing. These sorts of considerations in turn rely on comparisons of the benefits and burdens going to different groups (or individuals) and comparisons of their relative needs, efforts, etc.

Our morality therefore contains three main kinds of moral considerations, each of which emphasizes certain morally important aspects of our behavior, but no one of which captures all the factors that must be taken into account in making moral judgments. Utilitarian standards consider only the aggregate social welfare but ignore the individual and how that welfare is distributed. Moral rights consider the individual but discount both aggregate well-being and distributive considerations. Standards of justice consider distributive issues but they ignore aggregate social welfare and the individual as such. These three kinds of moral considerations do not seem to be reducible to each other yet all three seem to be necessary parts of our morality. That is, there are some moral problems for which utilitarian considerations are decisive, while for other problems the decisive considerations are either the rights of individuals or the justice of the distributions involved. This suggests that moral reasoning should incorporate all three kinds of moral considerations, even though only one or the other may turn out to be relevant or decisive in a particular situation. One simple strategy for ensuring that all three kinds of considerations are incorporated into one's moral reasoning is to inquire systematically into

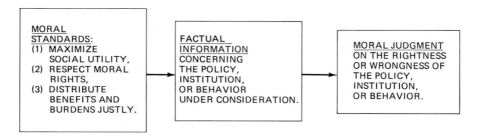

FIGURE 2-1

the utility, rights, and justice involved in a given moral judgment as in Figure 2.1. One might, for example, ask a series of questions about an action that one is considering: (1) Does the action, as far as possible, maximize social benefits and minimize social injuries? (2) Is the action consistent with the moral rights of those whom it will affect? (3) Will the action lead to a just distribution of benefits and burdens?

Bringing together different moral standards in this way, however, requires that one keep in mind how they relate to each other. As we have seen, moral rights identify areas in which other people generally may not interfere even if they can show that they would derive greater benefits from such interference. Generally speaking, therefore, standards concerned with moral rights have greater weight than either utilitarian standards or standards of justice. And standards of justice are generally accorded greater weight than utilitarian considerations.

But these relationships hold only in general. If a certain action (or policy or institution) promises to generate sufficiently large social benefits or to prevent sufficiently large social harm, the enormity of these utilitarian consequences may justify limited infringements of the rights of some individuals. Moreover, sufficiently large social costs and benefits may also be significant enough to justify some departures from standards of justice; and the correction of large and widespread injustices may be important enough to justify limited infringements on some individual rights.

We have at this time no comprehensive moral theory capable of determining precisely when utilitarian considerations become "sufficiently large" to outweigh narrow infringements on a conflicting right or standard of justice, or when considerations of justice become "important enough" to outweigh infringements on conflicting rights. Moral philosophers have been unable to agree on any absolute rules for making such judgments. There are, however, a number of rough criteria that can guide us in these matters. Suppose, for example, that only by invading my employees' right to privacy (with hidden cameras and legal on-the-job phone taps) will I be able to stop the continuing theft of several life-saving drugs that some of them are clearly stealing. How can I determine whether the utilitarian benefits are here "sufficiently large" to justify infringing on their right? First, I might ask whether the *kinds* of utilitarian values involved are clearly more important than the *kinds* of values protected by the right (or distributed by the standard of justice). The utilitarian benefits in the present example, for instance, include the saving of human life, while the right to privacy protects (let us suppose) the values of freedom from shame and blackmail and of freedom to live one's life as one chooses. Considering this I might decide that human life is here clearly the more important kind of value. Secondly, I might then ask whether the more important kind of value also involves substantially more people. For example, since the recovered drugs will (we assume) save several hundred lives, while the invasion of privacy will affect only a dozen people, the utilitarian values do involve substantially more people. Thirdly, I can ask whether the actual injuries sustained by the persons whose rights are violated (or to whom an injustice is done) will be minor. For example, suppose that I can ensure that my employees suffer no shame, blackmail, or restriction on their freedom as a result of my uncovering information about their private lives (I intend to destroy all such information). Then it would appear that they will not be injured in any major way by my invasion of their privacy.

There are, then, rough criteria that can guide our thinking when it appears that in a certain situation utilitarian considerations might be sufficiently important to override conflicting rights or standards of justice; and similar criteria can be used to determine whether in a certain situation considerations of justice should override an individual's rights. But these criteria remain rough and intuitive. They lie at the edges of the light that ethics can shed on moral reasoning.

QUESTIONS FOR REVIEW AND DISCUSSION

1. Define the following concepts: utilitarianism, utility, intrinsic good, instrumental good, basic need, mere wants, rule-utilitarianism, rights, legal rights, moral rights, negative rights, positive rights, contractual rights, categorical imperative (both versions), the libertarian view on rights, distributive justice, the fundamental (or formal) principle of distributive justice, material principle of justice, egalitarian justice, capitalist justice, socialist justice, libertarian justice, justice as fairness, principle of equal liberty, difference principle, principle of fair equality of opportunity, the "original position," retributive justice, compensatory justice.

2. "Utilitarianism is the view that so long as an action provides me with more measurable economic benefits than costs, the action is morally right." Identify all of the mistakes contained in this statement.

3. In your view, does utilitarianism provide a more objective standard for determining right and wrong than moral rights do? Explain your answer fully. Does utilitarianism provide a more objective standard than principles of justice? Explain.

4. "Every principle of distributive justice whether that of the egalitarian, or the capitalist, or the socialist, or the libertarian, or of Rawls, in the end is illegitimately advocating some type of equality." Do you agree or disagree? Explain.

CASES FOR DISCUSSION

The Ford Motor Car

Ford Motor Company is the second largest producer of automobiles. With annual sales of over six million cars and trucks worldwide, it has revenues of over $30 billion per year. In 1960, Ford's market position was eroded by competition from domestic and foreign subcompacts, especially Volkswagens. Lee Iacocca, president of Ford, determined to regain Ford's share of the market by having a new subcompact, the Pinto, in production by 1970.

Although the normal preproduction testing and development of an automobile takes about forty-three months, Iacocca managed to bring the Pinto to the production stage in a little over two years. Internal memos showed that Ford crash-tested early models of the Pinto before production "at a top-secret site, more than forty times and . . . every test made at over 25 mph without special structural alteration of the car . . . resulted in a ruptured fuel tank."[1] Stray sparks could easily ignite any spilling gasoline and engulf the car in flames. Several years later, a spokesman for Ford acknowledged "that early model Pintos did not pass rear-impact tests at 20 mph."[2]

Nonetheless, the company went on with production of the Pinto as designed, since it met all applicable federal safety standards then in effect and was comparable in safety to other cars then being produced. Moreover, a later Ford company study released by J.C. Echold, director of automotive safety for Ford, claimed that an improved design that would have rendered the Pinto and other similar cars less likely to burst into flames on collision would not be cost-effective for society. Entitled "Fatalities Associated with Crash Induced Fuel Leakage and Fires," the Ford study (which was intended to counter the prospect of stiffer government regulations on gasoline tank design) claimed that the costs of the design improvement ($11 per vehicle) far outweighed its social benefits:

> The total benefit is shown to be just under $50 million, while the associated cost is $137 million. Thus the cost is almost three times the benefits, even using a number of highly favorable benefit assumptions.

BENEFITS:

Savings	—	180 burn deaths, 180 serious burn injuries, 2100 burned vehicles.
Unit cost	—	$200,000 per death, $67,000 per injury, $700 per vehicle.
Total Benefits	—	180 X ($200,000) plus
		180 X ($ 67,000) plus
		2100 X ($ 700) = $49.15 million

[1] Mark Dowie, "Pinto Madness," *Mother Jones,* September/October 1977, p. 20. See also Joanne Gamdin, "Jury Slaps Massive 'Fine' on Ford in '72 Pinto Crash," *Business Insurance,* 20 February 1978, p. 76.

[2] "Ford Rebuts Pinto Criticism," *The National Underwriter,* 9 September 1977.

COSTS:

Sales	—	11 million cars, 1.5 million light trucks
Unit Cost	—	$11 per car, $11 per truck
Total Costs	—	11,000,000 × ($11) plus
		1,500,000 × ($11) = $137 million

[From memorandum attached to statement of J.C. Echold] [3]

Ford's estimate of the number of deaths, injuries, and vehicles that would be lost as a result of fires from fuel leakage were based on statistical studies. The $200,000 value attributed to the loss of life was based on a study of the National Highway Traffic Safety Administration, which broke down the estimated social costs of a death as follows: [4]

COMPONENT	1971 COSTS
Future Productivity Losses	
Direct	$132,000
Indirect	41,300
Medical Costs	
Hospital	700
Other	425
Property Damage	1,500
Insurance Administration	4,700
Legal and Court	3,000
Employer Losses	1,000
Victim's Pain and Suffering	10,000
Funeral	900
Assets (Lost Consumption)	5,000
Miscellaneous Accident Cost	200
TOTAL PER FATALITY:	$200,725

On May 28, 1972, Mrs. Lily Gray was driving a six-month-old Pinto on Interstate 15 near San Bernardino, California. In the car with her was Richard Grimshaw, a thirteen-year-old boy. Mrs. Gray was a unique person. She had adopted two girls, worked 40 hours a week, was den-mother for all the teenagers in the neighborhood, sold refreshments at the Bobby Sox games, and had maintained a twenty-two-year long happy marriage.

Mrs. Gray was driving at about 55 mph when the Pinto stalled and was rear-ended by a 1963 Ford convertible. On impact, the Pinto gas tank ruptured and the car burst into flames. Inside the car, Mrs. Gray was burned to death and Richard Grimshaw was severely burned over 90 per cent of his body. It was a hundred-to-one shot, but, although badly disfigured, Richard survived the accident and subsequently underwent seventy painful surgical operations. At least fifty-three persons

[3] Ralph Drayton, "One Manufacturer's Approach to Automobile Safety Standards," *CTLA News,* VIII, no. 2, February 1968: 11.

[4] Dowie, "Pinto Madness," p. 28.

have died in accidents involving Pinto fires and many more have been severely burnt.[5]

1. Using the Ford figures given in the memo calculate the probability that a vehicle would be involved in a burn death (that is, the number of burn deaths divided by the total number of cars and trucks sold). In your opinion, is there a limit to the amount that Ford should have been willing to invest in order to reduce this figure to zero? If your answer is yes, then determine from your answer what price you place on life and compare your price to the government's. If your answer is no, then discuss whether your answer implies that no matter how much it would take to make such cars, automakers should make cars completely accident-proof.

2. In your opinion, was the management of Ford morally responsible for Mrs. Gray's "burn death"? Explain. Was there something wrong with the utilitarian analysis Ford management used? Explain. Would it have made any difference from a moral point of view if Ford management had informed its buyers of the risks of fire? Explain.

3. Suppose that you were on Mr. J.C. Echold's staff and before the Pinto reached the production stage you were assigned the task of writing an analysis of the overall desirability of producing and marketing the Pinto as planned. One part of your report is to be subtitled "ethical and social desirability." What would you write in this part?

A South African Investment

In April 1977, the Interfaith Center on Corporate Responsibility announced that some of its subscribing members owned stock in Texaco, Inc. and in Standard Oil Co. of California (SoCal), and that these members would introduce shareholders' resolutions at the next annual stockholders' meeting of Texaco and SoCal that would require that these companies and their affiliates terminate their operations in South Africa. The effort to get Texaco and SoCal out of South Africa was primarily directed and coordinated by Tim Smith, project director of the Interfaith Center on Corporate Responsibility. The stockholders' resolution that Tim Smith would have the Interfaith shareholders introduce at the annual meetings of Texaco and SoCal read as follows:

> Whereas in South Africa the black majority is controlled and oppressed by a white minority that comprises 18 percent of the population;
> Whereas South Africa's apartheid system legalizes racial discrimination in all aspects of life and deprives the black population of their most basic human rights, such as, Africans cannot vote, cannot collectively bargain, must live in racially segregated areas, are paid grossly discriminatory wages, are assigned 13 percent of the land while 87 percent of the land is reserved for the white population;

[5] "Ford Fights Pinto Case: Jury gives 128 million," *Auto News*, 13 February 1978, pp. 3, 44.

Whereas black opposition to apartheid and black demands for full political, legal, and social rights in their country has risen dramatically within the last year;

Whereas widespread killing, arrests, and repression have been the response of the white South African government to nationwide demonstrations for democratic rights;

Whereas Prime Minister Vorster has openly declared his intention to maintain apartheid and deny political rights to South African blacks;

Whereas we believe that U.S. business investments in the Republic of South Africa, including our company's operations, provide significant economic support and moral legitimacy to South Africa's apartheid government;

Therefore be it resolved: that the shareholders request the Board of Directors to establish the following as corporate policy:

> "Texaco [and Standard Oil of California] and any of its subsidiaries or affiliates shall terminate its present operations in the Republic of South Africa as expeditiously as possible unless and until the South African government has committed itself to ending the legally enforced form of racism called apartheid and has taken meaningful steps toward the achievement of full political, legal, and social rights for the majority population (African, Asian, colored)."

The resolution was occasioned by the fact that Texaco and SoCal were the joint owners of Caltex Petroleum Co. (each owns 50 percent of Caltex), an affiliate that operates oil refineries in South Africa and that in 1973 was worth about $100 million. In 1975 Caltex announced that it was planning to expand its refinery plant in Milnerto, South Africa, from a capacity of 58,000 barrels a day to an increased capacity of 108,000 barrels a day. The expansion would cost $135 million and would increase South Africa's *total* refining capacity by 11 percent. Caltex would be obliged by South African law to bring in at least $100 million of these investment funds from outside the country.

The management of Texaco and SoCal were both opposed to the resolution that would have required them to pull out of South Africa and to abandon their Caltex expansion plans, which, by some estimates, promised an annual return of 20 percent on the original investment. They therefore recommended that stockholders vote against the resolution. The managements of both Texaco and SoCal argued that Caltex was committed to improving the economic working conditions of its black employees and that their continued presence in South Africa did not constitute an "endorsement" of South Africa's "policies." The commitment of Caltex to improving the condition of its employees was evidenced, the companies claimed, by its adherence to the 1977 "Sullivan principles."

Early in 1977, Caltex was one of several dozen corporations who had adopted a code of conduct drafted by the Reverend Dr. Leon Sullivan, a civil rights activist who is a minister of Philadelphia's large Zion Baptist Church. The Code was based on these six principles that the corporations affirmed for their plants:[1]

---

[1] Jack Magarrell, "U.S. Adopts Stand on Apartheid: Backed on Many Campuses," *The Chronicle of Higher Education,* 12 March 1979.

  I. Nonsegregation of the races in all eating, comfort, and work facilities.
 II. Equal and fair employment practices for all employees.
III. Equal pay for all employees doing equal or comparable work for the same period of time.
 IV. Initiation of and development of training programs that will prepare, in substantial numbers, blacks and other nonwhites for supervisory, administrative, clerical, and technical jobs.
  V. Increasing the number of blacks and other nonwhites in management and supervisory positions.
 VI. Improving the quality of employees' lives outside the work environment in such areas as housing, transportation, schooling, recreation, and health facilities.

These companies agree to further implement these principles. Where implementation requires a modification of existing South African working conditions, we will seek such modification through appropriate channels.

The code had been approved by the South African government since the principles were to operate within "existing South African working conditions," that is, within South African laws. South African laws requiring separate facilities and South African laws prohibiting blacks from becoming apprentices, for example, would continue to apply where in force.[2] Also, the principle of equal pay for equal work would probably require few changes where blacks and whites did not have equal work.

Caltex, however, was apparently committed to improving the economic position of its workers. It had moved 40 percent of its 742 black workers into refinery jobs formerly held by whites, although most blacks had remained in the lower six job categories (a total of 29 had moved into the top four white-collar and skilled categories).[3] The company had also kept its wages well above the averages determined in studies conducted by the South African University of Port Elizabeth. A basic argument that Texaco and SoCal advanced in favor of remaining in South Africa, then, was that their continued presence in South Africa advanced the economic welfare of blacks.

Texaco believes that continuation of Caltex's operations in South Africa is in the best interests of Caltex's employees of all races in South Africa. . . . In management's opinion, if Caltex were to withdraw from South Africa in an attempt to achieve political changes in that country, as the proposal directs, . . . such withdrawal would endanger prospects for the future of all Caltex employees in South Africa regardless of race. We are convinced that the resulting dislocation and hardship would fall most heavily on the nonwhite communities. In this regard, and contrary to the implications of the stockholders' statement, Caltex employment policies include equal pay for equal

[2] See Herman Nickel, "The Case for Doing Business in South Africa," *Fortune,* 19 June 1968, p. 72.
[3] Investor Responsibility Research Center, *Analysis E Supplement No. 9,* 7 April 1977, p. E 114.

work and the same level of benefit plans for all employees as well as a continuing and successful program to advance employees to positions of responsibility on the basis of ability, not race. [Statement of Texaco management] [4]

It is undeniable that the presence of foreign corporations in South Africa had helped to improve the real earnings of black industrial workers. Between 1970 and 1975, black incomes in Johannesburg rose 118 percent, while between 1975 and 1980 black per capita income was expected to rise 30 percent. In addition, the gap between black and white incomes in South Africa had narrowed. Between 1970 and 1976, the gap in industry narrowed from 1:5.8 to 1:4.4; in construction from 1:6.6 to 1:5.2; and in the mining sector from 1:19.8 to 1:7.7. [5] If the flow of foreign investment came to a halt, however, the South African normal yearly growth rate of 6 percent would drop to about 3 percent and the results would undoubtedly hit blacks the hardest. [6] Unemployment would rise (American companies employ 60,000 blacks), and whatever benefits blacks had gained would be lost.

Tim Smith and the Interfaith stockholders were aware of these facts. The basic issue for them, however, was not whether Caltex adhered to the six Sullivan principles or whether its presence in South Africa improved the economic position of blacks:

> The issue in South Africa at this time is black political power; it is not slightly higher wages or better benefits or training programs, unless these lead to basic social change. As one South African church leader put it, "These [six] principles attempt to polish my chains and make them more comfortable. I want to cut my chains and cast them away." . . . We must look not just at wages but at the transfer of technology, the taxes paid to South Africa, the effect of U.S. foreign policy, and the provision of strategic products to the racist government. If these criteria become part of the "principles" of U.S. investors, it should be clear that on balance many of the corporations strengthen and support white minority rule. This form of support should be challenged, and American economic complicity in apartheid ended. [Statement of Tim Smith] [7]

In short, the issue was one of human rights. The white South African government was committed to denying blacks their basic rights, and the continued presence of American companies supported this system of white rule.

> Nonwhites in South Africa are rightless persons in the land of their birth. . . . [The black African] has no rights in "white areas." He cannot vote, cannot own land, and may not have his family with him unless he has government permission. . . . The two major black political parties have been banned and hundreds of persons detained for political offenses . . . strikes by Africans are

---

[4] *Texaco Proxy Statement,* 1977, item 3.

[5] Nickel, "Doing Business in South Africa," p. 64.

[6] *Ibid.,* p. 63.

[7] Timothy Smith, "Whitewash for Apartheid from Twelve U.S. Firms," *Business and Society Review,* Summer 1977, pp. 59, 60.

illegal, and meaningful collective bargaining is outlawed. . . . by investing in South Africa, American companies inevitably strengthen the status quo of [this] white supremacy. . . . The leasing of a computer, the establishment of a new plant, the selling of supplies to the military—all have political over-tones. . . . And among the country's white community, the overriding goal of politics is maintenance of white control. In the words of Prime Minister John Vorster during the 1970 election campaign: "We are building a nation for whites only. Black people are entitled to political rights but only over their own people—not my people." [Statement of Tim Smith][8]

There was no doubt that the continuing operations of Caltex provided some economic support for the South African government. South African law required oil refineries in South Africa to set aside a percentage of their oil for government purchase. In 1975, about 7 percent of Caltex's oil sales went to the government of South Africa. As a whole, the South African economy relied on oil for 25 percent of its energy needs. Moreover, Caltex represented almost 11 percent of the total U.S. investment in South Africa. If Caltex closed down its operations in South Africa, this would certainly have had great impact on the economy especially if other companies then lost confidence in the South African economy and subsequently also withdrew from South Africa. Finally, Caltex also supported the South African government through corporate taxes.

1. In your judgment, are the possible utilitarian benefits of building the Caltex plant more important than the possible violations of moral rights and of justice that may be involved? Justify your answer fully by identifying the possible benefits and the possible violations of rights and justice that you believe may be associated with the building of the plant, and explaining which you think are more important.

2. If you were a stockholder in Texaco or Standard Oil, how do you think you ought to vote on the stockholders' resolution of the Interfaith Center? Justify your answer fully.

3. What kind of response should the managements of Texaco and SoCal make to the Interfaith Center?

4. In your judgment, does the management of a company have any responsibilities (i.e., duties) beyond ensuring a high return for its stockholders? Should the management of a company look primarily to the law and to the rate of return on its investment as the ultimate criteria for deciding what investments it should make? Why or why not?

Buying a Home in Hartford, Connecticut[1]

The Hartford, Connecticut metropolitan area in 1973 was composed of two distinct regions: the central 'inner" city and the outlying suburbs. Between 1960 and 1970 the minority population of Hartford's inner city had grown substantially;

---

[8]Timothy Smith, "South Africa: The Churches vs. the Corporations," *Business and Society Review,* 1971, pp. 54, 55, 56.
[1]This case is based entirely on the materials in U.S. Commission on Civil Rights, *Mortgage Money: Who Gets It? A Case Study in Mortgage Lending Discrimination in Hartford, Connecticut* (Washington, DC: U.S. Government Printing Office, 1974).

simultaneously, whites had moved out of the inner city into the suburbs. As a result, during the 1960s, the black population of the inner city climbed from 25,000 to over 44,000 and the Puerto Rican population went from 2,300 to over 8,500; the white population of the inner city during the same period declined from 134,700 to 103,320, a drop of almost 25 percent. By 1970, dwellings in the Hartford metropolitan area were distributed as follows:[2]

TABLE 2.1

Ethnic Population	In City Dwellings		In Suburban Dwellings	
White	103,319	(65.4%)	496,486	(98.1%)
Black	44,091	(27.9%)	6,427	(1.3%)
Puerto Rican	8,543	(5.4%)	693	(.1%)
TOTAL	158,017	(100%)	505,874	(100%)

Housing was racially segregated even within the inner city: Blacks and Puerto Ricans lived mostly in the northern part of the city, while the southern and western sections were predominantly white.

Houses in the inner city where minorities lived were by and large older than those in the suburbs. Moreover, twice as many inner-city dwellings as suburban dwellings were "overcrowded," and inner-city dwellings had lower average values than those in the suburbs:[3]

TABLE 2.2

Value of Dwelling	% of Dwellings In City	% of Dwellings in Suburbs
$0 – $10,000	1.2%	.9%
$10,000 – 14,999	7.6	4.1
$15,000 – 19,999	34.7	16.6
$20,000 – 24,999	32.5	26.4
$25,000 – 34,999	18.0	31.7
$35,000 or more	6.0	20.2

Most minorities living in the inner city did not own their own homes: Eighty-five percent of inner-city blacks and 97 percent of inner-city Puerto Ricans rented their houses.

Minorities remained in the inner city and failed to buy homes, in part, because of their incomes. Although the median income for all inner-city families in 1970 was $9,100 a year, the median for inner-city blacks was $7,000 and for inner-city Puerto Ricans it was $5,250. The median income for all suburban families, however, was $13,300. For suburban blacks it was $12,600 and for suburban Puerto

[2]*Ibid.*, p. 6.
[3]*Ibid.*, p. 7.

Ricans it was $12,400. Seventy percent of these suburbanites owned their own homes.

Yet economics alone did not seem to account for the difficulty blacks and Puerto Ricans encountered in purchasing homes and in moving to desirable suburban housing. Thirty percent of inner-city black families and 20 percent of inner-city Puerto Ricans in 1970 had incomes that should have qualified them to afford housing costing as much as $25,000.[4] At least 50 percent of suburban dwellings, and 75 percent of inner-city dwellings are valued at less than $25,000. Many blamed their situation on the city's financial and real estate institutions.

Families who want to purchase housing usually have to deal with two groups: real estate agents and loan officers. Real estate agents represent sellers and deal directly with buyers looking for a home. Loan officers at lending institutions (that is, at banks and at savings and loan associations) analyze the credit-worthiness of buyers who need a loan in order to purchase housing. The loan officer then recommends for or against the loan to a loan committee, which generally follows the officer's recommendation.

Many people felt that the policies of Hartford real estate agents and loan officers were biased against inner-city minority groups. Hartford's real estate agents readily admitted that they automatically ran credit checks on minority families, but not on white families.[5] The city's real estate agents argued, however, that lending institutions expected real estate agents to "screen" each buyer before he or she came to the lending institution. Since real estate agents wanted to remain on good terms with the city's lending institutions, they tried to discourage families from buying houses when they felt the family did not have the characteristics that lending institutions desired. Minority families often did not have these characteristics.

Although I am black, I contacted a white real estate agent because I wanted to purchase a house in a white suburb. The agent reviewed my credit reports, which showed that three years before I had been late in making certain payments due to an illness. After reading my report, the agent advised me against buying a house in the suburbs and steered me toward what he said was a "more suitable" section of town (a black neighborhood). The agent said that he felt banks would be more willing to approve my loan if I was purchasing a house in that section of town. [Reconstructed statement of Hartford home buyer][6]

My husband and I are black. When we saw an advertisement for a house we liked, we contacted the white real estate agent with whom the house was listed. When we met with the agent, he asked my husband what his income and employment was. The agent then told us that he was afraid we didn't meet the "income standards of the community" in which the house was located. Then without telling us what the house was selling for, nor asking how much we had for a down payment, he leafed briefly through his list-

[4]*Ibid.*

[5]*Ibid.*, p. 10.

[6]Based on interview materials in *ibid.*, p. 10.

ings and announced that he didn't have anything he "felt was suitable" for us. [Reconstructed statement of Hartford home buyer] [7]

Loan officers also had to rely on their subjective impressions in determining whether or not to approve a family's loan. A standard government text on mortgage credit risk analysis, for example, advised loan officers that:

> In judging a borrower's reasons for requesting a loan, the lender should consider the strength of his attachment to the property and his probable future attitudes toward it . . . A borrower's relationship to his family and friends is a significant element of risk although it is difficult to rate. Evaluators usually consider whether a borrower has an established reputation, a harmonious home life, associates with good reputations, and if he is active in civic affairs or whether he has been dishonest and untruthful in the past, has a troubled family life, and associates of doubtful reputation. [8]

Consequently, loan officers often based their loan recommendations on—as one officer puts it—a "feeling about the applicant." These impressions often led them to recommend against inner-city minority applications. These tendencies were magnified by the career ambitions of many loan officers:

> My future career is determined in part by the default rate on the applications I recommend for approval to our loan committee. Consequently, I try to avoid approving applications that I feel might be rejected by the loan committee. This would reflect adversely on me and might hinder my career advancement. [Reconstructed statement of Hartford loan officer] [9]

Many minority families relied on the incomes of both wife and husband in order to quality for a home loan. Some Hartford lending institutions, however, were reluctant to extend a loan on the basis of a working wife's income unless they were assured that the wife would not later stop working in order to have a child. Such assurance could be provided by a so-called "baby letter," that is, a physician's statement attesting to the wife or husband's sterility, the couple's use of approved birth control methods, or their willingness to have an abortion.

> My husband and I are Puerto Ricans. We are both in our late twenties and have been working for the last seven years. He makes about $10,000 a year and I make about $9,500. We are making monthly car payments of $200. When we applied to a savings and loan association for a 90 percent loan on a $16,000 house, we were told that the loan would be approved only if my salary was counted as part of the family income. But in order to count my income, the institution said, I had to give them a baby letter. But my husband and I are

[7]Based on interview materials in *ibid.*, p. 11.

[8]U.S. Department of Housing and Urban Development, *Mortgage Credit Risk Analysis and Servicing of Delinquent Mortgages,* by Anthony D. Grezzo. (Washington, DC: U.S. Government Printing Office, 1972), p. 14, quoted in *ibid.*, p. 12.

[9]Based on interview materials in *ibid.*, p. 13.

Catholics. We felt it was wrong for us to have to undergo sterilization or go against our religion in order to get a loan. [Based on interview of Hartford couple] [10]

1. In your view, is the distribution of housing in Hartford, Connecticut just or unjust by Rawls's principles? Does the distribution violate the criteria of equality? Of contribution? Of need and ability? Of free choice? Were the government's recommended criteria just? Was the reliance on "feelings" by loan officers just? Was the "baby letter" requirement just? Explain your answers fully.

2. To what extent were the loan officers morally responsible for any of the injustices described in the case? To what extent were the real estate agents morally responsible? Explain your answers fully.

3. In your opinion, what kind of compensation would be just for the various injuries inflicted on the various persons described in the case?

4. What specific kinds of policies would you recommend that the real estate agents and loan officers follow in the future?

Wage Differences at Robert Hall

Robert Hall Clothes, Inc., owns a chain of retail stores that specializes in clothing for the family.[11] One of the chain's stores is located in Wilmington, Delaware.

The Robert Hall store in Wilmington has a department for men's and boys' clothing and another department for women's and girls' clothing. The departments are physically separated and are staffed by different personnel: Only men are allowed to work in the men's department and only women in the women's department. The personnel of the store were sexually segregated because the store's managers felt that the frequent physical contact between clerks and customers would embarrass both and would inhibit sales unless they were of the same sex.

The clothing in the men's department is generally of a higher and more expensive quality than the clothing in the women's department. Competitive factors may account for this: There are fewer men's stores than women's stores. Because of these differences in merchandise, the store's profit margin on the men's clothing was higher than its margin on the women's clothing. As a result, the men's department consistently showed a larger dollar volume in gross sales and a greater gross profit, as is indicated in Table 2.3.

Because of the differences shown in Table 2.3, women personnel brought in lower sales and profits per hour. In fact, male salespersons brought in substantially more than the females did (Tables 2.4 and 2.5).

[10] *Ibid.*, p. 23.

[11] Information for this case is drawn entirely from *Hodgson v. Robert Hall Clothes, Inc.*, 473 F. 2nd 589, cert. denied, 42 U.S.L.W. 3198 (9 October 1973) and 326 F. supp. 1264 (D. Del. 1971).

TABLE 2.3

Year	Men's Department			Women's Department		
	Sales	Gross Profit	% Profit	Sales	Gross Profit	% Profit
1963	$210,639	$ 85,328	40.5	$177,742	$58,547	32.9
1964	178,867	73,608	41.2	142,788	44,612	31.2
1965	206,472	89,930	43.6	148,252	49,608	33.5
1966	217,765	97,447	44.7	166,479	55,463	33.3
1967	244,922	111,498	45.5	206,680	69,190	33.5
1968	263,663	123,681	46.9	230,156	79,846	34.7
1969	316,242	248,001	46.8	254,379	91,687	36.4

TABLE 2.4

Year	Male Sales Per Hour	Female Sales Per Hour	Excess M over F
1963	$38.31	$27.31	40%
1964	40.22	30.36	32%
1965	54.77	33.30	64%
1966	59.58	34.31	73%
1967	63.14	36.92	71%
1968	62.27	37.20	70%
1969	73.00	41.26	77%

TABLE 2.5

Year	Male Gross Profits Per Hour	Female Gross Profits Per Hour	Excess M Over F
1963	$15.52	$ 9.00	72%
1964	16.55	9.49	74%
1965	23.85	11.14	114%
1966	26.66	11.43	134%
1967	28.74	12.36	133%
1968	29.21	12.91	127%
1969	34.16	15.03	127%

As a result of these differences in the income produced by the two departments, the management of Robert Hall paid their male salespersons more than their female personnel. (Management learned in 1973 that it was entirely legal for them to do this if they wanted.) Although the wage differences between males and females were substantial, they were not as large as the percentage differences between male and female sales and profits. Over the years, Robert Hall set the wages given in Table 2.6.

TABLE 2.6

Year	Male Earnings Per Hour	Female Earnings Per Hour	Excess M Over F
1963	$2.18	$1.75	25%
1964	2.46	1.86	32%
1965	2.67	1.80	48%
1966	2.92	1.95	50%
1967	2.88	1.98	45%
1968	2.97	2.02	47%
1969	3.13	2.16	45%

The management of Robert Hall could argue that their female clerks were paid less because the commodities they sold could not bear the same selling costs that the commodities sold in the men's department could bear. On the other hand, the female clerks argued, the skills, sales efforts and responsibilities required of male and female clerks, were "substantially" the same.

1. In your judgment, do the managers of the Robert Hall store have any ethical obligations to change their salary policies? If you do not think they should change, then explain why their salary policy is ethically justified; if you think they should change, then explain why they have an obligation to change and describe the kinds of changes they should make. Would it make any difference to your analysis if instead of two departments in the same store, it involved two different Robert Hall stores, one for men and one for women? Would it make a difference if two stores (one for men and one for women) owned by different companies were involved? Explain each of your answers in terms of the relevant ethical principles upon which you are relying.

2. Suppose that there were very few males applying for clerk's jobs in Wilmington, while females were flooding the clerking job market. Would this competitive factor justify paying males more than females? Why? Suppose that 95 percent of the women in Wilmington who were applying for clerk's jobs were single women with children who were on welfare, while 95 percent of the men were single with no families to support. Would this "need" factor justify paying females more than males? Why? Suppose for the sake of argument that men were better at selling than women; would this justify different salaries?

3. If you think the managers of the Robert Hall store should pay their male and female clerks equal wages because they do "substantially the same work," then do you also think that ideally each worker's salary should be pegged to the work he or she individually performs (such as, by having each worker sell on commission)? Why? Would a commission system be preferable from a utilitarian point of view considering the substantial bookkeeping expenses it would involve? From the point of view of justice? What does the phrase "substantially the same" mean to you?

PART TWO
THE MARKET
AND BUSINESS

American business transactions are for the most part carried out within market structures. Businesses acquire supplies, raw materials, and machinery in industrial markets; they go to labor markets to find workers; they transfer their finished products to retailers in wholesale markets; and the final transfer to consumers is made in retail markets. The next two chapters examine the ethical aspects of these market activities. Chapter Three discusses the morality of the market system as a whole: How is it justified and what are its shortcomings from an ethical point of view? Chapter Four discusses the ethics of various market practices. There the emphasis is no longer on the ethics of the market system considered as a whole, but on the ethics of particular practices within the market system: Price-fixing, manipulation of supply, price discrimination, bribery, market concentration.

CHAPTER THREE
THE BUSINESS SYSTEMS

INTRODUCTION

The Humphrey-Javits bill was introduced into the Ninety-fourth Congress in the fall of 1975. If enacted, the bill would create an Economic Planning Board that would establish national objectives in the areas of employment, price stability, growth, and income distribution, and that would develop a "plan" for coordinating all economic activities so as to achieve these objectives. The objectives and plan would be submitted to Congress for approval and, if approved, would be carried out by the president through "appropriate actions."

The Humphrey-Javits bill was hailed by Arthur Schlesinger and many others as a long-overdue cure for the many problems created by a "free market system" and a much needed move toward national planning. Schlesinger wrote:

> The unregulated market place is patently unable to deal with urgent problems in our day. It has manifestly failed, for example, to control inflation while avoiding mass unemployment . . . Nor can the unregulated market place contain the administrative power over prices exerted by concentrated industries. Nor can the unregulated market place cope with problems such as oil that are essentially political rather than economic in character. Nor can the unregulated market place bring about the reconstruction and expansion of our mass transit system, which would be both helpful in reemployment and essential in the conservation of energy. Nor can the unregulated market place meet the nation's needs for health care, education, housing, welfare, solvent cities, and environmental protection . . . It is the obvious impotence of the unregulated market place in face of the hard problems of our time that has led . . . Senators Hubert Humphrey and Jacob Javits to introduce [this bill] . . . When

laissez-faire zealots object that planning will infallibly get us into a mess, one can only comment that it is hard to imagine a greater mess than the refusal to plan has got us into already: the worst inflation in a generation, the highest unemployment in thirty-five years, the worst decline in real output in nearly forty years, the worst deficit in the balance of payments ever, the worst peacetime budgetary deficits ever, the worst energy shortages ever, the worst crises in municipal finance ever. Is more of this the glorious future that . . . [the opponents of this bill] are holding out to the American people?[1]

Businessmen, however, were almost universally against the bill. T.A. Murphy, chairman of the board of General Motors, argued, for example, that the "free enterprise system" would be the "victim" of the Humphrey-Javits bill. In the interests of "individual freedom" and of "efficiency," the bill should be defeated, and the economic system should leave businesses free to respond to consumer demand:

No one questions the need for government intervention in situations where one person's unrestricted freedom can seriously inhibit the rights of others. . . [But] the areas in which one's individual free choice unduly impairs the rights of others are far more limited than government planners commonly assume. (If, for example, I were to prefer a car with lighter and consequently less expensive bumpers, it is hard to see how my free choice would materially impinge on the welfare of anyone else. Nonetheless, my choice has been restricted by government regulation.) . . . There really are only two ways to allocate resources in a society: by consumer choice or by government edict. The decisions are either decentralized and flowing from the bottom up or they are centralized and flowing from the top down. It really comes down to the question of who is to decide: the individual consumer speaking through the market place or the economic planner speaking through the legislative and administrative process. In the interests of individual freedom as well as efficiency, I come down on the side of the customer deciding for himself. The history of attempts to control the allocation of resources through the political process is dismal. . . . An adverse effect on our material prosperity, however, is not the only or even the most important reason for rejecting national planning. We are concerned ultimately with the threat to individual freedom . . . comprehensive national planning must ultimately involve the coercive powers of vast federal agencies.[2]

The controversy over the Humphrey-Javits bill was in fact only an episode in a great and continuing debate over the American business system: Should government regulate and coordinate the activities of business firms, or should business firms be left free to pursue their own interests within unregulated markets? Should the business system be a "planned" economy or should it be a "free market" economy? The arguments Schlesinger and Murphy advanced are classic examples of the two opposed viewpoints on this critical issue. One side argued that *unregulated*

---

[1] Arthur Schlesinger, Jr., "Laissez Faire, Planning, and Reality," *The Wall Street Journal,* 30 July 1975.

[2] T.A. Murphy, "In Opposition to the Humphrey-Javits Bill," *The Wall Street Journal,* 18 August 1975, p. 9.

market systems are defective because they encourage unemployment, price-fixing, shortages, irrational resource use, and an unjust distribution of wealth. The other side argued that *regulation* is defective because it violates the individual's right to freedom and it leads to an inefficient allocation of resources. This chapter examines these arguments for and against free markets and government regulation.

Ideologies

In analyzing these arguments on free markets and government, we will, in effect, be analyzing what sociologists refer to as "business ideologies." An ideology is a system of normative beliefs shared by members of some social group. The ideology expresses the group's answers to questions about human nature (such as, are humans motivated only by economic incentives?), about the basic purpose of our social institutions (as, what is the purpose of government? of business? of the market?), about how societies actually function (as, are markets free? does big business control government?), and about the values society should try to protect (as, freedom? productivity? equality?). A business ideology, then, is a normative system of beliefs on these matters, but specifically one which is held by business groups such as managers.

The importance of analyzing business ideologies is obvious: A business person's ideology often determines the business decisions he or she makes, and through these decisions the ideology influences the person's behavior. The business person's ideology, for example, will color the person's perceptions of the groups with whom he or she has to deal (employees, government officials, the poor, competitors, consumers); it will encourage the person to give in to certain pressures from these groups (perhaps even to support them) and to oppose others; it will make him or her look upon some actions as justified and legitimate and look on other actions (both those of the person and those of other groups) as unjustified and illegitimate. If a person's ideology is never examined, it will nonetheless have a deep and pervasive influence on the person's decision-making, an influence that may go largely unnoticed and that may derive from what is actually a false and ethically objectionable ideology.

Two main business ideologies have been identified by recent researchers: the "classical ideology" and the "managerial ideology."[3] The classical or "laissez-faire" ideology stresses the achievements of free enterprise and competition, and is generally hostile to government interference and to labor unions. It is the predominant (but not universal) ideology of older owners of small businesses. The "managerial ideology" stresses the social responsibilities of business. It tends to emphasize social cooperation, especially between business and government, and it tends to accept labor rights and to stress the importance of "humanizing" the workplace. It is the predominant (but not universal) ideology of the managers of large corporations. Both the classical and the managerial ideologies incorporate various ideas drawn

---

[3] Francis X. Sutton, Seymour E. Harris, Carl Kayser, and James Tobin, *The American Business Creed* (Cambridge: Harvard University Press, 1956).

from the works of Adam Smith, John Locke, John Keynes, and the other thinkers whose normative arguments we will examine and evaluate in this chapter. It would be a valuable exercise for the reader to identify the ideology he or she holds and to examine and criticize its elements as he or she reads through this chapter.

Market Systems Versus Command Systems

Markets are meant to solve a fundamental economic problem that all societies face: that of coordinating the economic activities of society's many members.[4] Who will produce what goods for what people? Modern societies solve this problem in two main ways: by a *command* system or by a *market* system.[5]

In a command system, a single authority (a person or a committee) makes the decisions about what is to be produced, who will produce it, and who will get it. The authority then communicates these decisions to the members of the system in the form of enforcible commands or directives, and transfers between the members then take place in accordance with the commands. This is, for example, the way in which the internal economic activities of vertically integrated business corporations may be coordinated. In the integrated corporation, a management group may decide what the various divisions will produce and what products each division will supply to the other divisions. These decisions are then communicated to the organization, perhaps in the form of a "budget." Command systems can also be extended to an entire economy. For five years during the Second World War, the United States and Great Britain both employed command systems to coordinate production among war-related industries.[6] And from 1928 to 1953 the Soviet Union imposed a series of plans upon its entire economy that told each firm exactly what labor and material resources it was to acquire, what goods it was to produce from these, and how it was to allocate its finished products among other firms and consumers.[7] The purpose of the USSR's "central planning system" was to industrialize the economy as rapidly as possible: Whereas in 1928 the Soviet Union was the fifth largest producer of industrial goods, it is now second after the United States.

The modern alternative to command is the "free market."[8] Within a free market system, individual firms—each privately owned and each desirous of making a profit—make their own decisions about what they will produce and how they will

---

[4] Robert L. Heilbroner, *The Economic Problem*, 3rd. ed. (Englewood Cliffs, NJ: Prentice-Hall Inc., 1972), pp. 14–28; see also Paul A. Samuelson, *Economics*, 9th ed. (New York: McGraw-Hill Book Company, 1973), pp. 17–18.

[5] See Charles E. Lindblom, *Politics and Markets* (New York: Basic Books Inc., Publishers, 1977), chapters 2, 3, 5, and 6 for a discussion contrasting these two abstractions, and for a subtle criticism of their adequacy.

[6] George Dalton, *Economic Systems and Society: Capitalism, Communism, and the Third World* (New York: Penguin Books, 1974), pp. 122–24; Otis L. Graham, Jr. *Toward a Planned Society: From Roosevelt to Nixon* (New York: Oxford University Press, 1976), pp. 69–86.

[7] *Ibid.*, pp. 121–31.

[8] Lindblom, *Politics and Markets*, p. 33.

produce it. Each firm then exchanges its goods with other firms and with consumers at the most advantageous prices it can get. Price levels serve to coordinate production by encouraging investment in highly profitable industries and discouraging it in unprofitable ones.

Free market systems, in theory, are based on two main components: a private property system and a voluntary exchange system.[9] If a society is to employ a market system, it must maintain a system of property laws (including contract law) that will assign to private individuals the right to make decisions about the firms and commodities they own, and that reassigns these rights when individuals exchange their goods with each other. And, of course, a free market system cannot exist unless individuals are legally free to come together in "markets" to voluntarily exchange their goods with each other.

In a pure free market system, there would be no constraints whatsoever on the property one could own and what one could do with the property one owns, nor on the voluntary exchanges one could make. Slavery would be entirely legal, as would prostitution. There are, however, no pure market systems. Some things may not be owned (such as slaves), some things may not be done with one's own property (such as pollution), some exchanges are illegal (as children's labor), and some exchanges are imposed (as in taxation). Such limitations on free markets are, of course, intrusions of a command system: Government concern for the public welfare leads it to issue directives concerning which goods may or may not be produced or exchanged. The result is government regulation of one form or another.

Since the eighteenth century, debates have raged over whether government commands should intervene in the market or whether market systems should remain free of all government intervention.[10] Should economies be partially or wholly coordinated by a government-authored command system? Or should private property rights and free exchanges be allowed to operate with few or no restrictions? The debate over the Humphrey-Javits bill was essentially a debate over these issues.

Two main arguments are usually advanced in favor of the free market system. The first argument, which originated with John Locke, is based on a theory of moral rights that employs many of the concepts we examined in the second section of Chapter Two. The second, which was first clearly proposed by Adam Smith, is based on the utilitarian benefits free markets provide to society, an argument that rests on the utilitarian principles we discussed in the first section of Chapter Two. A more recent utilitarian defense of free markets is based on the social Darwinism popularized a century after Smith. All of these arguments are examined in what follows.

---

[9] Milton Friedman, *Capitalism and Freedom* (Chicago: The University of Chicago Press, 1962), p. 14; see also, John Chamberlain, *The Roots of Capitalism* (New York: D. Van Nostrand Company, 1959), pp. 7–42.

[10] Joseph Schumpeter, *A History of Economic Analysis* (New York: Oxford University Press, 1954), pp. 370–72 and 397–99. For a treatment of 20th century controversies see Graham, *Toward a Planned Society.*

3.1 FREE MARKETS AND RIGHTS: JOHN LOCKE

One of the strongest cases for an unregulated market derives from the idea that human beings have certain "natural rights" that only a free market system can preserve. The two natural rights that free markets are supposed to protect are the right to freedom and the right to private property. Free markets are supposed to preserve the right to freedom insofar as they enable each individual to voluntarily exchange goods with others free from the coercive power of government. And they are supposed to preserve the right to private property insofar as each individual is free to decide what will be done with what he or she owns without interference from government.

John Locke (1632-1704), an English political philosopher, is generally credited with developing the idea that human beings have a "natural right" to liberty and a "natural right" to private property.[11] Locke argued that if there were no governments, human beings would find themselves in a "state of nature." In this state of nature each man would be the political equal of all others and would be perfectly free of any constraints other than the "law of nature," that is, the moral principles that God gave to humanity and that each man can discover by the use of his own God-given reason. As he puts it, in a state of nature all men would be in:

> A *state of perfect freedom* to order their actions and dispose of their possessions and persons as they think fit, within the bounds of the law of nature, without asking leave, or depending upon the will of any other man. A *state* also *of equality,* wherein all the power and jurisdiction is reciprocal, no one having more than another . . . without subordination or subjection [to another] . . . But . . . the *state of nature* has a law of nature to govern it, which obliges everyone: and reason, which is that law, teaches all mankind, who will but consult it, that being all equal and independent, no one ought to harm another in his life, health, liberty, or possessions.[12]

The law of nature, according to Locke, "teaches" each man that he has a right to liberty and that, consequently, "no one can be put out of this [natural] estate and subjected to the political power of another without his own consent."[13] The law of nature also informs us that each man has rights of ownership over his own body, his own labor, and the products of his labor and that these ownership rights are "natural," that is, they are not invented or created by government nor are they the result of a government grant:

> Every man has a *property* in his own *person:* This nobody has a right to but himself. The *labor* of his body, and the *work* of his hands, we may say, are

[11] The literature on Locke is extensive; see Richard I. Aaron, *John Locke,* 3rd ed. (London: Oxford University Press, 1971), pp. 352–76 for bibliographic materials.

[12] John Locke, *Two Treatises of Government,* ed. Peter Laslett, rev. ed. (New York: Cambridge University Press, 1963), pp. 309, 311.

[13] *Ibid.,* p. 374.

properly his. Whatsoever then he removes out of the state that nature has provided and left it in, he has mixed his *labor* with, and joined to it something that is his own, and thereby makes it his property. . . . [For] this *labor* being the unquestionable property of the laborer, no man but he can have a right to what that [labor] is once joined to, at least where there is enough, and as good, left in common for others.[14]

The state of nature, however, is a perilous state, in which individuals are in constant danger of being harmed by others, "for all being kings as much as he, every man his equal, and the greater part no strict observers of equity and justice, the enjoyment of the property he has in this state is very unsafe, very insecure."[15] Consequently, individuals inevitably organize themselves into a political body and create a government whose primary purpose is to provide the protection of their natural rights that is lacking in the state of nature. Since the citizen consents to government "only with an intention . . . to preserve himself, his liberty and property . . . the power of the society or legislature constituted by them can never be supposed to extend farther" than what is needed to preserve these rights.[16] Government, that is, cannot interfere with any citizen's natural right to liberty and natural right to property except insofar as such interference is needed to protect one person's liberty or property from being invaded by others.

Although Locke himself never explicitly used his theory of natural rights to argue for free markets, several twentieth-century authors have employed his theory for this purpose.[17] Friedrich A. Hayek, Murray Rothbard, Gottfried Dietze, Eric Mack, and many others claim that each person has the right to liberty and to property which Locke credited to every human being and that, consequently, government must leave individuals free to exchange their labor and their property as they voluntarily choose.[18] Only a free private enterprise exchange economy in which government stays out of the market and in which government protects the property rights of private individuals allows for such voluntary exchanges. The existence of the Lockean rights to liberty and property, then, implies that societies should incorporate private property institutions and free markets.

[14] *Ibid.,* p. 328-9.

[15] *Ibid.,* p. 395.

[16] *Ibid.,* p. 398.

[17] C.B. Macpherson, however, argues that Locke was attempting to establish the morality and rationality of a capitalist system; see his *The Political Theory of Possessive Individualism: Hobbes to Locke* (Oxford: The Clarendon Press, 1962).

[18] Friedrich A. Hayek, *The Road to Serfdom* (Chicago: University of Chicago Press, 1944); Murray N. Rothbard, *For a New Liberty* (New York: Collier Books, 1978); Gottfried Dietz, *In Defense of Property* (Baltimore: The Johns Hopkins Press, 1971); Eric Mack, "Liberty and Justice," in *Justice and Economic Distribution,* eds. John Arthur and William Shaw (Englewood Cliffs, NJ: Prentice-Hall, Inc., 1978), pp. 183-93; John Hospers, *Libertarianism* (Los Angeles: Nash, 1971); T.R. Machan, *Human Rights and Human Liberties* (Chicago: Nelson-Hall, 1975).

Criticisms of Lockean Rights

Criticisms of the Lockean defense of free markets have focused on three of its major weaknesses: (1) the assumption that individuals have the "natural rights" Locke claimed they have, (2) the conflict between these negative rights and positive rights, and (3) the conflict between these Lockean rights and the principles of justice.

First, then, the Lockean defense of free markets rests on the unproven assumption that people have rights to liberty and property that take precedence over all other rights. If humans do not have the overriding rights to liberty and property, then the fact that free markets would preserve the rights does not mean a great deal. Neither Locke nor his twentieth-century followers, however, has provided the arguments needed to establish that human beings have such "natural" rights. Locke himself merely asserted that "reason . . . teaches all mankind, who will but consult it" that these rights exist.[19] Instead of arguing for these rights, therefore, Locke had to fall back on the bare assertion that the existence of these rights is "self-evident": all rational human beings are supposed to be able to intuit that the alleged rights to liberty and to property exist. Unfortunately, many rational human beings have tried and failed to have this intuition.[20]

Secondly, even if human beings have a natural right to liberty and property, it does not follow that this right must override all other rights. The right to liberty and property is a "negative" right in the sense we defined in Chapter Two. But as we saw there, negative rights can conflict with people's positive rights. The negative right to liberty, for example, may conflict with someone else's positive right to food, medical care, housing, or clean air. Why must we believe that in such cases the negative right has greater priority than the positive right? Critics argue, in fact, that we have no reason to believe that the rights to liberty and property are overriding. Consequently we also have no reason to be persuaded by the argument that free markets must be preserved because they protect this alleged right.[21]

The third major criticism of the Lockean defense of free markets is based on the idea that free markets create unjust inequalities.[22] In a free market economy a person's productive power will be proportioned to the amount of labor or property

---

[19] Locke, *Two Treatises*, p. 311; for a fuller treatment of Locke's views on the law of nature, see John Locke, *Essays on the Law of Nature*, ed. W. von Leyden (Oxford: The Clarendon Press, 1954).

[20] William K. Frankena, *Ethics*, 2nd ed. (Englewood Cliffs, NJ: Prentice-Hall, Inc., 1973), pp. 102–5.

[21] For versions of this argument see Lindblom, *Politics and Markets*, pp. 45–51.

[22] Arthur M. Okun, *Equality and Efficiency* (Washington, DC: The Brookings Institution, 1975), pp. 1–4; see also Paul Baron and Paul Sweezy, *Monopoly Capitalism* (New York: Monthly Review, 1966), ch. 10; Frank Ackerman and Andrew Zimbalist, "Capitalism and Inequality in the United States," in *The Capitalist System*, 2nd ed., Richard C. Edwards, Michael Reich, Thomas E. Weisskopf, eds. (Englewood Cliffs, NJ: Prentice-Hall, Inc., 1978), pp. 297–307; Jonathan H. Turner and Charles E. Starnes, *Inequality: Privilege & Poverty in America* (Pacific Palisades, CA: Goodyear Publishing Company, Inc., 1976), pp. 44–45, 134–38.

he or she already possesses. Those individuals who have accumulated a great deal of wealth and who have access to education and training will be able to accumulate even more wealth by purchasing more productive assets. And individuals who own no property, who are unable to work or who are unskilled (such as the handicapped, the infirm, the poor, the aged) will be unable to buy any goods at all without help from the government. As a result, without government intervention the gap between the richest and the poorest will widen until large disparities of wealth emerge. Unless government intervenes to adjust the distribution of property that results from "free markets," large groups of citizens will remain at a subsistence level while others grow ever wealthier.

To prove their point, critics point to the large poverty class found in "capitalist" nations like the United States. In 1973, for example, the number of persons living at or below the poverty line defined by the Council of Economic Advisors was 23 million or about 11 per cent of the population. On the other hand, the top 1 per cent of the population held 25 per cent of all U.S. personal wealth. Critics also point to the skewed distribution of wealth and income among each quintile of the population that has emerged each time researchers have investigated the American population, as Table 3.1 summarizes.

TABLE 3.1   Distribution of Income and Wealth in American Society

Income Group	Percent Of Total Wealth (1962)	Percent Of Total Income (1970)	Percent Of Income From Property (1962)	Percent Of Stock Dividends (1962)	Average Family Income (1971)
Highest Fifth	57.2	41.6	65	82	24,559
Fourth Fifth	15.6	23.5	11	4	13,991
Middle Fifth	11.4	17.4	10	9	10,272
Second Fifth	8.6	12.0	8	4	7,025
Lowest Fifth	7.2	5.5	4	2	3,247

Source: Jonathan Turner and Charles E. Starnes, INEQUALITY: PRIVILEGE AND POWER IN AMERICA (Pacific Palisades, CA: Goodyear Publishing Co., Inc., 1976), passim.

The data uncovered by these investigations, critics contend, reveal the inadequacies of relying on markets to provide a just distribution of income and wealth. The deficiencies of the market, they claim, must be corrected by government action.

3.2 THE MARXIST CRITICISMS

Karl Marx (1818–1883) is undoubtedly the harshest and most influential critic of the inequalities that private property institutions and free markets are accused of creating.[23] Writing at the height of the Industrial Revolution, Marx was an eyewitness of the wrenching and exploitative effects that industrialization had upon the laboring peasant classes of England and Europe. In his writings he detailed the suffering and misery that capitalism was imposing upon its workers: exploitative working hours; pulmonary diseases and premature deaths caused by unsanitary factory conditions; seven-year-olds working twelve to fifteen hours a day; thirty seamstresses working thirty hours without a break in a room made for ten people.[24]

Marx claimed, however, that these instances of worker exploitation were merely symptoms of the underlying extremes of inequality that capitalism necessarily produces. According to Marx, capitalist systems offer only two sources of income: sale of one's own labor and ownership of the means of production (buildings, machinery, land, raw materials). Since workers cannot produce anything without access to the means of production, they are forced to sell their labor to the owner in return for a wage. The owner, however, does not pay workers the full value of their labor, only what they need to subsist. The difference ("surplus") between the value of their labor and the subsistence wages they receive is retained by the owner and is the source of the owner's profits. Thus the owner is able to exploit workers by appropriating from them the surplus they produce, using as leverage his ownership of the means of production. As a result, those who own the means of production gradually become wealthier, and workers become relatively poorer.

Alienation

The living conditions that capitalism imposed on the lower working classes contrasted sharply with Marx's view of how human beings should live. Marx held that human beings should be enabled to realize their human nature by freely developing their potential for self-expression and by satisfying their real human needs.[25] In order to develop their capacity for expressing themselves in what they make and in what they do, people should be able to engage in activities that develop

---

[23] The current revival of interest in Marx has resulted in a number of excellent studies: David McLellan, *Karl Marx: His Life and Thought* (New York: Harper and Row Publishers, Inc., 1973); John McMurtry, *The Structure of Marx's World-View* (Princeton: Princeton University Press, 1978); Anthony Cutler, Barry Hindess, Paul Hirst, and Arthur Hussain, *Marx's Capital and Capitalism Today* (London: Routledge and Kegan Paul, 1977); Ernest Mandel, *An Introduction to Marxist Economic Theory* (New York: Pathfinder Press, 1970); Shlomo Avineri, *The Social and Political Thought of Karl Marx* (New York: Cambridge University Press, 1968); Robert Heilbroner, *Marxism: For and Against* (New York: W.W. Norton & Co., Inc., 1980).

[24] For these and other illustrations cited by Marx see his *Capital*, Vol. I., trans. Samuel Moore and Edward Aveling (Chicago: Charles H. Kerr & Company, 1906), pp. 268–82.

[25] McMurtry, *Structure of Marx's World-View*, pp. 19–37.

their productive potential and should have control over what they produce. To satisfy their needs they must know what their real human needs are and be able to form satisfying social relationships. In Marx's view, capitalism "alienated" the lower working classes by neither allowing them to develop their productive potential nor satisfying their real human needs.

According to Marx, capitalist economies produce four forms of "alienation" in workers, that is, four forms of "separation" from what is essentially theirs.[26] First, capitalist societies give control of the worker's products to others. The objects that the worker produces by his labor are taken away by the capitalist employer and used for purposes that are antagonistic to the worker's own interests. As Marx wrote:

> The life that he has given to the object sets itself against him as an alien and hostile force . . . Labor certainly produces marvels for the rich, but it produces privation for the worker. It produces palaces, but hovels for the worker. It produces beauty, but deformity for the worker. It replaces human labor with machines, but it casts some of the workers back into a barbarous kind of work and turns others into machines. It produces intelligence, but also stupidity and cretinism for the workers.[27]

Secondly, capitalism alienates the worker from his own activity. Labor markets force him into earning his living by accepting work that he finds dissatisfying, unfulfilling, and that is controlled by someone else's choices. Marx asks:

> What constitutes the alienation of laboring? That working is *external* to the worker, that it is not part of his nature and that, consequently, he does not fulfill himself in his work, but denies himself, has a feeling of misery rather than well-being, does not develop freely his mental and physical energies but is physically exhausted and mentally debased . . . its alien character is clearly shown by the fact that as soon as there is no physical or other compulsion it is avoided like a plague . . . it is not his own work but work for someone else.[28]

Thirdly, capitalism alienates people from themselves by instilling in them false views of what their real human needs and desires are. Marx describes this alienation from one's own true self in a graphic portrait of the principles of the capitalist economist:

> [His] principal thesis is the renunciation of life and of human needs. The less you eat, drink, buy books, go the theater or to balls, or to the public house, and the less you think, love, theorize, sing, paint, play, etc., the more you will

---

[26] Karl Marx, "Estranged Labor," in *The Economic and Philosophic Manuscripts of 1844,* trans. by Martin Milligan, ed. Dirk Struik (New York: International Publishers, 1964) pp. 106–19.

[27] *Ibid.,* pp. 108–9.

[28] *Ibid.,* pp. 110–11.

be able to save and the greater will become your treasure which neither moth nor dust will corrupt—your capital. The less you are, the less you express your life, the more you have, the greater is your alienated life, and the greater is the saving of your alienated being.[29]

And, fourthly, capitalist societies alienate human beings from each other by separating them into antagonistic and unequal social classes.[30] According to Marx, capitalism divides humanity into a "proletariat" laboring class and a "bourgeois" class of owners and employers: "Society as a whole is more and more splitting up into two great hostile camps, into two great classes directly facing each other: bourgeoisie and proletariat."[31]

Capitalist ownership and unregulated markets, then, necessarily produce inequalities of wealth and power: a "bourgeois" class of owners who own the means of production and who accumulate ever greater amounts of capital; and a "proletariat" class of workers who must sell their labor to subsist and who are alienated from what they produce, from their own work, from their own human needs, and from their fellow human beings. Although private property and free markets may secure the "freedom" of the wealthy owner class, they do so by creating an alienated laboring class.

The Real Purpose of Government

The actual function that governments have historically served, according to Marx, is that of protecting the interests of the ruling economic class. It may be a popular belief that government exists to protect freedom and equality and that it rules by consent (as Locke suggested), but in fact, such beliefs are ideological myths which hide the reality of the control the wealthiest class exercises over the political process. To back up his claim Marx offered a breathtakingly comprehensive analysis of society which we can only sketch here.

Every society, according to Marx, can be analyzed in terms of its two main components: its *economic substructure,* and its *social superstructure.*[32] The economic substructure of a society consists of the materials and social controls that society uses to produce its economic goods. Marx refers to the materials (land, labor, natural resources, machinery, energy, technology) used in production as the "forces of production." Societies during the Middle Ages, for example, were based on agricultural economies in which the forces of production were primitive farming methods, manual labor, and hand tools. Modern societies are based on an industrial

---

[29] *Ibid.,* p. 150.

[30] *Ibid.,* p. 116.

[31] Karl Marx and Friedrich Engels, *Manifesto of the Communist Party* (New York: International Publishers, 1948), p. 9.

[32] The classic expression of this distinction is Karl Marx, *A Contribution to the Critique of Political Economy,* trans. N.I. Stone (New York: The International Library Publishing Co., 1904), pp. 11-13.

economy that uses assembly-line manufacturing techniques, electricity, and factory machinery.

The social controls used in producing goods (that is, the social controls by which society organizes and controls its workers) Marx called the "relations of production." There are, Marx suggests, two main types of relations of production: (1) control based on *ownership* of the materials used to produce goods and (2) control based on *authority* to command. In medieval society, for example, the feudal lords controlled their serfs through (1) the ownership the lords exercised over the manor farms on which the serfs worked and (2) the legal authority the lords exercised over their serfs who were legally bound to live on the manor lands and to obey the lord of the manor. In modern industrial society, capitalist owners control their factory laborers because (1) the capitalists own the machinery on which laborers must work if they are to survive and (2) the laborer must enter a wage contract by which he gives the owner (or his manager) the legal authority to command him. According to Marx, a society's relations of production define the main classes that exist in that society. In medieval society, for example, the relations of production created the ruling class of lords and the exploited serf class, while in industrial society the relations of production created the capitalist class of owners (whom Marx called the "bourgeoisie") and the exploited working class of wage-earners (whom Marx called the "proletariat").

Marx also claims that the *kinds* of relations of production a society adopts depends on the *kinds* of forces of production that society has. That is, the methods a society uses to produce goods determine the way that society organizes and controls its workers. For example, the fact that medieval society had to depend on manual farming methods to survive forced it to adopt a social system in which a small class of lords organized and directed the large class of serfs who provided the manual labor society needed on its farms. Similarly, the fact that modern society depends on mass production methods has forced us to adopt a social system in which a small class of owners accumulates the capital needed to build large factories, and in which a large class of workers provides the labor these mechanized factory assembly-lines require. In short, a society's forces of production determine its relations of production, and these relations of production then determine its social classes.

So much for the economic substructure: What is the "social superstructure" of a society and how is it determined? A society's superstructure consists of its government and its popular ideologies. And, Marx claims, the ruling class created by the economic substructure will inevitably control this superstructure. That is, the members of the ruling class will control the government and ensure that it uses force to protect their privileged position; and, at the same time, they will popularize those ideologies that justify their position of privilege. Medieval kings, for example, were selected from the class of lords and they enforced feudal law, even while the lords helped spread the ideology that their noble status was justified because of the aristocratic blood that ran in their veins. Similarly, in modern societies, Marx suggested, the class of owners is instrumental in the selection of government officials and the government then enforces the property system on which the wealth of this class depends; moreover, the ownership class, through its economists and its popularizing writers, inculcates the ideologies of free enterprise and of respect for private property, both of which support their privileged positions. Modern government, then, is not created by "consent" as Locke had claimed but by a kind of economic determination.

According to Marx, a society's government and its ideologies are designed to protect the interests of its ruling economic classes. These classes, in turn, are created by the society's underlying relations of production, and these relations of production in their turn are determined by the underlying forces of production. In fact, Marx claimed, all major historical changes are ultimately produced by changes in society's forces of production: Economic or "material" forces determine the course of history, as they determine the functions of government. As new material forces of production are found or invented (such as the steam engine or the assembly line), the old forces are pushed out of the way (as water-power and hand-crafts), and society reorganizes itself around the newly fashioned economic methods of production. New legal structures and social classes are created (as the corporation and the managerial class) and the old legal structures and social classes are demolished (as the manor and the aristocracy). Great "ideological" battles took place for men's minds during these periods of "transformation," but the new ideas always triumph: History always follows the lead of the newest forces of production. This Marxist view of history as determined by changes in the economic methods by which humanity produces the materials on which it must live is now generally referred to as "historical materialism."

Immiseration of Workers

Marx also claimed that so long as production in modern economies is not planned but is left to depend on private ownership and free markets, the result could only be a series of related disasters that would all tend to harm the working class. This claim rested on his analysis of two basic features of modern capitalism.[33] First, in modern capitalist systems productive assets (factories, land, technology, etc.) are privately controlled by self-interested owners, each of whom seeks to increase his assets by competing in free markets against other self-interested owners. Secondly, in modern capitalist systems, commodities are mass produced in factories by a highly organized group of laborers who, if they are to live, must work on the modern factory assembly lines controlled by the self-seeking owners. Such economic systems, in which self-interested owners *compete* in free markets while their organized workers *combine* to produce massive amounts of goods, Marx argues, is a "contradiction" that will inevitably generate three tendencies that collectively leave the worker in a "miserable" state. First, such societies will exhibit an increasing concentration of industrial power in a relatively few hands.[34] As self-interested private owners struggle to increase the assets they control, little businesses will gradu-

[33] See McMurtry, *Structure of Marx's World-View,* pp. 72–89.
[34] Marx, *Capital,* Vol. I, pp. 681–89.

ally be taken over by larger firms that will keep expanding in size. As time passes, Marx predicted, the small businessman will become less important and the owners of a few large firms will come to control the bulk of society's markets and assets. The rich, that is, will get richer.

Secondly, capitalist societies will experience repeated cycles of economic downturns or "crises."[35] Since the production of workers is highly organized, the firm of each owner can produce large amounts of surplus. And since owners are self-interested and competitive, each one will try to produce as much as he can in his firm without coordinating his production with that of other owners. As a result, firms will periodically produce an oversupply of goods. These will flood the market and a depression or a recession will result as the economy slows down to absorb the surplus.

Thirdly, Marx argues, the position of the worker in capitalist societies will gradually worsen.[36] This gradual decline will result from the self-interested desire of capitalist owners to increase their assets at the expense of their workers. This self-interest will lead owners to replace workers with machines, thereby creating a rising level of unemployment, which society will be unable to curb. Self-interest will also keep owners from increasing their workers' wages in proportion to the increase in productivity that mechanization makes possible. The combined effects of increased concentration, of cyclic crises, of rising unemployment, and of declining relative compensation are what Marx refers to as the "immiseration" of the worker. The solution to all these problems, according to Marx, is collective ownership of society's productive assets and the use of central planning to replace unregulated markets.[37]

Marx's theory has, of course, been subjected to intense and detailed criticism. The most telling criticism is that the immiseration of workers that he predicted has not in fact occurred. Workers in capitalist countries are much better off now than their fathers were a century ago. Nonetheless, contemporary Marxist writers point out that many of Marx's predictions have turned out correct. Factory workers today continue to find their work alienating insofar as it is dehumanizing, meaningless, and lacking in personal satisfaction.[38] Unemployment, inflation, recessions, and other "crises" continue to plague our economy.[39] Advertisements incessantly attempt to instill in us desires for things that we do not really need.[40] And inequality and discrimination persist.[41]

[35] Marx, *Capital*, Vol. II, pp. 86–87.

[36] Marx, *Capital*, Vol. I, pp. 689 ff.

[37] Marx and Engels, *Manifesto*, p. 30.

[38] See *Work in America: Report of the Special Task Force to the Secretary of Health, Education and Welfare* (Cambridge, MA: MIT Press, 1973).

[39] See Thomas E. Weisskopf, "Sources of Cyclical Downturns and Inflation" and Arthur MacEwan, "World Capitalism and the Crisis of the 1970s," in *The Capitalist System*, 2nd ed., Richard C. Edwards, Michael Reich, and Thomas E. Weisskopf, eds. (Englewood Cliffs, NJ: Prentice-Hall, Inc., 1978); pp. 441-61.

[40] Herbert Marcuse, *One Dimensional Man* (Boston: Beacon Press, 1964), pp. 225–46.

[41] Frank Ackerman and Andrew Zimbalist, "Capitalism and Inequality in the United States," in *The Capitalist System,* eds. Edwards, Reich, Weisskopf, pp. 297–307; and Michael Reich, "The Economics of Racism," in *ibid.,* pp. 381–88.

The Replies

Proponents of the free market have traditionally answered the criticisms that free markets generate injustices by arguing that the criticisms wrongly assume that justice means either equality or distribution according to need. This assumption is unprovable, they claim.[42] There are too many difficulties in the way of establishing acceptable principles of justice. Should distributive justice be determined in terms of effort, or ability, or need? These questions cannot be answered in any objective way, they claim, so any attempt to replace free markets with some distributive principle will, in the final analysis, be an imposition of someone's subjective preferences upon the other members of society. And this, of course, will violate the (negative) right every individual has to be free of the coercion of others.

Other defenders of free markets argue that justice can be given a clear meaning but one which supports free markets. Justice really means distribution according to contribution.[43] When markets are free and functioning competitively, some have argued, they will pay each worker the value of his or her contribution because each person's wage will be determined by what the person adds to the output of the economy. Consequently, they argue, justice *requires* free markets.

A third kind of reply that free market proponents have made to the criticism that markets generate unjust inequalities is that, although inequalities may be endemic to private ownership and free markets, the benefits that private ownership and free markets make possible are more important.[44] The free market enables resources to be allocated efficiently without coercion and this is a greater benefit than equality.

Thus the persuasiveness of the Lockean argument that unregulated markets should be supported because they protect the right to liberty and property depends, in the end, on the importance attributed to several ethical factors. How important are the rights to liberty and to property as compared to a just distribution of income and wealth? How important are the negative rights of liberty and property as compared to the positive rights of needy workers and of those who own no property? And how important is efficiency as compared to the claims of justice?

3.3 THE UTILITY OF FREE MARKETS: ADAM SMITH

The second major defense of unregulated markets rests on the utilitarian argument that unregulated markets and private property will produce greater benefits than any amount of regulation could. In a system with free markets and private property,

---

[42] Irving Kristol, "A Capitalist Conception of Justice," in *Ethics, Free Enterprise and Public Policy*, Richard T. DeGeorge and Joseph A. Pickler, eds. (New York: Oxford University Press, 1978), p. 65; see also H.B. Acton, *The Morals of Markets* (London: Longman Group Limited, 1971), pp. 68–72.

[43] John Bates Clark, *The Distribution of Wealth* (New York: The Macmillan Co., 1899), pp. 7-9, 106–7; for a critique of this argument, see Okun, *Equality and Efficiency*, pp. 40–47.

[44] Milton Friedman, *Capitalism and Freedom*, pp. 168–72.

buyers will seek to purchase what they want for themselves at the lowest prices they can find. It will therefore pay private businesses to produce and sell what consumers want and to do this at the lowest possible prices. To keep their prices down, private businesses will try to cut back on the costly resources they consume. Thus, the free market, coupled with private property, ensures that the economy is producing what consumers want, that prices are at the lowest levels possible, and that resources are efficiently used. The economic utility of society's members is thereby maximized.

Adam Smith (1723-1790), the "father of modern economics," is the originator of this utilitarian argument for the free market.[45] According to Smith, when private individuals are left free to seek their own interests in free markets, they will inevitably be led to further the public welfare by an "invisible hand":

> By directing [his] industry in such a manner as its produce may be of the greatest value, [the individual] intends only his own gain, and he is in this, as in many other cases, led by an invisible hand to promote an end that was no part of his intention . . . By pursuing his own interest he frequently promotes that of society more effectively than when he really intends to promote it.[46]

The "invisible hand," of course, is market competition. Every producer seeks to make his living by using his private resources to produce and sell those goods that he perceives people want to buy. In a competitive market a multiplicity of such private businesses must all compete with each other for the same buyers. To attract customers, therefore, each seller is forced not only to supply what consumers want, but to drop the price of his goods as close as possible to "what it really costs the person who brings it to market."[47] And to increase his profits each producer must pare his costs, thereby reducing the resources he consumes. The competition produced by a multiplicity of self-interested private sellers, then, serves to lower prices, conserve resources, and make producers respond to consumer desires. Motivated only by self-interest, private businesses are led to serve society. As Smith put the matter in a famous passage:

> It is not from the benevolence of the butcher, the baker, and the brewer that we expect our dinner, but from their regard for their own self-interest. We address ourselves not to their humanity, but to their self-love, and never talk to them of our own necessities, but of their advantages.[48]

[45] See S. Hollander, *The Economics of Adam Smith* (Toronto: University of Toronto Press, 1973).

[46] Adam Smith, *An Inquiry into the Nature and Causes of the Wealth of Nations* [1776] (New York: The Modern Library, n.d.), p. 423.

[47] *Ibid.*, p. 55.

[48] *Ibid.*, p. 14.

Smith also argued that a system of competitive markets will allocate resources efficiently among the various industries of a society.[49] For when the supply of a certain commodity is not enough to meet the demand, buyers will bid the price of the commodity upward until it rises above what Smith called the "natural price" (that is, the price that just covers the costs of producing the commodity including the going rate of profit obtainable in other markets). Producers of that commodity will then reap profits higher than those available to producers of other commodities. The higher profits will induce producers of those other products to switch their resources into the production of the more profitable commodity. As a result, the shortage of that commodity disappears and its price will sink back to its "natural" level. Conversely, when the supply of a commodity is greater than the quantity demanded, its price will fall, inducing its producers to switch their resources into the production of other more profitable commodities. The fluctuating prices of commodities in a system of competitive markets, then, forces producers to allocate their resources to those industries where they are most in demand and to withdraw resources from industries where there is an oversupply of commodities. The market, in short, allocates resources so as to most efficiently meet consumer demand, thereby promoting social utility.

The best policy of a government that hopes to advance the public welfare, therefore, is to do nothing: to let each individual pursue his or her self-interest in "natural liberty."[50] Any interventions into the market by government can only serve to interrupt the self-regulating effect of competition and reduce its many beneficial consequences.

In the early twentieth century, the economists Ludwig von Mises and Friedrich A. Hayek supplemented Smith's market theories by an ingenious argument.[51] They argued that not only does a system of free markets and private ownership serve to allocate resources efficiently, but it is in principle impossible for the government or any human being to allocate resources with the same efficiency. Human beings cannot allocate resources efficiently because they can never have enough information nor calculate fast enough to coordinate in an efficient way the hundreds of thousands of daily exchanges required by a complex industrial economy. In a free market, high prices indicate that additional resources are needed to meet consumer demand, and they motivate producers to allocate their resources to those consumers. The market thereby allocates resources efficiently from day to day through the pricing mechanism. If a human agency were to try to do the same thing, von Mises and Hayek argued, the agency would have to know from day to day what things each consumer desired, what materials each producer would need

---

[49] *Ibid.,* pp. 55-58.

[50] *Ibid.,* p. 651.

[51] Friedrich A. Hayek, "The Price System as a Mechanism for Using Knowledge," and Ludwig von Mises, "Economic Calculation in Socialism," both in *Comparative Economic Systems: Models and Cases,* ed. Morris Bornstein (Homewood, IL: Richard D. Irwin, Inc., 1965), pp. 39–50 and 79–85.

to produce the countless things consumers desired, and would then have to calculate how best to allocate resources among interrelated producers so as to enable them to meet consumer desires. The infinite quantity of detailed bits of information and the astronomical number of calculations that such an agency would need, von Mises and Hayek claimed, were beyond the capacity of any human beings. Thus, not only do free markets allocate goods efficiently, but it is quite impossible for government planners to duplicate their performance.

Criticisms of Adam Smith

Critics of Smith's classic utilitarian argument in defense of free markets and private property have attacked it on a variety of fronts. The most common criticism is that the argument rests on unrealistic assumptions.[52] Smith's arguments assume, first, that the impersonal forces of supply and demand will force prices down to their lowest levels because the sellers of products are so numerous and each enterprise is so small that no one seller can control the price of a product. This assumption was perhaps true enough in Smith's day, when the largest firms employed only a few dozen men and a multitude of small shops and petty merchants competed for the consumer's attention. But today many industries and resources are completely or partially monopolized, and the small firm is no longer the rule. In these monopolized industries where one or a few large enterprises are able to set their own prices, it is no longer true that prices necessarily move to their lowest levels. The monopoly power of the industrial giants enables them to keep prices at artificially high levels and to keep production at artificially low levels.

Secondly, critics claim, Smith's arguments assume that all the resources used to produce a product will be paid for by the manufacturer and that the manufacturer will try to reduce these costs in order to maximize his profits. As a result, there will be a tendency toward a more efficient utilitization of society's resources. But this assumption is also proved false when the manufacturer of a product consumes resources for which he or she does not have to pay and on which he or she therefore does not try to economize. For example, when manufacturers use up clean air by polluting it, or when they impose health costs by dumping harmful chemicals into rivers, lakes, and seas, they are using up resources of society for which they do not pay. Consequently, there is no reason for them to attempt to minimize these costs and social waste is the result. Such waste is a particular instance of a more general problem that Smith's analysis ignored. Smith failed to take into account the external effects that business activities often have on their surrounding environment. Pollution is one example of such effects, but there are others, such as the effects on society of introducing advanced technology, the psychological effects increased mechanization has had on laborers, the harmful effects that handling dangerous products has on the health of workers, and the economic shocks that result when natural resources are depleted for short-term gains. Smith ignored these external effects of the firm and assumed that the firm is a self-contained agent whose activities affect only itself and its buyers.

[52] These criticisms can be found in any standard economic textbook.

Thirdly, critics claim, Smith's analysis wrongly assumes that every human being is motivated only by a "natural" and self-interested desire for profit. Smith assumes that in all his dealings a person "intends only his own gain." Human nature follows the rule of "economic rationality": Give away as little as you can in return for as much as you can get. Since a human being "intends only his own gain" anyway, the best economic arrangement will be one that recognizes this "natural" motivation and allows it free play in competitive markets that force self-interest to serve the public interest. But this theory of human nature, critics have claimed, is clearly false. First, human beings regularly show a concern for the good of others and constrain their self-interest for the sake of the rights of others. Even when buying and selling in markets the constraints of honesty and fairness affect our conduct. Second, the critics claim, it is not necessarily "rational" to follow the rule "give away as little as you can for as much as you can get." In numerous situations everyone is better off when everyone shows concern for others, and it is then rational to show such concern. Third, socialist critics have argued, if human beings often behave like "rational economic men," this is not because such behavior is natural, but because the widespread adoption of competitive market relations forces humans to relate to each other as "rational economic men." The market system of a society *makes* humans selfish and this widespread selfishness then makes us think the profit motive is "natural." But in actual fact human beings are born with a natural tendency to show concern for other members of their species (in their families, for example).

As for the argument of von Mises and Hayek that human planners cannot allocate resources efficiently, the examples of French, Dutch, Swedish, and Soviet planning have demonstrated that planning is not quite as impossible as von Mises and Hayek imagined.[53] Moreover, the argument of von Mises and Hayek was answered on theoretical grounds by the socialist economist Oskar Lange who demonstrated that a "central planning board" could efficiently allocate goods in an economy without having to know everything about consumers and producers and without engaging in impossibly elaborate calculations.[54] All that is necessary is for the central planners to receive reports on the sizes of the inventories of producers, and price their commodities accordingly. Surplus inventories would indicate that lowering of prices was necessary, while inventory shortages would indicate that prices should be raised. By setting the prices of all commodities in this way, the central planning board could create an efficient flow of resources throughout the economy.

The Keynesian Criticism

The most influential criticism of Adam Smith's classical assumptions came from John Maynard Keynes (1883-1946), an English economist.[55] Smith assumed

[53] See Vaclav Holesovsky, *Economic Systems, Analysis, and Comparison* (New York: McGraw-Hill Book Company, 1977), chs. 9 and 10.

[54] Oskar Lange, "On the Economic Theory of Socialism," in Bornstein, ed., *Comparative Economic Systems*, pp. 86-94.

[55] The standard work on Keynes is Alvin H. Hansen, *A Guide to Keynes* (New York: McGraw-Hill Book Company, 1953).

that without any help from the government, the automatic play of market forces would ensure full employment of all economic resources including labor. If some resources are not being used, then their costs will drop and entrepreneurs will be induced to expand their output by using these cheapened resources. The purchase of these resources will in turn create the incomes that will enable people to buy the products made from them. Thus, all available resources will be used and demand will always expand to absorb the supply of commodities made from them (a relationship which is now called "Say's Law"). Since Keynes, however, economists have argued that without government intervention, the demand for goods may not be high enough to absorb the supply. The result will be rising unemployment and a slide into economic depression.

Keynes argued that the total demand for goods and services is the sum of the demand of three sectors of the economy: households, businesses, and government.[56] The aggregate demand of these three sectors may be less than the aggregate amounts of goods and services supplied by the economy at the full employment level. This mismatch between aggregate demand and aggregate supply will occur when households prefer to save some of their income in liquid securities instead of spending it on goods and services. When, as a consequence, aggregate demand is less than aggregate supply, the result will be a contraction of supply. Businesses will realize they are not selling all their goods, so they will cut back on production and thereby cut back on employment. As production falls, the incomes of households will also fall, but the amounts households are willing to save will fall even faster. Eventually, the economy will reach a stable point of equilibrium at which demand once again equals supply but at which there is widespread unemployment of labor and other resources.

Government, according to Keynes, can influence the propensity to save that lowers aggregate demand and creates unemployment. Government can prevent excess savings through its influence on interest rates and it can influence interest rates by regulating the money supply: The higher the supply of money the lower the rates at which it will be lent. Secondly, government can directly affect the amount of money households have available to them by raising or lowering taxes. And thirdly, government spending can close any gap between aggregate demand and aggregate supply by taking up the slack in demand from households and businesses (and, incidentally, creating inflation).

Thus, contrary to Smith's claims, government intervention in the economy is a necessary instrument for maximizing society's utility. Free markets alone are not necessarily the most efficient means for coordinating the use of society's resources. Government spending and fiscal policies can serve to create the demand needed to stave off unemployment. These views were the kernels of "Keynesian economics."

Keynes's views, however, have themselves fallen on hard times. During the

---

[56] John Maynard Keynes, *The General Theory of Employment, Interest, and Money* (London: Macmillan & Co., Ltd., 1936). For an accessible summary of Keynes's views, see his article, "The General Theory of Employment," *Quarterly Journal of Economics,* 51 (September 1937): 209–23.

1970s, the United States (and other Western economies) have been confronted with the simultaneous occurrence of inflation and unemployment. The standard Keynesian analysis would lead us to believe that these two should not occur together: Increased government spending, although inflationary, should serve to enlarge demand and thereby alleviate unemployment. However, during the 1970s the standard Keynesian remedy for unemployment (increased government spending) has had the expected effect of creating increasing inflation but has not cured unemployment.

Various diagnoses have been offered for the apparent failure of Keynesian economics to deal with the twin problems of inflation and unemployment.[57] John Hicks, a former Keynesian enthusiast, for example, has suggested that in many industries today prices and wages are no longer determined by market forces as Keynes assumed: They are, instead, set by producers and unions.[58] The ultimate effect of this price-setting is continuing inflation in the face of continued unemployment. Whether this analysis of Hicks' is correct or not, it is at least clear that we can no longer rely so heavily on Keynes to support economic planning.

The Utility of Survival of the Fittest: Social Darwinism

Nineteenth-century social Darwinists added a new twist to utilitarian justifications of free markets by arguing that free markets have beneficial consequences over and above those which Adam Smith identified. They argued that economic competition produces human progress. The doctrines of social Darwinism were named after Charles Darwin (1809–1882) who argued that the various species of living things were evolving as the result of the action of an environment that favored the survival of some things while destroying others: "This preservation of favorable individual differences and variations, and the destruction of those which are injurious, I have called natural selection or the survival of the fittest."[59] The environmental factors that resulted in the "survival of the fittest" were the competitive pressures of the animal world. As a result of this competitive "struggle for existence," Darwin held, species gradually change, since only the "fittest" survive to pass their favorable characteristics on to their progeny.

Even before Darwin published his theories, the philosopher Herbert Spencer (1820-1903) and other thinkers had already begun to suggest that the evolutionary processes that Darwin described were also operative in human societies. Spencer claimed in *Social Statics* that just as competition in the animal world ensures that only the fittest survive, so free competition in the economic world ensures that only the most capable individuals survive and rise to the top. The implication is that:

---

[57] For a nontechnical review of some of these approaches see Walter Guzzardi, Jr., "The New Down-to-Earth Economics," *Fortune*, 31 December 1978, pp. 72–79.

[58] John Hicks, *The Crisis in Keynesian Economics* (Oxford: Basil Blackwell, 1974), p. 25.

[59] Charles Darwin, *The Origin of Species by Means of Natural Selection* (New York: D. Appleton and Company, 1883), p. 63.

Inconvenience, suffering, and death are the penalties attached by Nature to ignorance as well as to incompetence and are also the means of remedying these. Partly by weeding out those of lowest development, and partly by subjecting those who remain to the never-ceasing discipline of experience, Nature secures the growth of a race who shall both understand the conditions of existence, and be able to act up to them.[60]

Those individuals whose aggressive business dealings enable them to succeed in the competitive world of business are the "fittest" and therefore the best. And just as survival of the fittest ensures the continuing progress and improvement of an animal species, so the free competition that enriches some individuals and reduces others to poverty will result in the gradual improvement of the human race. Government must not be allowed to interfere with this stern competition since this would only impede progress. In particular, government must not lend economic aid to those who fall behind in the competition for survival. For if these economic misfits survive, they will pass on their inferior qualities and the human race will decline.

It was easy enough for later thinkers to revise Spencer's views so as to rid them of their apparent callousness. Modern versions of Spencerism hold that competition is good not because it destroys the weak individual, but because it weeds out the weak *firm*. Economic competition ensures that the "best" business firms survive and, as a result, the economic system gradually improves. The lesson of modern social Darwinism is the same: Government must stay out of the market because competition is beneficial.

The shortcomings of Spencer's views were obvious even to his contemporaries.[61] Critics were quick to point out that the skills and traits that help individuals and firms advance and "survive" in the business world are not necessarily those which will help humanity survive on the planet. Advancement in the business world might be achieved through a ruthless disregard for other human beings. The survival of humanity, on the other hand, may well depend on the development of cooperative attitudes and on the mutual willingness of people to help each other.

The basic problem underlying the views of the social Darwinist, however, is the fundamental normative assumption that "survival of the fittest" means "survival of the best." That is, whatever results from the workings of nature is necessarily good. The fallacy, which modern authors call the "naturalistic fallacy," implies, of course, that whatever happens naturally is always for the best. It is a basic failure of logic, however, to infer that what *is* necessarily *ought* to be or that what nature creates is necessarily for the best.

---

[60] Herbert Spencer, *Social Statics, Abridged and Revised* (New York: D. Appleton and Company, 1893), pp. 204–5; for an account of Spencerism in America see Richard Hofstadter, *Social Darwinism in American Thought* (Boston: Beacon Press, 1955).

[61] See the essays collected in R.J. Wilson, *Darwinism and the American Intellectual* (Homewood, IL: The Dorsey Press, 1967); see also Donald Fleming, "Social Darwinism," in *Paths of American Thoughts,* eds. Arthur Schlesinger, Jr. and Morton White (Boston: Houghton Mifflin Company, 1970), pp. 123–46.

3.4 CONCLUSION:
THE MIXED ECONOMY

The debate for and against free markets and private property still rages on. While critics continue to point to their defects, proponents continue to praise their virtues. It is inevitable, perhaps, that the controversy has led many economists to advocate retention of market systems and private ownership but modification of their workings through government regulation so as to rid them of their most obvious defects. The resulting amalgam of government regulation, partially free markets, and limited property rights is appropriately referred to as the "mixed economy."[62]

Basically, a mixed economy retains a market and private property system but relies heavily on government policies to remedy their deficiencies. Government transfers (of private income) are used to get rid of the worst aspects of inequality by drawing money from the wealthy in the form of income taxes and distributing it to the disadvantaged in the form of welfare. Minimum wage laws, safety laws, union laws, and other forms of labor legislation are used to protect workers from exploitation. Monopolies are regulated, nationalized, or outlawed. Government monetary and fiscal policies attempt to ensure full employment. And government regulatory agencies police firms to ensure they do not engage in socially harmful behavior.

How effective are these sorts of policies? A comparison of the American economy with other economies which have gone much further down the road toward implementing the policies of a "mixed economy" may be helpful. Sweden, West Germany, Denmark, Japan, and Switzerland are all highly regulated nations with mixed economies. The MIT economist, Lester G. Thurow, has made the following comparisons of the U.S. with these nations.[63] In terms of per capita GNP, the United States has been surpassed by Sweden, Switzerland, Denmark, Norway, and West Germany. Yet the United States has greater inequality in the distribution of income than these countries. The top 10 percent of all U.S. households, for example, receive fifteen times as much income as the bottom 10 percent, whereas in Sweden the ratio is seven times, in West Germany it is eleven times, and in Japan it is ten times. Although inequality in the U.S. is comparatively high, productivity has been on a comparative decline. During the 1970s, Sweden's productivity growth rate was 11 percent more than ours, and Japan's was 25 percent more than ours.

Although these brief comparisons do not tell the whole story, they indicate at least that a mixed economy may have some advantages. Moreover, if we compare the performance of the U.S. economy at different periods in its history, the same conclusion is indicated. *Prior* to the intrusion of government regulation and social

---

[62] See, for example, Paul Samuelson, *Economics,* 9th ed. (New York: McGraw-Hill Book Company, 1973), p. 845.

[63] Lester C. Thurow, *The Zero-Sum Society* (New York: Basic Books, Inc., 1980), pp. 3–9.

welfare programs, the *highest* per capita growth rate in GNP that the U.S. experienced during a single decade was the 22 percent rate of growth that occurred between 1900 and 1910. Yet during the decade of the 1940s, when the U.S. economy was run as a command wartime economy, the growth rate in per capita GNP climbed to 36 percent (the highest ever), and during the decade of the 1960s, when the U.S. introduced its major social-welfare programs, the per capita GNP growth rate was at a 30 percent level. Again, these comparisons do not tell the whole story but they suggest that the "mixed economy" is not altogether a bad thing.

The desirability of the policies of the mixed economy also continues to be subject to the same debates that swirl around the concepts of free markets, private property, and government intervention. Since 1980 these debates have begun to focus on the "productivity crisis" that the United States is currently undergoing.[64] During the two decades between 1948 and 1968, worker output per hour increased at a rate of 3.2 percent each year; between 1968 and 1973 the annual rate of increase slipped to 1.9 percent; and from 1973 to 1979 it averaged only .7 percent.[65] Some have blamed this crisis on government intervention in the marketplace. According to these critics, environmental legislation and worker health laws have forced companies to invest heavily in "nonproductive" pollution-control equipment and in worker safety and have thereby drained off capital that should have been used to upgrade or replace inefficient plants and machines. Others have argued that much of the problem can be traced to the short-term strategies of business managers who have been reluctant to invest in risky research and development and in retooling programs that might hurt their short-run profit picture, and who have been more interested in expanding their companies through mergers and acquisitions that create no new value.[66]

Followers of Smith and of Locke continue to insist that the level of government intervention tolerated by the mixed economy does more harm than good. Their opponents continue to counter that in our mixed economy government favors business interests and that allowing businesses to set their own policies exacerbates our economic problems. On balance, however, it appears that the mixed economy comes closest to combining the utilitarian benefits of free markets with the respect for human rights and for justice that are the characteristic strengths of planned economies.

QUESTIONS FOR REVIEW AND DISCUSSION

1. Define: ideology, laissez-faire ideology, managerial ideology, command economy, free market system, private property system, state of nature, natural rights, Locke's natural right to property, surplus value, alienation, bourgeois,

---

[64] See "The Productivity Crisis," *Newsweek*, 8 September 1980, pp. 50–69, especially the debate between Friedman and Samuelson capsulized on pp. 68–69.

[65] "The Reindustrialization of America," *Business Week*, 30 June 1980, p. 65.

[66] For analyses of these viewpoints see James Fallows, "American Industry, What Ails It, How to Save It," *The Atlantic*, September 1980, pp. 35–50.

proletariat, economic substructure, social superstructure, forces of production, relations of production, historical materialism, immiseration of
workers, invisible hand, natural price, natural liberty, aggregate demand,
aggregate supply, Keynesian economics, survival of the fittest, social Darwinism, naturalistic fallacy, mixed economy, productivity crisis.

2. Contrast the views of Locke, Marx, Smith, Keynes, and Spencer on the nature
and proper functions of government and on its relationship to business.
Which views seem to you to provide the most adequate analysis of contemporary relations between business and government? Explain your answer fully.

3. "Locke's views on property, Smith's views on free markets, and Marx's views
on capitalism obviously do not hold true when applied to the organizational
structure and the operations of modern corporations." Comment on this
statement. What reforms, if any, would Locke, Smith, and Marx advocate
with respect to current corporate organization and performance?

4. "Equality, justice, and a respect for rights are characteristics of the American
economic system." Would you agree or disagree with this statement? Why?

5. "Free markets allocate economic goods in the most socially beneficial way
and ensure progress." To what extent is this statement true? To what extent
do you think it is false?

CASES FOR DISCUSSION

The Chrysler Loan

On July 31, 1979, John Riccardo, chairman of Chrysler Corporation, announced that Chrysler had lost $207.1 million in the second quarter of 1979. A
quarter earlier, Chrysler had lost $53.8 million. Analysts were predicting that by
the end of the year Chrysler's losses would total $400 to $600 million, more than
double the previous year's deficit of $204.6 million. To continue operating,
Riccardo said, the company was forced to request $1 billion in cash from the federal
government.[1]

Chrysler Corporation is the nation's third largest automobile manufacturer. In
1978 Chrysler posted sales of $16,340,700,000 and employed 250,000 workers. It
ranked as the tenth largest industrial firm in the United States and as the fourteenth
largest in the world. If the company failed the effects would be widespread.

Many analysts blamed Chrysler's problems on its own management's mistakes.[2] During the 1960s, Lynn Townsend, Chrysler's chairman at that time, had
attempted to expand into overseas markets by investing in several European companies which were failing: Sima in France and Rootes Motors in Britain. These investments further hurt the company by draining off cash funds that the company later
needed for its operations at home. Then throughout the 1970s, Chrysler repeatedly
miscalculated consumer demands. In 1971, when both GM and Ford introduced

---

[1] "Chrysler Drives for a Tax Break," *Time*, 16 July 1979, p. 55.

[2] *Fortune*, 27 August 1979, pp. 30–31.

their subcompact models, Chrysler chose to redesign its big cars because large cars promised higher profit margins. The large Chrysler cars came on the market in 1973, the year the Arab oil embargo shifted the market away from large gas guzzlers towards the kinds of small cars that Ford and GM were marketing. In 1976 Chrysler finally began to market a line of compact cars (the Volare and Aspen) but by that time consumers had begun to turn away from small cars toward large cars again. In 1978 Chrysler repeated its mistake: In that year it announced production of large New Yorker and St. Regis model cars. By the time these large cars were rolling off the assembly lines, gasoline shortages had forced consumers to return to small cars. By mid-year 1979, Chrysler's share of the market had dropped to about 11.8 percent (the lowest level since 1962), and its inventories of unsold large cars had climbed to eighty thousand units, for which it was paying $2 million per week in storage costs. Moreover, Chrysler could sell only a limited number of its highly popular four-cylinder subcompacts (Omnis and Horizons) because contracts negotiated with suppliers two years before had locked it into a low production schedule. This series of miscalculations was clearly reflected in Chrysler's earnings during the 1970s which are indicated in Table 3.2. The losses posted by Chrysler had led Moody's investors service and Standard & Poor's to rate Chrysler as a riskier and more speculative investment. This in turn forced Chrysler to pay higher interest rates when borrowing money and made borrowing more difficult.

TABLE 3.2

	Chrysler Net Income*
1973:	$ 255 million
1974:	(52)*
1975:	(260)
1976:	423
1977:	163
1978:	(205)
1979:	(1,097)

*Parentheses indicate losses.

Source: CHRYSLER CORPORATION REPORT TO SHARE-HOLDERS FOR THE YEAR ENDED DECEMBER 31, 1979 (Highland Park, Michigan: Chrysler Corporation, 1979), p. 25.

Chrysler management claimed that its financial problems were the result of government regulations. Arthur Laffer, a well-known economist, prepared a Chrysler-sponsored study that argued that the nation's safety, fuel-efficiency, and pollution requirements had hit Chrysler harder than GM and Ford. Although all three automakers had to spend roughly similar amounts in developing the technology to meet government standards, the two larger companies were able to spread these fixed costs over more units than Chrysler. According to the study, the fixed costs of complying with government regulations came to $620 per car for Chrysler as compared to $340 per car for GM. John Riccardo, Chrysler's chairman, argued his company's case as follows:

> Because of the hundreds of millions committed for new plants and new products, and the hundreds of millions invested to meet regulations, Chrysler faces a temporary shortage of funds. Chrysler has no choice but to seek temporary assistance from the heavy burden regulation places on us. We want equity restored to the competitive system because the system is anticompetitive as it stands now. We're not asking for a handout, a bail-out, or welfare. Chrysler is asking for temporary assistance for 1979 and 1980 equal to the cost of meeting government regulations for those two years. [Statement of John Riccardo] [3]

Chrysler's management also pointed out that if Chrysler did not get the financial aid it was seeking, there was a high probability that the company would go bankrupt and that this would have a disastrous effect on American society. A Congressional Budget Office study concluded that if Chrysler were to shut down, 360,000 workers would immediately be out of jobs, and "ripple effects" would put an equal number out of work in other parts of the economy.[4] Some areas would be hit harder than others; unemployment in Detroit could hit 16 percent while some small company towns in the midwest might have to shut down completely.[5] A Department of Transportation study argued that unemployment compensation combined with losses in personal and corporate taxes could cost city, state, and federal governments up to $16 billion by 1982.[6] John Riccardo stressed these reasons in his pleas for government aid:

> [To] turn our back on 140 thousand of our own employees would be irresponsibility. To close the doors in fifty-two American communities in which Chrysler is a major factor of the local economy would be irresponsibility. To deny employment to the 150 thousand people who work for the dealers who sell Chrysler products would be irresponsibility. To curtail the income of the hundreds of thousands who supply goods and services to Chrysler would be irresponsibility.... A Congressional Budget Office study shows that people with jobs at Chrysler, or jobs that depend on Chrysler, contribute 11 billion dollars each year in tax revenues to our country. Without those jobs they would be collecting 2 billion dollars instead in unemployment benefits. [Statement of John Riccardo] [7]

In addition, $1.1 billion of the pension benefits Chrysler had set up for its workers were unfunded. Of this, $250 million was uninsured and these benefits would be lost to its workers if the company were to shut down.

[3] Advertisement, *San Jose Mercury,* 21 August 1979, p. 8B.

[4] "Chrysler's Crisis Bailout," *Time,* 20 August 1979, p. 41.

[5] Peter Bohr, "Chrysler's Pie-in-the-Sky Plan for Survival," *Fortune,* 22 October 1979, p. 50.

[6] *Ibid.*

[7] Advertisement, *San Jose Mercury,* 21 August 1979, p. 8B.

In September of 1979, John Riccardo resigned as chairman of Chrysler, stating that he was too "closely associated with the past management of a troubled company" and that his continued presence at Chrysler might "hinder the final passage of our request" for federal aid.[8] He was succeeded by Lee A. Iacocca who had been serving as president of the company. Lee Iacocca's views on Chrysler's problems and the necessity of government aid essentially coincided with the views of his predecessor:

> It wasn't management mistakes (although there were some), or superior competition in the market place (there was some of that too), that brought the company to its knees. It was the relentless hammer of more and more government regulation. . . . [The] central and critical issue at stake in Chrysler's survival is people and jobs. If government wants to do something about unemployment, if it wants to keep the nation's urban areas and cities alive, if it wants to prevent increased welfare dependency and government spending, if it wants to offset an $8 billion imbalance of automotive trade with Japan, let it approve Chrysler's legitimate and amply precedented request for temporary assistance. [Statement of Lee Iacocca][9]

The claims Chrysler's management was making on its behalf were not accepted by all observers. *Fortune Magazine,* for example, pointed out that "[Chrysler] does not explain why so many foreign automakers, smaller than Chrysler, have managed to meet the same [government] standards and earn a profit."[10] *Fortune Magazine* also argued that Chrysler's real costs of meeting government regulations (which *Fortune* estimated at $137 million in 1979) did not begin to account for the staggering $1 billion loss that Chrysler projected for 1979.

The basic objections against giving government aid to Chrysler, however, were ideological: Government aid to businesses, critics held, is contrary to the basic principles of a free enterprise system in which firms are financed and managed, not by the government, but by private individuals. Thomas Murphy, chairman of GM, for example, opposed government aid because "federal assistance shouldn't violate the fundamental principles of the American system of free enterprise. . . . I don't think that's in accordance with what really made this country great."[11] Senator William Proxmire argued that "you just can't have a free-enterprise system without failures. Are we going to guarantee businessmen against their own incompetence by eliminating any incentive for avoiding the specter of bankruptcy?"[12] Jack Meany, president of Norris Industries, urged that "the right solution is to let the natural forces take place. In general, I don't think the government should underwrite private enterprise's failures. If we do that, we aren't going to have private enterprise."[13]

[8] *Facts on File,* 21 September 1979, p. 699.

[9] Lee Iacocca, "Manager's Journal," *Wall Street Journal,* 3 December 1979.

[10] *Fortune,* 27 August 1979, p. 30.

[11] *Wall Street Journal,* 6 August 1979.

[12] *Newsweek,* 13 August 1979, p. 55.

[13] *Wall Street Journal,* 17 September 1979, p. 1.

Business Week editorialized that unless companies were allowed to fail, the "discipline" of market forces "simply vanishes"; that the loan would give Chrysler an "unfair advantage" over other car makers; that it would set a "dangerous precedent"; and that it would put the government on the "expensive" course of "futilely" pumping money into failing enterprises for the sake of saving jobs.[14]

Milton Friedman, an economist and an enthusiastic advocate of free enterprise also attacked the idea of government aid to Chrysler. If Chrysler should be forced to shut down, he argued:

> No doubt many related enterprises will suffer losses, along with Chrysler stockholders, but that is a risk they knowingly run in order to be able to enjoy profits. . . . If Chrysler is not bailed out, the facilities worth using would be taken over by people who would be risking their money in the belief that they can make more effective and productive use of them than Chrysler's present management. In the process, they would create new jobs. If Chrysler is bailed out, it will cost the taxpayer money. The cost may be hidden in the form of loan guarantees, but it is real, nonetheless. It includes the possible loss if Chrysler cannot repay the loan. It includes also the slightly higher interest rate that the government will have to pay because it has increased its liabilities. Bailing out Chrysler will not change the total amount of capital available to the economy. But it will divert capital to Chrysler from other more productive uses. . . . The private-enterprise economic system is often described as a profit system. That is a misnomer. It is a profit and *loss* system. If anything, the loss part is even more vital than the profit part. That is where it differs most from a government-controlled system. . . . This system produced the remarkable growth in the productivity of the U.S. economy during the past two centuries. Our increasing rejection of this system in favor of a government-controlled economy is a major reason why productivity in recent years has gone into reverse. [Statement of Milton Friedman][15]

Other economists attacked this approach as doctrinaire. Paul Samuelson, for example, wrote:

> [The] hard-boiled consistent advocate of laissez-faire will say: "let the losers bite the dust. Ours is a profit-and-loss system" . . . this kind of answer can be given without really thinking about the matter or knowing any facts . . . [It] means accepting a particular set of understood dogmas and sticking with them through thick or thin . . . Then there are the pragmatists . . . They say we must think about the workers who will be thrown out of jobs and about the merchants who will thereby lose business in a cumulative chain of lost spending and responding . . . My own counsel is to go very slow in weighing the Chrysler petition. Let's ascertain all the key facts first. [Statement of Paul Samuelson][16]

[14]*Business Week*, 20 August 1979, p. 132.

[15]Milton Friedman, "Chrysler: Are Jobs the Issue?," *Newsweek*, 10 September 1979, p. 66.

[16]Paul Samuelson, "Judging Corporate Handouts," *Newsweek*, 13 August 1979, p. 58.

And John Kenneth Galbraith in his inimitable style dryly predicted that in the end ideological objections would give way to corporate interests:

> This request, one cannot doubt, will be granted. Even the finest and firmest free enterprise principles, we know, can be bent as needed to pecuniary and corporate need. And government handouts, however debilitating to the poor, have never been thought inimical to the wealthy. However, . . . if, as taxpayers, we are to invest one billion dollars in Chrysler, could we not be accorded an appropriate equity or ownership position? This is thought a reasonable claim by people who are putting up capital. And . . . in this high noon of the great conservative revolt, could we not ask that all corporations and all corporate executives that approve, or acquiesce by their silence in this expansive new public activity, refrain most scrupulously from any more of this criticism of big government? [Statement of John Kenneth Galbraith][17]

Chrysler's request for government aid was supported by its smooth and experienced lobbying efforts.[18] The Chrysler lobby team was headed by former congressman Joe Waggoner, Jr., of Louisiana, a once-influential member of the House Ways and Means Committee. The team also included Thomas Hale Boggs, Jr., son of the late majority leader of the House, and Ernest Christian, Jr., former legislative counsel in the Nixon administration. Waggoner, Boggs, and Christian had all maintained significant contacts in Washington. By September over a dozen of the sixty lawyers in Boggs's law firm were busy contacting Democratic congressmen, while Christian and others rallied Republican support. Moreover, while still chairman, Riccardo had spent long hours with Michigan's two Democratic senators, Donald Riegle and Carl Levin, and with Detroit mayor Coleman Young, all of whom subsequently also pleaded Chrysler's cause both locally and in Washington. In early June, Chrysler had stepped up its efforts by mobilizing a lobby consisting of dealers, suppliers, and the United Auto Workers. All were urged to contact their congressmen in order to "let them know how important Chrysler's business is." Before his retirement, Riccardo himself was spending four and five days a week in Washington visiting federal officials and congressmen, including Treasury Secretary G. William Miller, Rep. Henry Reuss, chairman of the House Banking Committee, Rep. Al Ullman, chairman of the House Ways and Means Committee, and Senator Russell B. Long, chairman of the Finance Committee. These, together with the governors of several midwestern states in which major Chrysler plants were located, all helped to further Chrysler's request for aid.

Chrysler's efforts eventually paid off.[19] On August 9, 1979, President Carter rejected Chrysler's initial request for $1 billion in cash as an advance against future tax credits but offered to extend Chrysler a federal loan guarantee. On September 15, Chrysler submitted a request for $1.2 billion in federal loan guarantees and was

---

[17]"Letters to the Editor," *Wall Street Journal,* 13 August 1979.

[18]See *Fortune,* 27 August 1979, pp. 30–31; and *Wall Street Journal,* 6 September 1979, p. 1.

[19]See *Facts on File,* 7 September 1979, p. 662; 21 September 1979, p. 699; 9 November 1979, p. 845.

again turned down by the Carter administration with the admonition that any such request "would have to be well below $1 billion." But on November 1, the Carter administration reversed its position and offered Chrysler a $1.5 billion federal loan guarantee on condition that Chrysler raise an additional $1.5 billion of new unguaranteed capital and on condition that the government (the treasury secretary) be given the authority to change Chrysler's management if it failed to exercise "reasonable business judgment." Five days earlier, Chrysler had agreed to give Douglas A. Fraser, president of the United Auto Workers, a position on its board of directors in return for several wage concessions that the union had granted Chrysler. Thus, both government and labor would now exercise a measure of authority over Chrysler's management. Chrysler accepted the government offer and the plan was subsequently ratified by Congress in the closing days of December, 1979.

The aid bill approved by Congress in December set up a government "loan guarantee board" with substantial control over Chrysler's affairs. The board can require the company to close plants, to drop existing automobile models, to cut spending for future products, to desist from acquiring new subsidiaries or from selling off old ones; it can veto contracts over $10 million, it can inspect all Chrysler records, and it can place government personnel on Chrysler's own board of directors to gain a majority. Almost all of Chrysler's assets were put up as collateral to the government. In case of bankruptcy, the federal government could end up owning these assets.

1. As far as possible, identify the real factors (social, organizational, political, economic, managerial, etc.) that, in your view, explain the difficulties Chrysler was experiencing in July, 1979. Identify the factors (social, organizational, political, etc.) that, in your view, were the factors that determined the outcome of the case in December, 1979. Which of the various analyses of government and economics (that is, Locke's, Smith's, Keynes's, etc.) studied in the chapter provide the best understanding of the events which led up to the difficulties of July 1979, and of the events which led up to the outcome of December 1979? Explain your answers.

2. Define, compare, and contrast the ideological views implied by the various statements of each of the parties quoted in the case study. How did those ideological views influence the kinds of policy recommendations each party made? What elements of the philosophies examined in the chapter appear in these ideological views?

3. In your opinion, was the final resolution of the case desirable from an ethical point of view (that is, the decision to grant the loan, the decision to give the treasury secretary a say in management, the decision to give the union a seat on the board of directors)? Justify your answer fully in terms of the utilities, the rights, and the just or unjust factors involved.

Humboldt County Private Enterprise

Mack Barber (not his real name) owns forty acres of rolling wooded land in Humboldt County in California. He uses it to grow marijuana.

Mr. Barber is in his early forties, married, and holds degrees from two universities. For several years he held a responsible position working for an engineering firm. Several years ago he gave it all up, "dropped out," and he and his wife, Rebecca, moved to the woods of Humboldt, and began to grow a few plants of marijuana for their own use. Eventually they decided to go into the business of producing marijuana, as many of their neighbors were doing in response to the depressed economic conditions of the area (unemployment was running as high as 22 percent).

> Like me, most of the growers raised marijuana just for their own use until four years ago when the word got out and it became so profitable people grew it to sell. . . . What's happened is a lot of good people have become independent of the welfare system because of this crop. . . . A good year for me would be 20 pounds. A nice, comfortable year is 10 to 15 pounds. [Statement of Mack Barber] [1]

This particular kind of marijuana—"sinsemilla"—grown by Mr. Barber sells for from $1,000 to $2,500 a pound, depending on market supply and demand factors. The plants are germinated indoors in January or February, transplanted outdoors in April, and harvested in September and October. The climate in Humboldt County is particularly favorable for growing sinsemilla. Sinsemilla is a seedless form of marijuana that produces unusual amounts of tetrahydrocannabinol, the mild hallucinogenic that gives marijuana its desirable qualities and that makes Humboldt County marijuana one of the most sought-after varieties of marijuana. Humboldt sinsemilla is known to be exported and marketed in Alaska, New York, Southern California, and Florida; the four corners of the United States. [2]

Experts estimate that the marijuana industry brought $300 million into Humboldt County in 1979 alone. By comparison, the second largest agricultural commodity (hay) brought in only $7 million. Only timber and possibly fishing are larger industries. As the marijuana business grew from a few small plots in 1975 and became a multimillion dollar industry in 1979, the employment picture in Humboldt County also improved dramatically. The jobless rate declined from a high of 22 percent in 1975 to about 9 percent in 1979. Many observers believe this decline was brought about by the absorption of several thousand persons into the marijuana industry. [3]

The marijuana industry of Humboldt County has created a considerable stir. Because of its economic importance and because large numbers of people believe they should not be prohibited from smoking marijuana if they freely choose to, Humboldt County supervisors have often discouraged police efforts to restrict marijuana growers by voting against funding for such efforts. As one supervisor put it:

[1] Ed Pope "Grower Brings New Life to Land," *San Jose Mercury,* 21 October 1979, page 3A.

[2] Ed Pope, "Harvest Tension Grows for Pot Farmers," *San Jose Mercury,* 26 November 1979, page 12A.

[3] Ed Pope, "Marijuana is Cash Crop for North Coast Farmers," *San Jose Mercury,* 21 October 1979, page 3A.

Some responsible businessmen think it (the marijuana industry) is very important to the economy. You know: people who sell cars, hardware, fencing and garden tools. [Statement of county supervisor][4]

Or, as a woman resident put it: "There are people who feel very strongly that this is their [rightful] living." Many other residents also felt that if the farmers wanted to use their private property to grow and sell marijuana, that was their right.

The sheriff's department, however, has tried to step up its efforts to enforce California law, which prohibits growing or selling marijuana. During harvest season, the sheriff's department flies over the county in airplanes and helicopters to locate marijuana farms. Once a farm is located, the department "raids" it, confiscates and destroys the marijuana farmer's crop, and destroys his watering system. Many residents see this as an unfortunate use of the county's very limited public resources.

Robert Cogan, an attorney for some of the farmers, sees these raids as ways of suppressing the political impact of the predominantly left-wing farmers:

> The raids take away their source of income; they will reduce the growers' participation in the upcoming election, prevent them from spending money in the campaign and financially backing their candidates and make them withdraw even further from this society . . . [The average marijuana farmer only] makes between $5,000 and $10,000 off any crop he harvests and he is lucky if he brings in more than one of every five crops he plants. [Statement of Robert Cogan][5]

In addition, of course, the raids restrict supply, thereby making it more difficult and expensive for users of marijuana to obtain what they want.

1. How would Marx analyze the events recounted in the case? How would Smith analyze these events? How would Locke analyze these events? To what extent, if at all, are these analyses correct?

2. In your view, should government prohibit economic activities like growing and selling marijuana? Why or why not? What sorts of business activities should government prohibit; what sort should it not prohibit? Justify your position fully. Identify the ideology implied by your position.

3. From an ethical point of view, what recommendations would you make to the various parties involved in the case? Explain your recommendations in terms of the utilities, the rights, and the just or unjust distributions involved.

[4] *Ibid.*
[5] *Ibid.*

CHAPTER FOUR
ETHICS
IN THE
MARKETPLACE

INTRODUCTION

PHILADELPHIA—A federal judge imposed stiff fines on three paper-products manufacturers—Continental Group, Inc., Chase Bag Co., and American Bag and Paper Corp.—for conspiring between 1950 and 1976 to fix the prices of certain paper bags. In addition, the judge imposed jail sentences and fines on officers of the three companies.[1]

ATLANTA—A federal district court here fined Wells Fargo Armed Service Corporation $375,000 and Brink's Inc., $625,000 after the two pleaded no contest in a criminal antitrust case. The armored car companies were charged last June by a federal grand jury with conspiring to allocate customers and to rig bids in violation of federal antitrust laws.[2]

WASHINGTON—A federal district court ordered seven major international shipping lines and thirteen executives charged with price-fixing to pay $6.1 million in penalties, the largest criminal fine ever imposed under the Sherman Antitrust Act. . . . The previous record was $3.5 million imposed on seven corporations in the ready-mix concrete trade in Ohio.[3]

HARTFORD—A federal judge imposed stiff jail penalties and hundreds of thousands of dollars in fines on eight companies and on eleven of their offi-

[1] *The Wall Street Journal,* 21 September 1978, p. 2.
[2] *The Wall Street Journal,* 24 April 1978, p. 8.
[3] *The New York Times,* 9 June 1979, pp. 31, 39.

cers charged with price-fixing in the electrical wiring devices industry. . . . Commenting on the good character records of the defendants, all first-time offenders, the judge said those who have reaped public esteem during years of secret price-fixing must pay for their crime. Several defense lawyers said their firms made only scant profits in recent years.[4]

WASHINGTON—Four steel companies have agreed to pay the federal government $440,000 to settle Federal Trade Commission charges that they violated a 1951 FTC order barring illegal collusion. . . . U.S. Steel Corp., Bethlehem Steel Corp., Laclede Steel Co., and Armco Steel Corp. . . . according to the suit, . . . fixed the price of certain steel products in Texas and other states, allocated the market for reinforcing-bar materials in Texas and other states and rigged bidding for the sale of the materials.[5]

WASHINGTON—Binney & Smith, Inc. and Milton Bradley Co. have agreed to pay $1.2 million to school systems across the country to settle government charges that they fixed the prices of art supplies at artificially high levels. . . . The FTC charged that from at least 1972 through at least 1978, Binney & Smith [maker of Crayola crayons] and some of its competitors agreed on the prices of chalk, crayons, watercolors, and tempera paints.[6]

If free markets are justified, it is because they allocate resources and distribute commodities in ways that maximize the economic utility of society's members, while allowing both buyers and sellers a high degree of freedom of choice. These beneficial aspects of a market system depend on the competitive nature of the system. Should firms join together and use their combined power to fix prices, to drive out competitors with unfair practices, or to earn monopolistic profits at the expense of consumers, the market ceases to be competitive and the result is both a decline in social utility as well as a restriction of people's freedom to make economic choices.

In view of the key role of competition in the American economy, both factually and from a normative point of view, it is surprising that anticompetitive practices are so common. One survey of major corporate executives indicated that 60 percent of those sampled believed that many businesses engage in price-fixing.[7] During 1975 and 1976 over 60 major firms were prosecuted by federal agencies for anticompetitive practices.[8] This chapter examines such practices, the underlying rationale for prohibiting them and the values that market competition is meant to achieve.

[4] *The Wall Street Journal,* 6 February 1978, p. 8.

[5] *The Wall Street Journal,* 2 July 1980, p. 38.

[6] *The Wall Street Journal,* 27 May 1980, p. 48.

[7] Ralph Nader and Mark J. Green, "Crime in the Suites," *New Republic,* 29 April 1972, pp. 17–21.

[8] Marshall Clinard, *Illegal Corporate Behavior* (Washington, DC: U.S. Government Printing Office, 1979), p. 184.

Before studying the ethics of anticompetitive practices it is essential that one have a precise understanding of the complex meaning of market competition. We all have, of course, an intuitive understanding of competition: It is a rivalry between two or more parties trying to obtain something that only one of them can possess. Competition exists in political elections, in football games, on the battlefield, and in courses in which grades are distributed "on the curve." Market competition, however, involves more than mere rivalry between two or more firms. To get a clearer idea of the nature of market competition we will examine three abstract models describing three degrees of competition in a market: perfect competition, pure monopoly, and oligopoly. We will examine, also, the ethical issues raised by each type of competition.

4.1 PERFECT COMPETITION

A perfectly competitive free market would be one in which no single firm has a significant effect on the prices that other firms charge.[9] Perfectly competitive free markets are characterized by six features:

1. There are many buyers and many sellers trading in the market.
2. All buyers and sellers can freely enter or leave the market.
3. No buyer or seller has a substantial share of the market.
4. The commodities of each seller are so similar that buyers do not care from which seller they buy.
5. All costs of production have been paid by each seller.
6. Prices are free to rise or fall without interference from government.

The last feature is what makes a market qualify as a "free" market.

In any market, the amount customers buy, or "demand," increases when prices go down, while the amount producers sell or "supply" decreases when prices go down. In the perfectly competitive free market, these fluctuations tend to move toward what is called the "equilibrium price," that is, the price at which the amount of goods buyers want to buy is equal to the amount of goods sellers want to sell. The market at this point is "cleared" since every seller finds a buyer and vice versa.

Why would prices gravitate toward equilibrium levels in a perfectly competitive market? The well-known supply and demand curves explain this phenomenon.

A *demand* curve is a line on a graph indicating the amounts of a commodity that consumers (or buyers) are willing to buy at each price. As we mentioned above, the higher the price of a commodity, the less of it buyers will want to purchase, so the curve slopes down to the right. In the imaginary curve in Figure 4.1, for example, buyers will buy 100 tons of potatoes if they sell at $5 per basket, but they will buy 600 tons if they sell at $1 per basket.

---

[9]The elementary account that follows can be found in any standard economics textbook, for instance, Werner Sichel and Peter Eckstein, *Basic Economic Concepts: Microeconomics,* 2nd ed. (Chicago: Rand McNally College Publishing Company, 1977), pp. 171–77.

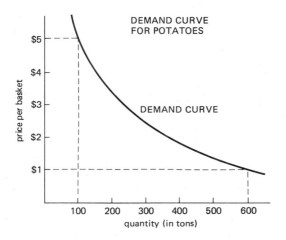

FIGURE 4-1

How is the demand curve determined? The curve is found by determining for each quantity of a commodity, the maximum price consumers are willing to pay for the satisfactions they expect to derive from that quantity of goods. At any point above their demand curve, buyers would see themselves as losers, that is, as paying out more in costs than what they are gaining in satisfactions. At any point below the demand curve they would see themselves as winners, that is, as paying out less in costs than what they get in return. ("Costs" here refer to whatever other satisfactions the consumer had to forgo in order to pay for the commodity.) Consequently, if prices rise *above* the demand curve, buyers will tend to leave the market and invest their resources in other markets. But if prices fall below the demand curve, new buyers will tend to flock into the market since they perceive an opportunity to increase their satisfactions at a low cost.

A *supply* curve, on the other hand, is a line on a graph indicating the amounts of a commodity that producers or sellers are willing to supply at various prices. The higher the price, the more sellers want to supply, so the curve slopes down to the left. In the imaginary curve traced in Figure 4.2, for example, farmers will grow only 100 tons of potatoes if they think potatoes will sell at only $1 per basket; but they will grow 500 tons if they expect potatoes to sell at $4 per basket.

The supply curve is calculated by determining for each amount of a commodity how much producers must charge in order to cover all the costs of producing those amounts of the commodity. The curve represents, therefore, the minimum price producers can accept without sustaining losses. ("Costs" here include not only the costs of labor, materials, distribution, etc., but also the "normal" profits sellers must make to motivate them to invest their resources in producing the commodity and to forgo the opportunity of making profits by investing in other markets.) For this reason, at any point below the supply curve, producers would see themselves as losers: They would be receiving less than the costs they must pay to produce the commodity. Therefore, if prices fall to points below the supply curve, producers

145

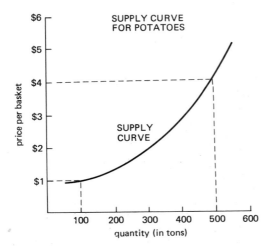

FIGURE 4-2

will tend to leave the market and go to invest their resources in other markets. On the other hand, if prices rise above the supply curve, then new producers will come crowding into the market, attracted by the opportunity to invest their resources in a market where they can derive higher profits than in other markets.

Sellers and buyers, of course, trade in the same markets, so their respective supply and demand curves can be superimposed on the same graph. Typically, when this is done, the supply and demand curves will meet and cross at some point. The point at which they meet is the point at which the price buyers are willing to pay for a certain amount of goods exactly matches the price sellers are willing to accept for that same amount (that is, the "equilibrium price"). This point of intersection, as indicated in Figure 4.3, where the point, "E," at which the supply and demand curves meet, is the so-called "point of equilibrium" or "equilibrium price." It is at $2 on the graph.

We mentioned that in a perfectly competitive free market, prices, the amounts supplied, and the amounts demanded will all tend to move toward the point of equilibrium. Why does this happen? Notice in Figure 4.3 that if the *prices* of potatoes rise above the point of equilibrium, say to $4 per basket, producers will supply more goods (500 tons) than at the equilibrium price level (300 tons). But at that high price, consumers will purchase fewer goods (only 100 tons) than at the equilibrium price. The result will be a surplus of unsold goods (500 − 100 = 400 tons of unsold potatoes). To get rid of their unsold surplus, sellers will be forced to lower their prices and decrease production. Eventually, equilibrium prices and amounts will be reached.

On the other hand, if the price drops below the point of equilibrium in Figure 4.3, say to $1 per basket, then producers will start supplying less than consumers want at that price. The result will be an excessive demand and shortages will appear. Subsequently, prices will rise and the rising prices will attract more producers into

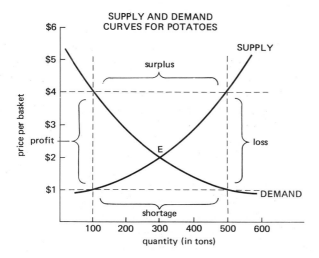

SUPPLY AND DEMAND
CURVES FOR POTATOES

FIGURE 4-3

the market, thereby raising supplies. Eventually, again, equilibrium will reassert itself.

Notice also what happens in Figure 4.3 if the *amount* being supplied, say 100 tons, for some reason is less than the equilibrium amount. The cost of supplying such an amount ($1 per basket) is much less than what consumers are willing to pay ($4 per basket) for that same amount. Consequently, prices will rise to the level the consumer is willing to pay ($4), and the difference ($3) will be abnormally high profits. The high profits, however, will attract outside producers into the market, thereby increasing the amounts supplied and bringing about a corresponding decrease in the price consumers are willing to pay for the increased amounts of goods that become available. Gradually, the amounts supplied will increase to the equilibrium point, and prices will drop to equilibrium prices.

The opposite happens if the amount being supplied, say 500 tons, is for some reason more than the equilibrium amount. Under these circumstances sellers will have to lower their prices to the very low levels that consumers are willing to pay for such large amounts. At such low price levels, the producers will leave the market to invest their resources in other more profitable markets, thereby lowering the supply, raising the price, and once again reestablishing equilibrium levels.

At this point the reader may be trying to think of an industry that fits the descriptions of perfect competition we have just given. The reader will have some difficulty finding one. Only a few agricultural markets, such as grain markets and potato markets, come close to embodying the six features that characterize a perfectly competitive market.[10] The fact is that the model of perfect competition is a theoretical construct of the economist which does not exist. But although the model

[10] Daniel B. Suits, "Agriculture," in *The Structure of American Industry*, 5th ed., ed. Walter Adams (New York: Macmillan Inc., 1977), pp. 1–39.

does not describe real markets, it does provide us with a clear understanding of the advantages of competition and an understanding of why it is desirable to keep markets as competitive as possible.

Perfect Competition, Utility, and Freedom

Free markets (that is, markets without government intervention), as we saw in the preceding chapter, have been defended on two main grounds: on the grounds that they provide important utilitarian benefits, and on the grounds that they protect the right to freedom. These two defenses apply only to the perfectly competitive free market. Noncompetitive "free" markets neither advance society's welfare, nor do they enhance the freedom of their participants. In this section we will examine exactly how the competitive market maximizes the utility of its participants and how it enhances their freedom. In the next section we will see why noncompetitive "free" markets fail to achieve these two moral objectives.

Perfectly competitive markets are capable of two major achievements: (1) They allocate resources efficiently and they distribute goods efficiently and (2) they allow a high degree of freedom. Efficiency is achieved in a system of perfectly competitive markets in three main ways.[11]

First, a perfectly competitive market system motivates firms to invest resources in those industries where consumer demand is high and to move resources away from industries where consumer demand is low. Resources will be attracted into markets where high consumer demand creates shortages that raise prices above equilibrium, and they will flee markets where low consumer demand leads to surpluses that lower prices below equilibrium. The perfectly competitive market system allocates resources efficiently in accordance with consumer demands and needs: The consumer is "sovereign" over the market.

Secondly, perfectly competitive markets encourage firms both to minimize the amount of resources consumed in producing a commodity and to use the most efficient technology available. Firms are motivated to use resources sparingly because they will want to lower their costs and thereby increase their profit margin. Moreover, in order not to lose buyers to other firms, each firm will reduce its profits to the lowest levels consistent with the survival of the firm. The perfectly competitive market encourages an efficient use of the seller's resources as well.

Thirdly, perfectly competitive markets distribute commodities among buyers in such a way that all buyers receive the most satisfying bundle of commodities they can purchase, given the commodities available to them and the money they can spend on these commodities. For when faced by a system of perfectly competitive markets, each buyer will buy up those proportions of each commodity that correspond with the buyer's desire for the commodity when weighed against the buyer's desires for other commodities. And when buyers have completed their buy-

---

[11]See Robert Dorfman, *Prices and Markets,* 2nd ed. (Englewood Cliffs, NJ: Prentice-Hall, Inc., 1972), pp. 170–226.

ing they will each know that they cannot improve on their purchases by trading their goods with other consumers, since all consumers can buy the same goods at the same prices. Thus, perfectly competitive markets enable consumers to attain a level of satisfaction upon which they cannot improve given the constraints of their budgets and the range of available goods. An efficient distribution of commodities is thereby achieved.

Not only do perfectly competitive markets encourage an allocation, use, and distribution of goods that will maximize consumer utility, but they also secure certain freedoms for individuals and firms. First, in a perfectly competitive market, sellers are free (by definition) to enter or leave the market. That is, individuals who want to engage in a certain business are not prevented from doing so, provided they have the expertise and the financial resources required.[12] Secondly, in perfectly competitive markets, consumers are free to purchase as much or as little of each available commodity as they choose. Goods are not rationed out in fixed quantities to everyone (by the government), nor are consumers forced (by government allocation) to accept products they do not want.[13] Thirdly, no single seller so dominates the perfectly competitive market that he or she is able to force buyers to accept the seller's terms or go without.[14] In a perfectly competitive market, industrial power is decentralized among many firms so that prices and quantities are not dependent on the whim of one or a few businesses.

4.2 MONOPOLY COMPETITION

What happens when a free market (that is, one without government intervention) ceases to be perfectly competitive? We will begin to answer this question in this section by examining the opposite extreme of a perfectly competitive market: The "free" (unregulated) monopoly market. We will then examine some less extreme varieties of noncompetition.

We noted earlier that a perfectly competitive market is characterized by six conditions. In a monopoly, three of these conditions are not present.[15] First, instead of many sellers, there is only one. Secondly, other sellers are not able to freely enter the market. Instead, there are barriers to entry such as patent laws, which give only one seller the right to produce a commodity, or high capitalization costs, which make it too expensive for a new seller to start a business in that industry. Thirdly, in a monopoly, a single seller has a substantial (100 percent) share of the market.

[12] Russell G. Warren, *Antitrust in Theory and Practice* (Columbus, OH: Grid, Inc., 1975), pp. 58–59.

[13] Milton Friedman, *Capitalism and Freedom* (Chicago: The University of Chicago Press, 1962), p. 14.

[14] Warren, *Antitrust,* pp. 76–77.

[15] Again, any standard economics textbook can be consulted for these elementary ideas, for example, H. Robert Heller, *The Economic System* (New York: Macmillan Inc., 1972), p. 109.

A nice example of a monopoly is the market in aluminum that developed during the first few decades of this century. Alcoa (the Aluminum Company of America) held the patents for the production of virgin aluminum in the United States until 1909, by which time it was firmly entrenched as the sole domestic producer of aluminum. Moreover, although its patents ran out in 1909, other manufacturers were never able to move successfully into the production of aluminum because their start-up costs would have been too high and they lacked Alcoa's experience, trade connections, and trained personnel. Alcoa remained the sole domestic producer of virgin aluminum until the 1940s (when it was successfully prosecuted under the Sherman Antitrust Act). For similar historical reasons, Western Electric has today emerged as the sole monopoly producer of certain telephone products.

Monopolies can also be created through mergers. At the turn of the century, for example, the leading oil refineries merged into a "holding company" (Standard Oil) which acquired monopoly control over oil refining. The monopoly was broken up when the Supreme Court charged the company with monopolization.

Monopoly markets, then, are those in which a single firm is the only seller in the market and which new sellers are barred from entering. A seller in a monopoly market, therefore, can control the prices of the available goods. A monopoly seller, for example, can set prices above their equilibrium level at, say, $3. By limiting supply to only those amounts buyers will purchase at the monopolist's high prices (300 units), the monopoly firm can ensure that it sells all its products, and that it will reap substantial profits from its business. Figure 4.4 illustrates the situation in a monopoly market: The monopoly firm will fix its output at a quantity that is less than equilibrium and at which demand is so high that it allows the firm to reap an excess "monopoly profit" by charging prices that are far above the supply curve and above the equilibrium price. The monopoly firm will, of course,

FIGURE 4-4

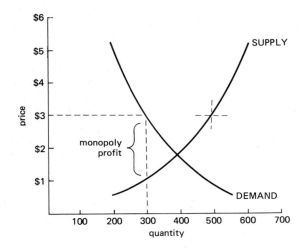

figure out what price-amount ratios will ensure it the highest total profits (that is, the profit-per-unit multiplied by the number of units), and will then fix its prices and production at those levels.

If entry into the market were open, of course, these excess profits would draw other producers into the market, resulting in an increased supply of goods and a drop in prices until equilibrium was attained. In a monopoly market, where entry is closed or prohibitive, this does not happen and prices remain high.

Monopoly Competition, Utility, and Freedom

How well does a free monopoly market succeed in achieving the utilitarian benefits and enhancement of freedom that characterize perfectly competitive free markets? Not well. Unregulated monopoly markets normally fail to achieve these two moral values.

The most obvious result of a monopoly is a decline in the efficiency with which it allocates and distributes goods. First, the monopoly market allows resources to be used in ways that will produce shortages of those things buyers want and cause them to be sold at higher prices than necessary. The high profits in a monopoly market indicate a shortage of goods but because other firms are blocked from entering the market, their resources cannot be used to make up the shortages indicated by the high profits. This means that the resources of these other firms are deflected into other nonmonopoly markets that already have an adequate supply of goods. Shortages, therefore, continue to exist. Moreover, the monopoly market allows the monopoly firm to set its prices well above costs, instead of forcing the firm to lower its prices to cost levels. The result is an inflated price for the consumer, a price that the consumer is forced to accept because the absence of other sellers has limited his or her choices. These excess profits absorbed by the monopolist are resources that are not needed to supply the amounts of goods the consumer is getting.

Secondly, monopoly markets do not encourage suppliers to use resources in ways that will minimize the resources consumed to produce a certain amount of a commodity. A monopoly firm is not encouraged to reduce its costs and is therefore not motivated to find less costly methods of production. Since profits are high anyway, there is little incentive for it to develop new technology that might reduce costs or that might give it a competitive edge over other firms. For there are no other competing firms.

Thirdly, a monopoly market allows the seller to introduce price differentials that block consumers from putting together the most satisfying bundle of commodities they can purchase given the commodities available and the money they can spend. Since everyone must buy from the monopoly firm, the firm can set its prices so that some buyers are forced to pay a higher price for the same goods than others. The monopoly firm, for example, can adjust its prices so that those consumers who have a greater desire for its goods must pay a higher price for the same goods than those consumers who have a lesser desire for them. As a consequence, those who have the greater desire now buy less, and those who have the lesser desire now buy more, than either would buy at an equal price. The result is that some consumers are no longer able to purchase the most satisfying bundle of goods they could buy.

Monopoly markets do more than bring about a decline in social utility. They also embody restrictions on freedom. First, monopoly markets by definition are markets that other sellers are not free to enter. Secondly, monopoly markets enable the monopoly firm to force on its buyers goods that they may not want, in quantities they may not desire. The monopoly firm, for example, can force consumers to purchase commodity X only if they also purchase commodity Y from the firm. Thirdly, monopoly markets are dominated by a single seller whose decisions determine the prices and quantities of a commodity offered for sale. The monopoly firm's power over the market is absolute.

A monopoly market, then, is one that no longer maximizes a society's utility and does not embody the kind of freedom characteristic of perfectly competitive markets. Instead of maximizing utility, monopoly markets provide incentives for waste, misallocation of resources, and profit-gouging. Instead of offering economic freedom, monopoly markets create an inequality of power that allows the monopoly firm to dictate terms to the consumer. The producer replaces the consumer as "sovereign" of the market.

4.3 OLIGOPOLISTIC COMPETITION

Few industries are monopolies. Most markets are not dominated by a single firm, but, more usually, by as many as four firms or more. Such markets lie somewhere on the spectrum between the two extremes of the perfectly competitive market with innumerable sellers and the pure monopoly market with only one seller. Market structures of this "impure" type are referred to collectively as "imperfectly competitive markets," of which the most important kind is the "oligopoly."[16]

In an oligopoly, three of the six conditions that characterize the purely competitive market are once again not present. First, instead of many sellers, there are only a few significant sellers. That is, most of the market is shared by a relatively small number of firms. Secondly, sellers are not able to freely enter the market. Although more than one seller is present in an oligopoly market, new sellers find it exceedingly difficult to break into the industry. This may be due to the prohibitively high costs of starting a business in that industry, it may be due to long-term contracts which have tied up all the buyers to the firms already in the industry, or it may be due to enduring loyalties created by brand-name advertising. Thirdly, in an oligopoly, a substantial share of the market is controlled by a relatively small number of large firms. The share may be anywhere between 25 percent and 90 percent, and the corporations controlling this share may range from two to fifty, depending on the industry.

[16] See Heller, *ibid.*, pp. 97–103.

Oligopoly markets which are dominated by a few large firms are said to be "highly concentrated." Examples of such oligopoly markets are not hard to find. The firms that dominate the highly concentrated American industries tend, by and large, to be among the largest corporations in the United States. Table 4.1 provides a list of some of the corporations dominant in various oligopoly industries during the 1970s, together with the approximate percentage of the markets controlled by these firms. As the reader can see, these include many of the basic American industries, and the most well-known and largest American firms.

Although oligopolies can form in a variety of ways, the most common causes of an oligopolistic market structure are horizontal mergers.[17] A horizontal merger is simply the unification of two or more companies that were formerly competing in the same line of business. If enough companies in a competitive industry merge, the industry can become an oligopoly composed of a very few very large firms. During the 1950s, for example, the 108 competing banks in Philadelphia began to merge, until by 1963 the number of bank firms had been reduced to 42.[18] The Philadelphia National Bank emerged as the second largest bank (as a result of nine mergers) and the Girard Bank emerged as the third largest (as a result of six mergers). In the early 1960s, the Philadelphia National Bank and the Girard Bank proposed to merge into a single firm. If the merger had been approved (it was stopped through legal action), the two banks together would have controlled well over a third of the banking activities of metropolitan Philadelphia.

How do oligopoly industries affect the market? Because an oligopoly has a relatively small number of firms, it is relatively easy for the managers of these firms to join forces and act as a unit. By explicitly or tacitly agreeing to set their prices at the same level and to restrict their output accordingly, the oligopolists can function more like a single firm. This uniting of forces, together with the barriers to entry that are characteristic of oligopoly industries, can result in the same high prices and low supply levels characteristic of monopoly markets. As a consequence, the same decline in utility and loss of freedom can be brought about in oligopoly markets that is found in monopolies.

Explicit Agreements

Prices in an oligopoly can be set at profitable levels through explicit agreements that restrain competition. The managers of the few firms operating in an oligopoly can meet and jointly agree to fix prices at a level much higher than what each would be forced to take in a perfectly competitive market. The greater the degree of market concentration present in an industry, the fewer the managers that have to be brought into such a price-fixing agreement, and the easier it is for them to come to an agreement. Such agreements, of course, reproduce the effects of a monopoly and consequently curtail market efficiency and market freedom as defined in the first section of this chapter.

[17]See George J. Stigler, "Monopoly and Oligopoly by Merger," *The American Economic Review,* 40 (Proceedings of the American Economic Association, 1950): 23–34.

[18]Warren, *Antitrust,* p. 271.

TABLE 4.1 Major Oligopoly Industries.

Industry Market and Leading Market Firms	Approximate Percent of Market Shared By These Firms
MOTOR VEHICLES	90%
General Motors	
Ford	
Chrysler	
COMPUTERS, TYPEWRITERS	70%
IBM	
SOUP	75%
Campbell	
COPYING EQUIPMENT	85%
Xerox	
RAZORS, TOILETRIES	70%
Gillette	
TELEPHONE EQUIPMENT	98%
Western Electric	
HEAVY ELECTRICAL EQUIPMENT	75%
General Electric	
Westinghouse	
PETROLEUM REFINING	35%
Standard Oil (New Jersey)	
Texaco	
Gulf	
Mobil	
IRON AND STEEL	50%
U.S. Steel	
Bethlehem	
Armco	
Republic	
DRUGS	70%
American Home Products	
Merck	
Pfizer	
Lilly	
SOAPS, DETERGENTS	65%
Proctor and Gamble	
Colgate	
Lever	

154

TABLE 4.1 (continued)

Industry Market and Leading Market Firms	Approximate Percent of Market Shared By These Firms
AIRCRAFT	70%
Boeing	
McDonnell-Douglas	
ALUMINUM	80%
Alcoa	
Kaiser	
Reynolds	
PHOTOGRAPHIC SUPPLIES	80%
Eastman Kodak	
TIRES AND TUBES	75%
Goodyear	
Firestone	
Uniroyal	
DRY CEREALS	60%
General Mills	
Kellogg	

Sources: William G. Shepherd, MARKET POWER AND ECONOMIC WELFARE (New York: Random House, 1970), pp. 152–154; Philip I. Blumberg, THE MEGACORPORATION IN AMERICAN SOCIETY (Englewood Cliffs, N.J.: Prentice-Hall, Inc., 1975), p. 66.

If the freedom and social utility that competitive markets achieve are important values for society, then it is crucial that the officers of oligopoly firms refrain from engaging in practices that restrict competition. Only if markets remain competitive will they exhibit the freedom and utility that justify their existence. The beneficial aspects of a free market will be reaped by society only so long as oligopoly firms refrain from engaging in collusive practices that destroy the competitive structure of markets. For these reasons, most ethicians have concluded that it is unethical for businesses to unite in collusive arrangements that do away with competition and reproduce the effects of monopoly markets. In particular, the following sorts of market practices have been identified as unethical:

Price-Fixing When firms are operating in an oligopoly market, it is easy enough for their managers to meet secretly and agree to set their prices at artificially high levels. This is straightforward price-fixing. In 1978, for example, several managers of firms manufacturing paper bags used for packaging foods, coffee, and other goods were fined for getting together and conspiring to fix the prices of those paper bags.[19] The managers worked for Continental Group, Inc., Chase Bag Co.,

[19]"Paper Companies Get Heavy Fines for Price-Fixing," *The Wall Street Journal*, 21 September 1978, p. 2.

American Bag and Paper Corp., and Harley Corp., four of the dominant firms in paper bag markets.

Manipulation of Supply   Firms in an oligopoly industry might agree to limit their production so that prices rise to levels higher than those that would result from free competition. When hardwood manufacturers met periodically in trade associations early in this century, they would often agree on output policies that would secure high profits.[20] The American Column and Lumber Company was eventually prosecuted under the Sherman Antitrust law to force it to desist from this practice. Such a "manipulation of supply" would also result in market shortages.

Exclusive Dealing Arrangements   A firm institutes an exclusive dealing arrangement when it sells to a buyer on condition that the buyer will not purchase any products from certain other sellers. During the 1940s, for instance, American Can Company would lease its can closing machines (at very low prices) only to those customers who agreed not to purchase any cans from Continental Can Company, its major competitor.[21]

Tying Arrangements   A firm enters into a tying arrangement when it sells a buyer a certain commodity only on condition that the buyer agrees to purchase certain other commodities from the firm. Chicken Delight, for example, franchises home delivery and pick-up food stores whose major product is chicken cooked in a special mix. In 1970, Chicken Delight would sell a franchise license to a person only if the person also agreed to purchase a certain numbers of cookers, fryers, and other supplies.[22] The firm was subsequently forced to stop the practice through legal action.

Retail Price Maintenance   If a manufacturer sells to retailers only on condition that they all charge the same set retail prices for its goods, it is engaging in "retail price maintenance." Eastman Kodak Company, for example, until stopped by the Federal Trade Commission, used to establish the prices at which retailers had to sell its "Kodachrome" and "Magazine Cine-Kodak Film."[23] Retail price maintenance dampens competition between retailers and removes from the manufacturer the competitive pressure to lower prices and cut costs.

Price Discrimination   To charge different prices to different buyers for identical goods or services is to engage in price discrimination. Price discrimination was used by Continental Pie Company during the 1960s in an attempt to undersell Utah

[20] Almarin Phillips, *Market Structure, Organization, and Performance* (Cambridge: Harvard University Press, 1962), pp. 138–60.

[21] Warren, *Antitrust*, pp. 233–35.

[22] *Ibid.*, pp. 218–19.

[23] *Ibid.*, pp. 161–62.

Pie Company which had managed to take away much of the Salt Lake City business of Continental Baking Company.[24] For several years, Continental sold its pies to Salt Lake City customers at prices substantially lower than those it charged for the same goods sold to customers in other areas. The Supreme Court found such pricing practices "predatory." Price differences should be based on true differences in the cost of manufacturing, packaging, marketing, transporting, or servicing goods.

Tacit Agreements

Although most of the forms of explicit market agreement enumerated above are illegal, the more common types of price-setting in oligopolies are accomplished through some unspoken form of cooperation against which it is difficult to legislate. How does this take place? The managers of the major firms in an oligopoly can learn by hard experience that competition is not in their personal financial interests. Price-cutting competition, they find, will only lead to minimal profits. The firms in an oligopoly, therefore, may each come to the conclusion that cooperation is in the best interests of all. Each firm may then reach the independent conclusion that they will all benefit if when one major firm raises its prices, all other firms set their prices at the same high levels. Through this process of "price-setting," all the major firms will retain their share of the market and they will all gain by the higher price. Since the 1930s, for example, the major tobacco companies have charged identical list prices for cigarettes. When one company decides it has a reason to raise or lower its cigarette prices, the other companies will always follow suit within a short period of time. The officials of these companies, however, have made no explicit agreement to act in concert; without ever having talked the matter over among themselves, each realizes that all will benefit so long as they continue to act in a unified fashion. In 1945, incidentally, the Supreme Court found the dominant cigarette companies guilty of tacit collusion, but the companies reverted to identical pricing after the case was settled.[25]

To coordinate their prices, some oligopoly industries will recognize one firm as the industry's "price leader."[26] Each firm will tacitly agree to set its prices at the levels announced by the price leader, knowing that all other firms will also follow its price leadership. Since each oligopolist knows it will not have to compete with another firm's lower prices, it is not forced to reduce its margin of profit to the levels to which open competition would reduce them. There need be no overt collusion involved in this form of price-setting, only an unspoken understanding that all firms will follow the price leadership of the dominant firm and will not engage in the price-lowering tactics of competition.

Whether prices in an oligopoly market are set by explicit agreements or by implicit understandings, it is clear that social utility declines to the extent that prices

[24]*Ibid.*, p. 332.

[25]William H. Nicholls, "The Tobacco Case of 1946," *American Economic Review*, 39 (1949): 284–96.

[26]Jesse W. Markham, "The Nature and Significance of Price Leadership," *The American Economic Review*, 41 (1951): 891–905.

are artificially raised above the levels that would be set by a perfectly competitive market. Consumers must pay the inflated prices of the oligopolists, resources are no longer efficiently allocated and used, and the freedom of both consumers and potential competitors diminishes.

Bribery

When used to secure the sale of a product, political bribery can also introduce diseconomies into the operations of markets. This is a form of market defect that received a great deal of public attention during the late 1970s when it was discovered that a sizable group of companies had attempted to land contracts with overseas governments by paying bribes to various government officials. Lockheed Aircraft Corporation, for example, paid several million dollars to government officials in Saudi Arabia, Japan, Italy, and Holland in order to influence aircraft sales in those countries.[27]

When bribes are used to secure the purchase of a commodity, the net effect is a decline in market competition.[28] The product of the briber no longer competes equally with the product of other sellers on the basis of its price or its merits. Instead, the bribe serves as a barrier to prevent other sellers from entering the briber's government market. Because of the bribe, the government involved buys only from the firm who supplies the bribe and the briber becomes in effect a monopoly seller.

If a briber succeeds in preventing other sellers from receiving equal entry into a government market, it becomes possible for the briber to engage in the inefficiencies characteristic of monopolies. The bribing firm can impose higher prices, engage in waste, and neglect quality and cost controls since the monopoly secured by the bribe will secure a sizable profit without need of making the price or quality of its products competitive with those of other sellers.

Bribes used to secure the sale of products by shutting out other sellers differ, of course, from bribes used for other purposes. An official may insist on being paid to perform his or her legal duties on behalf of a petitioner as when, for example, a customs officer asks for a "tip" to expedite the processing of an import permit. Or a government official may offer to lower a costly tariff in return for an under-the-table payment. The previous analysis would not apply to bribes of this sort, which are being used for a purpose other than to erect market barriers.

In determining the ethical nature of payments used for purposes other than to shut out other competitors from a market, the following considerations are relevant:

1. Is the offer of a payment initiated by the payer (the one who pays the money) or does the payee (the one who receives the money) demand the payment by threatening injury to the payer's interests? In the latter case, the payment is

[27]Willard F. Mueller, "Conglomerates: A Nonindustry," [pp. 442–481] in *The Structure of American Industry*, ed. Adams, p. 459.

[28]Neil H. Jacoby, Peter Nehemkis, and Richard Eells, *Bribery and Extortion in World Business* (New York: Macmillan Inc., 1977), p. 183.

not a bribe but a form of extortion and if the threatened injury is large enough, the payer may not be morally responsible for his or her act, or the moral responsibility may at least be diminished.

2. Is the payment made to induce the payee to act in a manner that violates his or her official sworn duty to act in the best interests of the public, or is the payment made to induce the payee to perform what is already his or her official duty? If the payee is being induced to violate his or her official duty, then the payer is cooperating in an immoral act since the payee has entered an agreement to fulfill these duties.

3. Is the nature and purpose of the payment considered ethically unobjectionable in the local culture? If a form of payment is a locally accepted public custom *and* there is a proportionately serious reason for making the payment (it is not intended to erect a market barrier nor to induce an official to violate his or her public duties), then it would appear to be ethically permissible on utilitarian grounds. (It might, however, constitute a legal violation of the Foreign Corrupt Practices Act of 1977.)

4.4 OLIGOPOLIES AND PUBLIC POLICY

It is the high degree of market concentration in oligopoly industries that places a great deal of economic power in the hands of a small number of firms and that enables them to collude, overtly or tacitly. It is not clear, however, how great this economic power is or how much it is used. Some authors have argued that the economic power held by oligopoly corporations is actually quite small and insufficient to affect society, while others have claimed that several social factors inhibit the use of this power. One's opinion of what, if anything, should be done about the high degree of market concentration in oligopoly industries depends largely on one's views concerning the extent and the use of oligopoly power.

The Do-Nothing View

Some observers hold that nothing should be done about the economic power held by oligopoly corporations because that power is actually not as large as it may first appear. Several reasons have been given to support this claim. First, it is argued that, although competition *within* industries has declined, it has been replaced by competition *between* industries with substitutable products.[29] The steel industry, for example, is now in competition with the aluminum and cement industries. Consequently, although there may be a high degree of market concentration in a single industry like steel, a high level of competition is still maintained by its relation to other competing industries.

Secondly, as John Kenneth Galbraith has argued, the economic power of any large corporation may be balanced and restrained by the "countervailing power" of

---

[29] See J.M. Clarm, "Toward a Concept of Workable Competition," *American Economic Review*, 30 (1940): 241-56.

other large corporate groups in society.[30] Government and unions, for example, both restrain the power of big businesses. And although a business corporation may have a large share of an industrial market, it is faced by buyers that are equally large and equally powerful. A large steel company, for example, must sell to equally large automobile companies. This balance of power between large corporate groups, Galbraith claims, effectively reduces the economic power any one corporate giant can exert.

The Antitrust View

Other observers are less sanguine about the economic power exerted by oligopoly corporations. They argue that prices and profits in concentrated industries are higher than they should be. The solution, they argue, is to reinstate competitive pressures by forcing the large companies to divest themselves of their holdings, thereby breaking them up into smaller firms.[31]

By breaking the large corporations into smaller units, they argue, there will be many more firms competing in those industries that are currently highly concentrated. The result will be a competitive market that will bring down prices and will encourage greater innovation and cost-cutting methods.

The Regulation View

A third group of observers holds that oligopoly corporations should not be broken up because their large size has beneficial consequences that would be lost if they were forced to decentralize.[32] In particular, they argue, mass production and mass distribution of goods can be carried out only by using the highly centralized accumulation of assets and manpower that the large corporation makes possible. Moreover, the concentration of assets allows large firms to take advantage of the economies made possible by large-scale production in large plants. These savings are passed on to consumers in the form of cheaper and more plentiful products.

Although firms should not be broken up, it does not follow that they should not be regulated. According to this third view, concentration gives large firms an economic power that allows them to fix prices and engage in other forms of behavior that are not in the public interest. To ensure that consumers are not harmed by large firms, regulatory agencies and legislation should be set up to restrain and control the activities of large corporations.

Some observers, in fact, advocate that where large firms cannot be effectively

---

[30] John Kenneth Galbraith, *American Capitalism: The Concept of Countervailing Power*, rev. ed. (Cambridge, Mass.: The Riverside Press, 1956), pp. 112-13.

[31] See John M. Blair, *Economic Concentration: Structure, Behavior, and Public Policy* (New York: Harcourt Brace Jovanovich, Inc. 1972).

[32] J.A. Schumpeter, *Capitalism, Socialism, and Democracy* (New York: Harper, 1943), pp. 79 ff.

controlled by the usual forms of regulation, then regulation should take the form of nationalization. That is, the government should take over the operation of firms in those industries where only public ownership can ensure that firms operate in the public interest.

Other advocates of regulation, however, argue that nationalization is itself not in the public interests.[33] Public ownership of firms, they claim, inevitably leads to the creation of unresponsive and inefficient bureaucracies. Moreover, publicly owned enterprises are not subject to competitive market pressures and this results in higher prices and higher costs.

Which of these three views is correct: the do-nothing view, the antitrust view, or the regulation view? Readers will have to decide this issue for themselves, since at the moment there does not appear to be sufficient evidence to answer this question unequivocally. Whichever of these three views the reader may find most persuasive, it is clear that the social benefits generated by free markets cannot be secured unless the managers of firms maintain competitive market relationships between themselves. The ethical rules prohibiting collusion are at bottom rules meant to ensure that markets are structured competitively. These rules may be voluntarily followed or legally enforced. They are justified insofar as society is justified in pursuing the utilitarian benefits and the rights to freedom that competitive markets can secure.

QUESTIONS FOR REVIEW AND DISCUSSION

1. Define the following concepts: perfect competition, demand curve, supply curve, equilibrium point, monopoly competition, oligopolistic competition, price-fixing, manipulation of supply, tying arrangements, retail price maintenance, price discrimination, price-setting, price leadership, extortion, countervailing power, do-nothing view on oligopoly power, antitrust view on oligopoly power, regulation view on oligopoly power.

2. "From an ethical point of view big business is always bad business." Discuss the pros and cons of this statement.

3. What kind of public policy do you think the United States should have with respect to business competition? Develop moral arguments to support your answer (that is, arguments which show that the kinds of policies you favor will advance the public welfare, or that they will secure certain important rights, or that they will ensure certain forms of justice).

4. In your judgment, should an American company operating in a foreign country in which collusive price-fixing is not illegal obey the U.S. laws against collusion? Explain your answer.

---

[33] L. Von Mises, *Planned Chaos* (New York: Foundations for Economic Education, 1947).

CASES FOR DISCUSSION

General Electric Prices

Clarence Burke began working for the heavy-equipment division of General Electric as soon as he graduated from college in 1926. Clarence was an energetic, hard-driving, and tenacious person and looked forward to a promising career at GE. The heavy electrical equipment division at GE was the oldest part of the company, around which the rest had been built, and it still accounted for a quarter of its sales. Moreover, GE dominated the heavy electrical equipment markets: It held 40 to 45 percent of the heavy equipment markets, followed by Westinghouse who held 30 to 35 percent, then Allis-Chalmers and Federal Pacific who held 10 percent apiece. By the 1950s, the combined sales of these companies would average $1,750,000,000 per year in the heavy electrical equipment markets alone.[1]

Long before Clarence Burke began working for GE, the company was involved in a series of antitrust suits that continued through the 1940s. These suits are summarized in Table 4.2. In November 1946, as a response to these suits, GE formulated an antitrust directive which stated that it "is the policy of this company to conform to the antitrust laws." The directive (which came to be known as "directive 20.5") was repeatedly revised and filled out until it eventually read:

Directive Policy on the Compliance by the Company and its Employees with the Antitrust Laws No. 20.5

It is the policy of the company to comply strictly in all respects with the antitrust laws. There shall be no exception to this policy nor shall it be compromised or qualified by any employee acting for or on behalf of the company. No employee shall enter into any understanding, agreement, plan, or scheme, express or implied, formal or informal, with any competitor, in regard to prices, terms or conditions of sale, production, distribution, territories, or customers; nor exchange or discuss with a competitor prices, terms, or conditions of sale, or any other competitive information; nor engage in any other conduct that in the opinion of the company's counsel violates any of the antitrust laws.[2]

Every manager was periodically asked to indicate in writing that he was adhering to the policy. The standard written letter the manager would sign stated:

I have received a copy of directive policy general No. 20.5, dated _____ .
I have read and understood this policy. I am observing it and will observe it in the future.[3]

---

[1] U.S. Congress, Senate, *Administered Prices: Hearings before the Subcommittee on Antitrust and Monopoly of the Committee on the Judiciary,* 87th Congress, 1st session, May--June, 1961, p. 17111. Hereafter cited as "Administered Prices."

[2] *Ibid.,* p. 17120.

[3] *Ibid.,* p. 16737.

TABLE 4.2 General Electric Antitrust Suits

Title Of Case	Date	Comment
General Electric Co., et al.	1911	Price-fixing conspiracy in electric lamps enjoined Oct. 12, 1911.
General Electric Co., et al.	1924	Electric lamp price-fixing conspiracy; Nov. 23, 1926, dismissed.
Radio Corp. of America, et al.	1930	Consent decree Mar. 7, 1932, enjoined activities in conspiracy to monopolize radio communication and apparatus.
Corning Glass Works, et al.	1940	Glass bulb cartel; Sept. 9, 1941, nolo contendere; fines in case totaled $47,000.
General Electric Co., et al.	1940	Conspiracy to fix prices in hard metal compositions and tools and dies made therefrom; dismissed Jan. 6, 1949.
General Electric Co., et al.	1941	Jan. 19, 1949, court held GE had monopolized incandescent lamp industry; Aug. 6, 1953, court enjoined illegal practices and ordered patents dedicated to public.
General Electric Co., et al.	1941	Cartel found guilty Oct. 18, 1948, of price-fixing, division of markets, and production limitation in hard metal alloys, tools and dies, fines in case totaled $56,000.
General Electric Co., et al.	1942	Consent decree Mar. 26, 1954, canceled foreign and domestic agreements in fluorescent electric lamp cartel and ordered compulsory royalty-free licensing of patents.
Line Material Co., et al.	1945	Decree Oct. 4, 1948, enjoined activities in price-fixing conspiracy in drop-out fuse cutouts.

TABLE 4.2 (continued)

Title Of Case	Date	Comment
General Electric Co., et al.	1945	Consent decree, Oct. 6, 1953, enjoined activities in electrical equipment cartel and required nonexclusive reasonable royalty patent licenses.
Electrical Apparatus Export Association, et al.	1945	Consent decree Mar. 12, 1947, enjoined price-fixing and market allocations and other activities of electrical equipment cartel.
General Cable Corp.	1947	Consent decree Aug. 25, 1948, enjoined present and future cartel patent pooling, and price-fixing agreements in high-tension cable and accessories.
General Electric Co., et al.	1948	Nov. 4, 1949, nolo contendere; fines in case totaled $40,000; electrical switches and equipment price-fixing conspiracy.
General Electric Co., et al.	1948	Consent decree Nov. 14, 1949, enjoined activities in electrical switches and equipment price-fixing conspiracy.
General Electric Co., et al.	1948	May 27, 1952, nolo contendere; fines in case totaled $78,000; monopoly in street-lighting equipment.
General Electric Co., et al.	1948	Consent decree May 27, 1952, enjoined customer allocation and price-fixing street-lighting equipment.

Source: U.S. Congress, Senate, ADMINISTERED PRICES: HEARINGS BEFORE THE SUB-COMMITTEE ON ANTITRUST AND MONOPOLY OF THE COMMITTEE ON THE JUDICIARY, 87th CONGRESS FIRST SESSION, May–June, 1961, p. 17688

The letter was not signed under oath, of course, nor was a manager responsible to his or her immediate local superior for adhering to the policy. The letter was sent out from GE's central offices, and was returned to the central offices by mail. Any disciplinary action taken to enforce the directive also had to originate at the home office.

In 1945 Clarence Burke was promoted to Sales Manager of GE's distribution transformer department. Here he worked under H.L. "Buster" Brown, general manager in charge of sales for all transformer departments. In July 1945, a month after Clarence entered his new position as department sales manager, his superior, Mr. Brown, told him he would be expected to attend the regularly scheduled meetings of the National Electrical Manufacturers Association in Pittsburgh, meetings which were also attended by the sales managers of the other three or four major producers of electrical equipment. Conversations at the meetings gradually began to turn to prices and soon the managers were making informal agreements to quote "an agreed upon price" to all their customers. Clarence Burke went along and accepted the practice, especially after the managers were assured by "Buster" Brown that the company's antitrust directive did not refer to the sorts of informal agreements they were making: The only agreements that were illegal, according to Brown, were those which "gouged the public." Several years later Clarence Burke recalled that he and others had "understood" that what they were doing was what the company wanted.[4]

Clarence Burke was not the only GE manager who moved into price-fixing arrangements with the other major electrical companies. By the late 1950s, W.W. Ginn, a GE vice-president, was meeting with competitors to fix prices for power transformers; Frank Stehlik, a GE general manager, was meeting to fix prices for power switchgear assemblies; W.F. Oswalt, another general manager, was fixing industrial control equipment prices; and G.L. Roark, a GE marketing manager, was fixing prices for power switching equipment. In fact, as later investigations showed, the managers of all the principal companies manufacturing heavy electrical equipment (General Electric, Westinghouse, Allis-Chalmers, and Federal Pacific) were meeting regularly to set prices for their products.[5] Throughout the late 1940s, Clarence Burke was gradually introduced to the details of a practice that was accepted in the entire industry, as well as in his own company:

> I was taught [the techniques] by my superiors back as far as 1945, who took me to meetings with them and told me that, instead of showing Pittsburgh [the place of the meetings] in your expense account, let's all show so-and-so. . . . From then on it was just inbred in me. . . . I ascertained that it [was the usual way to act] because my superiors at Pittsfield were doing it and asking me to do it. So it was their practice. [Statement of C. Burke][6]

In 1950, the general manager of GE's switchgear division, R.F. Tinnerholm, offered to move Clarence Burke to the more prestigious position of sales manager in a department of GE's switchgear division:

> I was offered the position of manager of sales of the specialty transformer division in Fort Wayne, Indiana, and I accepted and I went there on February

[4]Richard Austin Smith, "The Incredible Electrical Conspiracy," *Fortune,* April 1961, p. 136.

[5]*New York Times,* 7 February 1961, p. 26.

[6]*Administered Prices,* pp. 16772–73.

1, 1950. . . . They wanted to replace the manager of marketing. . . . Walter F. Rauber, I think his name is; they had determined to replace him, and since I had had switchgear experience and had had large apparatus experience, they determined that I was a logical replacement for Mr. Rauber. . . . I was interviewed [by] . . . R.F. Tinnerholm, who was then manager of the switchgear division. . . . Mr. Tinnerholm . . . spelled it out very clearly: Mr. Rauber (to use his words as I remember it) was so "religious" that, since he had signed this slip of paper saying that he would observe policy 20.5, he would not talk with competitors. So he was "not broad enough for the job" and they would expect me to be "broad enough" to hold down that job. [Statement of Clarence Burke] [7]

Part of what had led many managers to adopt price-fixing were the pressures they felt on them to meet corporate goals. Clarence Burke recalled several years later that the general manager of GE's switchgear division always insisted on a "reach budget," that is, a budget that increased the percent of net profit to sales over what it had been the year before. Burke claimed that he and the other managers felt that if they wanted to "get ahead" and have the "good will" of their superiors, they would have to attain these goals; and the only way to attain these, they felt, was to get together with their competitors.[8]

The price-fixing agreements that the four main electrical switchgear companies entered into in 1950, according to Burke, were intended to "stabilize" prices and to ensure at the same time that each company retained its share of the market. Managers of the four companies met in a hotel room at least once a month and arranged to take turns submitting the lowest bids for upcoming contracts so that GE would wind up with 45 percent of the jobs, Westinghouse with 35 percent, Allis-Chalmers with 10 percent, and Federal Pacific with 10 percent. These were the approximate percentages of the market that each company had controlled before the agreements.

A major fear of the companies was that without the agreements, they might be forced into what Burke termed "a ruinous cutthroat competition." That fear seemed to be borne out in 1954 when GE decided to withdraw from the price-fixing meetings. The result was a financial disaster for the industry, as each company rushed to undersell the others, until prices were being cut by as much as 50 percent. After two years, the damaging effect of the price war led the four electrical companies to resort to fixing prices again in order to "restore stability" to the market:

The latter part of 1953 [General Electric] served notice on the rest of the industry people that [we] would not meet with them any more. . . . Through 1954 there were no meetings . . . and that is when prices began to deteriorate gradually. . . . Prices began to get farther and farther off book until the latter part of 1954 they were about 15 percent off book. Then in January 1955 they really went down to the bottom, about 45 to 50 percent off book. . . . That summer—and I think it was June or July 1955—Mr. Burens [general

---

[7]*Ibid.*, p. 16736.
[8]Smith, "Incredible Electrical Conspiracy," p. 172.

manager of GE's switchgear division] asked me to come over to his office, and he told me that he had to start meeting with competition again. . . . And he said something to the effect that he had no other alternative. [Statement of Clarence Burke][9]

The meetings resumed until the winter of 1957 when Westinghouse decided to withdraw from the price-fixing agreements and the market once again went down. Within months prices fell by 60 percent. In the fall of 1958, however, the agreements were reestablished and prices moved back to their prior levels where they remained until the price-fixing meetings were finally ended in 1960. General Electric's profits during the years of these price-fixing agreements are indicated in Table 4.3.[10]

TABLE 4.3 Net Profit and Rate of Return on Stockholder's Equity, and Profit in Percent of Sales, 1940 and 1947–60 for General Electric Company

Year	Net Profit After Taxes	Rate of Return	Profit in Percent of Sales
	Thousands	Percent	Percent
1940	$ 56,494	17.1	. . . . . .
1947	101,221	22.5	6.6
1948	131,594	25.4	7.1
1949	129,946	21.8	7.0
1950	177,722	26.6	8.0
1951	133,699	18.7	5.1
1952	165,181	18.4	5.5
1953	174,128	18.5	4.9
1954	204,482	20.9	6.1
1955	209,055	19.7	6.0
1956	213,837	19.4	5.2
1957	247,972	21.1	5.7
1958	243,050	19.4	5.9
1959	280,348	20.6	6.4
1960	200,165	13.6	4.8

Source: U.S. Congress, Senate, ADMINISTERED PRICES: HEARINGS BEFORE THE SUBCOMMITTEE ON ANTITRUST AND MONOPOLY OF THE COMMITTEE ON THE JUDICIARY, 87th CONGRESS, FIRST SESSION, May–June, 1961, p. 17743.

Clarence Burke was not entirely unconcerned about his involvement in the price-fixing agreements. His reflections turned on what he saw as the effects of these agreements:

I will have to say that we did not charge everything [the market could bear]. Our purpose in meeting with competitors was not to dig the customers or any-

[9]*Administered Prices*, p. 16740.
[10]*Ibid.*, p. 17743.

thing. It was just to get what was a fair market value and would produce a fair profit for the industry and would keep the industry healthy. And I think if you will look over the records of the industry during that period, you will see that it did not make any huge profits. General Electric Company's maximum was less than 6 cents on the sales dollar. We were not meeting for the purpose of getting the most that the traffic could bear. It was to get a value for our product ... I knew I violated the technicalities of the law. I salved my own conscience by saying I was not violating the spirit of the law. Because I was not establishing prices that would gouge the public, and I thought the spirit of the law was to prevent you from establishing abnormal prices, from making huge profits. [Statement of Clarence Burke] [11]

In June 1960 a federal grand jury indicted the companies and managers involved in the price-fixing agreements. Clarence Burke was granted immunity in return for his willingness to testify against the other companies and managers. Seven executives of the companies pleaded guilty and were sentenced to jail; thirty-eight other managers were fined, and fines were brought against the companies. Although Clarence Burke was not prosecuted by the government he was fired by GE:

[The vice president of relations services] gave me this talk about how it would be to my advantage to resign from the General Electric Company. . . . They made it very clear that this had nothing to do with disciplinary action on 20.5 or because we pleaded guilty in the antitrust case. It was just the fact that because of the adverse publicity that had been received, that they could never put me in a position that my talents warranted. Therefore I would be better off if I resigned. . . . I asked him what the alternative to resigning was, and he said, "Well, if you don't resign you are off the payroll at 5 o'clock today." And that was between 4:30 and 5. [Statement of Clarence Burke] [12]

Between 1960 and 1963, a pattern of strong competition emerged in many of the markets that had been subject to the price-fixing agreements. Prices fell by 15 to 20 percent.[13] Then, in May 1963, General Electric published a pricing system that (as internal GE documents later revealed) it hoped would once again make it possible for the industry to set prices, but this time without entering into explicit collusion. The pricing system which GE published stated that (1) all of its book prices would be published, (2) all bids and discounts would be exactly 76 percent of book prices, (3) if GE offered any buyer a lower discount, it would be contractually (hence legally) bound to penalize itself, because it publicly guaranteed every customer that it would apply any lower discounts retroactively on all sales of the preceding six months, (4) all sales and orders would be published. Westinghouse immediately adopted the same pricing system, and the managers of the two firms now coordinated their prices by using public communications and public penalties

---

[11] *Ibid.*, pp. 16745 and 16790.
[12] *Ibid.*, p. 16785.
[13] *Ibid.*, p. 17093.

instead of the secret methods that had sent some of them to jail in 1961. This pricing system continued at least until 1976.[14]

1. Where would you estimate the equilibrium price was during the price-fixing schemes (at 10 percent below the list price? 30 percent? 60 percent?). Identify the conditions within GE and within the industry which encouraged the price-fixing schemes.

2. Evaluate the price-fixing scheme from an ethical point of view (your evaluation should describe the effects of the scheme on society's welfare, on the moral rights of society's members, and on the distribution of benefits and burdens within society). In your judgment, did Clarence Burke act wrongly? Why? Was he morally responsible for his actions? Why?

3. Why was GE's written policy on antitrust ineffective? In his book, *White Collar Crime,* Edwin Sutherland hypothesized that "criminal behavior [in business] is learned in association with those who define such behavior favorably and in isolation from those who define it unfavorably. . . . As a part of the process of learning practical business, a young man with idealism and thoughtfulness for others is inducted into white collar crime." (pp. 234 and 240.) To what extent was this hypothesis verified in the case of GE? What implications, if any, does this have for moral responsibility within GE? Within any business?

4. Apart from their legality, did the price-setting scheme set up in 1963 differ in any morally relevant ways from the earlier price-fixing schemes?

5. What internal policies might have changed GE's moral climate? What public policies might have changed the industry's practices?

A Japanese Bribe

In July of 1976, Kukeo Tanaka, former prime minister of Japan, was arrested on charges of taking bribes ($1.8 million) from Lockheed Aircraft Company to secure the purchase of several Lockheed jets. Tanaka's secretary and several other government officials were arrested with him. The Japanese public reacted with angry demands for a complete disclosure of Tanaka's dealings. By the end of the year, they had ousted Tanaka's successor, Takeo Miki, who was widely believed to have been trying to conceal Tanaka's actions.

In Holland that same year, Prince Bernhard, husband of Queen Juliana, resigned from three hundred positions he held in government, military, and private organizations. The reason: He was alleged to have accepted $1.1 million in bribes from Lockheed in connection with the sale of 138 F–104 starfighter jets.

In Italy, Giovani Leone, president in 1970, and Aldo Moro and Mariano Rumor, both prime ministers, were accused of accepting bribes from Lockheed in

[14]William G. Shepherd and Clair Wilcox, *Public Policies Toward Business,* 6th ed. (Homewood, IL.: Richard D. Irwin, Inc., 1979), p. 215.

connection with the purchase of $100 million worth of aircraft in the late 1960s. All were excluded from government.

Scandinavia, South Africa, Turkey, Greece, and Nigeria were also among the fifteen countries in which Lockheed admitted to having handed out payments and at least $202 million in "commissions" since 1970.

Lockheed Aircraft's involvement in the Japanese bribes was revealed to have begun in 1958 when Lockheed and Grumman Aircraft (also an American firm) were competing for a Japanese Air Force jet aircraft contract. According to the testimony of Mr. William Findley, a partner in Arthur Young & Co. (auditors for Lockheed), Lockheed in 1958 engaged the services of Yoshio Kodama, an ultra right-wing war criminal and reputed underworld figure with strong political ties to officials in the ruling Liberal Democratic Party. With Kodama's help, Lockheed secured the government contract. Seventeen years later, it was revealed that the CIA had been informed at the time (by an American embassy employee) that Lockheed had made several bribes while negotiating the contract.[1]

In 1972, Lockheed again hired Kodama as a consultant to help secure the sale of its aircraft in Japan. Lockheed was desperate to sell planes to any major Japanese airline since it was scrambling to recover from a series of financial disasters. Cost overruns on a government contract had pushed Lockheed to the brink of bankruptcy in 1970. Only through a controversial emergency government loan guarantee of $250 million in 1971 did the company narrowly avert disaster. Mr. A. Carl Kotchian, president of Lockheed from 1967 to 1975, was especially anxious to make the sales since the company had been unable to get as many contracts in other parts of the world as it had wanted.

> This bleak situation all but dictated a strong push for sales in the biggest untapped market left—Japan. This push, if successful, might well bring in revenues upwards of $400 million. Such a cash inflow would go a long way towards helping to restore Lockheed's fiscal health, and it would, of course, save the jobs of thousands of the firm's employees. [Statement of Mr. Kotchian][2]

Kodama eventually succeeded in engineering a contract for Lockheed with All-Nippon Airways, even beating out McDonnell Douglas, which was actively competing with Lockheed for the same sales. To ensure the sale, Kodama asked for and received from Lockheed about $9 million during the period from 1972 to 1975. Much of the money allegedly went to then prime minister Kukeo Tanaka and other government officials, who were supposed to intercede with All-Nippon Airlines on behalf of Lockheed.

According to Mr. Carl Kotchian, "I knew from the beginning that this money

[1] James Post, *Corporate Behavior and Social Change* (Reston, VA: Reston Publishing Co., 1978), p. 207.

[2] A. Carl Kotchian, "The Payoff: Lockheed's 70–Day Mission to Tokyo," *Saturday Review,* 9 July 1977, p. 8.

was going to the office of the prime minister."[3] He was, however, persuaded that that by paying the money, he was sure to get the contract from All-Nippon Airways. The negotiations eventually netted over $1.3 billion in contracts for Lockheed.

In addition to Kodama, Lockheed had also been advised by Toshiharu Okubo, an official of the private trading company, Marubeni, which acted as Lockheed's official representative. Mr. A. Carl Kotchian later defended the payments, which he saw as one of many "Japanese business practices" that he had accepted on the advice of his local consultants. The payments, the company was convinced, were in keeping with local "business practices."[4]

> Further, as I've noted, such disbursements *did not violate American laws.* I should also like to stress that my decision to make such payments stemmed from my judgment that the (contracts) . . . would provide Lockheed workers with jobs and thus redound to the benefit of their dependents, their communities, and stockholders of the corporation. I should like to emphasize that the payments to the so-called "high Japanese government officials" were all requested by Okubo and were *not brought up from my side.* When he told me "five hundred million yen is necessary for such sales," from a purely ethical and moral standpoint I would have declined such a request. However, in that case, I would *most certainly* have sacrificed commercial success. . . . [If] Lockheed had not remained competitive by the rules of the game as then played, we would not have sold [our planes]. . . . I knew that if we wanted our product to have a chance to win on its own merits, we had to follow the functioning system. [Statement of A. Carl Kotchian][5]

In August 1975 investigations by the United States government led Lockheed to admit it had made $22 million in secret payoffs.[6] Subsequent Senate investigations in February 1976 made Lockheed's involvement with Japanese government officials public.[7] Japan subsequently canceled their billion dollar contract with Lockheed.

In June 1979 Lockheed pleaded guilty to concealing the Japanese bribes from the government by falsely writing them off as "marketing costs."[8] The Internal Revenue Code states in part, "No deduction shall be allowed . . . for any payment made, directly or indirectly, to an official or employee of any government . . . if the payment constitutes an illegal bribe or kickback."[9] Lockheed was not charged specifically with bribery because the U.S. law forbidding bribery was

---

[3]*Ibid.*

[4]"Lockheed Says It Paid $22 Million to Get Contracts," *The Wall Street Journal,* 4 August 1975.

[5]Kotchian, "The Payoff," p. 12.

[6]*The Wall Street Journal, op. cit.*

[7]"Payoffs: The Growing Scandal, *Newsweek,* 23 February 1976.

[8]"Lockheed Pleads Guilty to Making Secret Payoffs," *San Francisco Chronicle,* 2 June 1979.

[9]Internal Revenue Code 1975, Section 162C.

not enacted until 1978. Lockheed pleaded guilty to four counts of fraud and four counts of making false statements to the government. Mr. Kotchian was not indicted, but under pressure from the board of directors, he was forced to resign from Lockheed. In Japan, Kodama was arrested along with Tanaka.

1. Explain fully the effects that payments like those which Lockheed made to the Japanese have on the structure of a market.

2. In your view, were Lockheed's payments to the various Japanese parties "bribes" or "extortions"? Explain your response fully.

3. In your judgment, did Mr. A. Carl Kotchian act rightly from a moral point of view? (Your answer should take into account the effects of the payments on the welfare of the societies affected, on the rights and duties of the various parties involved, and on the distribution of benefits and burdens among the groups involved.) In your judgment, was Mr. Kotchian morally responsible for his actions? Was he, in the end, treated fairly?

4. In its October 27, 1980, issue, *Business Week* argued that every corporation has a "corporate culture," i.e., a set of values that set a pattern for its employees' activities, opinions, and actions, and which are instilled in succeeding generations of employees (pp. 148–160). Describe, if you can, the "corporate culture" of Lockheed and relate that culture to Mr. Kotchian's actions. Describe some strategies for changing that culture in ways that might make foreign payments less likely.

PART THREE
BUSINESS AND ITS EXTERNAL EXCHANGES, ECOLOGY, AND CONSUMERS

The process of producing goods forces businesses to engage in exchanges and interactions with two main external environments: the natural environment and a consumer environment. It is from the natural environment that business ultimately draws the raw materials which it transforms into its finished products. These finished products are then externally promoted and sold to consumers. The natural environment therefore provides the raw material input of business while the consumer environment absorbs its finished output.

The next two chapters explore the ethical issues raised by these exchanges and interactions. Chapter Five discusses the two basic problems related to the natural environment: pollution and resource depletion. Chapter Six discusses several consumer issues, including product quality and advertising.

CHAPTER FIVE
ETHICS
AND THE
ENVIRONMENT

INTRODUCTION

Modern industry has provided us with a material prosperity unequaled in our history. It has also created unparalleled environmental threats to ourselves and to future generations. The very technology that has enabled us to manipulate and control nature has also polluted our air and waterways, exterminated or endangered entire species, depleted our natural resources, and defaced the landscape. No metropolitan area in the United States today is free of the irritations of smog.[1] The atmosphere has become the receptable for tons of particulate materials and gases that industrial smokestacks spew into the air each day. The water that gushes out of city faucets inevitably has the sour taste of the chlorine required to make it drinkable. The Great Lakes are dead or in the process of dying.[2] The water of the lower Mississippi River carries such high levels of industrial effluents that it is now suspected of being a major cause of cancer.[3] The Hudson River has been the recipient of 500,000 pounds of deadly polychlorinated biphenyls, traces of which have now begun to appear in Eastern seafoods.[4]

[1] J.L. Bregman and S. Lenormand, *The Pollution Paradox* (New York: Spartan Books, 1966), p. 54.

[2] "Great Lakes Study Finds Cleaning Up Could Take Decade," *New York Times,* 12 March 1976, p. 31; The International Reference Group on Great Lakes Pollution from Land Use Activities, *Environment Management Strategy for the Great Lakes* (Windsor, Ontario: International Joint Commission, 1978), p. 19.

[3] T. Page, R. Harris, and S. Epstein, "Drinking Water and Cancer Mortality in Louisiana," *Science,* 193 (1976): 55–57.

[4] R. Severo, "PCB Clean Up Cost Put at $20 Million," *New York Times,* 26 April 1976, p. 1; "PCB Found in Fish on Market Along East Coast," *New York Times,* 13 August 1976, p. A9.

Not only is the environment being contaminated, but resources are also being rapidly depleted. Our industrialized economy depends on a constant input of raw materials and energy. In 1974 the United States alone consumed the equivalent of 13,769,000,000 barrels of oil. In addition, each U.S. citizen that year accounted for the consumption of 1,300 pounds of metal and 18,500 pounds of other minerals.[5] Yet as the shortages that plagued the 1970s have shown, these resources are not inexhaustible. Many experts estimate that over the next one hundred years many of our essential resources will be completely depleted or will become so scarce that their recovery will be prohibitively expensive.[6]

So intractable and difficult are the problems raised by these environmental threats, that many observers believe that they cannot be solved. William Pollard, a physicist, for example, despairs of our being able to deal adequately with these problems:

> My own view is that [mankind] will not do so until he has suffered greatly and much that he now relies upon has been destroyed. As the earth in a short few decades becomes twice as crowded with human beings as it is now, and as human societies are confronted with dwindling resources in the midst of mounting accumulations of wastes, and a steadily deteriorating environment, we can only foresee social paroxysms of an intensity greater than any we have so far known. The problems are so varied and so vast and the means for their solutions so far beyond the resources of the scientific and technological know-how on which we have relied that there simply is not time to avoid the impending catastrophe. We stand, therefore, on the threshold of a time of judgment more severe, undoubtedly, than any mankind has ever faced before in history.[7]

Environmental issues, then, raise large and complicated ethical and technological questions for our business society. What is the extent of the environmental damage produced by present and projected industrial technology? How large a threat does this damage pose to our welfare? What values must we give up in order to halt or slow such damage? Whose rights are violated by pollution and who should be given the responsibility of paying for the costs of polluting the environment? How long will our natural resources last? What obligations do firms have to future generations to preserve the environment and conserve our resources?

This chapter explores these environmental issues. It begins with an overview of various technical aspects of environmental resource use. This is followed by a discussion of the ethical basis of environmental protection. The final sections discuss two controversial issues: our obligations to future generations and the prospects for continued economic growth.

[5] R.C. Kirby and A.S. Prokopovitsh, "Technological Insurance Against Shortages in Minerals and Metals," *Science,* 191 (1976): 713–19.

[6] L.D. Roper, *Where Have all the Metals Gone?* (Blacksburg, VA: University Publications, 1976).

[7] William G. Pollard, "The Uniqueness of the Earth," in *Earth Might Be Fair,* ed. Ian G. Barbour (Englewood Cliffs, NJ: Prentice-Hall, Inc., 1972), pp. 95–96; see also Robert L. Heilbroner, *An Inquiry into the Human Prospect* (New York: W.W. Norton & Co., Inc., 1974).

5.1 THE DIMENSIONS OF POLLUTION AND RESOURCE DEPLETION

The life, health, and happiness of humans as well as of plants and animals are threatened by our uses of the environment. The threats that concern us here are of two main varieties: pollution of the environment and resource depletion. Pollution refers to the undesirable and unintended contamination of the environment by the manufacture or use of commodities. Resource depletion, on the other hand, refers to the consumption of finite or scarce resources. In a certain sense, pollution is really a type of resource depletion, since contamination of air, water, or land diminishes their beneficial qualities. But for purposes of discussion, we will keep the two issues distinct.

Air Pollution

Air pollution is not new—it has been with us since the industrial revolution introduced the world to the belching factory smokestack. But the costs of air pollution have increased almost exponentially. Today, air pollutants affect vegetation, decreasing agricultural yields and inflicting losses on the timber industry; they deteriorate exposed construction materials through corrosion, discoloration, and rot; and they are hazardous to health and life, raising medical costs and lessening the enjoyment of living.[8]

Studies have indicated that air pollution may have potentially disastrous long-range effects on climate through the creation of a "greenhouse effect" that threatens to trap heat in the atmosphere and raise temperatures worldwide.[9] When carbon dioxide is released into the atmosphere by the burning of fossil fuels such as coal, it absorbs solar energy that would otherwise be reflected back into space, thereby increasing the temperature of the world. It is estimated that if coal is once again widely used, the temperature of the globe by 2020 may rise high enough to expand the world's deserts and to melt the polar ice caps, causing sea levels to rise and flood coastal lowlands.[10]

The effects of air pollution were summarized a few years ago in a report of the Department of Health, Education, and Welfare:

At levels frequently found in heavy traffic, carbon monoxide produces headaches, loss of visual acuity, and decreased muscular coordination.

[8] John R. Holum, *Topics and Terms in Environmental Problems* (New York: John Wiley & Sons, Inc., 1977), pp. 16–17; the best study of the health effects of air pollution is Lester Lave and Eugene Seskind, *Air Pollution and Human Health* (Baltimore: Johns Hopkins University Press, 1977); for a review of the literature see Lester Lave and Eugene Seskind, "Air Pollution and Human Health," *Science,* 169 (21 August 1970): 723–33.

[9] Conservation Foundation, *Implications of Rising Carbon Dioxide Content of the Atmosphere* (New York, 1963).

[10] V. Siegenthaler and H. Oeschger, "Predicting Future Atmospheric Carbon Dioxide Levels," *Science,* 199 (1978): 388–95.

Sulfur oxides, found wherever coal and oil are common fuels, corrode metal and stone and, at concentrations frequently found in our larger cities, reduce visibility, injure vegetation, and contribute to the incidence of respiratory diseases and to premature death.

Besides their contribution to photochemical smog, described below, nitrogen oxides are responsible for the whiskey-brown haze that not only destroys the view in some of our cities, but endangers the takeoff and landing of planes. At concentrations higher than those usually experienced, these oxides can interfere with respiratory function and, it is suspected, contribute to respiratory disease. They are formed in the combustion of all types of fuel.

Hydrocarbons are a very large class of chemicals, some of which, in particle form, have produced cancer in laboratory animals, and others of which, discharged chiefly by the automobile, play a major role in the formation of photochemical smog.

Photochemical smog is a complex mixture of gases and particles manufactured by sunlight out of the raw materials—nitrogen oxides and hydrocarbons—discharged to the atmosphere chiefly by the automobile. Smog, whose effects have been observed in every region of the United States, can severely damage crops and trees, deteriorate rubber and other materials, reduce visibility, cause the eyes to smart and the throat to sting, and, it is thought, reduce resistance to respiratory disease.

Particulate matter not only soils our clothes, shows up on our window sills, and scatters light to blur the image of what we see, it acts as a catalyst in the formation of other pollutants, it contributes to the corrosion of metals, and, in proper particle size, can carry into our lungs irritant gases which might otherwise have been harmlessly dissipated in the upper respiratory tract. Some particulates contain poisons whose effects on man are gradual, often the result of the accumulation of years.[11]

The major sources of air pollution are automobiles and industrial smokestacks. In 1968, auto emission accounted for somewhere between 40 percent and 60 percent of all air pollution, mostly in the form of carbon monoxide, a toxic gas.[12] In congested urban areas such as Los Angeles, estimates of the proportion of air pollution caused by automobiles rise to as much as 70 percent. Industrial pollution is derived principally from power plants and from plants that refine and manufacture basic metals.[13] Electrical power plants that depend on fossil fuels such as oil, coal, or natural gas throw tons of sulfur oxides, nitrogen oxides, and ashes into the air. When taken into the lungs, sulfur oxides form sulfuric acid, which damages the linings of the lungs and causes emphysema and bronchitis.[14] Copper refineries and smelters emit large quantities of copper oxides and ash. Steel, nickel, cement, and chemical plants throw various particulate contaminants into the air. The major sources of air pollutants for 1974 are summarized in Table 5.1.

[11] Quoted in *No Deposit–No Return,* Huey D. Johnson, ed. (Reading, MA: Addison-Wesley Publishing Co., Inc., 1970), pp. 166–67.

[12] Fred Luthans and Richard M. Hodgetts, *Social Issues in Business,* 2nd ed. (New York: Macmillan Inc., 1976), p. 249.

[13] Council on Environmental Quality, *Environmental Quality,* ninth annual report (Washington, DC: U.S. Government Printing Office, 1978), pp. 72–76.

[14] Arthur Stern, ed., *Air Pollution* (New York: Academic Press, Inc., 1968), pp. 11–15.

TABLE 5.1 Sources of Air Pollution

Transportation	99.1 Million Tons
Power Production	43.8 " "
Industrial Processes	33.6 " "
Solid Waste Disposal	3.6 " "
Miscellaneous	18.3 " "

Source: Council on Environmental Quality, ENVIRONMENTAL QUALITY (Washington, D.C.: U.S. Government Printing Office, 1973).

The quantities of each of the major kinds of pollutants emitted in 1974 are summarized in Table 5.2.

TABLE 5.2 Quantities of Air Pollutants

Particulates	19.5 Million Tons
Sulfur Oxides	31.4 " "
Carbon Monoxide	94.6 " "
Hydrocarbons	30.4 " "
Nitrogen Oxides	22.5 " "

Source: Council on Environmental Quality, ENVIRONMENTAL QUALITY (Washington, D.C.: U.S. Government Printing Office, 1973).

The combined costs of air pollution are high. The Environmental Protection Agency has estimated that the 1968 costs of medical care and lost work time due to air pollution were six billion dollars; damages to exterior coverings, forests, and crops were another five billion dollars; and the decline in property values attributable to air pollution added another five and a half billion dollars annually, for a total of $16.5 billion.[15] If air pollution were not controlled, the agency estimated that 1977 costs would have totaled $25 billion (in 1970 dollars). Besides these economically measurable costs, there are the less easily quantified costs of loss of life and health. In 1952, between 4,000 and 5,000 persons died when an air inversion left the polluted air trapped above London for four days; several less severe episodes between 1952 and 1962 accounted for perhaps 4,000 more deaths in London; a "killer smog" in 1953 killed 200 in New York City, and a second episode in 1966 killed 168 persons.[16] Studies have indicated that if the concentrations of sulfur

[15] U.S. Environmental Protection Agency, "The Challenge of the Environment: A Primer on EPA's Statutory Authority," in *A Managerial Odyssey: Problems in Business and its Environment,* Arthur Elkins and Dennis W. Callaghan, eds. (Reading, MA: Addison-Wesley Publishing Co., Inc., 1975), p. 252.

[16] For descriptions of these and other air pollution disasters see H.R. Lewis, *With Every Breath You Take* (New York: Crown, 1965).

oxides and particulates over our major cities were cut in half from their 1960 levels, this would add an average of one year to the lives of each of its residents.[17] If air pollution in urban areas were reduced to the levels of those rural regions that enjoy clean air, the death rates for asthma, bronchitis, and emphysema would drop by about 50 percent;[18] deaths from heart disease would drop by about 15 percent;[19] deaths from lung cancer could drop by as much as 90 percent.[20]

Water Pollution

The contamination of waterways is also an old problem, one that has been with us since civilization began using water to dispose of its wastes and sewage. Water pollutants today have several sources and consist of a variety of different materials.[21]

Salt brines from mines and oil wells, as well as mixtures of sodium chloride and calcium chloride used to keep winter roads clear of snow, all eventually drain into water sources where they raise the saline content.[22] The high saline levels in ponds, lakes, and rivers kill whatever fish, vegetation, or other organisms inhabited them. Highly salinated water also poses major health hazards when it finds its way into city water supplies and is drunk by persons afflicted with heart disease, hypertension, cirrhosis of the liver, or renal disease.

Water drainage from coal mining operations contains sulfuric acid as well as iron and sulfate particles. Continuous-casting and hot-rolling mills employ acids to scrub metals, and these acids are then rinsed off with water. The acidic water from these sources is sometimes flushed into streams and rivers. The high acid levels produced in waterways by these practices are lethal to most organisms living within the aquatic environment.[23]

Organic wastes in water are comprised in large part of untreated human wastes and sewage, but a substantial amount is also derived from industrial processing of various food products, from the pulp and paper industry, and from animal feedlots.[24] Organic wastes that find their way into water resources are consumed by various types of bacteria, which in the process deplete the water of its oxygen. The oxygen-depeleted water then becomes incapable of supporting fish life and other organisms.

---

[17] Seskin, *Air Pollution and Human Health.*

[18] Lave and Seskin, *Ibid.*, pp. 723–33.

[19] *Ibid.*

[20] P. Stocks and J.M. Campbell, *British Medical Journal*, II (1955): 923.

[21] Holum, *Topics and Terms in Environmental Problems*, p. 655.

[22] Richard H. Wagner, *Environment and Man*, 2nd ed. (New York: W.W. Norton & Co., Inc., 1974), p. 99.

[23] X.M. Mackenthun, *The Practice of Water Pollution* (Washington, DC: U.S. Government Printing Office, 1969), ch. 8.

[24] Wagner, *Environment*, pp. 102–7.

Phosphorus compounds also contaminate many of our water sources.[25] Phosphorus compounds are found in cleansing detergents used both domestically and industrially, in fertilizers used for agricultural purposes, and in untreated human and animal sewage. Lakes with high concentrations of phosphorus give rise to explosive expansions of algae populations that choke waterways, drive out other forms of life, deplete the water of its oxygen, and severely restrict water visibility.

Various inorganic pollutants pose serious health hazards when they make their way into water used for drinking and eating purposes. Mercury has been finding its way into fresh water supplies and the oceans, put there by run-off from the combustion of fossil fuels, by past pulp mill uses of mercury-based fungicides, and by the use of certain pesticides.[26] Mercury is transformed into organic compounds by microorganisms, and becomes increasingly concentrated as it moves up the food chain to fish and birds. When consumed by humans, these compounds can cause brain damage, paralysis, and death. The Allied Chemical Company was recently found to be discharging large quantities of kepone into Virginia's James River.[27] Kepone is a chlorine compound that is toxic to fish life and causes nerve damage, sterility, and possibly cancer in humans. Cadmium from zinc refineries, from the agricultural use of certain fertilizers, and from battery manufacturers, also makes its way into water sources, where it becomes concentrated in the tissues of fish and shellfish.[28] Cadmium causes a degenerate bone disease that cripples some victims and kills others; it induces severe cramps, vomiting, and diarrhea, and it produces high blood pressure and heart disease. A few years ago, Reserve Mining Company was found to be depositing asbestos-contaminated wastes in the waters of Lake Superior, which provides the drinking supply of several towns.[29] Asbestos fibers may cause cancer of the gastrointestinal tract.

Heat is also a water pollutant.[30] Water is used as a coolant in various industrial manufacturing processes and by the electrical power industry, a major heat polluter. Transferring heat into water raises the water's thermal energy to levels that decrease its ability to hold the dissolved oxygen that aquatic organisms require. In addition, the alternating rise and fall of temperatures prevents the water from being populated by fish, since most water organisms are adapted only to stable water temperatures.

Oil spills are a form of water pollution whose occurrence has become more

[25] J.H. Ryther, "Nitrogen, Phosphorus, and Eutrophication in the Coastal Marine Environment," *Science*, 171, no. 3975 (1971): 1008–13.

[26] L.J. Carter, "Chemical Plants Leave Unexpected Legacy for Two Virginia Rivers," *Science*, 198 (1977): 1015–20; J. Holmes, "Mercury Is Heavier Than You Think," *Esquire*, May 1971; T. Aaronson, "Mercury in the Environment," *Environment*, May 1971.

[27] F.S. Sterrett and C.A. Boss, "Careless Kepone," *Environment*, 19 (1977): 30–37.

[28] L. Friberg, *Cadmium in the Environment* (Cleveland, OH: C.R.C. Press, 1971).

[29] See Presson S. Shane, "Case Study–Silver Bay: Reserve Mining Company," in *Ethical Issues in Business*, Thomas Donaldson and Patricia H. Werhane, eds. (Englewood Cliffs, NJ: Prentice-Hall, Inc., 1979), p. 358–61.

[30] C.T. Hill, "Thermal Pollution and Its Control," in *The Social Cost of Power Production* (New York: Macmillan Inc., 1975); J.R. Clark, "Thermal Pollution and Aquatic Life," *Scientific American*, March 1969.

frequent as our dependence on oil has increased.[31] Oil spills result from off-shore drilling as well as from oil tanker accidents. A few years ago two Standard Oil of California tankers collided in San Francisco Bay, spilling hundreds of thousands of gallons of oil along 50 miles of California coastlines; eight months later a Navy tanker spilled 230,000 gallons on the beaches of San Clemente and the following month a Swedish tanker spilled 15,000–30,000 more gallons of oil into San Francisco Bay. The contamination produced by oil spills affects various forms of marine and bird life, requires expensive clean-up operations for residents, and imposes costly losses on nearby tourist industries.

In the past, the oceans have been used as disposal sites for intermediate- and low-level radioactive wastes (which are more fully discussed below). Oceanographers have now begun to find in seawater traces of plutonium, cesium, and other radioactive materials that have apparently leaked from the sealed drums in which radioactive wastes are disposed.[32]

How much have the various forms of water pollution recited in this litany cost us, and what benefits might we expect from their removal? Unfortunately, there are few reliable estimates of the costs of water pollution. The best estimate, made by the Environmental Protection Agency in 1973, was that (in 1973 dollars) the total costs of annual water pollution in the United States are $10.1 billion per year.[33] About 60 percent of these costs derive from estimated loss of recreational benefits.

Noise Pollution

Noise is unwanted and damaging sound.[34] Although tolerance levels differ, on the average noise becomes uncomfortable at about 120 decibels (about the sound of an automobile horn three feet away, or of a large pneumatic riveter four feet away). Noise becomes painful at about 140 decibels (a jet takeoff at 80 feet), although hearing can be damaged at lower levels. Nervous systems begin to be affected adversely at about 70 decibels, and 55 decibels will disturb but not necessarily awaken a sleeping person.

Noise increases tensions, it can affect blood pressure, and it seems to be related to heart deterioration.[35] As a consequence, noise pollution exacts heavy medical costs. In addition, institutions that require low noise levels—such as schools, hospitals, or libraries—must invest heavily in insulation, while residents in high noise-pollution areas pay by having their rest disturbed, and businesses pay by the lowered work efficiency of their distracted employees.

[31] A.E. Nash, Dean E. Mann, and Phil. G. Olsen, *Oil Pollution and the Public Interest* (Berkeley: Institute of Government Studies, University of California, 1972).

[32] D. Burnham, "Radioactive Material Found in Oceans," *New York Times,* 31 May 1976, p. 13.

[33] H.T. Heintz, A. Hershaft, and G. Horak, *National Damages of Air and Water Pollution* (Washington, DC: Environmental Protection Agency, 1976).

[34] See H. Still, *In Quest of Quiet* (Harrisburg, PA: Stackpole Books, 1970).

[35] See J.D. Miller, *Effects of Noise on People* (Washington, DC: U.S. Government Printing Office, 1971).

Noise has a variety of sources, the most ubiquitous of which are those connected with transportation, such as jet aircraft, automobiles, subways, railroads, and trucks. Industrial machines, domestic appliances (such as air-conditioners), emergency sirens, and construction equipment also contribute their share.

Toxic Substances

Hazardous or toxic substances are substances that can cause an increase in mortality rates or an increase in irreversible or incapacitating illness, or that have other seriously adverse health or environmental effects. These include acidic chemicals, inorganic metals (such as mercury or arsenic), flammable solvents, pesticides, herbicides, phenols, explosives, and so on. (Radioactive wastes are also classified as hazardous substances but these will be discussed separately below.) 2, 4, 5-T and Silvex, for example, are two widely used herbicides that contain dioxin—a deadly poison (one hundred times more deadly than strychnine) and a carcinogen. Until 1979 these herbicides were being sprayed on forests in Oregon, where they are believed to have led to an abnormal number of miscarriages in local women and to have caused a range of reproductive defects in animals. A second example: In the late 1970s, toxic chemical wastes buried by Hooker Chemical Company at sites near Niagara Falls, N.Y., were found to have leaked from the sites and to have contaminated the surrounding residential areas including homes, schools, playing fields, and underground water supplies. The wastes included dioxin, pesticides, carbon tetrachloride, and other carcinogenic or toxic chemicals that were suspected of having induced spontaneous abortions, nerve damage, and congenital malformations among families living nearby.[36]

The Environmental Protection Agency estimates that 10 to 15 percent of the 344 million metric wet tons of industrial wastes produced each year are toxic, an estimated total of 51 million tons per year.[37] These wastes have been deposited in 32,000 to 50,000 sites, whose precise locations, contents, and characteristics are not entirely known. Altogether about 80 percent of industrial wastes are estimated to have been deposited in the past in ponds, lagoons, and landfills that are not secure. In many places, wastes have been migrating out of the sites, sometimes seeping into the underlying groundwater, where the chemicals have contaminated the water supply of the surrounding community. The costs of cleaning up these dumps have been estimated at between $28.4 billion and $55 billion.

Nuclear Wastes

Light-water nuclear reactors contain radioactive materials, including known carcinogens such as strontium 90, cesium 137, barium 140, and iodine 131. Extremely high levels of radiation from these elements can kill a person, lower dosages

[36] For these and other similar examples see Council on Environmental Quality, *Environmental Quality-1979* (Washington, DC: U.S. Government Printing Office, 1979), p. 175; "The Poisoning of America," *Time*, 22 September 1980, pp. 58–69; M.H. Brown, "The Poisoned Land," *New West*, 22 September 1980, pp. 52–64.

[37] *Environmental Quality-1979*, p. 181.

(especially if radioactive dust particles are inhaled or ingested) can cause thyroid, lung, or bone cancer and can cause genetic damage that will be transmitted to future generations. To this date nuclear plants have operated safely without any catastrophic release of large quantities of radioactive materials. Estimates of the probable risk of such a catastrophic accident are highly controversial, and considerable doubt has been cast on these probability estimates, especially since the accident at Three Mile Island.[38] Even without catastrophic accidents, however, small amounts of radioactive materials are routinely released into the environment during the normal operations of a nuclear plant and during the mining, processing, and transporting of nuclear fuels. The government has estimated that between the years 1975 and 2000 at least one thousand people will die of cancer from these routine emissions; other estimates, however, place these figures at substantially higher levels.[39]

Plutonium is produced as a waste by-product in the spent fuel of light-water reactors. A 1000-megawatt reactor, for example, will generate about 265 pounds (120 kilograms) of plutonium wastes each year that must be disposed of. Plutonium is a highly toxic and extremely carcinogenic substance. A particle weighing 10 millionths of a gram, if inhaled, can cause death within a few weeks. Twenty pounds, if properly distributed, could give lung cancer to everyone on earth. Plutonium is also the basic constituent of atomic bombs. As nuclear power plants proliferate around the world, therefore, the probability has increased that plutonium will fall into the hands of criminal terrorists or other hostile groups, who may use it to construct an atomic weapon or to lethally contaminate large populated areas.[40]

Nuclear power plant wastes are of three main types: high-level wastes, transuranic wastes, and low-level wastes.[41] High-level wastes emit gamma rays, which can penetrate all but the thickest shielding. These include cesium 137 and strontium 90—which both become harmless after about 1,000 years—and plutonium—which remains hazardous for 250,000 to 1,000,000 years. All of these are highly carcinogenic. Nuclear reactors have already produced about 612,000 gallons of liquid and 2,300 tons of solid high-level wastes each year. These wastes must be isolated from the environment until they are no longer hazardous. It is unknown at this time whether there is any safe and permanent method for disposing of these wastes.[42]

[38] See U.S. Nuclear Regulatory Commission, "NRC Statement on Risk Assessment and the Reactor Safety Study Report in Light of the Risk Assessment Review Group Report," 18 January 1979.

[39] U.S. Nuclear Regulatory Commission, "Final Generic Environmental Statement on the Use of Plutonium Recycle in Mixed Oxide Fuel in Light Water Cooled Reactors," NUREG-0002, vol. 1, August 1976.

[40] See Theodore B. Taylor and Mason Willrich, *Nuclear Theft: Risks and Safeguards* (Cambridge, MA: Ballinger Publishing Co., 1974).

[41] For a nontechnical review of the literature on nuclear waste products see Scott Fenn, *The Nuclear Power Debate* (Washington, DC: Investor Responsibility Research Center, 1980); see also William Ramsay, *Unpaid Costs of Electrical Energy* (Baltimore: Johns Hopkins University Press for Resources for the Future, 1978).

[42] Thomas O'Toole, "Glass, Salt Challenged as Radioactive Waste Disposal Methods," *The Washington Post,* 24 December 1978.

Transuranic wastes contain smaller quantities of the elements found in high-level wastes. These come from spent fuel processing and from various military weapons processes. Until recently, transuranic wastes were buried in shallow trenches. It has been discovered, however, that radioactive materials have been migrating out of these trenches, and they may eventually have to be exhumed and redisposed of at a cost of several hundred million dollars.[43]

Low-level wastes consist of the contaminated clothing and used equipment from reactor sites and of the tailings from mining and milling uranium. About 16 million cubic feet of these wastes have been produced at reactor sites, and an additional 500 million cubic feet of uranium tailings (about 140 million tons) have accumulated in the open at mine sites. About 10 million additional tons of mill tailings are produced each year. Uranium tailings continue to emit radioactive radon for several hundred thousand years. In addition, all nuclear plants (including equipment, buildings, and land) become low-level nuclear wastes themselves after an operating life of thirty to thirty-five years. The entire plant must then be decommissioned and, since it remains radioactive for thousands of years, the dismantled plant and land site must be maintained under constant security for the next several centuries.[44]

More than one author has suggested that the safe disposal of nuclear wastes is soluble only if we assume that none of our descendants will ever accidentally drill into nuclear repositories or enter them during times of war, that records of their locations will be preserved for the next several centuries, that the wastes will not accidentally flow together and begin reacting, that geological events, ice-sheets, or other unforeseen earth movements never uncover the wastes, that our engineering estimates of the properties of metal, glass, and cement containers are accurate, and that our medical predictions concerning safe levels of radiation exposure prove correct.[45]

Depletion of Species

It is well known that human beings have depleted dozens of plant and animal species to the point of extinction. Since 1600 A.D. , at least thirty-six species of mammals and ninety-four species of birds have become extinct.[46] Several more species, such as whales and salmon, today find themselves threatened by commercial predators. Forests are also being decimated by the timber industry. Between the years 1600 and 1900 half of the forested land area in the United States was

---

[43] U.S. General Accounting Office, GAO Report to Congress B-164052, "Cleaning Up the Remains of Nuclear Facilities—A Multibillion Dollar Problem," EMD-77-46 (Washington, DC: U.S. Government Printing Office, 1977), 16 June 1977.

[44] Sam H. Schurr, et al., *Energy in America's Future* (Baltimore: The Johns Hopkins University Press, 1979), p. 35.

[45] Ellen Winchester, "Nuclear Wastes," *Sierra,* July/August 1979.

[46] J. Fisher, N. Simon, and J. Vincent, *Wildlife in Danger* (New York: The Viking Press, 1969).

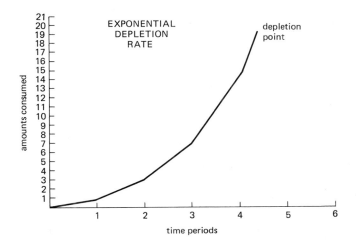

FIGURE 5-1

cleared.[47] Experts estimate that the planet's rain forests are being destroyed at the rate of about one percent a year.[48]

Depletion of Fossil Fuels

Fossil fuels have been depleted at an exponentially rising rate. That is, the rate at which they have been used doubled with the passage of a regular fixed time period. This type of "exponential depletion" is illustrated in Figure 5.1. If continued, an exponentially rising rate of depletion will end with the complete and catastrophic depletion of the resource in a relatively short time frame.[49] If the current exponentially increasing rate of use of fossil fuels continues, the estimated world reserves of coal will be depleted in about one hundred years, estimated world reserves of oil will be exhausted in about forty years, and estimated reserves of natural gas will last only about thirty years.[50]

Many researchers, however, have pointed out that our consumption of fossil fuels will probably not continue rising at historical exponential rates.[51] Instead, as

[47]C.S. Wong, "Atmospheric Input of Carbon Dioxide from Burning Wood," *Science,* 200 (1978): 197–200.

[48]G.M. Woodwell, "The Carbon Dioxide Question," *Scientific American,* 238 (1978): 34–43.

[49]An exponential rate of depletion is assumed in the Club of Rome report; Donella H. Meadows, Dennis L. Meadows, Jergen Randers, and William W. Behrens III, *The Limits to Growth* (New York: Universe Books, 1972).

[50]W. Jackson Davis, *The Seventh Year* (New York: W.W. Norton & Co., Inc., 1979), pp. 38–40; see also, U.S. Congress Office of Technology Assessment, *World Petroleum Availability: 1980-2000* (Washington, DC: U.S. Government Printing Office, 1980).

[51]M.K. Hubbert, "U.S. Energy Resources: A Review as of 1972," Document No. 93–40 (92–72) (Washington, DC: U.S. Government Printing Office, 1974).

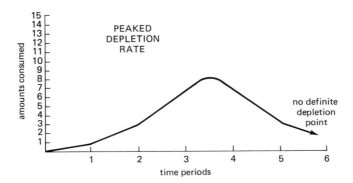

FIGURE 5-2

reserves shrink, they will become increasingly difficult, and therefore more costly, to extract. Consequently, although the rates at which reserves are depleted will continue to rise exponentially for a period, the rising costs of extraction will eventually cause the rates to peak and then begin to decline, without complete depletion ever being attained. Figure 5.2 illustrates this type of "peaked depletion" rate, in which consumption of the resource gradually peters out as the resource becomes increasingly difficult to extract, rather than culminating in complete and sudden depletion within a relatively short period of time. If we assume that the rate at which we consume our resources is more adequately mirrored by the "peaked" model than by the "exponential" model, then fossil fuels will not be depleted within the short time frame predicted by an exponential growth model. The extraction of estimated reserves of coal will probably peak in about 150 years and then continue, but at a declining rate for another 150 years; the extraction of estimated reserves of oil will probably peak in about 40 years and then gradually decline; the extraction of estimated U.S. reserves of natural gas has already peaked (in 1975) and is now expected to decline gradually over the next 30 or 40 years.[52] Rising energy prices have already lowered domestic consumption of oil and natural gas.

Depletion of Minerals

The depletion of metal reserves, like the depletion of fossil fuels, can also be calculated either on the basis of an "exponential growth" model or on the basis of a "peaked growth" model. If we assume that the current exponentially rising rates of depletion will continue, then aluminum will be exhausted in the year 2003, copper will be exhausted in 1993, iron in 2065, lead in 1993, manganese in 2018, molybdenum in 2006, nickel in 2025, tin in 1987, tungsten in 2000, and zinc in 1990.[53]

However, as with fossil fuels, we should probably assume that the rate at which metals are consumed will not continue to grow exponentially, but that consumption rates will peak and then decline as metals become rarer and more difficult

---

[52] Davis, *The Seventh Year,* pp. 44–46; see also Schurr et al., *Energy in America's Future,* pp. 225–246, for more detailed estimates.

[53] *Ibid.,* p. 128.

to extract. If we use this "peaked" model analysis and restrict ourselves solely to U.S. reserves, then the essential fact to note is that extraction rates of aluminum, iron, lead, manganese, mercury, tungsten, and zinc all seem to have peaked and are already on the decline.[54] We can expect that by the year 2000 we will have exhausted perhaps 90 percent of our aluminum, 80 percent of our iron, 70 percent of our lead, 90 percent of our manganese, 80 percent of our mercury, 90 percent of our tungsten, and 70 percent of our zinc.[55] The remaining reserves will be exceedingly difficult and costly to extract.

There are physical limits, then, to our natural resources: They cannot be exploited indefinitely. Eventually, they will either run out or the costs of extraction will make it unfeasible to mine them. Substitute materials may be found for many of these resources, but it is unlikely that substitutes will be found for all of them. And whatever substitutes are developed will also be limited, so the day of reckoning will only be delayed.

5.2 THE ETHICS OF POLLUTION CONTROL

Business institutions have traditionally been able to ignore environmental effects for several reasons. First, businesses have been able to treat things like air and water as *free* goods; that is, as goods that no one owns and that each firm can therefore use without reimbursing anyone for their use. Since 1969, for example, a DuPont plant in West Virginia had been dumping 10,000 tons of chemical wastes each month into the Gulf of Mexico, until it was stopped in 1974.[56] The waters of the Gulf provided a free dumping site for whose damages DuPont did not have to pay. Because such resources are not privately owned, they lack the protection that a private owner would normally provide, and businesses are able to ignore the damages they inflict on them. Secondly, businesses have seen the environment as an *unlimited* good. That is, the "carrying capacity" of air and water is relatively large, and each firm's contribution of pollution to these resources is relatively small and insignificant.[57] The amount of chemicals DuPont was dumping into the Gulf, for example, might be relatively small compared to the size of the Gulf and the effects viewed as being negligible. When the effects of its activities are seen as so slight, a firm will tend to ignore these effects. However, when *every* firm reasons in this way, the combined "negligible" effects of each firm's activities may become enormous, and potentially disastrous. The carrying capacity of the air and water is soon exceeded and these "free" and "unlimited" goods rapidly deteriorate.

Of course, pollution problems are not rooted only in business activities. Pol-

---

[54]*Ibid.*, pp. 131–32.

[55]*Ibid.*

[56]Lester A. Sobel, *Jobs, Money, and Pollution* (New York: Facts on File, 1977), p. 170.

[57]The term is Garrit Hardin's; see his "The Tragedy of the Commons," *Science,* 162 No. 3859 (13 December 1968): 1243–48.

lution also results from the use that consumers make of products and from human waste products.[58] A primary source of air pollution, for example, is automobile use, and a primary source of water pollution is sewage. We are truly *all* polluters.[59] And since every human being pollutes, pollution problems have increased as our population has multiplied. The world's population grew from 1 billion in 1850 to 2 billion in 1930 to 4 billion in 1975, and will continue to grow to 14 billion by 2030.[60] This population explosion has put severe strains on the air and water resources into which we each dump our share of pollutants. These strains, moreover, have been aggravated by our tendency to concentrate our populations in urban centers. All over the world, urban areas are growing rapidly, and the high population densities urbanization has created multiplies the pollution burdens placed on air and water resources.[61]

The problems of pollution, then, have a variety of origins and their treatment requires a similarly variegated set of solutions. Our focus in what follows, however, will concentrate on a single range of problems: the ethical issues raised by pollution from commercial and industrial enterprises.

Ecological Ethics

The problem of pollution (and of environmental issues in general) is seen by some researchers as a problem that can best be framed in terms of our duty to recognize and preserve the "ecological systems" within which we live.[62] An ecological system is an interrelated and interdependent set of organisms and environments, such as a lake—in which the fish depend on small aquatic organisms, which in turn live off of decaying plant and fish waste products.[63] Because the various parts of an ecological system are interrelated, the activities of one of its parts will affect all the other parts. And because the various parts are interdependent, the survival of each part depends on the survival of the other parts. Now business firms (and all other social institutions) are parts of a larger ecological system, "spaceship earth."[64] Busi-

---

[58] Neil H. Jacoby, "The Environmental Crisis," *The Center Magazine,* 3, no. 6 (November-December 1970): 39-43.

[59] J.H. Dales, *Pollution, Property, and Prices* (Toronto: University of Toronto Press, 1968), p. 10.

[60] Gordon Taylor, *The Doomsday Book: Can the World Survive?* (New York: The World Publishing Co., 1970), p. 12.

[61] Carl J. George and Daniel McKinely, *Urban Ecology: In Search of an Asphalt Rose* (New York: McGraw-Hill Book Company, 1974).

[62] Barry Commoner, *The Closing Circle* (New York: Alfred A. Knopf, Inc., 1971), ch. 2.

[63] See Edward J. Kormondy, *Concepts of Ecology* (Englewood Cliffs, NJ: Prentice-Hall, 1969).

[64] Matthew Edel, *Economics and the Environment* (Englewood Cliffs, NJ: Prentice-Hall, Inc., 1973); for the term "Spaceship earth," see Kenneth Boulding, "The Economics of the Coming Spaceship Earth," in *Environmental Quality in a Growing Economy,* ed. Henry Jarret (Baltimore: Johns Hopkins Press for Resources for the Future, 1966).

ness firms depend upon the natural environment for their energy, material resources, and waste disposal. And that environment in turn is affected by the commercial activities of business firms. The activities of eighteenth-century European manufacturers of beaver hats, for example, led to the wholesale destruction of beavers in the United States, which in turn led to the drying up of the innumerable swamp lands that had been created by beaver dams.[65] Unless businesses recognize the interrelationships and interdependencies of the ecological systems within which they operate, and unless they ensure that their activities will not seriously injure these systems, we cannot hope to deal with the problem of pollution.

The fact that we are only a part of a larger ecological system has led some writers to insist that we should recognize our moral duty to protect the welfare not only of human beings, but also of *other nonhuman parts* of this system.[66] This insistence on the adoption of an "ecological ethic" is not based on the idea that the welfare of humans depends on the well-being of our ecological systems, but, rather, on the idea that ecological systems deserve to be preserved *for their own sake.* Thus, some writers have claimed that not only human beings, but animals, too, have moral rights.[67] Others have argued that even nonsentient objects such as trees and mountains should be recognized as having rights.[68] And still others have argued that the entire "environmental system" has a right to have its "integrity, stability, and beauty" preserved.[69]

These attempts to extend moral rights to nonhumans are, of course, highly controversial, and some authors have even labeled them "incredible."[70] But we do not have to rely on these unusual views to develop an environmental ethic. For our purposes, we need only examine two traditional approaches to environmental issues.[71] One is based on a theory of human rights, and the other is based on utilitarian considerations.

---

[65] George Perkins, *Man and Nature* (1864) (Cambridge: Harvard University Press, 1965), p. 76.

[66] For discussion and criticisms of these views, see Holmes Rolston III, "Is There an Ecological Ethic?," *Ethics,* 85, no. 2 (January 1975): 9–109; W.K. Frankena, "Ethics and the Environment," in *Ethics and Problems of the 21st Century,* K.E. Goodpaster and K.M. Sayre, eds. (Notre Dame, IN: University of Notre Dame Press, 1979), pp. 3–20; William T. Blackstone, "The Search for an Environmental Ethic," in *Matters of Life and Death,* Tom Regan, ed. (New York: Random House, Inc., 1980), pp. 299–335.

[67] Peter Singer, *Animal Liberation* (New York: Random House, Inc., 1975); *Animal Rights and Human Obligations,* Tom Regan and Peter Singer, eds. (Englewood Cliffs, NJ: Prentice-Hall, Inc., 1976).

[68] Christopher D. Stone, *Should Trees Have Standing?* (Los Altos, CA: William Kaufmann Co., 1974).

[69] Aldo Leopold, "The Land Ethic," in *A Sand Country Almanac* (New York: Oxford University Press, 1949), pp. 201–26; see also Mark Sagoff, "On Preserving the Natural Environment," *The Yale Law Journal,* vol. 84, no. 2, 1974.

[70] Frankena, "Ethics and the Environment."

[71] For a comprehensive treatment of the ethics of environmental issues, see John Passmore, *Man's Responsibility for Nature* (New York: Charles Scribner's Sons, 1974).

Environmental Rights
and Absolute Bans

In an influential article, William T. Blackstone has argued that the possession of a livable environment is not merely a *desirable* state of affairs, but something to which each human being has a *right*. [72] That is, a livable environment is not merely something that we would all like to have: It is something that others have a duty to allow us to have. They have this duty, Blackstone argues, because we each have a right to a livable environment, and our right imposes on others the correlative duty of not interfering in our exercise of that right. This is a right, moreover, which should be incorporated into our legal system.

Why do human beings have this right? According to Blackstone, a person has a moral right to a thing when possession of that thing is "essential in permitting him to live a human life (that is, in permitting him to fulfill his capacities as a rational and free being)." [73] At this time in our history, it has become clear that a livable environment is essential to the fulfillment of our human capacities. Consequently, human beings have a moral right to a decent environment, and it should become a legal right.

Moreover, Blackstone adds, this moral and legal right should override people's legal property rights. Our great and increasing ability to manipulate the environment has revealed that unless we limit the legal freedom to engage in practices that destroy the environment, we shall lose the very possibility of human life and the possibility of exercising other rights, such as the right to liberty and to equality.

Several states have introduced amendments to their constitution that grant to their citizens an "environmental right" much like Blackstone advocates. Article One of the Constitution of Pennsylvania, for example, was amended a few years ago to read:

> The people have a right to clean air, pure water, and to the preservation of the natural scenic, historic, and aesthetic values of the environment. Pennsylvania's natural resources . . . are the common property of all the people, including generations yet to come. As trustee of these resources, the commonwealth shall preserve and maintain them for the benefit of all people.

To a large extent, something like Blackstone's concept of "environmental rights" was recognized in federal law through the 1970s. [74] Section 101(b) of the National Environmental Policy Act of 1969, for example, states that one of its purposes is to "assure for all Americans safe, healthful, productive, and aesthetically

---

[72] William T. Blackstone, "Ethics and Ecology," in *Philosophy and Environmental Crisis*, William T. Blackstone, ed. (Athens, GA: University of Georgia Press, 1974).

[73] *Ibid.*, p. 31; see also, William T. Blackstone, "Equality and Human Rights," *Monist*, vol. 52, no. 4 (1968); and William T. Blackstone, "Human Rights and Human Dignity," in *Human Dignity*, Laszlo and Grotesky, eds.

[74] See William H. Rodgers, Jr., *Handbook on Environmental Law* (St. Paul, MN: West Publishing Co., 1977).

and culturally pleasing surroundings." Subsequent acts tried to achieve this purpose. The Water Pollution Control Act of 1972 required firms, by 1977, to use the "best practicable technology" to get rid of pollution (that is, technology used by several of the least polluting plants in an industry); the Clean Water Act of 1977 required that by 1984 firms must eliminate all toxic and nonconventional wastes with the use of the "best available technology" (that is, technology used by the one least polluting plant). The Air Quality Act of 1967 and the Clean Air Amendments of 1970 established similar limits to air pollution from stationary sources and automobiles, and provided the machinery for enforcing these limits. These federal laws did *not* rest on a utilitarian cost-benefit analysis. That is, they did not say that firms should reduce pollution so long as the benefits outweigh the costs; instead they simply imposed absolute bans on pollution regardless of the costs involved. Such absolute restrictions can only be justified by an appeal to people's rights.

Federal statutes in effect impose absolute limits upon the property rights of owners of firms, and Blackstone's arguments provide a plausible rationale for limiting property rights in these absolute ways for the sake of a human right to a clean environment. Blackstone's argument obviously rests on a Kantian theory of rights: Since humans have a moral duty to treat each other as ends and not as means, they have a correlative duty to respect and promote the development of another's capacity to freely and rationally choose for himself.

The main difficulty with Blackstone's view, however, is that it fails to provide any nuanced guidance on several pressing environmental choices. How much pollution control is really needed? Should we have an *absolute* ban on pollution? How far should we go in limiting property rights for the sake of the environment? What goods, if any, should we cease manufacturing in order to halt or slow environmental damage? Who should pay for the costs of preserving the environment? Blackstone's theory gives us no way of handling these questions because it imposes a simple and absolute ban on pollution.

Utilitarianism and Partial Controls

Utilitarianism provides a way of answering the questions that Blackstone's theory of environmental rights leaves unanswered. A fundamentally utilitarian approach to environmental problems is to see them as market defects. If an industry pollutes the environment, the market prices of its commodities will no longer reflect the true cost of producing the commodities; the result is a misallocation of resources, a rise in waste, and an inefficient distribution of commodities. Consequently, society as a whole is harmed as its overall economic welfare declines.[75] Utilitarians therefore argue that individuals should avoid pollution because they

---

[75] There are a number of texts describing this approach. A compact treatment is Edwin S. Mills, *The Economics of Environmental Quality* (New York: W.W. Norton & Co., Inc., 1978), ch. 3; more informational treatments can be found in *Economics of the Environment,* Robert Dorfman and Nancy Dorfman, eds. (New York: W.W. Norton & Co., Inc., 1977).

should avoid harming society's welfare.[76] The following paragraphs explain this utilitarian argument in greater detail, and explain the more nuanced approach to pollution that utilitarian cost-benefit analysis seems to provide.

Private Costs and Social Costs

Economists often distinguish between what it cost a private manufacturer to make a product and what the manufacture of that product cost society as a whole. Suppose, for example, that an electric firm consumes a certain amount of fuel, labor, and equipment to produce one kilowatt of electricity. The cost of these resources are its *private* costs: The price it must pay out of its own pocket to manufacture one kilowatt of electricity. But producing the kilowatt of electricity may also involve other "external" costs for which the firm does not pay.[77] When the firm burns fuel, for example, it may generate smoke and soot that settles on surrounding neighbors, who have to bear the costs of cleaning up the grime and of paying for any medical problems the smoke creates. From the viewpoint of society as a whole, then, the costs of producing the kilowatt of electricity include not only the "internal" costs of fuel, labor, and equipment for which the manufacturer pays, but also the "external" costs of clean-up and medical care that the neighbors pay. This *sum total* of costs (the private internal costs plus the neighbors' external costs) are the *social* costs of producing the kilowatt of electricity: the total price society must pay to manufacture one kilowatt of electricity. Of course, private costs and social costs do not always diverge as in this example: Sometimes the two coincide. If a producer pays for *all* the costs involved in manufacturing a product, for example, or if manufacturing a product imposes no external costs, then the producer's costs and the total social costs will be the same.

Thus, when a firm pollutes its environment in any way, the firm's private costs are always *less* than the total social costs involved. Whether the pollution is localized and immediate, as in the neighborhood effects described in the example above, or whether the pollution is global and long-range as in the "hot-house" effects predicted to follow from introducing too much carbon dioxide into the atmosphere, pollution always imposes "external" costs, that is, costs for which the person who produces the pollution does not have to pay. Pollution is fundamentally a problem of this divergence between private and social costs.

Why should this divergence be a problem? It is a problem because when the private costs of manufacturing a product diverge from the social costs involved in its manufacture, markets no longer price commodities accurately; consequently, they no longer allocate resources efficiently. As a result, society's welfare declines. To understand why markets become inefficient when private and social costs diverge, let us suppose that the electrical power industry is perfectly competitive (it is

---

[76] Mills, *Economics of Environmental Quality*, pp. 68–70.

[77] For a compact review of the literature on external costs, see E.J. Mishan, "The Postwar Literature on Externalities: An Interpretative Essay," *Journal of Economic Literature*, 9, no. 1 (March 1971): 1–28.

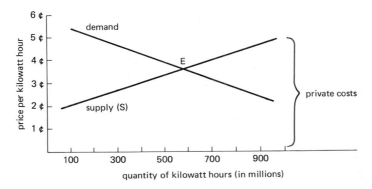

FIGURE 5-3

not, but let us suppose it is).[78] Suppose, then, that market supply curve, S, in Figure 5.3 reflects the private costs producers must pay to manufacture each kilowatt of electricity. The market price will then be at the equilibrium point E, where the supply curve based on these private costs crosses the demand curve.

In the hypothetical situation in Figure 5.3, the curves intersect at the market price of 3.5 cents and at an output of 600 million kilowatt hours. But suppose that besides the private costs that producers incur in manufacturing electricity, the manufacture of electricity also imposes "external" costs on their neighbors in the form of environmental pollution. If these external costs were added to the private costs of producers, then a new supply curve, S', would result that would take into account all the costs of manufacturing each kilowatt hour of electricity, as in Figure 5.4.

The new supply curve in Figure 5.4, S', which is above the supply curve, S (which includes only the manufacturers' private costs), shows the quantities of electricity that would be supplied if all the costs of producing the electricity were taken into account, and the prices that would have to be charged for each kilowatt hour if all costs were thus taken into account. As the new curve, S', indicates, when all the costs are taken into account, the market price of the commodity, 4.5 cents, will be *higher,* and the output, 350 million kilowatt hours, will be *lower,* than when only private costs are incorporated. Thus, when *only* private costs are taken into account the electricity is *underpriced* and it is *overproduced.* And this in turn means that the electricity market is no longer allocating resources and distributing commodities so as to maximize utility. Three deficiencies, in particular, can be noted.

First, allocation of resources in markets that do not take all costs into account is not optimal, because from the point of view of society as a whole, more of the commodity is being produced than society would demand if society had availa-

[78] Not only is the electrical power industry completely monopolized, but in the short run, at least, demand is relatively inelastic. Over the *long run* demand may have the more elastic characteristics we assume in the example.

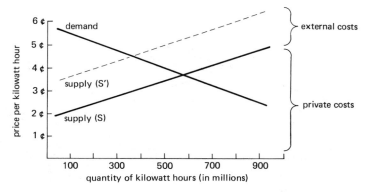

FIGURE 5-4

ble an accurate measure of what it is actually paying to produce the commodity. Since the commodity is being overproduced, more of society's resources are being consumed to produce the commodity than is optimal. The resources being consumed by overproduction of the commodity are resources that could be used to produce other commodities for which there would be greater demand if prices accurately reflected costs. Resources are thereby being misallocated.

Secondly, when external costs are not taken into account by producers, producers ignore these costs and make no attempt to minimize them. So long as the firm does not have to pay for external costs, it has no incentive to use technology that might decrease or eliminate them. Consequently, the resources being consumed by these external costs (such as clean air) are being unnecessarily wasted. There may be technologically feasible ways of producing the same commodities without imposing as many external costs, but the producer will make no attempt to find them.

Thirdly, when the production of a commodity imposes external costs on third parties, goods are no longer efficiently distributed to consumers. External costs introduce effective price differentials into markets: Everyone does not pay equal prices for the same commodities. The neighbors who live near our imaginary electric plant, for example, pay not only the prices the plant charges everyone else for electricity, but also the costs the smoke from the burning fuel imposes on them in the form of extra cleaning bills, medical bills, painting bills, etc. Because they must pay for these extra external costs, of course, they have fewer funds to pay for their share of market commodities. Consequently, their share of goods is not proportioned to their desires and needs as compared to the shares of those who do not have to pay the extra external costs.

Pollution, then, imposes "external costs" and this in turn means that the private costs of production are less than the social costs. As a consequence, markets do not impose an optimal discipline on producers, and the result is a drop in social utility. Pollution of the environment, then, is a violation of the utilitarian principles that underlie a market system.

Remedies: The Duties of the Firm

The remedy for external costs, according to the utilitarian argument sketched above, is to ensure that the costs of pollution are internalized, that is, that they are absorbed by the producer and taken into account when determining the price of his goods.[79] In this way goods will be accurately priced, market forces will provide the incentives that will encourage producers to minimize external costs, and some consumers will no longer end up paying more than others for the same commodities.

There are various ways of internalizing the external costs of pollution. One way is for the polluting agent to pay to all of those being harmed, voluntarily or by law, an amount equal to the costs the pollution imposes on them. When Union Oil's drilling in the Santa Barbara channel on the California coast led to an oil spill, the total costs that the spill imposed on local residents and on state and federal agencies were estimated at about $16,400,000 (including costs of cleanup, containment, administration, damage to tourism and fishing, recreational and property damages, and loss of marine life).[80] Union Oil paid about $10,400,000 of these costs voluntarily by paying for all cleanup and containment of the oil, and it paid about $6,300,000 in damages to the affected parties as the result of litigation.[81] Thus, the costs of the oil spill were "internalized," in part through voluntary action and in part through legal action. When the polluting firm pays those on whom its manufacturing processes impose costs, as Union Oil did, it is led to figure these costs into its own subsequent price determinations. Market mechanisms then lead it to come up with ways of cutting down pollution in order to cut down its costs. Since the Santa Barbara oil spill, for example, Union Oil and other petroleum firms have invested considerable amounts of money in developing methods to minimize pollution damage from oil spills.

A problem with this way of internalizing the costs of pollution, however, is that when several polluters are involved, it is not always clear just who is being damaged by whom. How much of the environmental damage caused by several polluters should be counted as damages to my property and how much should be counted as damages to your property, when the damages are inflicted on things such as air or public bodies of water, and for how much of the damage should each polluter be held responsible? Moreover, the administrative and legal costs of assessing damages for each distinct polluter and of granting separate compensations to each distinct claimant can become substantial.

A second remedy is for the polluter to stop pollution at its source by installing pollution-control devices. In this way, the external costs of polluting the environment are translated into the internal costs the firm itself pays to install pollution

[79] See E.J. Mishan, *Economics for Social Decisions* (New York: Praeger Publishers, Inc., 1973), pp. 85 ff.

[80] Walter J. Mead and Philip E. Sorensen, "The Economic Cost of the Santa Barbara Oil Spill," paper presented to the *Santa Barbara Oil Symposium*, University of California, Santa Barbara, December 1970.

[81] S. Prakash Sethi, *Up Against the Corporate Wall* (Englewood Cliffs, NJ: Prentice-Hall, Inc., 1977), p. 21.

controls. Once costs are internalized in this way, market mechanisms again provide cost-cutting incentives and ensure that prices reflect the true costs of producing the commodity. In addition, the installation of pollution-control devices serves to eliminate the long-range and potentially disastrous worldwide effects of pollution.

Justice

This utilitarian way of dealing with pollution (that is, by internalizing costs) seems to be consistent with the requirements of distributive justice insofar as distributive justice favors equality. Observers have noted that pollution often has the effect of increasing inequality.[82] If a firm pollutes, its stockholders benefit because their firm does not have to absorb the external costs of pollution and this leaves them with greater profits, and those customers who purchase the firm's products also benefit because the firm does not charge them for all the costs involved in making the product. The *beneficiaries* of pollution, therefore, tend to be those who can afford to buy a firm's stock and its products. On the other hand, the external *costs* of pollution are borne largely by the poor.[83] Property values in polluted neighborhoods are generally lower, and consequently they are inhabited by the poor and abandoned by the wealthy. Pollution, therefore, may produce a net flow of benefits away from the poor and toward the well-off, thereby increasing inequality. To the extent that this occurs, pollution violates distributive justice. Internalizing the costs of pollution, as utilitarianism requires, would rectify matters by removing the burdens of external costs from the backs of the poor and placing them in the hands of the wealthy: the firm's stockholders and its customers. By and large, therefore, the utilitarian claim that the external costs of pollution should be internalized is consistent with the requirements of distributive justice.

We should note, however, that if a firm makes basic goods (food products, clothing, gasoline, automobiles) for which the poor must allocate a larger proportion of their budgets than the affluent, then internalizing costs may place a heavier burden on the poor than on the affluent, because the prices of these basic goods will rise. The poor may also suffer if the costs of pollution control rise so high that unemployment results (although current studies indicate that the unemployment effects of pollution-control programs are transitory and minimal).[84] There is some rudimentary evidence that tends to show that current pollution-control measures place greater burdens on the poor than on the wealthy.[85] This suggests the need to integrate distributional criteria into our pollution-control programs.

Internalizing external costs also seems to be consistent with the requirements of retributive and compensatory justice.[86] Retributive justice requires that those

---

[82] See Mishan, "The Postwar Literature on Externalities," p. 24.

[83] William J. Baumal and Wallace E. Oates, *Economics, Environmental Policy, and the Quality of Life* (Englewood Cliffs, NJ: Prentice-Hall, Inc., 1979), p. 177.

[84] *Ibid.,* pp. 180–82.

[85] *Ibid.,* pp. 182–84.

[86] Mishan, "The Postwar Literature on Externalities," p. 24.

who are responsible for and who benefit from an injury should bear the burdens of rectifying the injury, while compensatory justice requires that those who have been injured should be compensated by those who injure them. Taken together, these requirements imply that (1) the costs of pollution control should be borne by those who cause pollution and who have benefited from pollution activities, while (2) the benefits of pollution control should flow to those who have had to bear the external costs of pollution. Internalizing external costs seems to meet these two requirements: (1) The costs of pollution control are borne by stockholders and by customers, both of whom benefit from the polluting activities of the firm, and (2) the benefits of pollution control flow to those neighbors who once had to put up with the firm's pollution.

Costs and Benefits

The technology for pollution control has developed effective but costly methods for abating pollution. Up to 60 percent of water pollutants can be removed through "primary" screening and sedimentation processes; up to 90 percent can be removed through more expensive "secondary" biological and chemical processes; and amounts over 95 percent can be removed through even more expensive "tertiary" chemical treatment.[87] Air pollution abatement techniques include: the use of fuels and combustion procedures that burn more cleanly; mechanical filters that screen or isolate dust particles in the air; "scrubbing" processes that pass polluted air through liquids that remove pollutants; and chemical treatment that transforms gases into more easily removed compounds.[88]

It is possible, however, for a firm to invest *too much* in pollution control devices. Suppose, for example, that the pollution from a certain firm causes $100 worth of environmental damage, and suppose that the only device that can eliminate this pollution would cost the firm at least $1,000. Then, obviously, the firm should not install the device, for if it does so, the economic utility of society will decline: The costs of eliminating the pollution will be greater than the benefits society will reap, thereby resulting in a shrinkage of total utility.

How much should a firm invest in pollution control, then? Consider that the costs of controlling pollution and the benefits derived from pollution control are inversely related.[89] As one rises, the other falls. Why is this so? Think for a moment that if a body of water is highly polluted, it will probably be quite easy and consequently quite cheap to filter out a certain limited amount of pollutants. To filter out a few more pollutants, however, will require finer and therefore additional and more expensive filters. Costs will keep climbing for each additional level of purity desired, and getting out the last few molecules of impurities would require astronomically expensive additional equipment. However, getting out those last traces of

[87] Mills, *Economics of Environmental Quality*, pp. 111–12.

[88] Frederick D. Sturdivant, *Business and Society* (Homewood, IL: Richard D. Irwin, Inc., 1977), p. 307.

[89] See Mills, *Economics of Environmental Quality*, pp. 83–91.

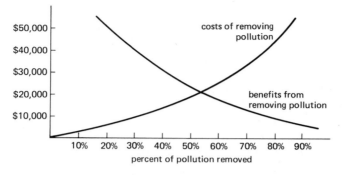

FIGURE 5-5

impurities will probably not matter much to people and will therefore be unnecessary. At the other end of the scale, however, getting rid of the first gross amounts of pollutants will be highly beneficial to people: The costs of damages from these pollutants are substantial. Consequently, if we plot as curves on a graph the costs of removing pollution and the benefits of removing pollution (which are equivalent to the external costs removed) the result will be two intersecting curves as illustrated in Figure 5.5. What is the optimal amount of pollution control? Obviously, the point at which the two lines cross. At this point, the costs of pollution control exactly equal its benefits. If the firm invests additional resources in removing pollution, society's net utility will decline. Beyond this point, the firm should resort to directly or indirectly (that is, through taxes or other forms of social investment) paying society for the costs of polluting the environment.

To enable the firm to make such cost-benefit analyses, researchers have devised an array of theoretical methods and techniques for calculating the costs and benefits of removing pollution. These make use of estimates of consumer surplus, rents, market prices and "shadow prices," adjustment for "transfers," discounted future values, and recognition of risk factors.[90] Thomas Klein summarizes the procedures for cost-benefit analysis as follows:

1. Identify costs and benefits of the proposed program and the person or sectors incurring or receiving them. Trace transfers.
2. Evaluate the costs and benefits in terms of their value to beneficiaries and donors. The standard of measure is the value of each marginal unit to demanders and suppliers ideally captured in competitive prices. Useful refinements involve:
   a. Incorporating time values through the use of a discount rate.
   b. Recognizing risk by factoring possible outcomes according to probabilities and, where dependent, probability trees.
3. Add up costs and benefits to determine the net social benefit of a project or program.[91]

[90] See E.J. Mishan, *Cost-Benefit Analysis: An Introduction* (New York: Praeger Publishers, Inc., 1971).

[91] Thomas A. Klein, *Social Costs and Benefits of Business* (Englewood Cliffs, NJ: Prentice-Hall, Inc., 1977), p. 118.

In order to avoid "erratic" and "costly" use of these procedures, Klein recommends that firms introduce a system of "social accounting" that "routinely measures, records, and reports external effects to management and other parties."[92]

It is at this point, however, that a fundamental difficulty in the utilitarian approach to pollution emerges. The cost-benefit analyses just described assume that the costs and benefits of reducing pollution can be accurately measured.[93] In some cases (limited and local in character) cost-benefit measurements are available: The costs and benefits of cleaning up the oil spilled by Union Oil at Santa Barbara, for example, were more or less measurable. But the costs and benefits of pollution removal are difficult to measure when they involve damages to human health and loss of life: What is the price of life?[94]

Measurement is also difficult when the effects of pollution are uncertain and, consequently, difficult to predict: What will be the effects of increasing the carbon dioxide content of our atmosphere by burning more coal, as the United States is now starting to do? In fact, perhaps the major problem involved in obtaining the measurements needed to apply cost-benefit analysis to pollution problems is the problem of estimating and evaluating *risk* (that is, the probability of future costly consequences).[95] Many new technologies carry with them unknown degrees of risk to present and future generations. The use of nuclear technology, for example, involves some probability of damages to health and loss of life for present and future generations: There are the risks of health damages from mining and the use and disposal of radioactive materials, plus the risks of sabotage and of a proliferation of the materials used in atomic weapons. But there are insurmountable obstacles in the way of measuring these risks accurately. We cannot use trial and error (a usual method for learning what the probabilities of an event are) to learn the risk, for example, of a nuclear accident, since the lesson would obviously be too costly and some of the health effects of radioactivity would not appear until decades after it is too late to correct them. Moreover, the mathematical models that we must rely on to measure risk in the absence of trial and error learning are not useful when all the possible things that can go wrong with a technology are not known. Human error, carelessness, and malice have been involved in most nuclear mishaps. The human factor is notoriously impossible to predict, and therefore impossible to incorporate into a measurement of the risks associated with using nuclear power. Moreover, even if the numerical risk associated with a new technology were known, it is unclear how much weight it should be given in a social cost-benefit analysis. Imagine, for example, that society currently accepts with some indifference a .01 risk of death

---

[92] *Ibid.*, p. 119; the literature on social accounting for business firms is vast; see U.S. Department of Commerce, *Corporate Social Reporting in the United States and Western Europe* (Washington, DC: U.S. Government Printing Office, 1979); Committee on Social Measurement, *The Measurement of Corporate Social Performance* (New York: American Institute of Certified Public Accountants, Inc., 1977).

[93] See Boyd Collier, *Measurement of Environmental Deterioration* (August, TX: Bureau of Business Research, The University of Texas at Austin, 1971).

[94] See Michael D. Boyles, "The Price of Life," *Ethics*, 89, no. 1 (October 1978): 20–34; Mishan, *Economics for Social Decisions*, pp. 101–8.

[95] Much of the material in this and the following paragraphs is based on the superb analysis in Robert E. Goodwin, "No Moral Nukes," *Ethics*, 90, no. 3 (April 1980): 417–49.

associated with driving. Does it then follow that society also should be indifferent to accepting a .01 risk of death from the introduction of a certain new technology? Obviously not, because risk is cumulative: The new technology will *double* society's risk of death to .02, and while society may be indifferent to carrying a .01 risk of death, it may find a .02 risk unacceptable. Knowing the risk of a certain costly future event does not, then, necessarily tell us the value that society will place on that risk once it is added to the other risks society already runs. And, to make matters worse, individuals differ substantially in their aversion to risk: Some individuals *like* to gamble while others find it extremely distasteful.

The almost insurmountable problems involved in getting accurate pollution measurements are illustrated by the lack of any federal estimates of the *benefits* produced by pollution control activities.[96] The present financial *costs* of pollution control are fairly easy to obtain by examining reports on expenditures for pollution equipment. Total 1978 expenditures for pollution control, including government and private expenditures, were $46.7 billion.[97] But the *benefits* associated with these expenditures have never been accurately measured. The federal government estimated that the annual benefits from air pollution control alone were approximately $21.4 billion in 1978, and earlier studies had estimated the annual benefits of water pollution control alone would be $12.3 billion by 1978.[98] But these estimates are based on exceedingly unreliable methodologies and deliberately omit many of the effects of pollution, especially long-range global effects such as the effects of carbon dioxide build-up and ozone depletion, as well as the health benefits from the elimination of chemical contamination in drinking water.

The problems involved in getting accurate measurements of the benefits of pollution control are also illustrated by the difficulties businesses have encountered in trying to construct a "social audit" (a report of the social costs and social benefits of the firm's activities). Those who advocate that a corporation should measure and report the social impacts of its activities have been forced to "recognize that the goal of measuring all impacts of all actions upon all conditions and all publics, using standard techniques and units, considerably exceeds current capabilities and that compromises and modifications are inevitable."[99] Due to this inability to measure benefits, so-called "social audits" are usually nothing more than qualitative descriptions of what a firm is doing. But without definite quantitative measurements of the benefits deriving from its attempts to reduce pollution, a firm has no way of knowing whether its efforts are cost-effective from a social point of view.

These failures of measurement pose significant technical problems for utilitarian approaches to pollution. In addition, the use of utilitarian cost-benefit analysis is sometimes based on assumptions that are inconsistent with people's moral

[96] Council on Environmental Quality, *Environmental Quality*, eighth annual report (Washington DC: U.S. Government Printing Office, 1979), pp. 323–25.

[97] Council of Environmental Quality, *Environmental Quality–1979*, p. 667.

[98] *Ibid.*, p. 655.

[99] Committee on Social Measurement, *The Measurement of Corporate Social Performance*, p. 31.

rights. Advocates of utilitarian cost-benefit analysis sometimes assume that if the benefits of a certain technology or manufacturing process "clearly" outweigh its costs, then it is morally permissible to impose the process on unwilling citizens. A recent government report, for example, makes the following recommendations:

> Because nuclear problems are such highly emotional issues and becoming even more so, as evidenced by the states that have indicated an unwillingness to permit nuclear waste disposal within their boundaries, it may be impossible to get the public and political support necessary for a given state to accept nuclear waste. Ultimately, if state approval for waste repository sites cannot be obtained within an established time, the federal government might have to mandate selections. While such action would not be easy it may be necessary if the waste problem is to be solved in a reasonable time.[100]

But recommendations of this type seem to violate the basic moral right that underlies democratic societies: Persons have a moral right to be treated only as they have consented to be treated beforehand (see Chapter Two, second section). If people have not consented to take on the costs of a technology (and indicate this unwillingness, for example, through local legislation, hearings, or opinion surveys), then their moral right of consent is violated when these costs are imposed on them anyway. Using only cost-benefit analysis to determine whether a new technology or manufacturing process should be used, then, ignores the question of whether the costs involved are *voluntarily* accepted by those who must bear them, or whether they are unilaterally *imposed* on them by others.

It should be noted that although the right of consent seems to imply that decisions concerning pollution control always should be left in the hands of the ordinary citizen, this implication is not necessarily correct. For people can give their informed consent to a risky project only if they have an adequate understanding of the project and its attendant risks. But contemporary technology is often so complex that even experts disagree when estimating and assessing the risks it may involve (scientists disagree wildly, for example, over the safety of using nuclear power). So it may be impossible for ordinary citizens to understand and assess the risks that a certain polluting technology will impose on them, and, consequently, it may be impossible, in principle, for them to give their informed consent to it.

In view of all the problems raised by utilitarian approaches to pollution, then, it may be that alternative approaches are more adequate. In particular, it may be that the absolute bans on pollution which are currently incorporated in federal laws, and the rights theory on which these absolute bans rest, are, for the present at least, a more adequate approach to pollution issues than utilitarianism. Alternatively, some writers have suggested that when risks cannot be reliably estimated it is best to choose only those projects that carry no risk of irreversible damages. For example, if there is a probability that the pollution from a certain technology may bring about catastrophic consequences that will continue to plague us forever, then

---

[100] U.S. General Accounting Office, *The Nation's Nuclear Waste* (Washington, DC: U.S. Printing Office, 1979), p. 12.

the technology should be rejected in favor of other technologies that will not close off our options in the same permanent way. Others suggest that when risks cannot be assessed, we should, in justice, identify those who are most vulnerable and who would have to bear the heaviest costs if things should go wrong, and then take steps to ensure that they are protected. Future generations and children, for example, should be protected against our polluting choices. Finally, others suggest that when risks cannot be measured, the only rational procedure is to first assume that the worst will happen and then choose the option that will leave us best off when the worst happens (this is the so-called "maximin rule" of probability theory). It is unclear which of these alternative approaches should be adopted when utilitarian cost-benefit analysis fails.

5.3 THE ETHICS OF CONSERVING DEPLETABLE RESOURCES

Conservation refers to the saving or rationing of natural resources for later uses. Conservation, therefore, looks primarily to the future: To the need to limit consumption now in order to have resources available for tomorrow.

In a sense, pollution control is a form of conservation. Pollution "consumes" pure air and water, and pollution control "conserves" them for the future. But there are basic differences between the problems of pollution and the problems of *resource depletion* that make the term "conservation" more applicable to the latter problems than to the former. With some notable exceptions (such as nuclear wastes), most forms of pollution affect present generations and their control will benefit present generations. The depletion of most scarce resources, however, lies far in the future, and the effects of their depletion will be felt primarily by posterity, and not by present generations. Consequently, our concern over the depletion of resources is primarily a concern for *future* generations and for the benefits that will be available to them. For this reason, conservation is more applicable to the problems of resource depletion than to those of pollution.[101] Moreover (again with notable exceptions), pollution is a problem concerned primarily with "renewable" resources, insofar as air and water can be "renewed" by ceasing to dump pollutants into them and allowing them time to recover. Tomorrow's supply, therefore, will be created anew over and over if we take the proper precautions. Resource depletion, however, is concerned with finite, nonrenewable resources. And the only store of a finite, nonrenewable resource that will be around tomorrow is that which is left over from today. Conservation, therefore, is the only way of ensuring a supply for tomorrow's generations.

Resource depletion forces two main kinds of questions on us, then: First, why ought we to conserve resources for future generations, and second, how much should we conserve?

---

[101] Passmore, *Man's Responsibility for Nature*, p. 74.

Rights of Future Generations

It might appear that we have an obligation to conserve resources for future generations because they have an equal right to the limited resources of this planet. And if future generations have an equal right to the world's resources, then by depleting these resources, we are taking what is actually theirs and violating their equal right to these resources.

A number of writers, however, have claimed that it is a mistake to think that future generations have rights.[102] It is a mistake, consequently, to think that we should refrain from consuming natural resources because we are taking what future generations have a right to. Three main reasons have been advanced to show that future generations cannot have rights.

First, future generations cannot intelligently be said to have rights because they do not now exist and may never exist.[103] I may be able to *think* about future people, but I cannot hit them, punish them, injure them, or treat them wrongly. Future people exist only in the imagination, and imaginary entities cannot be acted upon in any way whatsoever except in imagination. Similarly, we cannot say that future people possess things now, when they do not yet exist to possess or have them. Since there is a possibility that future generations may never exist, they cannot "possess" rights.

Secondly, if future generations did have rights, then we might be led to the absurd conclusion that we must sacrifice our entire civilization for their sake.[104] Suppose that each of the infinite number of future generations had an equal right to the world's supply of oil. Then we would have to divide the oil equally among them all, and our share would be a few quarts at the most. We would then be put in the absurd position of having to shut down our entire Western civilization in order that each future person might be able to possess a few quarts of oil.

Thirdly, we can say that someone has a certain right only if we know that he or she has a certain interest which that right protects. The purpose of a right, after all, is to protect the interests of the right-holder. But we are virtually ignorant of what interests future generations will have. What wants will they have? The men and women of the future may be genetically fabricated to order, with desires, pleasures, and needs vastly different from our own. What kinds of resources will future technology require for supplying their wants? Science might come up with technologies for creating products from raw materials that we have in abundance—minerals in sea water, for example—and might find potentially unlimited energy sources such as nuclear fusion. Moreover, future generations might develop cheap and plentiful substitutes for the scarce resources that we now need. Since we are uncertain about these matters, we must remain ignorant about the interests future

---

[102] Martin Golding, "Obligations to Future Generations," *Monist,* 56, no. 1 (1972): 85–99; Richard T. DeGeorge, "The Environment, Rights, and Future Generations," in *Ethics and Problems of the 21st Century,* K.E. Goodpaster and K.M. Sayre, eds., pp. 93–105.

[103] DeGeorge, "The Environment, Rights, and Future Generations," pp. 97–98.

[104] *Ibid.*

generations will want to protect (who could have guessed eighty years ago that uranium rocks would one day be considered a "resource" in which people would have an interest?). Consequently, we are unable to say what rights future people might have.[105]

If these arguments are correct, then to the extent that we are uncertain what future generations will exist or what they will be like, they do not have any rights. It does not follow, however, that we have no obligations to any future generations since our obligations may be based on other grounds.

Justice to Future Generations

John Rawls argues that while it is unjust to impose disproportionately heavy burdens on present generations for the sake of future generations, it is also unjust for present generations to leave nothing for future generations. To determine a just way of distributing resources between generations, he suggests, the members of each generation should put themselves in the "original position" and, without knowing what generation they belong to, they should

> . . . ask what is reasonable for members of adjacent generations to expect of one another at each level of (historical) advance. They should try to piece together a just savings schedule by balancing how much at each stage (of history) they would be willing to save for their immediate descendants against what they would feel entitled to claim of their immediate predecessors. Thus imagining themselves to be parents, say, they are to ascertain how much they would set aside for their children by noting what they would believe themselves entitled to claim of their own parents.[106]

In general, Rawls claims, this method of ascertaining what earlier generations in justice owe to later generations will lead to the conclusion that what justice demands of us is merely that we hand to the next generation a situation on which we have improved, just as we received from the generation before us a situation on which they had improved:

> Each generation must not only preserve the gains of culture and civilization, and maintain intact those just institutions that have been established, but it must also put aside in each period of time a suitable amount of real capital accumulation. . . . (It should be kept in mind here that capital is not only factories, and machines, and so on, but also the knowledge and culture, as well as the techniques and skills, that make possible just institutions and the fair value of liberty.) This . . . is in return for what is received from previous generations that enables the later ones to enjoy better life in a more just society.[107]

---

[105] Golding, "Obligations to Future Generations," p. 99.

[106] John Rawls, *A Theory of Justice* (Cambridge: Harvard University Press, 1971), p. 289.

[107] *Ibid.*, pp. 285 and 288.

Justice, then, requires that we hand over to our immediate successors a world that is not in worse condition than the one we received from our ancestors.

This condition is reinforced by some basic utilitarian principles. Utilitarians have argued that each generation has a duty to maximize the future beneficial consequences of its actions and to minimize their future injurious consequences.[108] However, utilitarians have claimed, these future consequences should be "discounted" (given less weight) in proportion to their uncertainty and to their distance in the future.[109] Together, these utilitarian principles imply that we at least have an obligation to avoid those practices whose harmful consequences for the generation that immediately follows us are certain to outweigh the beneficial consequences our own generation derives from them. Our responsibility for more distant future generations, however, is diminished, especially insofar as we are unable to foresee what effects our present actions will have on them because we do not know what needs or technology they will have.

Unfortunately, we cannot rely on market mechanisms (that is, price rises) to ensure that scarce resources are conserved for future generations.[110] The market registers only the effective demands of present participants and the actual supplies presently being made available. The needs and demands of future generations, as well as the potential scarcities that lie far in the future, are so heavily "discounted" by markets that they hardly affect prices at all.[111] William Shepherd and Clair Wilcox provide a summary of the reasons that the private choices represented in markets and market prices fail to take into account the future scarcity of resources:

1. *Multiple access* If a resource can be used by several separate extractors, then the shared access will invariably lead the resource to be depleted too fast. . . . As with several people with straws in one milkshake, each owner's private interest is in taking it out as fast as possible. . . .

2. *Time preferences and myopia* Firms often have short time horizons, under the stress of commercial competition. This may underrepresent the legitimate interests of future generations. . . .

3. *Inadequate forecasting* Present users may simply fail to foresee future developments. This may reflect a lack of sufficient research interest and ability to discern future changes. . . .

4. *Special influences* Specific taxes and other incentive devices may encourage overly rapid use of resources. . . .

---

[108] J. Brenton Stearns, "Ecology and the Indefinite Unborn," *The Monist,* 56, no. 4 (October 1972): 612–625; Jan Narveson, "Utilitarianism and New Generations," *Mind,* 76 (1967): 62–67.

[109] Robert Scott, Jr., "Environmental Ethics and Obligations to Future Generations," in *Obligations to Future Generations,* R.I. Sikora and Brian Barry, eds. (Philadelphia: Temple University Press, 1978), pp. 74–90.

[110] Passmore, *Man's Responsibility for Nature,* p. 85.

[111] Joan Robinson, *Economic Philosophy* (London: Penguin Books, 1966), p. 115.

5. *External effects* There are important externalities in the uses of many re-sources, so that private users ignore major degrees of pollution and other external costs. . . .

6. *Distribution* Finally, private market decisions are based on the existing pattern of distribution of wealth and income. As resource users vote with their dollars, market demand will more strongly reflect the interests and preferences of the wealthy.[112]

The only means of conserving for the future, then, appear to be voluntary (or politically enforced) policies of conservation.

In practical terms, Rawls's view implies that while we should not sacrifice the cultural advances we have made, we should adopt voluntary or legal measures to conserve those resources and environmental benefits that we can reasonably assume our immediate posterity will need if they are to live lives with a variety of available choices comparable, at least, to ours. In particular, this would mean that we should preserve wildlife and endangered species; that we should take steps to ensure that the rate of consumption of fossil fuels and of minerals does not continue to rise; that we should cut down our consumption and production of those goods that depend on nonrenewable resources; that we should recycle nonrenewable resources; that we should search for substitutes for materials that we are too rapidly depleting.

Several General Motors programs of 1978 provide illustrations of the kinds of business policies that can embody these principles. The General Motors "social audit" for 1978 included the following description of its energy saving programs:

GM conservation efforts reduced the amount of energy used to build each vehicle by over 22 percent. Although some of these savings result from higher production volume, 16 percent comes directly from conservation programs. . . . Plant engineering and development groups are focusing on projects to reduce the energy used in [those operations which require the most energy]. Some examples:

—A pilot coal-gasification system has been installed at the Saginaw Steering Gear Division to evaluate the effectiveness of coal gas, both as a basic industrial fuel and for heat treating and paint drying.
—Methane gas from municipal wastes is being investigated as a potential supplemental fuel for operations which now must exclusively use natural gas.
—Several programs are underway to improve the energy efficiency of the melting cupolas in iron foundries. . . .
—Improved exhaust-air filtration systems being developed will remove particulates and allow recirculation of warm air into a plant, reducing the need to heat make-up air.[113]

---

[112] William G. Shepherd and Clair Wilcox, *Public Policies Toward Business,* 6th ed. (Homewood, IL: Richard D. Irwin, Inc., 1979), pp. 524–25.
[113] *1979 General Motors Public Interest Report* (New York: General Motors Corp., 1979), pp. 52–53.

Economic Growth?

But to many observers conservation measures fall far short of what is needed. Several writers have argued that if we are to preserve enough scarce resources that future generations can maintain their quality of life at a satisfactory level, we shall have to change our economies substantially, particularly by scaling down our pursuit of economic growth. E.F. Schumacher, for example, claims that the industrialized nations will have to convert from growth-oriented capital-intensive technologies to much more labor-intensive technologies in which humans do work machines now do.[114] Others argue that economic systems will have to abandon their goal of steadily increasing production, and put in its place the goal of decreasing production until it has been scaled down to "a steady state," that is, a point at which "the total population and the total stock of physical wealth are maintained constant at some desired levels by a 'minimal' rate of maintenance throughout (that is, by birth and death rates that are equal at the lowest feasible level, and by physical production and consumption rates that are equal at the lowest feasible level)."[115] The conclusion that economic growth must be abandoned if society is to be able to deal with the problems of diminishing resources has been challenged.[116] But it is at least arguable that adherence to continual economic growth promises to degrade the quality of life of future generations.[117]

The arguments for this claim are simple and stark. If the world's economies continue to pursue the goal of economic growth, the demand for depletable resources will continue to rise. But since world resources are finite, at some point supplies will simply run out. At this point, if the world's nations are still based on growth economies, we can expect a collapse of their major economic institutions (that is, of manufacturing and financial institutions, communication networks, the service industries) which in turn will bring down their political and social institutions (that is, centralized governments, education and cultural programs, scientific and technological development, health care).[118] Living standards will then decline precipitously in the wake of widespread starvation and political dislocations. Various scenarios for this sequence of events have been constructed, all of them more or less speculative and necessarily based on uncertain assumptions.[119] The most famous of these are the studies of the Club of Rome which has projected on computers the

[114] E.F. Schumacher, *Small is Beautiful* (London: Blond and Briggs, Ltd., 1973).

[115] Herman E. Daly, ed., *Toward A Steady-state Economy* (San Francisco: W.H. Freeman, 1974), p. 152; see also Robert L. Stirers, *The Sustainable Society: Ethics and Economic Growth* (Philadelphia: Westminster Press, 1976).

[116] See, for example, Wilfred Beckerman, *In Defense of Economic Growth* (London: Jonathan Cape, 1974); Rudolph Klein, "The Trouble with Zero Economic Growth," *New York Review of Books* (April 1974).

[117] E.J. Mishan, *The Economic Growth Debate: An Assessment* (London: George Allen & Unwin Ltd., 1977).

[118] See Davis, *The Seventh Year.*

[119] Several of these scenarios are reviewed in James Just and Lester Lave, "Review of Scenarios of Future U.S. Energy Use," *Annual Review of Energy,* 4 (1979): 501–36.

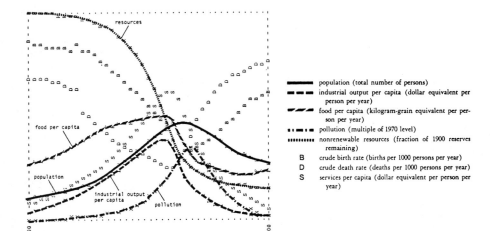

population (total number of persons)

industrial output per capita (dollar equivalent per
person per year)

food per capita (kilogram-grain equivalent per person per year)

pollution (multiple of 1970 level)

nonrenewable resources (fraction of 1900 reserves
remaining)

B   crude birth rate (births per 1000 persons per year)

D   crude death rate (deaths per 1000 persons per year)

S   services per capita (dollar equivalent per person per
year)

*The "standard" world model run assumes no major change in the physical,
economic, or social relationships that have historically governed the development of the world system. All variables plotted here follow historical
values from 1900 to 1970. Food, industrial output, and population grow
exponentially until the rapidly diminishing resource base forces a slowdown
in industrial growth. Because of natural delays in the system, both population and pollution continue to increase for some time after the peak of
industrialization. Population growth is finally halted by a rise in the death
rate due to decreased food and medical services.*

Figure 5.6 is from Donella H. Meadows et al., THE LIMITS TO GROWTH (New York: Universe
Books, 1974), pp. 123–24. Reprinted by permission of Universe Books.

FIGURE 5-6

results of continuing the economic growth patterns of the past, in the face of declining resources.[120] Figure 5.6 reproduces one of these computer projections.

In the computer-based graph of Figure 5.6, the horizontal axis represents
time, so that as we run from the year A.D. 1900 at the left, to the year A.D. 2100
at the right, we see what will happen to the world's population, industrial output,
food, pollution levels, nonrenewable resources, and so on, as time passes. During
the first half of the 1900s, population, output, food, and services continue to grow
while death rates, birth rates, and resources decline. At some point after 1950, however, a sudden and catastrophic collapse of output and services occurs as resources
suddenly run out. Population continues to rise, but a climbing death rate and declining food supply soon brings it down. The decline in industrial output causes a decline in pollution, but food supplies, industrial output, and population by 2100 are
below 1900 levels. "We can thus say with some confidence that, under the assumption of no major change in the present system, population and industrial
growth will certainly stop within the next century at the latest."[121]

The assumptions on which these doomsday scenarios are based have been sub-

[120]Meadows, Meadows, Randers, and Behrens, *The Limits to Growth* (New York:
Universe Books, 1974).

[121]*Ibid.*, p. 132.

jected to intense criticisms.[122] The computer programs and underlying equations on which the predictions are based make controversial assumptions about future population growth rates, the absence of future increases in output per unit of input, our inability to find substitutes for depleted resources, and the ineffectiveness of recyling. These assumptions can all be challenged. Although future generations will certainly have fewer of the natural resources on which we depend, we cannot be sure exactly what impact this will have on them. Probably the impact will not be as catastrophic as the initial prognostications of the Club of Rome indicated.[123] But we also cannot assume that the impact will be entirely benign.[124] Given this situation, at the very least a commitment to conservation seems to be in order. Whether a wholesale transformation of our economy is also necessary if civilization is to survive is a difficult and disturbing question that we may soon have to face.

Just as troubling are the moral questions raised by the distribution of dwindling energy supplies among the world's peoples. As is well known, and as the data in Table 5.3 confirm, the United States is the world's richest nation and the highest consumer of energy. The 6 percent of the world's population that lives within the United States consumes 35 percent of the world's annual energy supplies, while the 50 percent of the world's people who inhabit less developed nations must get along with about 8 percent of its energy supplies. Each person in the United States, in fact, consumes fifteen times more energy than a native South American, twenty-four times more than a native Asian, and thirty-one times more than a native African.

The high energy consumption rates of Americans are not paralleled by similarly high rates of energy production. As the data in Table 5.4 indicate, United States energy consumption is subsidized by other countries, in particular by the Caribbean, the Middle East, and Africa. That is, there is a net flow of energy *out of* these less-consuming populations and *into* the high-consumption population of the United States. Moreover, Americans use much of the energy supplies available to them for inessentials (unneeded products, unnecessary travel, household comforts, and conveniences) while the more frugal nations tend to use their supplies to meet basic needs (food, clothing, housing).

In view of the approaching scarcity of energy resources, these comparisons cannot help but raise the question of whether a high-consumption nation is morally justified in continuing to appropriate for its own use the nonrenewable energy resources of other more frugal nations that are too weak economically to use these resources or too weak militarily to protect them. Any attempt to answer this question obviously requires a detailed inquiry into the nature of the world's social, economic,

---

[122] H.S.D. Cole, Christopher Freeman, Marie Jahoda, and K.L.R. Pavitt, eds., *Models of Doom: A Critique of the Limits to Growth* (New York: Universe Books, 1973); William Nordhaus, "World Dynamics: Measurement Without Data," *Economic Journal,* 83 (December 1973): 1156–83.

[123] In a more recent study, the Club of Rome has moderated its predictions; see, Donella H. Meadows et al., *The Limits to Growth,* 2nd ed. (New York: Universe Books, 1974).

[124] Heilbroner, *The Human Prospect.*

TABLE 5.3 Per Capita GNP (1976) and Energy Consumption for Twenty-five Most Populated Nations

	GNP Per Capita ($)	Energy Consumption Per Capita (In Kilograms of Coal Equivalents)
United States	7,510	11,554
West Germany	7,380	5,922
France	6,550	4,380
Japan	4,910	3,679
United Kingdom	4,020	5,268
Italy	3,050	3,284
Spain	2,920	2,399
Poland	2,860	5,253
Soviet Union	2,760	5,259
Iran	1,930	1,490
Brazil	1,140	731
Mexico	1,090	1,227
Turkey	990	743
South Korea	670	1,020
China	410	706
Philippines	410	329
Nigeria	380	94
Thailand	380	308
Egypt	280	473
Indonesia	240	218
Pakistan	170	181
India	150	218
Burma	120	49
Bangladesh	110	32
Ethiopia	100	27

Sources: GNP Figures based on G.T. Korian, THE BOOK OF WORLD RANKINGS (New York: Facts on File, 1979), p. 82; Energy Consumption Figures based on United Nations, STATISTICAL YEARBOOK–1978 (New York: United Nations, 1979), pp. 389–392.

and political systems, an inquiry which is beyond the scope of this book. The question, however, is one that events may also soon force us to face.

QUESTIONS FOR REVIEW AND DISCUSSION

1. Define the following concepts: pollution, toxic substance, nuclear wastes, exponential depletion, peaked depletion, free good, unlimited good, ecological system, ecological ethic, right to a livable environment, absolute ban, private costs, social costs, external costs, to internalize costs, cost-benefit analysis, risk, social audit, right of consent, conservation, rights of future generations, justice toward future generations, multiple access, time preference, doomsday scenario, high-consumption nation.

2. Define the main forms of pollution and resource depletion and identify the major problems associated with each form.

TABLE 5.4 World Energy Production and Consumption (1972)

Region	% Of World Supplies Produced	% Of World Supplies Consumed	Per Capita Consumption (In Kilograms Of Coal)	Per Capita Surplus (+) or Deficit (−) (In Kilograms Of Coal)
North America	30.7	35.9	11,531	−1,210
Caribbean America	4.3	2.1	1,227	+ 1,560
Other America	1.1	1.7	759	− 290
Western Europe	7.8	19.4	4,000	−2,250
Middle East	16.2	1.3	857	+ 9,330
Far East	3.5	7.6	482	− 270
Oceana	1.2	1.2	4,275	− 60
Africa	5.8	1.8	363	+ 860
Communist Countries	29.4	29.0	1,800	+ 70

Source: United Nations, WORLD ENERGY SUPPLIES, 1969–1972 (New York: United Nations, 1974).

3. Compare and contrast the views of (a) an ecological ethic, (b) Blackstone's ethic of environmental rights, and (c) a utilitarian ethic of pollution control. Which view seems to you to be the most adequate? Explain your answer.

4. Do you agree with the claims that (1) future generations have no rights, and (2) the future generations to which we have obligations actually include only the generation which will immediately succeed us? Explain your answer. If you do not agree with these claims, then state your own views and provide arguments to support them.

5. In your judgment, should the major decisions on pollution and resource depletion (especially energy policy) be made by government experts? By scientific experts? By everyone? Provide moral arguments in support of your judgment.

6. "Any pollution law is unjust because it necessarily violates people's right to liberty and right to property." Discuss.

7. In their book, *Energy Future,* R. Strobaugh and D. Yergin claim that in the debate over nuclear power" the resolution of differing opinions over how to deal with uncertainty, over how much risk is acceptable or how safe is safe enough—all require judgments in which values play as large a role as scientific facts" (p. 100). Discuss this claim.

CASES FOR DISCUSSION

The Ozone Threat: Managing With Uncertainty

In June 1974, two California chemists, Mario J. Molina and F.S. Roland, announced that the fluorocarbons being added to the atmosphere could be expected to decrease the ozone layer surrounding the earth by 10 percent within the next fifty to eighty years.[1] Since the ozone layer about 15 miles above the earth's surface shields the earth from the sun's harmful ultraviolet rays, the decrease in ozone might allow these rays to reach the earth and induce skin cancer in humans. An earlier study in 1973 had predicted that a mere 5 percent decrease in ozone might produce at least 8,000 extra cases of skin cancer per year.[2] In addition, the 1973 study had speculated that increased solar radiation could damage the plankton in the oceans that produce much of the world's oxygen and might destroy many other plant and animal species. Other researchers suggested that an increase in solar radiation might lead to widespread climatic changes, including melting of polar ice, a consequent rise in sea levels and a flooding of coastal cities.[3]

Two months later in September 1974, two more scientists, R. Cicerone and R. Stolarski, published a new computer study in *Science* that predicted a 10 percent decrease in the ozone layer by 1990. Fears increased when a third major prediction in October 1974 found that if fluorocarbons continued to be added to the atmosphere at current rates, then by 1995, 40 percent of the ozone layer would be gone.[4]

All of these studies pointed out that much of the fluorocarbon gas that was entering the ozone layer came from the propellents used in aerosol spray cans. When released from the can, the fluorocarbon gas ($CFCl_3$) floats up into the stratosphere where ultraviolet light from the sun causes the gas to release free chlorine atoms. A single chlorine molecule then acts as a catalyst to make tens of thousands of ozone molecules (O_3) break down into simple oxygen molecules (O_2). Whereas ozone filters out ultraviolet light, oxygen does not. The small amounts of fluorocarbon gas being used as propellents in deodorant sprays, hair sprays, perfume sprays, and so on, then, could destroy vast amounts of ozone once it reached the stratosphere.

In August 1975 government researchers reported that various atmospheric and laboratory experiments strongly confirmed the ozone depletion theory postulated by Rowland and Molina. Balloon samples indicated that fluorocarbons had found their way into the stratosphere "in the predicted amounts" and that they were being broken down "as predicted and at the rates predicated by theory." Balloon tests also indicated that free chlorine atoms were being produced in the stratosphere as the ozone depletion theory predicted would happen.[5]

The DuPont Company was the largest producer of the one billion pounds of fluorocarbons (valued at $450 million) manufactured in the United States in 1974. By itself it accounted for about 50 percent of the fluorocarbon market, the rest being shared by five other manufacturers. In addition, DuPont was constructing a new $100 million fluorocarbon plant in Corpus Christi which, when completed,

[1] "Fluorocarbons and Ozone: New Predictions Ominous," *Science News*, 5 October 1974.

[2] "The Effects of Ozone Depletion," *Science*, 4 October 1974.

[3] "Fluorocarbon—Use Limit Urged by Panel to Avoid Cancer Risks, Climate Changes," *The Wall Street Journal*, 14 September 1976.

[4] "Fluorocarbons and Ozone: New Predictions Ominous."

[5] Jeffrey A. Tannenbaum, "Theory that Aerosols Deplete Ozone Shield is Attracting Support," *The Wall Street Journal*, 3 December 1975.

would be the largest such plant in the world. DuPont was, therefore, highly concerned by the threat of a ban.[6]

DuPont management quickly moved to meet the threat. DuPont's research director, Ray McCarthy, pointed out that the ozone depletion theory had not yet been fully established and large research gaps still remained. It was entirely possible that the computer models employed by the theories were mistaken, that the chlorine atoms found in the stratosphere had sources other than fluorocarbons and that the speculations concerning the effects of ozone depletion were exaggerated. McCarthy and other scientists claimed that it would be at least three to six years before proper proof of the theory was obtained. "I hope," McCarthy said, "that the measurements now planned and under way will prove effective in unequivocally providing information on reaction of chlorine in the stratosphere. If not, we will seek other methods which will give us that unequivocal proof."[7] Research should continue, but no regulations should be imposed until the necessary research had been completed.

> All we have are assumptions. Without experimental evidence, it would be an injustice if a few claims—which even the critics agree are hypotheses—were to be the basis of regulatory or consumer reaction. [Statement of Raymond L. McCarthy][8]

Other researchers, however, urged haste, since, if the ozone depletion theory was right, then there was little time left before its consequences would be almost irreversible. Ralph Cicerone, one of the authors of the ozone depletion theory, argued,

> Decision-makers do not have much room to hedge their bets . . . whatever the effects of fluorocarbons will be, the full impact will not be felt for a decade after release and it will persist for many decades. . . . Complete scientific proof to everyone's satisfaction will take years, so we are faced with a benefit-risk analysis. I have come to the reluctant conclusion that the risks are greater than the benefits and the evidence is already strong. [Statement of Ralph Cicerone][9]

DuPont lobbied to prevent the passage of legislation that would ban the fluorocarbons. In ten out of the fourteen states which had introduced fluorocarbon bills by the middle of 1975, the bills were defeated or tabled, in part as a result of industry lobbies.[10] When New York State succeeded in passing a bill banning fluoro-

[6]Walter Sullivan, "Federal Ban Urged on Spray-can Propellants," *The New York Times,* 21 November 1974.

[7]Janet Weinberg, "Ozone Verdict: On Faith or Fact," *Science News,* 17 May 1975, p. 324.

[8]"Industry Doubts Threat to Ozone," *The New York Times,* 2 November 1974.

[9]*Ibid.,* p. 324.

[10]Steven Greenhouse, "Aerosol Feels the Ozone Effect," *The New York Times,* 22 June 1975.

carbons unless proved safe, Raymond McCarthy of DuPont complained that "the bill gives the industry the real but impossible task of proving that something will never happen."[11]

To ensure that fluorocarbons would not be banned, DuPont embarked on an extensive advertising campaign conveying their side of the story: The ozone depletion theory was backed by little evidence. The chairman of the board of DuPont published the following statement in several major newspapers:

> The current controversy centers around the theory [of ozone depletion]. On one side are scientists, theorists, and some legislators who contend that these useful, inert gases, breaking down into chlorine, will lead eventually to an unnatural amount of ozone depletion. On the other side are scientists, researchers, and the aerosol industry who maintain there is no persuasive evidence to support this recently proposed theory of ozone depletion. And, they say, even if the theory has elements of correctness, other chemicals, reactions, and processes might be primarily responsible. Why, they ask, should an industry be prejudged and useful fluorocarbon products be destroyed before any answers are found? . . . As the world's leading supplier of fluorocarbon propellants, DuPont has an obvious stake in the outcome of the controversy. As a corporation we are committed to making products safely, and to supplying safe products to our customers. We have publicly announced that, should reputable evidence show that some fluorocarbons cause a health hazard through depletion of the ozone layer, we are prepared to stop production of the offending compounds. To date there is no experimental evidence to support the contention that . . . [these] compounds have caused a depletion of the ozone layer. . . . Nor will there be any hard answers until some hard facts are produced. In the meantime, aerosol products suffer under a cloud of presumed guilt, and other fluorocarbon-dependent industries are seriously threatened. We believe this is unfair. The "ban now—find out later" approach thrust upon an $8 billion segment of industry in this issue, both in the headlines and in many legislative proposals, is a disturbing trend. Businesses can be destroyed before scientific facts are assembled and evaluated; and many might never recover, even though these facts may vindicate them. Except where available evidence indicated that there may be immediate and substantial danger to health or environment, the nation cannot afford to act on this and other issues before the full facts are known. [Statement of Irving S. Shapiro, chairman of the board, DuPont] [12]

A federal ban against fluorocarbons was enacted on March 15, 1978. On that date, the government announced a ban effective in October on the use of fluorocarbons in 98 percent of all aerosol sprays, but allowed fluorocarbons to continue to be used as coolants in refrigerators, air-conditioners and in the manufacture of foams and solvents, uses which accounted for about 50 percent of the fluorocarbons being produced before the ban. Also, the ban permitted the sale of fluorocarbon sprays until April 1979, and, of course, it put no restrictions on foreign sales of fluorocarbons.

[11] *Ibid.*

[12] "The Ozone Layer vs the Aerosol Industry: DuPont Wants to See Them Both Survive," advertisement, *The New York Times,* 30 June 1975.

In November of 1979, the National Academy of Sciences announced that its researchers had found that the ozone layer was actually being depleted at twice the 7.6 per cent rate it had finally accepted as probable in 1976.[13] According to the academy's National Research Council's panel on stratospheric chemistry, current uses of fluorocarbon chemicals "will result in ozone depletion that is calculated to reach 16.5 per cent, half of which will occur over the next thirty years." The revised estimates were the results of improved atmospheric tests and improved mathematical models which had been used in a study done for the Environmental Protection Agency. These improved techniques also narrowed the range of uncertainty of the predictions to one chance out of twenty that the predictions could be wrong.

The main contributors of fluorocarbons to the atmosphere in 1980 were spray cans used in foreign countries and the increasing use of fluorocarbons both in the U.S. and elsewhere as refrigerants and as a medium for industrial solvents. The use of fluorocarbons for refrigeration, for example, increased by 25 percent during 1978 and 1979.

On October 7, 1980, the Environmental Protection Agency announced plans to propose a "no-growth" policy on the manufacture of fluorocarbons.[14] Charles Masten, director of DuPont's freon products division, denounced the proposal as "unwarranted at this time." According to Mr. Masten new evidence had been found that cast doubt on the validity of the ozone theory.

1. Describe the strategies which DuPont's management used to respond to the ozone controversy before the 1978 ban. Identify the social costs and risks associated with these strategies and the populations which bore these costs and risks. Identify the social benefits deriving from these strategies and the groups who derived these benefits. In your judgment did the social benefits outweigh the social costs and risks? Explain your answer fully.

2. Evaluate the moral quality of DuPont's strategies in terms of (a) the utilitarian costs and benefits associated with those strategies as compared to other alternative strategies, (b) the moral rights of the various parties affected, and (c) the just or unjust way in which benefits and burdens were distributed among various populations by these strategies.

3. In view of the uncertainty and differences of opinion surrounding the theory of ozone depletion, were the strategies that DuPont adopted to respond to the controversy morally blameworthy? In your judgment, would DuPont be morally responsible for any health injuries that may result from the depletion of the ozone layer twenty years later? Why?

4. Devise a practicable and morally adequate strategy by which DuPont could respond to the controversies renewed in 1979 and 1980.

[13]"Rate of Destruction Revised Upward for Earth's Ozone Layer," *San Jose Mercury,* 9 November 1979, p. 2F.

[14]"EPA Wants to Halt Growth of Substances that Harm Ozone," *San Jose Mercury,* 8 October 1980, p. 17A.

Reserve Mining Company began its operations in Silver Bay, Minnesota, in 1955. Silver Bay is located on the northwest shore of Lake Superior, 50 miles from Duluth, and 47 miles from Babbit where Reserve holds mining leases on land estimated to contain two billion tons of magnetic taconite ore. Reserve's taconite ore is a hard gray rock that is about one-third magnetite (a magnetic iron ore) and two-thirds silicates, a sandlike mineral that becomes waste after the magnetite is removed. Reserve removes the ore from the ground at Babbit, crushes it into small rocks, and hauls it by private railroad to Silver Bay. At Silver Bay the taconite is ground into a powdery sand and mixed with water to form a "slurry" which is then passed over magnets that remove the iron particles from the slurry. The remaining fluid silicate wastes, called "tailings," are then discharged into Lake Superior, where they are supposed to flow to the bottom of the lake since the solids in the slurry make it heavier than the lake water. These processes use about 350,000 gallons of lake water every minute, and have deposited about 67,000 tons of tailings into the lake each day.[1]

Reserve is owned by Armco Steel (the fourth largest U.S. steel producer) and Republic Steel (fifth largest), each of which owns 50 percent of the company and which together are its only customers. Altogether, Reserve supplies about 75 percent of Armco's iron ore needs and about 50 percent of Republic's. This means that Reserve provides 15 percent of the nation's domestically mined iron ore, or about 11 million tons of ore a year. During the mid-1970s, Reserve was making annual after-tax profits of about $20 million on its operations and had about $350 million invested in its mining and processing facilities.

When Reserve Mining Company opened its plant in 1955, local Minnesotans welcomed it and praised it as an industrial "pioneer." Reserve brought thousands of jobs into Silver Bay which had long been an economically depressed area. It revitalized Babbit, built hundreds of new houses for its employees, put in new water and sewer lines, paid for new schools and medical facilities, and provided low-interest loans for those who wanted to purchase their own homes. Not surprisingly, local residents liked Reserve and looked upon it as the "best employer" in the area. About 80 percent of the 3,200 local workers were employed by Reserve and constituted most of its $23 million annual payroll.[2]

Reserve's discharge of tailings into Lake Superior was approved in 1947 by the Minnesota Department of Conservation and Water Pollution Control. Reserve had stated at public hearings held at that time that the tailings would be contained within a 9 square mile area of the lake and that they would have no adverse effects on fish life nor on human health. Nonetheless, in 1967 the U.S. Department of the Interior directed its Great Lakes Regional Coordinator, Charles Stoddard, to undertake a study of the environmental impact of Reserve's operations. Although never

---

[1] Jack McWethy, "When Government and Industry Tangle Over the Environment," *U.S. News and World Report,* 10 January 1977, pp. 63–65.

[2] Quincy Dadisman, "The Battle of Lake Superior," *The Nation,* 11 May 1974, p. 592.

officially released, Stoddard's report was leaked to the press. According to accounts of the report's contents, Stoddard found "that suspended tailings were causing green water for distances of at least 18 miles southwest of the point of discharge, that lake currents were carrying some particles across state boundaries, that water quality standards for iron, lead, and copper were being violated, that bottom fauna important as fish food was adversely affected, that the tailings were lethal to the sac fry of rainbow trout and that eutrophication of the lake was accelerating."[3] The report ended by recommending that Reserve be given three years to stop discharging its taconite tailings into Lake Superior.

In May 1969 Secretary of the Interior, Stewart Udall, convened a series of "enforcement conferences" in Duluth to investigate the alleged illegal pollution of Lake Superior. During the first conference, Reserve president Edward Furness defended Reserve's practices as a safe technological necessity:

> A substantial part of the success of Reserve's taconite operations is the availability of large quantities of water. . . . Reserve's earliest studies showed that it wasn't possible to conduct its concentration process at Babbit, the site of our mine. . . . There simply was no water available in Babbit in the quantities required by a large-scale operation such as ours. Also, because of its location near the Superior National Forest and near the boundary waters, there was no area available to Reserve for tailings disposal. The only solution, engineering studies made clear, was to locate the processing plant at Silver Bay and bring the crude taconite there by rail from Babbit. . . . The tailings are inert, inorganic, insoluble [like] the material that is washed from sand beaches. . . . From a conservation standpoint, Reserve's use of Lake Superior is sound. There is no waste of water, no injury to water. . . . No agency, industry, or individual—public or private—is more interested in preserving the high quality of Lake Superior than is Reserve Mining Company. [Statement of Edward Furness, president of Reserve][4]

After hearing testimony from government officials, the first conference ended by recommending "further engineering and economic studies relating to possible ways and means of reducing to the maximum practicable extent the discharge of tailings into Lake Superior."

Immediately after the conference, Armco's managers began to formulate the strategies by which Reserve would respond to the developing criticisms. A memo written by Armco's manager of Air and Water Pollution Control at this time suggested some of the strategies they would pursue during the ensuing months and years:

> It appears there are several alternatives that must be weighed and considered, some of these are:

[3]John G. Mitchell, "Corporate Responsibility in Silver Bay," *Audubon,* 11 March 1975, p. 50.

[4]Federal Water Pollution Control Administration, *Proceedings, Conference—Pollution of Lake Superior and its Tributary Basin, Minnesota—Wisconsin—Michigan,* 13–15 May 1969, pp. 2–3.

1. By vigorous political activity, primarily in Washington, D.C., it may be possible to amend or modify the "conclusions" and "recommendations" [of the conference].
2. I would assume that if we (Reserve-Armco-Republic) were to fight this issue in the courts that the "public image" would suffer somewhat from the "robber baron" concept. Nevertheless, I believe this approach must be carefully studied.
3. A careful study should be made of the present processing techniques to determine if the production of "super-fine tailings" can be reduced.
4. We should indicate to the conference members the magnitude of the problem, the complexities involved, and the tremendous impact on the economy of the region. I suggest that we should also offer some "pilot" schemes that we believe may have merit in reducing the problem. By this technique we may be able to gain a few years' time.
5. Another obvious alternative available to management is to close down the existing facilities. If the federal government will assume a major part of the cost (equity) involved in this decision, it may have some merit for consideration.[5]

If Reserve were to have shut down its operations at this point, the economic impact would have been significant.[6] 1,500 workers would have lost their jobs at the Silver Bay plant and 1,600 would have lost their jobs at the Babbit Mine. Minnesota officials estimated that more than 10,000 other persons in the area depended on Reserve's operations. Based on an average family size of four, this meant over 50,000 people in the area could be affected. A shut-down would also affect the more distant operations of Armco and Republic which both depended on Reserve for their ore. Not only would the jobs of their own 98,000 steelworkers be threatened, but American industries might be forced either to purchase their steel from abroad, thereby further weakening the United States' balance of payments, or else face a domestic steel shortage.

While the enforcement conferences continued, various parties inquired about the fate of the original Stoddard report which had first alerted the public to Reserve's alleged pollution of Lake Superior. According to a Ralph Nader study group, release of the Stoddard report had been blocked in Washington by Minnesota Congressman John Blatnik and by Max Edwards, Assistant Secretary of the Interior for Water Research and Pollution Control.[7] Both of these men, according to the Nader study group, had been successfully lobbied by Reserve officials who had persuaded them to ensure that the damaging findings of the Stoddard report were never officially released.

The enforcement conferences dragged on for several years. During that time Reserve repeatedly put forward a plan to deal with the tailings by building a "deep pipe" from its Silver Bay plant to the bottom of Lake Superior. The waste tailings, Reserve claimed, would then flow harmlessly to the bottom of the lake through the

---

[5]*U.S.A. et al.* vs. *Reserve Mining Co. et al.,* U.S. District Court, District of Minnesota, Fifth Dist. Civil Action, No. 5-72, Civ. 19; State of Minnesota, Exhibit 74.

[6]"Ecology Versus Economy," *Newsweek,* 6 May 1974, p. 68.

[7]David Zwick, *Water Wasteland* (New York: Bantam Books, Inc., 1972), pp. 145-48.

pipe. Environmentalists rejected the plan since the tailings would still be contaminating the lake. Over the next several years Reserve repeatedly revised the plan and resubmitted "improved" versions for discussion.

On February 2, 1972, at the request of the Environmental Protection Agency (EPA) the Justice Department finally filed suit against Reserve. The suit alleged that Reserve wastes were illegally spreading throughout the western end of Lake Superior where they were reducing clarity, interfering with aquatic plant growth, and damaging fish life.

The focus of the suit changed dramatically on June 15, 1973, one month before the case was to come to trial. On that day the EPA released a report announcing that high concentrations of amosite asbestos fibers had been found in the drinking water of the two hundred thousand residents of Duluth, Two Harbors, Beaver Bay, Silver Bay and other communities which drew their drinking water from the parts of Lake Superior into which Reserve had been dumping their taconite tailings. Moreover, asbestos was found in the air around Silver Bay and other communities near Reserve. The report claimed that the asbestos fibers in the air and water originated in Reserve's operations and pointed out that asbestos fibers were known to cause lung cancer when inhaled and were suspected of causing stomach and intestinal cancers when ingested. Although adults who had been drinking the contaminated water for years were now already exposed, the report cautiously recommended that "an alternate source of drinking water be found for young children."[8]

The asbestos warnings of the EPA relied in part on the research of Doctor I.J. Selikoff and others who had found that among asbestos workers who twenty years earlier had inhaled asbestos fibers and who had accidentally ingested it in the course of their work, there were up to six times more fatal lung cancers and up to three times more fatal gastrointestinal cancers than in a normal population.[9] Once contracted, the cancers associated with asbestos are generally irreversible and generally fatal, but these asbestos-related diseases are not detectable until twenty or thirty years after exposure to asbestos.

The air around Silver Bay was found to contain anywhere between 2,000 and 11 million fibers of asbestos per cubic meter of air (the Occupational Safety and Health Agency limits work-place exposure to 5 million fibers per cubic meter) and the water around Duluth was found to contain 12.5 million fibers per liter. Reserve later claimed that it was not known what concentrations of asbestos would cause an increase in cancers *outside* of the work-place since all earlier research on asbestos exposure had been carried on in work-place situations. Moreover, since the plant had been operating for only seventeen years, any alleged health injuries would not become diagnosible for several more years.

The EPA warning frightened Duluth residents, who began buying bottled water in large quantities. City and state officials organized to truck in water from other

[8] *Minneapolis Tribune,* 5 May 1974, p. 13B.
[9] See I.J. Selikoff, E.C. Hammond, and J. Chung, "Carcinogenicity of Amosite Asbestos," *Archives of Environmental Health,* 25 (1972): 183–86.

sources and the federal government provided a grant of $100,000 for water for low-income residents. Two years later, Duluth built a $7 million water plant, financed largely by the federal government, which was designed to take water from Lake Superior and filter out the asbestos fibers. Some communities, however, continued to draw unfiltered water from the lake.

The residents of Silver Bay, most of whom were employed by Reserve, were less concerned about the danger of asbestos than about the more immediate danger of losing their jobs. Many were angered at the commotion being caused by Duluth residents and angry at state officials who had instigated the suit. Virtually all the residents living in the immediate vicinity of the plant were happy with Reserve's operations and unconcerned about the plant's air and water wastes.

The trial began on August 1, 1973, before the Federal District Court in Minneapolis, and the main issue soon became the alleged health hazards of Reserve's operations. Presiding Judge Miles Lord heard testimony from more than 100 witnesses and analyzed more than 1,600 exhibits. The proceedings eventually covered 20,000 pages of transcripts.

During the course of the trial Judge Lord asked Reserve for suggestions on alternative ways of handling the wastes from Reserve's operations. Reserve put forward several schemes while the trial dragged on. One plan that Reserve proposed in several versions was the plan to build a pipe from its Silver Bay plant to the bottom of Lake Superior (at a cost of $27 million and an additional $4.7 million in yearly operating costs) to carry the waste tailings to the bottom of the lake. The plan, however, was again totally unacceptable to environmentalists and Judge Lord later characterized it as a "presentation . . . to delay" the proceedings. A second Reserve proposal made in the final week of the trial was to build ponds on land a few miles from the lake and to dispose of the tailings in these ponds constructed at a cost of $172 million. Reserve's offer, however, was conditional on financial assistance from the government, on a guarantee that the court would find Reserve innocent and that environmental agencies would never again interfere with Reserve's operations, and on a guarantee that Reserve could continue operating during the five years it would take to build the ponds. The Court regarded this second proposal as "absurd" and "shocking."

On April 20, 1974, nine months after the trial began, an exasperated Judge Miles Lord reached his decision. Reserve's air discharges, he held, "substantially endanger the health of the people of Silver Bay and surrounding communities" and its continued discharge of asbestos in the water "endangers the health of the people who procure their drinking water from the western arm of Lake Superior"; consequently, "the Court must order an immediate curtailment of the discharge."[10] On April 21, Reserve Mining was forced to shut down its operations.

Reserve lawyers immediately appealed the Court decision. Forty-eight hours later the U.S. Court of Appeals for the Eighth Circuit granted a stay of the order to close, pending its final decision on the appeal. The Eighth Circuit Court stated that there is "vast uncertainty as to the medical consequences of low levels of exposure

---

[10]Mitchell, "Corporate Responsibility in Silver Bay," p. 54.

to asbestos fibers [and] unknowns may not be substituted for proof of a demonstrable hazard to the public health." At once, Reserve recommenced operations and its tailings once again flowed into the lake. However, eleven months later on March 14, 1975, the Eighth Circuit Court filed its own decision on the appeal:

> Reserve's discharges into the air and water give rise to a potential threat to the public health. The risk to public health is of sufficient gravity to be legally cognizable and calls for an abatement order on reasonable terms. [But] Reserve is entitled to a reasonable opportunity and a reasonable time period [two years] to convert its Minnesota taconite operations to on-land disposal of taconite tailings and to restrict air emissions at its Silver Bay plant or to close its existing Minnesota taconite-pelletizing operations.[11]

Several months after receiving the Appeals Court order to take steps to stop polluting, Reserve petitioned to construct a pool to serve as an on-land dumping site for its tailings at a place called "Mile Post 7" located seven miles from Lake Superior. The facility would cost $350 million. If its petition was refused, the company suggested, it might choose to close down permanently and throw its many employees out of work.

The Reserve petition was adamantly opposed by environmentalists and by state authorities who argued that run-off from the pool might still contaminate Lake Superior. The pool, they held, should be built 20 miles from the lake, even though construction at a more distant site might cost up to $667 million.[12] Consequently, state environmental agencies decided to refuse to approve Reserve's petition. However, several months later, Reserve appealed the decision and on January 31, 1977, the Minnesota District Court ordered the state agencies to approve the Mile Post 7 site.[13] Since Reserve had not yet done anything to stop its emissions, it was clear that it would miss the two-year time period granted by the court in 1975. Consequently, on May 21, 1977, federal officials agreed to give Reserve three more years to build its disposal site at the Mile Post 7 site and ruled it could continue discharging its wastes into Lake Superior until March, 1980.[14] Reserve eventually began work on the disposal site at Mile Post 7. Commenting on the costs of the new facility, Matthew R. Bahoretz, executive vice-president of Reserve said in November 1977:

> Obviously, our costs are going to increase, and that will make it more difficult for us to compete. Any time you have to make this kind of [nonproductive] investment merely for ecological improvements, it is a burden. . . . There's only so much gross national product to go around. It just seems wrong some way to spend so much of it to solve a problem that is a concern to such a small segment of the population.[15]

[11] Peter C. DuBois, "Iron Curtains?," *Barrons,* 25 August 1975, p. 16.

[12] "A Pollution Ruling that May Close a Plant," *Business Week,* 14 June 1976, p. 31.

[13] *New York Times,* 1 February 1977.

[14] *New York Times,* 22 May 1977.

[15] *Wall Street Journal,* 15 November 1977, p. 1.

The disposal facility was not yet completed in March, 1980, and Reserve was forced in that month to close down and finally stop dumping its wastes into Lake Superior. The plant remained closed until May, 1980, when it reopened and began shipping its waste tailings by rail and pipeline to the new pond enclosed by dams in a 6 square mile marshy area 7 miles from the shores of Lake Superior.

1. What strategies did Reserve's management use to respond to the allegations concerning its pollution of Lake Superior? Why did it probably adopt these strategies? What social benefits and what social costs (and risks) were associated with these strategies before the release of the EPA report on June 15, 1973? After the release of the report? In your view, did the benefits outweigh the costs either before or after June 15, 1973?

2. Reserve's final investment in pollution control ($350 million) was equivalent to the total capital investment in its mining and processing facilities. In your judgment would this investment have been worth it given only the information available before June 15, 1973? After June 15, 1973? Explain your answers fully. Comment on Mr. Bahoretz's November 1977 statement.

3. Evaluate the adequacy of Reserve's responses to the allegations concerning its pollution (a) in utilitarian terms, (b) in terms of the moral rights of those affected, and (c) in terms of the justice or injustice of the responses.

4. What morally appropriate and practicable courses of action would you have recommended for Reserve before June 15, 1973? After June 15, 1973?

Monarchs and Townspeople

In 1979, Synertex, a semiconductor company with headquarters in Sunnyvale, California, applied for a permit to build a $40 million research and manufacturing plant in Santa Cruz, California.[1] The plant was to be located across the street from Natural Bridges State Park.

Natural Bridges State Park contains a grove of eucalyptus trees which, for several centuries, has served as a major wintering site for the Monarch butterfly. Park rangers estimated that each winter 95,000 of the large black and orange Monarchs settled on the eucalyptus trees concentrated in the few acres of the small park. So many of the bright-colored butterflies would land on the trees that their branches would bend and often break from their weight. The Monarch butterflies migrated several hundred miles each year to reach the park where they remained from November to March. Up to two thousand tourists visit the park on weekends to see the butterflies. A few other sites on the California coast also serve as wintering grounds for the world-famous butterfly, but none is as popular or as well known.

The environmental report which Synertex had to make before its request for a permit would be considered concluded that operations at the plant would pose an unknown degree of risk for the butterflies. The plant would sometimes release into the air small amounts of hydrocarbons as well as sulfur and nitrogen oxides, and these would be blown in the direction of the park by prevailing winds 20 per-

[1]This case is based entirely on Ken Peterson, "It's Butterflies vs. Industry," *San Jose Mercury*, 25 October 1979, pp. 1A and 24A.

cent of the time. Although the fumes would be 99 percent diluted by the time they reached the butterfly groves, "there is no available data" on the effects these diluted fumes would have on the butterflies.

Since the plant would employ 350–400 workers, most townspeople strongly supported granting the permit. Synertex believed the site was ideal in view of the availability of needed labor, as well as the material and geographical resources the site provided. Synertex also believed that the risk to the butterflies was virtually nil and was willing to hire a biologist to monitor the effects its operations had on the butterflies. The firm was unwilling, however, to guarantee that it would shut down its $40 million plant if the butterflies were affected by its operations.

1. Discuss the costs and benefits of building the Synertex plant. In your judgment, did the benefits outweigh the costs? Explain.

2. Who should have the right to make the final decision in the Synertex case? Local townspeople? Tourists? State government? The federal government? Synertex management? Explain your answers.

3. Do wildlife issues differ in any important ways from pollution issues or from issues concerning the depletion of energy resources?

CHAPTER SIX
THE ETHICS
OF CONSUMER
PRODUCTION
AND MARKETING

INTRODUCTION

Ultra Sheen Permanent Creme Relaxer, which is manufactured by Johnson Products Company, is an emulsion sold to consumers for the purpose of straightening curly hair. In the early 1970s, the creme relaxer was being advertised as "gentle" and "easy" to use. In television ads a woman would declare that the creme relaxer "goes on cool while it really relaxes my hair. And the Conditioner and Hair Dress protects against moisture, so my hair doesn't go back." An FTC investigation, however, discovered that the basic ingredient in the relaxer is sodium hydroxide lye, which "breaks down the cells of the hair shaft . . . makes it brittle and causes partial or total hair loss." Far from being "gentle," the Johnson Creme Relaxer was alleged to be "a primary skin irritant. It is caustic to skin and breaks down the cells which form the epidermis. Ultra Sheen Relaxer in some instances causes skin and scalp irritation and burns, which may produce scars and permanent follicle damage. It also causes eye irritation and may impair vision." The FTC ordered that advertisements should stop misrepresenting the product and that customers should be informed of the product's dangers.[1]

Consumers are exposed daily to astonishingly high levels of risk from the use of household products. Each year 20 million people are injured in accidents involving household items; of these, 110,000 are permanently disabled and 30,000 are

---

[1] *FTC in the Matter of Johnson Products Company, Inc., and Bozell & Jacobs, Inc.,* Docket no. C-2788 (10 February 1976).

killed.[2] Product-related accidents are the major cause of death for people between the ages of one and thirty-six, far outstripping the deaths caused by cancer or heart disease. The total cost of these injuries is estimated to be about $5.5 billion per year.[3]

But product injuries make up only one category of costs imposed on unwary consumers. Consumers may also bear the costs of deceptive selling practices, of shoddy product construction, of warranties that are not honored, and of products that immediately break down. The story of a Puerto Rican woman in New York is illustrative:

> I bought a TV set from a First Avenue store. It was a used set which was sold as new. After seven days it broke down. The store took it back and returned it in two weeks. It broke down again and they took it for thirty days. They brought it back and it broke down one week later. They took it away and I asked for a refund because there was a guarantee of ninety days which had not run out. But they wouldn't give me back my $100 or bring me another TV.[4]

Consumers are also bombarded daily by an endless series of advertisements urging them to buy certain products. Although sometimes defended as sources of information, advertisements are also criticized on the grounds that they rarely do more than give the barest indications of the basic function a product is meant to serve and sometimes misrepresent and exaggerate its virtues. Economists argue that advertising expenditures are a waste of resources, while sociologists bemoan the cultural effects of advertising.[5]

This chapter examines the various ethical issues raised by product quality and advertising. The first few sections discuss various theories of the manufacturer's moral duties to consumers and the last sections discuss consumer advertising. Before we enter these discussions, however, it may be helpful to get a clearer idea of the nature of the issues involved.

Ethics and the Consumer: The Issues

Consumer analysts claim that there are today approximately 2.5 billion potentially dangerous items in American homes, an average of 45 in each home.[6] 175,000 people are mangled by power lawnmowers each year; 1,000 are electro-

---

[2] National Commission on Product Safety, *Final Report of the National Commission on Product Safety* (Washington, DC: U.S. Government Printing Office, 1970), p. 1.

[3] *Ibid.*

[4] David Caplovitz, *The Poor Pay More* (New York: The Free Press, 1967), p. 150.

[5] Several of these criticisms are surveyed in Stephen A. Greyser, "Advertising: Attacks and Counters," *Harvard Business Review,* 50 (10 March 1972): 22–28.

[6] James W. Bishop, Jr., and Henry W. Hubbard, *Let the Seller Beware* (Washington National Press, Inc., 1969), ch. 7.

cuted by electric appliances; 175,000 are burned by flammable clothing, and about 12,000 of these burn victims die; 2,000 are accidentally poisoned by household chemicals; 100,000 are cut by glass doors. Injuries from auto-related accidents average 70,000 each week; deaths average 1,000 per week; financial losses are estimated at $30 million per day.

Part of the responsibility for these injuries rests on consumers. Individuals are often careless in their use of products. "Do-it-yourselfers" use power saws without guards attached or flammable liquids near open flames. People often use tools and instruments that they do not have the skill, the knowledge, or the experience to handle.

But injuries also arise from flaws in product design, in the materials out of which products are made, or in the processes used to construct products. Insofar as manufacturing defects are the source of product-related injuries, consumer advocates claim, the duty of minimizing injuries should lie with the manufacturer. The producer is in the best position to know the hazards raised by a certain product and to eliminate the hazards at the point of manufacture. In addition, the producer's expertise makes the producer knowledgeable about the safest materials and manufacturing methods and enables him to build adequate safeguards into the design of the product. Finally, because the producer is intimately acquainted with the workings of the product, he or she can best inform the consumer on the safest way to use the product and on what precautions need to be taken.

Where, then, does the consumer's duties to protect his or her own interests end, and where does the manufacturer's duty to protect consumers' interests begin? Three different theories on the ethical duties of manufacturers have been developed, each one of which strikes a different balance between the consumer's duty to himself or herself and the manufacturer's duty to the consumer: the contract view, the "due care" view, and the social costs view. The contract view would place the greater responsibility on the consumer, while the "due care" and social costs views place the larger measure of responsibility on the manufacturer. We will examine each of these views.

6.1 THE CONTRACT VIEW
OF BUSINESS'S DUTIES
TO CONSUMERS

According to the contract view of the business firm's duties to its customers, the relationship between a business firm and its customers is essentially a contractual relationship, and the firm's moral duties to the customer are those created by this contractual relationship.[7] When a consumer buys a product, this view holds, the consumer voluntarily enters into a "sales contract" with the business firm. The firm

---

[7]For this approach, see Thomas Garrett, *Business Ethics* (Englewood Cliffs, NJ: Prentice-Hall, Inc., 1966), pp. 119–32.

freely and knowingly agrees to give the consumer a product with certain characteristics and the consumer in turn freely and knowingly agrees to pay a certain sum of money to the firm for the product. In virtue of having voluntarily entered this agreement, the firm then has a duty to provide a product with those characteristics, and the consumer has a correlative right to get a product with those characteristics.

The contract theory of the business firm's duties to its customers rests on the view that a contract is a free agreement that imposes on the parties the basic duty of complying with the terms of the agreement. We examined this view earlier (Chapter Two) and noted the two justifications Kant provided for the view: A person has a duty to do what he or she contracts to do, because failure to adhere to the terms of a contract is a practice (1) that cannot be universalized, and (2) that treats the other person as a means and not as an end.[8] Rawls's theory also provides a justification for the view, but one that is based on the idea that our freedom is expanded by the recognition of contractual rights and duties: An enforced system of social rules that requires people to do what they contract to do will provide them with the assurance that contracts will be kept. Only if they have such assurance will people feel able to trust each other's word, and on that basis to secure the benefits of the institution of contracts.[9]

We also noted in Chapter Two that traditional moralists have argued that the act of entering into a contract is subject to several secondary moral constraints:

1. Both of the parties to the contract must have full knowledge of the nature of the agreement they are entering.
2. Neither party to a contract must intentionally misrepresent the facts of the contractual situation to the other party.
3. Neither party to a contract must be forced to enter the contract under duress or undue influence.

These secondary constraints can be justified by the same sorts of arguments that Kant and Rawls use to justify the basic duty to perform one's contracts. Kant, for example, easily shows that misrepresentation in the making of a contract cannot be universalized, and Rawls argues that if misrepresentation were not prohibited, fear of deception would make members of a society feel less free to enter contracts. But these secondary constraints can also be justified on the grounds that a contract cannot exist unless these constraints are fulfilled. For a contract is essentially a *free agreement* struck between two parties. Since an agreement cannot exist unless both parties know what they are agreeing to, contracts require full knowledge and the absence of misrepresentation. And since freedom implies the absence of coercion, contracts must be made without duress or undue influence.

[8] Immanual Kant, *Groundwork of the Metaphysic of Morals*, trans. H.J. Paton (New York: Harper & Row, Publishers, Inc., 1964), pp. 90, 97; see also, Alan Donagan, *The Theory of Morality* (Chicago: The University of Chicago Press), 1977, p. 92.

[9] John Rawls, *A Theory of Justice* (Cambridge: Harvard University Press, Belknap Press, 1971), pp. 344–50.

The contractual theory of business's duties to consumers, then, claims that a business has four main moral duties: The basic duty of (1) complying with the terms of the sales contract, and the secondary duties of (2) disclosing the nature of the product, (3) avoiding misrepresentation, and (4) avoiding the use of duress and undue influence. By acting in accordance with these duties, a business respects the right of consumers to be treated as free and equal persons, that is, in accordance with their right to be treated only as they have freely consented to be treated.

The Duty to Comply

The most basic moral duty that a business firm owes its customers, according to the contract view, is the duty to provide consumers with a product that lives up to those claims that the firm expressly made about the product, which led the customer to enter the contract freely, and which formed the customer's understanding concerning what he or she was agreeing to buy. In the early 1970s, for example, Winthrop Laboratories marketed a painkiller that the firm advertised as "nonaddictive." Subsequently, a patient using the painkiller became addicted to it and shortly died from an overdose. A court in 1974 found Winthrop Laboratories liable for the patient's death because, although it had expressly stated that the drug was nonaddictive, Winthrop Laboratories had failed to live up to its duty to comply with this express contractual claim.[10]

As the above example suggests, our legal system has incorporated the moral view that firms have a duty to live up to the express claims they make about their products. The Uniform Commercial Code, for example, states in Section 2-314:

> Any affirmation of fact or promise made by the seller to the buyer that related to the goods and becomes part of the basis of the bargain creates an express warranty that the goods shall conform to the affirmation or promise.

In addition to the duties that result from the *express* claim a seller makes about the product, the contract view also holds that the seller has a duty to carry through on any *implied* claims he or she knowingly makes about the product. The seller, for example, has the moral duty to provide a product that can be used safely for the ordinary and special purposes for which the customer, relying on the seller's judgment, has been led to believe it can be used. The seller is morally bound to do whatever he or she knows the buyer understood the seller was promising, since at the point of sale sellers should have corrected any misunderstandings they were aware of.[11]

This idea of an "implied agreement" has also been incorporated into the law. Section 2-315 of the Uniform Commercial Code, for example, reads:

> Where the seller at the time of contracting has reason to know any particular purpose for which the goods are required and that the buyer is relying on the

---

[10]*Crocker* v. *Winthrop Laboratories, Division of Sterling Drug, Inc.,* 514 Southwestern 2d 429 (1974).

[11]See Donagan, *Theory of Morality,* p. 91.

seller's skill or judgment to select or furnish suitable goods, there is . . . an implied warranty that the goods shall be fit for such purpose.

The express or implied claims that a seller might make about the qualities possessed by the product range over a variety of areas and are affected by a number of factors. Frederick Sturdivant classifies these areas in terms of four variables: "The definition of product quality used here is: the degree to which product performance meets predetermined expectation with respect to (1) reliability, (2) service life, (3) maintainability, and (4) safety."[12]

Reliability Claims of reliability refer to the probability that a product will function as the consumer is led to expect that it will function. If a product incorporates a number of interdependent components, then the probability that it will function properly is equal to the result of multiplying together each component's probability of proper functioning.[13] As the number of components in a product multiplies, therefore, the manufacturer has a corresponding duty to ensure that each component functions in such a manner that the total product is as reliable as he or she implicitly or expressly claims it will be. This is especially the case when malfunction poses health or safety hazards. The U.S. Consumer Product Safety Commission lists hundreds of examples of hazards from product malfunctions in its yearly report.[14]

Service life Claims concerning the life of a product refer to the period of time during which the product will function as effectively as the consumer is led to expect it to function. Generally, the consumer implicitly understands that service life will depend on the amount of wear and tear to which one subjects the product. In addition, consumers also base some of their expectations of service life on the explicit guarantees the manufacturer attaches to the product.

A more subtle factor that influences service life is the factor of obsolescence.[15] Technological advances may render some products obsolete when a new product appears that carries out the same functions more efficiently. Or purely stylistic changes may make last year's product appear dated and less desirable. The contract view implies that a seller who knows that a certain product will become obsolete has a duty to correct any mistaken beliefs he or she knows buyers will form concerning the service life they may expect from the product.

Maintainability Claims of maintainability are claims concerning the ease with which the product can be repaired and kept in operating condition. Claims of main-

---

[12] Frederick D. Sturdivant, *Business and Society* (Homewood, IL: Richard D. Irwin, Inc., 1977), p. 259.

[13] *Ibid.*, p. 260.

[14] U.S. Consumer Products Safety Commission, *1979 Annual Report* (Washington, DC: U.S. Government Printing Office, 1979), pp. 81–101.

[15] A somewhat dated but still incisive discussion of this issue is found in Vance Packard, *The Wastemakers* (New York: David McKay Co., Inc., 1960).

tainability are often made in the form of an express warranty. Whirlpool Corporation, for example, appended this express warranty on one of its products:

> During your first year of ownership, all parts of the appliance (except the light bulbs) that we find are defective in materials or workmanship will be repaired or replaced by Whirlpool free of charge, and we will pay all labor charges. During the second year, we will continue to assume the same responsibility as stated above except you pay any labor charges.[16]

But sellers often also imply that a product may be easily repaired even after the expiration date of an express warranty. In fact, however, product repairs may be costly, or even impossible, due to the unavailability of parts.

Product safety   Implied and express claims of product safety refer to the degree of risk associated with using a product. Since the use of virtually any product involves some degree of risk, questions of safety are essentially questions of *acceptable known levels* of risk. That is, a product is safe if its attendant risks are known and judged to be "acceptable" or "reasonable" by the *buyer* in view of the benefits the buyer expects to derive from using the product. This implies that the seller complies with his or her part of a free agreement if the seller provides a product that involves only those risks he or she says it involves, and the buyer purchases it with that understanding. The National Commission on Product Safety, for example, characterized "reasonable risk" in these terms:

> Risks of bodily harm to users are not unreasonable when consumers understand that risks exist, can appraise their probability and severity, know how to cope with them, and voluntarily accept them to get benefits they could not obtain in less risky ways. When there is a risk of this character, consumers have reasonable opportunity to protect themselves; and public authorities should hesitate to substitute their value judgments about the desirability of the risk for those of the consumers who choose to incur it. But preventable risk is not reasonable (a) when consumers do not know that it exists; or (b) when, though aware of it, consumers are unable to estimate its frequency and severity; or (c) when consumers do not know how to cope with it, and hence are likely to incur harm unnecessarily; or (d) when risk is unnecessary in that it could be reduced or eliminated at a cost in money or in the performance of the product that consumers would willingly incur if they knew the facts and were given the choice.[17]

Thus the seller of a product (according to the contractual theory) has a moral duty to provide a product whose use involves *no greater risks* than those the seller *expressly* communicates to the buyer or those the seller *implicitly* communicates by the implicit claims made when marketing the product for a use whose normal risk

---

[16] Quoted in address by S.E. Upton (vice-president of Whirlpool Corporation) to the American Marketing Association in Cleveland, OH: 11 December 1969.

[17] National Commission on Product Safety, *Final Report,* quoted in William W. Lowrance, *Of Acceptable Risk* (Los Altos, CA: William Kaufmann, Inc., 1976), p. 80.

level is well known. If the label on a bottle, for example, indicates only that the contents are highly toxic ("Danger: Poison"), the product should not include additional risks from flammability. Or, if a firm makes and sells skis, use of the skis should not embody any unexpected additional risks other than the well-known risks which attend skiing (it should not, for example, involve the added possibility of being pierced by splinters should the skis fracture). In short, the seller has a duty to provide a product with a level of risk which is no higher than he or she expressly or implicitly claims it to be, and which the consumer freely and knowingly contracts to assume.

The Duty of Disclosure

An agreement cannot bind unless both parties to the agreement know what they are doing and freely choose to do it. This implies that the seller who intends to enter a contract with a customer has a duty to disclose exactly what the customer is buying and what the terms of the sale are. At a minimum, this means the seller has a duty to inform the buyer of any facts about the product that would affect the customer's decision to purchase the product. For example, if the product the consumer is buying possesses a defect that poses a risk to the user's health or safety, the consumer should be so informed. Some have argued that sellers should also disclose a product's components or ingredients, its performance characteristics, costs of operation, product ratings, and any other applicable standards.[18]

Behind the claim that entry into a sales contract requires full disclosure is the idea that an agreement is free only to the extent that one knows what alternatives are available: Freedom depends on knowledge. The more the buyer knows about the various products available on the market and the more comparisons the buyer is able to make among them, the more one can say that the buyer's agreement is voluntary.[19]

The view that sellers should provide a great deal of information for buyers, however, has been criticized on the grounds that information is costly and therefore should itself be treated as a product for which the consumer should either pay or do without. In short, consumers should freely contract to purchase information as they freely contract to purchase goods, and producers should not have to provide it for them.[20] The problem with the criticism is that the information on which a person bases his or her decision to enter a contract is a rather different kind of entity from the product exchanged through the contract. Since a contract must be entered into freely, and since free choice depends on knowledge, contractual transactions must be based on an open exchange of information. If consumers had to bargain for such information, the resulting contract would hardly be free.

---

[18] See Louis Stern, "Consumer Protection via Increased Information," *Journal of Marketing,* vol. 31, no. 2 (April 1967).

[19] Lawrence E. Hicks, *Coping with Packaging Laws* (New York: AMACOM, 1972). p. 17.

[20] See the discussions in Richard Posner, *Economic Analysis of Law,* 2d ed. (Boston: Little, Brown and Company, 1977), p. 83; and R. Posner, "Strict Liability: A Comment," *Journal of Legal Studies,* 2, no. 1 (January 1973): 21.

The Duty Not to Misrepresent

Misrepresentation, even more than the failure to disclose information, renders freedom of choice impossible. That is, misrepresentation is coercive: The person who is intentionally misled acts as the deceiver wants the person to act and not as the person would freely have chosen to act if he or she had known the truth. Since free choice is an essential ingredient of a binding contract, intentionally misrepresenting the nature of a commodity is wrong.

A seller misrepresents a commodity when he or she represents it in a way deliberately intended to deceive the buyer into thinking something about the product that the seller knows is false. The deception may be created by a verbal lie, as when a used model is described as "new," or it may be created by a gesture, as when an unmarked used model is displayed together with several new models. That is, the deliberate intent to misrepresent by false implication is as wrong as the explicit lie.

The varieties of misrepresentation seem to be limited only by the ingenuity of the greed that creates them.[21] A manufacturer may give a product a name that the manufacturer knows consumers will confuse with the brand-name of a higher-quality competing product; the manufacturer may write "wool" or "silk" on material made wholly or partly of cotton; the manufacturer may mark a fictitious "regular price" on an article that is always sold at a much lower "sale" price; a business may advertise an unusually low price for an object which the business actually intends to sell at a much higher price once the consumer is lured into the store; a store may advertise an object at an unusually low price, intending to "bait and switch" the unwary buyer over to a more expensive product; a producer may solicit paid "testimonials" from professionals who have never really used the product. We shall return to some of these issues below when we discuss advertising.

The Duty Not to Coerce

People often act irrationally when under the influence of fear or emotional stress. When a seller takes advantage of a buyer's fear or emotional stress to extract consent to an agreement that the buyer would not make if the buyer were thinking rationally, the seller is using duress or undue influence to coerce. An unscrupulous funeral director, for example, may skillfully induce guilt-ridden and grief-stricken survivors to invest in funeral services that they cannot afford. Since entry into a contract requires *freely* given consent, the seller has a duty to refrain from exploiting emotional states that may induce the buyer to act irrationally against his or her own best interests. For similar reasons, the seller also has the duty not to take advantage of gullibility, immaturity, ignorance, or any other factors that reduce or eliminate the buyer's ability to make free rational choices.

---

[21] See, for example, the many cases cited in George J. Alexander, *Honesty and Competition* (Syracuse, NY: Syracuse University Press, 1967).

Problems with the Contractual Theory

The main objections to the contract theory focus on the unreality of the assumptions on which the theory is based. First, critics argue, the theory unrealistically assumes that manufacturers make direct agreements with consumers. Nothing could be farther from the truth. Normally, a series of wholesalers and retailers stand between the manufacturer and the ultimate consumer. The manufacturer sells the product to the wholesaler, who sells it to the retailer, who finally sells it to the consumer. The manufacturer never enters into any direct contract with the consumer. How then can one say that manufacturers have contractual duties to the consumer?

Advocates of the contract view of manufacturer's duties have tried to respond to this criticism by arguing that manufacturers enter into "indirect" agreements with consumers. Manufacturers promote their products through their own advertising campaigns. These advertisements supply the promises that lead people to purchase products from retailers who merely function as "conduits" for the manufacturer's product. Consequently, through these advertisements, the manufacturer forges an indirect contractual relationship not only with the immediate retailers who purchase the manufacturer's product but also with the ultimate consumers of the product. The most famous application of this doctrine of broadened indirect contractual relationships is to be found in a 1960 court opinion, *Henningsen* v. *Bloomfield Motors.*[22] Mrs. Henningsen was driving a new Plymouth when it suddenly gave off a loud cracking noise. The steering wheel spun out of her hands, the car lurched to the right and crashed into a brick wall. Mrs. Henningsen sued the manufacturer, Chrysler Corporation. The court opinion read:

> Under modern conditions the ordinary layman, on responding to the importuning of colorful advertising, has neither the opportunity nor the capacity to inspect or to determine the fitness of an automobile for use; he must rely on the manufacturer who has control of its construction, and to some degree on the dealer who, to the limited extent called for by the manufacturer's instructions, inspects and services it before delivery. In such a marketing milieu his remedies and those of persons who properly claim through him should not depend "upon the intricacies of the law of sales. The obligation of the manufacturer should not be based alone on privity of contract [that is, on a direct contractual relationship]. It should rest, as was once said, upon 'the demands of social justice'." *Mazetti v. Armous & Co. (1913).* "If privity of contract is required," then, under the circumstances of modern merchandising, "privity of contract exists in the consciousness and understanding of all right-thinking persons . . . " Accordingly, we hold that under modern marketing conditions, when a manufacturer puts a new automobile in the stream of trade and promotes its purchase by the public, an implied warranty that it is reasonably suitable for use as such accompanies it into the hands of the ultimate purchaser. Absence of agency between the manufacturer and the dealer who makes the ultimate sale is immaterial.

[22] *Henningsen* v. *Bloomfield Motors, Inc.,* 32 New Jersey 358, 161 Atlantic 2d 69 (1960).

Thus, Chrysler Corporation was found liable for Mrs. Henningsen's injuries on the grounds that its advertising had created a contractual relationship with Mrs. Henningsen and on the grounds that this contract created an "implied warranty" about the car which Chrysler had a duty to fulfill.

A second objection to the contract theory focuses on the fact that a contract is a two-edged sword. If a consumer can freely agree to buy a product *with* certain qualities, the consumer can also freely agree to buy a product *without* those qualities. That is, freedom of contract allows a manufacturer to be released from his or her contractual obligations by explicitly *disclaiming* that the product is reliable, serviceable, safe, etc. Many manufacturers fix such disclaimers on their products. The Uniform Commercial Code, in fact, stipulates in Section 2-316:

a. Unless the circumstances indicate otherwise, all implied warranties are excluded by expressions like "as is," "with all faults," or other language that in common understanding calls the buyer's attention to the exclusion of warranties and makes plain that there is no implied warranty, and
b. When the buyer before entering into the contract has examined the goods or the sample or model as fully as he desired, or has refused to examine the goods, there is no implied warranty with regard to defects that on examination ought in the circumstances to have been revealed to him.

The contract view, then, implies that if the consumer has ample opportunity to examine the product and the disclaimers and voluntarily consents to buy it anyway, he or she assumes the responsibility for the defects disclaimed by the manufacturer, as well as for any defects the customer may carelessly have overlooked. Disclaimers can effectively nullify all contractual duties of the manufacturer.

A third objection to the contract theory criticizes the assumption that buyer and seller meet each other as equals in the sales agreement. The contractual theory assumes that buyers and sellers are equally skilled at evaluating the quality of a product and that buyers are able to adequately protect their interests against the seller. This is the assumption built into the requirement that contracts must be freely and knowingly entered into: Both parties must know what they are doing and neither must be coerced into doing it. This equality between buyer and seller that the contractual theory assumes, derives from the laissez-faire ideology that accompanied the historical development of contract theory.[23] Classical laissez-faire ideology held that the economy's markets are competitive and that in competitive markets the consumer's bargaining power is equal to that of the seller. Competition forces the seller to offer the consumer as good or better terms than the consumer could get from other competing sellers, so the consumer has the power to threaten to take his or her business to other sellers. Because of this equality between buyer and seller, it was fair that each be allowed to try to out-bargain the other and unfair to place restrictions on either. In practice, this laissez-faire ideology gave birth to the doctrine of "caveat emptor": let the buyer take care of himself.

[23] See Friedrich Kessler and Malcolm Pitman Sharp, *Contracts* (Boston: Little, Brown and Company, 1953), p. 1-9.

In fact, sellers and buyers do not exhibit the equality these doctrines assume. A consumer who must purchase hundreds of different kinds of commodities cannot hope to be as knowledgeable as a manufacturer who specializes in producing a single product. Consumers have neither the expertise nor the time to acquire and process the information on which they must base their purchase decisions. Consumers, as a consequence, must usually rely on the judgment of the seller in making their purchase decisions, and are particularly vulnerable to being harmed by the seller. Equality, far from being the rule, as the contract theory assumes, is usually the exception.

6.2 THE DUE CARE THEORY   *hopes to overcome objections above*

The "due care" theory of the manufacturer's duties to consumers is based on the idea that consumers and sellers do not meet as equals and that the consumer's interests are particularly vulnerable to being harmed by the manufacturer who has a knowledge and an expertise that the consumer does not have. Because manufacturers are in a more advantaged position, they have a duty to take special "care" to ensure that consumers' interests are not harmed by the products that they offer them. The doctrine of "caveat emptor" is here replaced with a weak version of the doctrine of "caveat vendor": let the seller take care of the buyer. A New York court decision neatly described the advantaged position of the manufacturer and the consequent vulnerability of the consumer:

> Today as never before the product in the hands of the consumer is often a most sophisticated and even mysterious article. Not only does it usually emerge as a sealed unit with an alluring exterior rather than as a visible assembly of component parts, but its functional validity and usefulness often depend on the application of electronic, chemical, or hydraulic principles far beyond the ken of the average consumer. Advances in the technologies of materials, of processes, of operational means have put it almost entirely out of the reach of the consumer to comprehend why or how the article operates, and thus even farther out of his reach to detect when there may be a defect or a danger present in its design or manufacture. In today's world it is often only the manufacturer who can fairly be said to know and to understand when an article is suitably designed and safely made for its intended purpose. Once floated on the market, many articles in a very real practical sense defy detection of defect, except possibly in the hands of an expert after laborious, and perhaps even destructive, disassembly. By way of direct illustration, how many automobile purchasers or users have any idea how a power steering mechanism operates or is intended to operate, with its "circulating work and piston assembly and its cross shaft splined to the Pitman arm"? We are accordingly persuaded that from the standpoint of justice as regards the operating aspect of today's products, responsibility should be laid on the manufacturer, subject to the limitations we set forth.[24]

[24] *Codling* v. *Paglia,* 32 New York 2d 330, 298 Northeastern 2d 622, 345 New York Supplement 2d 461 (1973).

The "due care" view holds, then, that because consumers must depend upon the greater expertise of the manufacturer, the manufacturer not only has a duty to deliver a product that lives up to the express and implied claims about it, but in addition the manufacturer has a duty to exercise due care to prevent others from being injured by the product, *even if the manufacturer explicitly disclaims such responsibility and the buyer agrees to the disclaimer.* The manufacturer violates this duty and is "negligent" when there is a failure to exercise the care that a reasonable person could have foreseen would be necessary to prevent others from being harmed by use of the product. Due care must enter into the design of the product, into the choice of reliable materials for constructing the product, into the manufacturing processes involved in putting the product together, into the quality controls used to test and monitor production, and into the warnings, labels, and instructions attached to the product. In each of these areas, according to the due care view, the manufacturer, in virtue of a greater expertise and knowledge, has a positive duty to take whatever steps are necessary to ensure that when the product leaves the plant it is as safe as possible, and the customer has a right to such assurance. Failure to take such steps is a breach of the moral duty to exercise due care and a violation of the injured person's right to expect such care, a right that rests on the consumer's need to rely on the manufacturer's expertise. Edgar Schein sketched out the basic elements of the "due care" theory several years ago when he wrote:

> . . . a professional is someone who knows better what is good for his client than the client himself does. . . . If we accept this definition of professionalism . . . we may speculate that it is the *vulnerability of the client* that has necessitated the development of moral and ethical codes surrounding the relationship. The client must be protected from exploitation in a situation in which he is unable to protect himself because he lacks the relevant knowledge to do so . . . If [a manufacturer] is . . . a professional, who is his client? With respect to whom is he exercising his expert knowledge and skills? Who needs protection against the possible misuse of these skills? . . . Many economists argue persuasively . . . that the consumer has not been in a position to know what he was buying and hence was, in fact, in a relatively vulnerable position . . . Clearly, then, one whole area of values deals with the relationship between the [manufacturer] and consumers.[25]

The due care view, of course, rests on the principle that individuals have a moral duty not to harm or injure others by their acts and that others have a moral right to expect such care from individuals. This principle has been justified from a variety of different positions. Rule-utilitarians have defended it on the grounds that if the rule is accepted, everyone's welfare will be advanced.[26] It has been argued for on the basis of Kant's theory, since it seems to follow from the categorical imperative that people should be treated as ends and not merely as means, that is, that

[25] Edgar H. Schein, "The Problem of Moral Education for the Business Manager," *Industrial Management Review,* 8 (1966): 3-11.

[26] See W.D. Ross, *The Right and the Good* (Oxford: The Clarendon Press, 1930), ch. 2.

they have a *positive* right to be helped when they cannot help themselves.[27] And Rawls has argued that individuals in the "original position" would agree to the principle because it would provide the basis for a secure social environment.[28] The judgment that individual producers have a duty not to harm or injure, therefore, is solidly based on several ethical principles.

The Duty to Exercise Due Care

According to the due care theory, manufacturers exercise sufficient care when they take adequate steps to prevent whatever injurious effects they can foresee that the use of their product may have on consumers after having conducted inquiries into the way the product will be used and after having attempted to anticipate any possible misuses of the product. A manufacturer, then, is *not* morally negligent when others are harmed by a product and the harm was not one that the manufacturer could possibly have foreseen or prevented. Nor is a manufacturer morally negligent after having taken all reasonable steps to protect the consumer and to ensure that the consumer is informed of any irremovable risks that might still attend the use of the product. A car manufacturer, for example, cannot be said to be negligent from a moral point of view when people carelessly misuse the cars the manufacturer produces. A car manufacturer would be morally negligent only if the manufacturer had allowed unreasonable dangers to remain in the design of the car that consumers cannot be expected to know about or that they cannot guard against by taking their own precautionary measures.

What specific responsibilities does the duty to exercise due care impose on the producer? In general, the producer's responsibilities would extend to three areas:[29]

Design The manufacturer should ascertain whether the design of an article conceals any dangers, whether it incorporates all feasible safety devices, and whether it uses materials that are adequate for the purposes the product is intended to serve. The manufacturer is responsible for being thoroughly acquainted with the design of the item, and to conduct research and tests extensive enough to uncover any risks that may be involved in employing the article under various conditions of use. This requires researching consumers and analyzing their behavior, testing the product under different conditions of consumer use, and selecting materials strong enough to stand up to all probable usages. The effects of aging and of wear should also be analyzed and taken into account in designing an article. Engineering staff should acquaint themselves with hazards that might result from prolonged use and wear, and

---

[27] Donagan, *Theory of Morality,* p. 83.

[28] Rawls, *Theory of Justice,* pp. 114–17; 333–42.

[29] Discussions of the requirements of "due care" may be found in a variety of texts, all of which, however, approach the issues from the point of view of legal liability: Irwin Gray, *Product Liability: A Management Response* (New York: AMACOM, 1975), ch. 6; Eugene R. Carrubba, *Assuring Product Integrity* (Lexington, MA: Lexington Books, 1975); Frank Nixon, *Managing to Achieve Quality and Reliability* (New York: McGraw-Hill Book Co., 1971).

should warn the consumer of any potential dangers. There is a duty to take the latest technological advances into account in designing a product, especially where advances can provide ways of designing a product that is less liable to harm or injure its users.

Production   The production manager should control the manufacturing processes to eliminate any defective items, to identify any weaknesses that become apparent during production, and to ensure that short-cuts, substitution of weaker materials, or other economizing measures are not taken during manufacture that would compromise the safety of the final product. To ensure this, there should be adequate quality controls over materials that are to be used in the manufacture of the product and over the various stages of manufacture.

Information   The manufacturer should fix labels, notices, or instructions on the product that will warn the user of all dangers involved in using or misusing the item and that will enable the user to adequately guard himself or herself against harm or injury. These instructions should be clear and simple, and warnings of any hazards involved in using or misusing the product should also be clear, simple, and prominent. In the case of drugs, manufacturers have a duty to warn physicians of any risks or of any dangerous side-effects that research or prolonged use have revealed. It is a breach of the duty not to harm or injure if the manufacturer attempts to conceal or down-play the dangers related to drug usage.

In determining the safeguards that should be built into a product, the manufacturer must also take into consideration the *capacities* of the persons who will use the product. If a manufacturer anticipates that a product will be used by persons who are immature, mentally deficient, or too inexperienced to be aware of the dangers attendant on the use of the product, then the manufacturer owes them a greater degree of care than if the anticipated users were of ordinary intelligence and prudence. Children, for example, cannot be expected to realize the dangers involved in using electrical equipment. Consequently, if a manufacturer anticipates that an electrical item will probably be used by children, steps must be taken to ensure that a person with a child's understanding will not be injured by the product.

If the possible harmful effects of using a product are serious, or if they cannot be adequately understood without expert opinion, then sale of the product should be carefully controlled. A firm should not oppose regulation of the sale of a product when regulation is the only effective means of ensuring that the users of the product are fully aware of the risks its use involves.

Problems with "Due Care"   *what is reasonable?*

The basic difficulty raised by the "due care" theory is that there is no clear method for determining when one has exercised enough "due care." That is, there is no hard and fast rule for determining how far a firm must go to ensure the safety of its product. Some authors have proposed the general utilitarian rule that the greater the probability of harm and the larger the population that might be harmed, the more the firm is obligated to do. But this fails to resolve some important issues. Every product involves at least some small risk of injury. If the manufacturer should try to eliminate even low-level risks, this would require that the manufacturer invest so much in each product that the product would be priced out of the reach of most consumers. Moreover, even *attempting* to balance higher risks against added costs involves measurement problems: How does one quantify risks to health and life?

A second difficulty raised by the "due care" theory is that it assumes that the manufacturer can discover the risks that attend the use of a product before the consumer buys and uses it. In fact, in a technologically innovative society new products will continually be introduced into the market whose defects cannot emerge until years or decades have passed. Only years after thousands of people were using and being exposed to asbestos, for example, did a correlation emerge between the incidence of cancer and exposure to asbestos. Although manufacturers may have greater expertise than consumers, their expertise does not make them omniscient. Who, then, is to bear the costs of injuries sustained from products whose defects neither the manufacturer nor the consumer could have uncovered beforehand?

Thirdly, the due care view appears to some to be paternalistic. For it assumes that the *manufacturer* should be the one who makes the important decisions for the consumer, at least with respect to the levels of risks that are proper for consumers to bear. But one may wonder whether such decisions should not be left up to the free choice of consumers who can decide for themselves whether or not they want to pay for additional risk reduction.

6.3 THE SOCIAL COSTS VIEW OF THE MANUFACTURER'S DUTIES

A third theory on the duties of the manufacturer would extend the manufacturer's duties beyond those imposed by contractual relationships and beyond those imposed by the duty to exercise due care in preventing injury or harm. This third theory holds that a manufacturer should pay the costs of *any* injuries sustained through any defects in the product, *even when the manufacturer exercised all due care in the design and manufacture of the product and has taken all reasonable precautions to warn users of every foreseen danger.* According to this third theory a manufacturer has a duty to assume the risks of even those injuries that arise out of defects in the product that no one could reasonably have foreseen or eliminated. The theory is a very strong version of the doctrine of "caveat vendor": let the seller take care of the buyer.

This third theory, which has formed the basis of the legal doctrine of "strict

---

[30]See, for example, Michael D. Smith, "The Morality of Strict Liability In Tort," *Business and Professional Ethics,* 3, no. 1 (December 1979): 3–5; for a review of the rich legal literature on this topic, see Richard A. Posner, "Strict Liability: A Comment," *The Journal of Legal Studies,* 2, no. 1 (January 1973): 205–21.

liability," is founded on utilitarian arguments.[30] The utilitarian arguments for this third theory hold that the "external" costs of injuries resulting from unavoidable defects in the design of an artifact constitute part of the costs society must pay for producing and using an artifact. By having the manufacturer bear the external costs that result from these injuries as well as the ordinary internal costs of design and manufacture, all costs will be internalized and added on as part of the price of the product. Internalizing all costs in this way, according to proponents of this theory, will lead to a more efficient use of society's resources. First, since the price will reflect *all* the costs of producing and using the artifact, market forces will ensure that the product is not overproduced, and that resources are not wasted on it. (Whereas if some costs were not included in the price, then manufacturers would tend to produce more than is needed.) Secondly, since manufacturers have to pay the costs of injuries, they will be motivated to exercise greater care and to thereby reduce the number of accidents. Manufacturers will therefore strive to cut down the social costs of injuries, and this means a more efficient care for our human resources. In order to produce the maximum benefits possible from our limited resources, therefore, the social costs of injuries from defective products should be internalized by passing them on to the manufacturer, even when the manufacturer has done all that could be done to eliminate such defects. And thirdly, internalizing the costs of injury in this way enables the manufacturer to distribute losses among all the users of a product instead of allowing losses to fall on individuals who may not be able to sustain the loss by themselves.   Ought implies can.

Underlying this third theory on the duties of the manufacturer are the standard utilitarian assumptions about the values of efficiency. The theory assumes that an efficient use of resources is so important for society that social costs should be allocated in whatever way will lead to a more efficient use and care of our resources. On this basis, the theory argues that a manufacturer should bear the social costs for injuries caused by defects in a product, even when no negligence was involved and no contractual relationship existed between the manufacturer and the user.

Problems with the Social Costs View

The major criticism of the social costs view of the manufacturer's duties is that is is unfair.[31] It is unfair, the critics charge, because it violates the basic canons of compensatory justice. Compensatory justice implies that a person should be forced to compensate an injured party only if the person could foresee and could have prevented the injury. By forcing manufacturers to pay for injuries that they could neither foresee nor prevent, the social costs theory (and the legal theory of 'strict liability' that flows from it) treats manufacturers unfairly. Moreover, insofar as the social costs theory encourages passing the costs of injuries on to all consumers (in the form of higher prices), consumers are also being treated unfairly.

A second criticism of the social costs theory attacks the assumption that pass-

[31] George P. Fletcher, "Fairness and Utility in Tort Theory," *Harvard Law Review*, 85, no. 3 (January 1972): 537-73.

ing the costs of all injuries on to manufacturers will reduce the number of accidents.[32] On the contrary, critics claim, by relieving consumers of the responsibility of paying for their own injuries, the social costs theory will encourage carelessness in consumers. And an increase in consumer carelessness will lead to an increase in consumer injuries.

The arguments for and against the social costs theory deserve much more discussion than we can give them here. The theory is essentially an attempt to come to grips with the problem of allocating the costs of injuries between two morally innocent parties: The manufacturer who could not foresee or prevent a product-related injury, and the consumer who could not guard himself or herself against the injury because the hazard was unknown. This allocation problem will arise in any society that, like ours, has come to rely upon a technology whose effects do not become evident until years after the technology is introduced. Unfortunately, it is also a problem that may have no "fair" solution.

6.4 ADVERTISING ETHICS

The advertising industry is a massive business. Over $20 billion is spent each year on advertising.[33] $8 billion is spent on television ads alone.[34] There are over six thousand advertising agencies doing business in the United States, many of which employ several thousand people.

Who pays for these advertising expenditures? In the end, advertising costs must be covered by the prices consumers pay for the goods they buy: The consumer pays. What does the consumer get for his or her advertising dollar? According to most consumers, they get very little. Surveys have shown that 66 percent of consumers feel that advertising does not reduce prices; 65 percent believe it makes people buy things they should not buy; 54 percent feel advertisements insult the intelligence, and 63 percent feel advertisements do not present the truth.[35] On the other hand, defenders of the advertising industry see things differently. Advertising, they claim, "is, before all else, communication."[36] Its basic function is to provide consumers with information about the products available to them, a beneficial service.[37]

Is advertising then a waste or a benefit? Does it harm consumers or help them?

---

[32] Posner, *Economic Analysis of Law,* pp. 139–42.

[33] Eli P. Cox, "Deflating the Puffer," *Business Topics,* Summer 1973, p. 32.

[34] *Broadcasting Yearbook 1979* (Hollywood, CA: Broadcasting Publications, Inc., 1979), p. A.2.

[35] Raymond A. Bauer and Stephen A. Greyser, *Advertising in America: The Consumer View* (Cambridge: Harvard University Press, 1968), p. 394.

[36] Walter Weir, *Truth in Advertising and Other Heresies* (New York: McGraw-Hill Book Company, 1963), p. 154.

[37] See also, J. Robert Moskin, ed., *The Case for Advertising* (New York: American Association of Advertising Agencies, 1973), *passim.*

A Definition

Commercial advertising is sometimes defined as a form of "information" and an advertiser as "one who gives information." The implication is that the defining function of advertising is to provide information to consumers.[38] This definition of advertising, however, fails to distinguish advertisements from, say, articles in publications like *Consumer Reports,* which compare, test, and objectively evaluate the durability, safety, defects, and usefulness of various products. Consider how little information is conveyed by the following advertisements:

> "When you say Budweiser, you've said it all."
> "Cadillac—the new look of leadership."
> "Be careful how you use it." (Hai Karate)
> "It's the real thing." (Coke)

Advertisements often do not include much objective information for the simple reason that their primary function is not that of providing unbiased information. The primary function of commercial advertisements, rather, is to sell a product to prospective buyers, and whatever information they happen to carry is subsidiary to this basic function and usually determined by it.

A more helpful way of characterizing commercial advertising is in terms of the buyer-seller relationship: Commercial advertising can be defined as a certain kind of communication between a seller and potential buyers. It is distinguished from other forms of communication by two features. First, it is publicly addressed to a mass audience as distinct from a private message to a specific individual. Because of this public feature, advertising necessarily has widespread social effects.

Secondly, advertising is intended to *induce* several members of its audience to buy the seller's products. An advertisement can succeed in this intent in two main ways: (1) by creating a desire for the seller's product in consumers and (2) by creating a belief in consumers that the product is a means of satisfying some desire the buyer already has.

Discussion of the ethical aspects of advertising can be organized around the various features identified in the definition above: its social effects, its creation of consumer desires, and its effects on consumer beliefs.

We will begin by discussing the *social effects* of advertising.

Social Effects of Advertising

Critics of advertising claim that it has several adverse effects on society: It degrades people's tastes, it wastes valuable resources, and it creates monopoly power. We will examine these criticisms one by one.

---

[38] Sturdivant, *Business and Society,* p. 243.

Psychological effects of advertising   A familiar criticism of advertising is that it debases the tastes of the public by presenting irritating and aesthetically unpleasant displays.[39] To be effective advertisements must often be intrusive, strident, and repetitive. So that they will be understood by the most simple-minded person, advertisements are often boring, insipid, and insult the intelligence of viewers. In illustrating the use of toothpaste, mouth washes, deodorants, and undergarments, for example, advertisements sometimes employ images that many people find vulgar, offensive, disgusting, and tasteless. Yet, although these sorts of criticisms may be quite accurate, they do not seem to raise important ethical issues. It is certainly unfortunate that advertisements do not measure up to our *aesthetic* norms, but this does not imply that they also violate our *ethical* norms.

More to the point is the criticism that advertising debases the tastes of consumers by gradually and subtly inculcating materialistic values and ideas about how happiness is achieved.[40] Since advertising necessarily emphasizes the consumption of material goods, people are led to forget the importance of their other, more basic, needs and of other more realistic ways of achieving self-fulfillment. As a result, personal efforts are diverted from "nonmaterialistic" aims and objectives that are more likely to increase the happiness of people, and are instead channeled into expanded material consumption. Consumer advocate Mary Gardiner Jones writes:

> The conscious appeal in the television commercial is essentially materialistic. Central to the message of the TV commercial is the premise that it is the acquisition of *things* that will gratify our basic and inner needs and aspirations. It is the message of the commercial that all of the major problems confronting an individual can be instantly eliminated by . . . the use of a product . . . A second inescapable premise of these ads is that we are all externally motivated, concerned to do and be like our neighbors or to emulate popular successful individuals . . . Personal success in the TV ad is externally contrived, not the product of years of study and training . . . In addition, . . . the TV commercial presents a very special and limited view of American society. Here, according to the TV commercial . . . is what the young and successful are wearing and how they furnish their homes . . . [But] the TV world [is] typically that of the white suburban middle-income, middle-class family.[41]

The difficulty with this criticism, however, is that it is uncertain whether advertising actually has the large psychological effects the criticism attributes to it.[42] A person's beliefs and attitudes are notoriously difficult to change without

---

[39] See Stephen A. Greyser, "Irritation in Advertising," *Journal of Advertising Research,* 13, no. 3 (February 1973): 7–20.

[40] David M. Potter, *People of Plenty* (Chicago: The University of Chicago Press, 1954), p. 188.

[41] Mary Gardiner Jones, "The Cultural and Social Impact of Advertising on American Society," in *Consumerism,* 2nd ed., David Aaker and George S. Day, eds. (New York: The Free Press, 1974), p. 431.

[42] Stephen A. Greyser, "Advertising: Attacks and Counters," *Harvard Business Review,* 50 (10 March 1972): 22–28.

there being in the first place a willingness to accept the message being offered. Thus, the success of advertising may depend more on its appeal to the values consumers already possess than on its ability to instill new values. If this is so, then advertising does not so much create society's values as reflect them.

Advertising and waste   A second major criticism brought against advertising is that it is wasteful.[43] Economists sometimes distinguish between "production costs" and "selling costs." Production costs are the costs of the resources consumed in producing or improving a product. Selling costs are the additional costs of resources that do not go into changing the product but are invested instead in persuading people to buy the product. The costs of resources consumed by advertising, critics claim, are essentially "selling costs": they are not used to improve the product but to merely persuade people to buy it. The resources consumed by advertisements do not add anything to the utility of the product. Such resources, critics conclude, are "wasted" because they are expended without adding to consumer utility in any way.

One reply made to this argument is that advertising does in fact produce something: It produces and transmits information on the availability and the nature of products.[44] But as many have pointed out, even in these respects, the information content of advertisements is minimal and could be transmitted by substantially less expensive means.[45]

Another more persuasive reply to the argument is that advertising serves to produce a beneficial rise in demand for *all* products. This rising general demand in turn makes mass production possible. The end result is a gradually expanding economy in which products are manufactured with ever greater efficiency and ever more cheaply. Advertising, then, adds to consumer utility by serving as an incentive to greater consumption and thereby indirectly motivating a greater productivity and efficiency and a lower price structure.[46]

There is, however, substantial uncertainty surrounding the question whether advertising is responsible for a rise in the total consumption of goods.[47] Studies have shown that advertising frequently fails to stimulate consumption of a product, and consumption in many industries has increased in spite of minimal advertising expenditures. Advertising thus appears to be effective for individual companies not because it *expands* consumption, but only because it *shifts* consumption away from one product to another. If this is true, then economists are correct when they claim

[43] For an informal discussion of this issue see Jules Backman, "Is Advertising Wasteful?," *Journal of Marketing*, (January 1968), pp. 2–8.

[44] Phillip Nelson, "The Economic Value of Advertising," in Yale Brozen, *Advertising and Society* (New York: New York University Press, 1974), pp. 43–66.

[45] Richard Caves, *American Industry: Structure, Conduct, Performance* (Englewood Cliffs, NJ: Prentice-Hall, Inc., 1972), p. 101.

[46] David M. Blank, "Some Comments on the Role of Advertising in the American Economy—A Plea for Reevaluation," in *Reflections on Progress in Marketing*, ed. L. George Smith (Chicago: American Marketing Association, 1964), p. 151.

[47] See the discussion in Thomas M. Garrett, *An Introduction to Some Ethical Problems of Modern American Advertising* (Rome: The Gregorian University Press, 1961), pp. 125–30.

that beyond the level needed to impart information, advertising becomes a waste of resources because it does nothing more than shift demand from one firm to another.[48]

Moreover, even if advertising were an effective spur to consumption, many authors have argued, this is not necessarily a blessing. E.F. Schumacher, Herman E. Daly, and other economists have claimed that the most pressing social need at present is finding ways of *decreasing* consumption.[49] Increasing consumption has led to a rapid industrial expansion that has polluted much of the natural environment and has rapidly depleted our nonrenewable resources. Unless we limit consumption, we will soon outrun the finite natural resources our planet possesses with disastrous consequences for us all. If this is so, then the claim that advertising induces ever higher levels of consumption is not in its favor.

Advertising and market power   Since the early 1950s, Nicholas Kaldor and others have claimed that the massive advertising campaigns of modern manufacturers enable them to achieve and maintain a monopoly (or oligopoly) power over their markets.[50] And monopolies, as we have seen, lead to higher consumer prices. Kaldor's argument was simple. Large manufacturers have the financial resources to mount massive and expensive advertising campaigns to introduce their products. These campaigns create in consumers a "loyalty" to the brand-name of the manufacturer, giving the manufacturer control of a major portion of the market. Small firms are then unable to break into the market because they cannot finance the expensive advertising campaigns that would be required to get consumers to switch their brand loyalties. As a result, a few large oligopoly firms emerge in control of consumer markets from which small firms are effectively barred. Advertising, then, is supposed to reduce competition, and to raise barriers to entry into markets.

But is there a connection between advertising and market power? If advertising does raise costs for consumers by encouraging monopoly markets, then there should be a statistical connection between the amount of advertising revenues spent by an industry and the degree of market concentration in that industry. The more concentrated and less competitive industries should exhibit high levels of advertising, while less concentrated and more competitive industries should exhibit correspondingly lower levels. Unfortunately, the statistical studies aimed at uncovering a connection between advertising intensity and market concentration have been inconclusive.[51] Some concentrated industries (soaps, cigarettes, breakfast cereals)

---

[48] *Ibid.,* p. 177.

[49] See E.F. Schumacher, *Small is Beautiful* (London: Blond and Briggs, Ltd., 1973); and Herman E. Daly, ed., *Toward a Steady-State Economy* (San Francisco: W. H. Freeman, 1979), 'Introduction.'

[50] Nicholas H. Kaldor, "The Economic Aspects of Advertising," *The Review of Economic Studies,* 18 (1950–51): 1–27; see also William S. Comanor and Thomas Wilson, *Advertising and Market Power* (Cambridge: Harvard University Press, 1975).

[51] See L.G. Telser, "Some Aspects of the Economics of Advertising," *Journal of Business* (April 1968), pp. 166–73; for a survey of studies on this issue, see James M. Ferguson, *Advertising and Competition: Theory Measurement and Fact* (Cambridge, MA: Ballinger Publishing Company, 1974), ch. 5.

expend large amounts on advertising, but others (drugs, cosmetics) do not. Moreover, in at least some oligopoly industries (the auto industry, for example) smaller firms spend more per unit on advertising than the large major firms. Whether advertising harms consumers by diminishing competition is an interesting but unsettled question.

The criticisms of advertising based on its social effects are inconclusive. They are inconclusive for the simple reason that it is unknown whether advertising has the capacity to produce the effects that the criticisms assume it has. To establish the case for or against advertising on the basis of its effects on society will require a great deal more research on the exact nature of the psychological and economic effects advertising has.

Advertising and the Creation of Consumer Desires

During the late 1950s, John K. Galbraith and others began to argue that advertising is manipulative: It is the creation of desires in consumers for the sole purpose of absorbing industrial output.[52] Galbraith distinguished two kinds of desires: those that have a "physical" basis, such as desires for food and shelter, and those that are "psychological in origin," such as the individual's desires for goods that "give him a sense of personal achievement, accord him a feeling of equality with his neighbors, direct his mind from thought, serve sexual aspiration, promise social acceptability, enhance his subjective feeling of health, contribute by conventional canons to personal beauty, or are otherwise psychologically rewarding."[53] The physically based desires originate in the buyer and are relatively immune to being changed by persuasion. The psychic desires, however, are capable of being managed, controlled and expanded by advertising. Since the demand created by physical needs is finite, producers soon produce enough to meet these needs. If production is to expand, therefore, producers must create new demand by manipulating the pliable psychic desires through advertising. Advertising is therefore used to create psychic desires for the sole purpose of "ensuring that people buy what is produced," that is, to absorb the output of an expanding industrial system.

The effect of this management of demand through advertising is to shift the focus of decision in the purchase of goods from the consumer where it is beyond control, to the firm where it is subject to control.[54] Production, then, is not molded to serve human desires; rather human desires are molded to serve the needs of production.

If this view of Galbraith's is correct, then advertising violates the individual's right to choose for himself or herself: Advertising manipulates the consumer. The con-

[52] See John Kenneth Galbraith, *The Affluent Society* (Boston: Houghton Mifflin Company, 1958).

[53] John Kenneth Galbraith, *The New Industrial State,* (New York: New American Library, 1967), p. 211.

[54] *Ibid.,* p. 215.

sumer is used merely as a means for advancing the ends and purposes of producers, and this diminishes the consumer's capacity to freely choose for himself or herself.[55]

It is not clear that Galbraith's argument is correct. As we have already seen, the psychological effects of advertising are still unclear. Consequently, it is unclear whether psychic desires can be manipulated by advertising in the wholesale way that Galbraith's argument assumes.[56]

Moreover, as F.A. von Hayek has pointed out, the "creation" of psychic wants did not originate with modern advertising.[57] New wants have always been "created" by the invention of novel and attractive products (such as, the first bow-and-arrow, the first painting, the first perfume), and such a creation of wants seems harmless enough.

However, although it is unclear whether advertising as a whole has the massive manipulative effects that Galbraith attributes to it, it is clear that some particular advertisements are at least *intended* to manipulate. They are intended, that is, to arouse in the consumer a psychological desire for the product without the consumer's knowledge and without the consumer being able to rationally weigh whether the product is in his or her own best interests. Advertisements that intentionally rely on "subliminal suggestion," or that attempt to make consumers associate unreal sexual or social fulfillment with a product, fall into this class, as do advertisements that are aimed at children. In 1972, for example, the Federal Trade Commission strongly criticized an advertisement for Vivarin tablets that implied that it would renew a woman's sexual attractiveness. The ad ran as follows:

> One day it dawned on me that I was boring my husband to death. It was hard for me to admit it—but it was true . . . Often by the time he came home at night I was feeling dull, tired, drowsy, and so Jim would look at television and, for the most part, act like I wasn't even there. And I wasn't. I decided that I had to do something. I had seen an advertisement for a tablet called Vivarin. It said that Vivarin was a non-habit-forming stimulant tablet that would give me a quick lift. Last week . . . I took a Vivarin tablet . . . just about an hour before Jim came home, and I found time to pretty up a little, too. It worked. All of a sudden Jim was coming home to a more exciting woman. Me. . . . The other day—it wasn't even my birthday—Jim sent me flowers with a note. The note began: "To my new wife . . . "[58]

The only active ingredient in Vivarin was the equivalent of the caffeine in two cups of coffee. Advertisements of this sort are manipulative, insofar as they circumvent conscious reasoning and seek to influence the consumer to do what the advertiser

---

[55] See the discussion of this issue in Stanley I. Benn, "Freedom and Persuasion," *The Australasian Journal of Philosophy,* vol. 45 (December 1967).

[56] See George Katova, *The Mass Consumption Society* (New York: McGraw-Hill Book Company, 1964), pp. 54–61.

[57] F.A. von Hayek, "The *Non Sequitur* of the 'Dependence Effect,'" *Southern Economic Journal* (April 1961).

[58] Quoted in Ivan L. Preston, *The Great American Blow-up* (Madison, WI: The University of Wisconsin Press, 1975), p. 216.

wants and not what is in the consumer's interests.[59] They violate, that is, the consumer's right to be treated as a free and equal rational being.

Advertising and Its Effects
on Consumer Beliefs

The most common criticism of advertising concerns its effect on the consumer's beliefs. Since advertising is a form of communication, it can be as truthful or as deceptive as any other form of communication. Most criticisms of advertising focus on the deceptive aspects of modern advertising.

Deceptive advertising can take several forms.[60] An advertisement can misrepresent the nature of the product by using deceptive mock-ups, by using untrue paid testimonials, by inserting the word "guarantee" where nothing is guaranteed, by quoting misleading prices, by failing to disclose defects in a product, by misleadingly disparaging a competitor's goods, or by simulating well-known brand-names. Some fraudulent forms of advertising involve more complex schemes. Bait advertisements, for example, announce the sale of goods that later prove not to be available or to be defective. Once the consumer is lured into the store, he or she is pressured to purchase another more expensive item.

A long ethical tradition has consistently condemned deception in advertising on the grounds that it violates consumers' rights to choose for themselves (a Kantian argument) and on the grounds that it generates a public distrust of advertising that diminishes the utility of this form and even of other forms of communication (the utilitarian argument).[61] The central problem, then, is not that of trying to understand why deceptive advertising is wrong as much as of trying to understand how it becomes deceptive and therefore unethical.

All communication involves three terms: (1) the author(s) who originates the communication, (2) the medium that carries the communication, and (3) the audience who receives the communication. Since advertising is a form of communication, it involves these three terms and the various ethical problems raised by the fact that it is a form of communication can be organized around these three elements:

The authors   Deception involves three necessary conditions in the author of a communication: (a) The author must intend to have the audience believe something false, (b) the author must know it is false, and (c) the author must knowingly do something that will lead the audience to believe the falsehood. This means that the deliberate intent to have an audience believe something false by merely implying it is as wrong as an express lie. It also means, however, that the advertiser cannot be

[59] Garrett, *Ethical Problems of Modern American Advertising,* pp. 46–51.

[60] See Preston, *The Great American Blow-up.*

[61] For a discussion of these arguments, see Sissela Bok, *Lying* (New York: Vintage Books, 1978).

held morally responsible for misinterpretations of an advertisement when these are the unintended and unforeseen results of unreasonable carelessness on the part of the audience. The "author" of an advertisement includes, of course, not only the heads of an advertising agency, but also the persons who create advertising copy and those who "endorse" a product. By offering their positive cooperation in the making of an advertisement, they become morally responsible for its effects.

The medium   Part of the responsibility for truth in advertising rests on the media that carry advertisements. As active participants in the transmission of a message, they also lend their positive cooperation to the success of the advertisement and so they, too, become morally responsible for its effects. They should, therefore, take steps to ensure that the contents of their advertisements are true and not misleading. In the drug industry, retail agents who serve as company sales agents to doctors and hospitals are in effect advertising "media" and are morally responsible for not misleading doctors with respect to the safety and possible hazards of the drugs they promote.

The audience   The meaning attributed to a message depends in part on the capacities of the person who receives the message. A clever and knowledgeable audience, for example, may be capable of correctly interpreting an advertisement that may be misleading to a less knowledgeable or less educated group. Consequently, the advertiser should take into account the interpretive capacities of the audience when he or she determines the content of an advertisement. Most buyers can be expected to be reasonably intelligent and to possess a healthy skepticism concerning the exaggerated claims advertisers make for their products. Advertisement that will reach the ignorant, the credulous, the immature, and the unthinking, however, should be designed to avoid misleading even those potential buyers whose judgment is limited. When matters of health or safety, or the possibility of significant injury to buyers is involved, special care should be exercised to ensure that advertisements do not mislead users into ignoring possible dangers.

The third category of issues ("The Audience") raises what is perhaps the most troubling problem in advertising ethics: To what extent do consumers possess the capacity to filter out the "puffery" and bias most advertising messages carry? When an advertisement for a Norelco electric shaver proclaims "You can't get any closer," do consumers automatically discount the vague, nonspecific, and false implication that Norelco was tested against every possible method of shaving and was found to leave facial hair shorter than any other method? Unfortunately, we have very little knowledge of the extent to which consumers are able to filter out the exaggerations advertisements contain.

The moral issues raised by advertising, then, are complex and involve several still unsolved problems. The following summarizes, however, the main factors that should be taken into consideration in determining the ethical nature of a given advertisement:

SOCIAL EFFECTS

1. What does the advertiser intend the effect of the advertisement to be?
2. What are the actual effects of the advertisement on individuals and on society as a whole?

EFFECTS ON DESIRE

1. Does the advertisement inform or does it also seek to persuade?
2. If it is persuasive, does it attempt to create an irrational and possibly injurious desire?

EFFECTS ON BELIEF

1. Is the content of the advertisement truthful?
2. Does the advertisement have a tendency to mislead those to whom it is directed?

QUESTIONS FOR REVIEW AND DISCUSSION

1. Define the following concepts: the contractual theory (of a seller's duties), the duty to comply, implied claim, reliability, service life, maintainability, product safety, reasonable risk, duty of disclosure, duty not to misrepresent, duty not to coerce, manufacturer's implied warranty, disclaimer, caveat emptor, due care theory (of a seller's duties), caveat vendor, professional, manufacturer's duty to exercise due care, social costs theory (of a seller's duties), advertisement, production costs, selling costs, to expand consumption, to shift consumption, Kaldor's theory of advertising and market power, brand loyalty, Galbraith's theory of the creation of consumer desires, bait advertisements, deception.
2. Discuss the arguments for and against the three main theories of a producer's duties to the consumer. In your judgment, which theory is most adequate? Are there any marketing areas where one theory is more appropriate than the others?
3. Who should decide (a) how much information should be provided by manufacturers, (b) how good products should be, (c) how truthful advertisements should be? The government? Manufacturers? Consumer groups? The free market? Explain your views.
4. "Advertising should be banned because it diminishes a consumer's freedom of choice." Discuss this claim. Review the materials available in your library and decide whether you agree that "criticisms of advertising based on its social effects are inconclusive."
5. Carefully examine two or more advertisements taken from current newspapers or magazines and assess the extent to which they meet what you would consider adequate ethical standards for advertising. Be prepared to defend your standards.

6. A manufacturer of electric coffee-pots recalled the pots (through newspaper announcements) when he found that the handles would sometimes fall off without warning and the boiling contents would spill. Only ten percent of the pots were returned. Does the manufacturer have any additional duties to those who did not return the pots? Explain your answer.

CASES FOR DISCUSSION

Drugs and Hair Dyes

In January 1978, the Food and Drug Administration (FDA) announced it was considering a regulation that would require hair dyes containing the chemical 4–MMPD (4-Methoxy-M-phenylenediamine sulfate) to carry the following label:

> Warning: Contains an ingredient that can penetrate your skin and has been determined to cause cancer in laboratory animals.

The warning promised to have a significant effect on the sales of the major manufacturers of permament hair dyes, including Clairol, Cosmair, Revlon, Alberto-Culver, Breck, Helene Curtis, and Tussy. The permanent hair dye sales of these companies had topped $300 million in 1977.

4–MMPD had been suspected of being carcinogenic since March 1975, when Dr. Bruce Ames announced that hair-dye ingredients caused mutations in bacterial genes.[1] Since chemicals that produce bacterial mutations are often also found to cause cancer, bacterial mutations are generally regarded as indications of a potentially carcinogenic substance.

The National Cancer Institute (NCI) subsequently tested 4–MMPD and found that it did indeed cause cancer in laboratory animals. Concurrently, the FDA sponsored studies that showed that about 3 percent of the 4–MMPD in dyes readily penetrates the scalp and enters the bloodstream; only 50 percent of the chemical is subsequently excreted.

In spite of these findings, however, the FDA was unable to do more than propose a warning label, since the 1938 Food, Drug, and Cosmetic Act, which regulates cosmetics, prohibits the FDA from banning the sale of hair dyes no matter how hazardous their contents. This prohibition was written into the law when a powerful cosmetic lobby convinced Congress in 1938 that hair dyes should be exempt from any law controlling cosmetics.[2] Moreover, the cosmetic industry contested the validity of the NCI tests on the grounds that the large doses of 4–MMPD administered to animals in the tests were "the equivalent of a woman drinking more than 25 bottles of hair dye a day, every day of her life." FDA officials countered that because

---

[1] "Are Hair Dyes Safe?," *Consumer Reports,* 44, no. 8 (August 1979): 456–60.

[2] Darla Miller, "Well, Does She or Doesn't She–Know If Her Hair Dye is Safe," *San Jose Mercury,* 5 December 1979, pp. 1C, 3C.

of test expenses, researchers must expose a few animals to large doses in order to determine the risk of exposing many humans to small doses. After a prolonged legal battle with the cosmetic industry, the FDA succeeded in imposing the proposed warning label.

When it was clear that the FDA would succeed in imposing the warning label, the major hair dye manufacturers implemented essentially similar strategies to avoid the label: They reformulated their hair dyes so that the new dyes contained no 4-MMPD. However, the companies refused to recall the old hair dyes that they had already distributed to retailers and that would continue to be sold over counters for several years. They would affix no warnings to these dyes.

The response of Revlon differed somewhat from that of other manufacturers. Revlon removed the offending 4-MMPD from its dyes and replaced it with a 4-EMPD (4-ethoxy-M-phenylenediamine sulfate), a substance with a chemical structure almost identical to 4-MMPD, but one that did not yet require a warning label.

Several chemical experts later claimed that Revlon's 4-EMPD had a potential for causing cancer similar to that of 4-MMPD.[3] The FDA subsequently tested 4-EMPD and found that it produced bacterial mutations similar to those that 4-MMPD had produced several years before. When questioned about the safety of 4-EMPD, Revlon at first contended that the NCI had tested 4-EMPD and had found it was not hazardous. NCI, however, denied that it had ever tested 4-EMPD. Revlon then corrected itself, and admitted that its own biologists had performed bacterial tests on 4-EMPD and, like the FDA, they had found that the substance caused mutations in bacterial genes.[4]

Until animal tests on 4-EMPD are completed, the FDA cannot move to require a warning label against the Revlon substance. Such tests take three to four years to complete, and processing a warning proposal takes another one or two years.

1. In your judgment, was the Food and Drug Administration right in ordering the warning label in January 1978, on the basis of the kinds of tests that it and the NCI had carried out? Defend your answer.

2. In your judgment, was it enough, from an ethical point of view, for the cosmetic companies to fix the warning on their labels or did their duties extend beyond this? Relate your answer to the three theories on the seller's duties discussed in the text and to the legitimacy of imposing risk.

3. In your judgment, should the FDA also have imposed some restrictions on the advertisements through which the cosmetic companies promoted their dyes? Explain your answer.

4. Comment on the ethical propriety of the strategies by which the cosmetic companies responded to the FDA announcement of January 1978 and to the requirement of a warning label.

5. Should government have the power to regulate business in the manner described in the case? Should the FDA have more or less control over cosmetic

[3]*Ibid.*
[4]"Are Hair Dyes Safe," p. 458.

companies? Comment on the business-government relationships illustrated by the case.

Marketing Infant Formula

Dear Friend,

In asking for your help in the boycott of Nestlé products, I speak for myself and for the Infant Formula Action Coalition (INFACT). Nestlé, the largest food processer in the world, is actively encouraging mothers in the developing countries in Africa, Asia, and South America to give up breast feeding and turn to powdered milk formula instead. But in such countries water is contaminated, sterilization procedures are unknown, illiteracy makes proper preparation impossible, and poor people try to stretch the powdered milk supply by overdiluting their baby's formula. The tragic results are widespread malnutrition and severe infant diarrhea that often ends in death. Despite worldwide protest, Nestlé continues to put profits first and refuses to halt this traffic with death. So we are trying, by boycott, to compel Nestlé to do what they won't do out of decency. INFACT and I ask you to do two things: Boycott *all* Nestlé products, and send a generous contribution to help us spread the word.

Most sincerely,

Benjamin Spock, M.D.[1]

Dr. Spock's letter supporting the boycott of Nestlé's products was one of several tactics used to get producers of infant formula to change their marketing practices in developing nations. In addition to Nestlé, four other companies have come under fire for their marketing of infant formula in third-world countries: Bristol-Myers, Abbott Laboratories, American Home Products, and Borden's.

Infant formula was developed in the 1920s to provide a medically acceptable alternative to breast milk for mothers who were not able to breast-feed their babies.[2] By the 1960s, 75 percent of all American babies were being fed infant formula, and two kinds of companies were producing and marketing the formulas: drug companies and food companies. The three main American drug companies producing infant formula (Bristol-Myers, Abbott Laboratories, and American Home Products) tended to emphasize dietary research in the development of their formulas and tended to market their formulas through medical channels: physicians, nurses, hospitals, clinics, professional health journals, and medical detail staff. The two main food companies (Nestlé–a Swiss company–and Borden's), on the other hand, entered the infant formula business as a way of diversifying the canned milk prod-

---

[1] Undated letter printed and distributed by the Newman Center, 1701 University Ave., S. E., Minneapolis, MN 55414.

[2] The information in this and the following paragraph is drawn from James E. Post, "The International Infant Formula Industry," pp. 215–41, in *Marketing and Promotion of Infant Formula in the Developing Nations, 1978: Hearing Before the Subcommittee on Health and Scientific Research of the Committee on Human Resources.* U.S. Congress, Senate, 95th Congress. Hereinafter this publication is cited as *"Hearings."*

ucts they were already producing and they tended to market their product through conventional consumer-oriented mass advertising.

During the 1960s birth rates in the United States and Europe began to level off, and infant formula producers turned to marketing their products in third-world countries where birth rates were still high and where a trend toward urbanization was making large populations accessible to modern mass-marketing techniques. Bristol-Myers pushed hard to extend its marketing into the Caribbean, Central America, and the Philippines; Abbott Laboratories moved into Africa and Southeast Asia; American Home Products expanded into Southeast Asia, Latin America, and Africa; Borden's went into Latin America, the Caribbean, and Southeast Asia; and Nestlé attempted to build up a significant presence in every national market. By the late 1970s Abbott Laboratories' infant formula sales in developing nations totaled about $20 million annually; American Home Products had sales of about $50 million worth of infant formula in developing nations; and Nestlé held about a 50 percent share of the entire infant formula world market estimated to total $1.5 billion in 1978. Borden's succeeded in developing only a narrow share of the infant formula market.

Many medical personnel in third-world countries were happy to see the appearance of the infant formulas. Prior to the introduction of the formulas, infants were regularly weaned from breast-feeding with rice water, sweetened cow's milk, and other supplemental foods, so the formulas provided a preferable method of weaning. Undernourished or sickly mothers, too, had not had a readily available alternative to supplement their breast milk until the formulas appeared. In addition, understaffed hospitals welcomed the appearance of the "mothercraft nurses" whom the formula manufacturers provided and who instructed new mothers on all aspects of hygenic child care and feeding. The nurses, dressed in white uniforms, provided the mothers with free samples (as hospitals do in the United States), and were often paid on a commission basis to promote the formulas. While the drug companies (Bristol-Myers, Abbott Laboratories, and American Home Products) promoted their formulas primarily through these medical avenues, Nestlé and the other food companies tended to rely primarily on intensive mass-media advertising including sound trucks, newspapers, television, radio, popular magazines, and billboards.

As infant formula manufacturers expanded their marketing into the developing countries in the early 1970s, health officials began to voice a concern that the incidence of malnutrition and diarrhea were rising among third-world babies due to an increasing reliance on infant formulas and a concomitant decline of breast-feeding. In a series of studies, Dr. Derrick B. Jelliffe and other nutrition experts claimed that the trend toward infant formulas was dangerous, and that breast milk was the only ideal food for growing infants because it contains both the nutrients essential to a child's health and the antibodies that protect the child against disease.[3] If a mother is unable to nurse her child, they argued, then commercial formulas would

---

[3] D.B. Jelliffe, *Child Nutrition in Developing Countries* (Washington, DC: U.S. Government Printing Office, 1966); D.B. Jelliffe, "World Trends in Infant Feeding," *American Journal of Clinical Nutrition,* 29 (1976): 1227.

provide a safe substitute only if they could be used under sanitary conditions and according to the instructions provided with the formulas. In underdeveloped countries, they claimed, these conditions were not available: Hygiene was lacking, sterilization procedures were not employed, and mothers lacked the education to read written instructions. These and other difficulties involved in the use of infant formula by third-world mothers were summarized in 1973 by Dr. Roy E. Brown:

> [As] with other so-called convenience foods, the general public must pay the commercial companies for that convenience. In a newly urbanized [third-world] family, the financial pressures may be extreme, and it is not uncommon for a well-meaning mother to be forced to cut her food costs by over-diluting or "stretching" the infant's formula . . . Added to this are several other related problems in formula preparation. The uneducated mother may easily misread or misunderstand the directions and incorrectly reconstitute the formula. In many new urban centers, the contaminated water supply will contaminate the formula. There is an associated problem with the cleansing of feeding bottles and nipples, and with refrigeration of the prepared formulas . . . The end result is not only poor nutrition but also recurrent bouts of diarrhea that will cause further dietary restriction, modification, and dilution and that will increase the likelihood of malnutrition and possible death.[4]

Dr. Jelliffe estimated that infant deaths in the third-world directly or indirectly attributable to the use of infant formula might be as high as ten million per year. Consequently steps should be taken to encourage breast-feeding among mothers in developing countries and to discourage the use of infant formula preparations.

Critics of the infant formula companies alleged that it was the aggressive marketing practices that the companies were using in the third-world that were encouraging mothers to use infant formula even when it endangered the life and health of their infants. Two kinds of practices drew special criticism: intensive consumer advertising that implied that the use of infant formula was nutritionally or socially superior to breast-feeding, and the use of medical personnel to endorse or promote the infant formulas directly to new mothers. Doug Clement, for example, an organizer of the Infant Formula Action Coalition that sponsored the Nestlé boycott, argued:

> Mass-media advertising is one way that these formula producers create a market for infant formula in the developing countries. Huge advertisements appear on the sides of panel trucks in Nigeria or stationwagons in Thailand. In Barbados, advertisements for Bristol-Myers' "Enfamil" were on the back covers of the 1975 and 1976 telephone books . . . In the maternity ward of Philippine hospitals there are full-color calendars and posters depicting bright, healthy babies next to large cans of Nestlé's "Lactogen" and "Pelargon" formulas. And in Uruguay newspaper ads display a new Nestlé formula: "Eledon" . . . [Radio] has become an extensive advertising medium for formula marketers in the third-world. In Kenya, for example, infant formula

---

[4] Roy E. Grown, "Breast Feeding in Modern Times," *The American Journal of Clinical Nutrition,* 26 (May 1973): 485–86.

ads made up almost 13 percent of all Swahili radio advertising in 1973; nine-tenths of this advertising was for Nestlé's Lactogen. In Malaysia, where the poor and rural tend to listen to the radio while the relatively rich and urban watch television, Nestlé ran three and a half times as many formula ads on radio as on TV in 1976. "Mothercraft nurses," hired by the companies to talk to new mothers about infant care and feeding . . . bring cans of their company's formula when they visit mothers on the maternity wards or in their homes, and often leave [free] samples behind. In their crisp white uniforms, the nurses are seen as medical authorities, and their explicit endorsement of bottle-feeding is a powerful reinforcement of the media message. Such advertising persuades third-world women that formula is the modern, healthy, and Western way to feed babies. Bottle-feeding becomes a status symbol; breast-feeding, a vulgar tradition. [Statement of Doug Clement][5]

All infant formula promotions in the third-world, these critics argued, should unequivocally emphasize the superiority of breast-feeding over bottle-feeding. None should encourage bottle-feeding.

In February 1978, a researcher for the Interfaith Center for Corporate Responsibility (a critic of the infant formula companies) analyzed the labels on several cans of infant formula available in stores in Guatemala. According to the researchers, the Spanish labels read as follows when translated into English:[6]

SIMILAC—American Home Products (no mention of breast-feeding):

There is no food equivalent that more closely resembles the milk of healthy well-fed mothers.
SIMILAC With Iron
Similar to Mother's milk

WYETH S-26—American Home Products (no mention of breast-feeding):

Nourishes the baby like the mother's breast.
S-26
A superior food for the infant offers the baby all the formula he wants, just as if you were giving him the breast.

NAN—Nestlé:

Maternal lactation is the most adequate for the baby but in case of its total or partial absence, or if for other reasons it is necessary to replace or complement it, you can use NAN with total confidence, a powdered food quantitatively and qualitatively similar to mother's milk, for use right from the infant's birth.

ENFAMIL—BRISTOL MYERS:

Breast milk is best for your infant and is the preferred feeding whenever possible. ENFAMIL is a sound nutritious substitute or supplement for

[5] Doug Clement, "Infant Formula Malnutrition: Threat to the Third-World," *The Christian Century*, 1 March 1978, p. 209.

[6] *Hearings*, pp. 720–21.

breast milk to be used when breast-feeding is unsuccessful, inappropriate, or stopped early.

During the early 1970s, Borden's was advertising "KLIM," its principal powdered milk product, in the Caribbean and other developing areas. Magazine and newspaper advertisements showed a picture of a smiling plump baby drinking from a bottle; below the picture of the baby was a slightly smaller picture of a can of Klim and the text: "Give him Klim and watch him grow! Klim is full of goodness to build strong bodies, bones, and teeth. Give your baby the best full cream powdered milk—give him Klim. KLIM IS GOOD FOR YOUR BABY AND YOUR GROWING CHILDREN TOO." The ad contained no mention of breast-feeding nor did it mention that Klim was not an infant formula but was simply a form of powdered milk. In Singapore radio ads often repeated the slogan: "Help your baby grow healthy and happy. Give him [Nestlé's] Lactogen with Honey." Newspaper advertisements carried the same slogan in large type beneath a picture of a plump smiling baby surrounded by a well-dressed family and a picture of a can of Lactogen infant formula; beneath the slogan in much smaller type was the text: "Mother's milk is always best for your baby but when breast-feeding is no longer possible, or when your breast-fed baby is growing so fast that he needs extra feeds, give him Lactogen with Honey and help him grow healthy and happy."

The infant formula companies also promoted their products through the use of "baby booklets" which were distributed to new mothers free of charge. Nestlé, for example, distributed booklets entitled *A Life Begins* and *Your Baby and You* that urged the mother to use "an occasional bottle-feed" when she could not breast-feed her baby "entirely" by herself. The pamphlets also drew attention to various reasons for discontinuing breast-feeding and for substituting formula.

Critics of the infant formula industry employed several strategies as they attempted to pressure the companies into changing their marketing practices. In England, the War On Want, a charity organization, published *The Baby Killer*, an exposé of the infant formula issue and a severe criticism of Nestlé. When a German translation appeared within a year retitled *Nestlé Kills Babies*, Nestlé sued the publishers for defamation and libel. Although Nestlé won the suit in 1976, the lawsuit drew substantial media coverage and focused attention on Nestlé's marketing practices. The following year, in the United States several consumer advocacy groups joined together to form INFACT (Infant Formula Action), a coalition that launched a national boycott of all Nestlé products.

Through 1975, 1976, and 1977, members of the Interfaith Center for Corporate Responsibility (an agency that tries to promote social responsibility in corporations) who held stock in Bristol-Myers, Borden's, Abbott, and American Home Products joined together to sponsor shareholders' resolutions requesting that these companies release information on their infant formula promotion policies. Although these resolutions were all voted down, the companies nonetheless eventually agreed to release the information requested. Subsequently, the Interfaith Center submitted resolutions to American Home Products and Abbott Laboratories asking that these companies cease advertising infant formula to third-world consumers, discontinue using medical personnel and free samples, and include clear instructions and warnings on all infant formula products. Although these resolutions were voted down, they generated substantial publicity for the Interfaith Center and the infant formula issue.

The companies producing infant formula responded to the criticisms in several ways. One response was to argue that withdrawing infant formulas from the third-world would create even greater problems. Abbott Laboratories, for example, argued that the availability of infant formula was a health necessity in third-world countries, and the critical problem was that of developing safe methods of making it available.

> Few would debate that breast-milk alternatives have been necessary . . . [in cases] related to maternal disease, infant deformities, serious illness, prematurity, and inadequacy of breast-milk. In these cases, a formula may be necessary to complement or replace breast-milk if the child is to progress normally. . . . [Another] problem is that women of low socioeconomic status in developing countries are often malnourished . . . they produce an at-risk newborn of low birth weight in up to 50 percent of the cases . . . If fed solely at the breast, low birth weight infants begin to exhibit signs of growth retardation, reduced activity and other symptoms of serious malnutrition at about three months . . . The infant's poor state of malnutrition is associated with higher susceptibility to infection and disease. . . . Over time we believe it will become increasingly clear that a high-quality infant formula, closely patterned after breast-milk and fed with breast-milk may be *nutritionally* preferable for many infants, if the intergenerational cycle of malnourished mothers, malnourished infant is to be broken. . . . So that this point of view is not misinterpreted, we reaffirm that every mother who can, should breast-feed. Even if the breast-milk eventually becomes inadequate, the mother should breast-feed so that the baby receives colostrum and as much benefit as possible from her natural milk . . . [However] in the case of significantly malnourished mothers with low birth weight infants, the advice that nothing but breast-feeding should be offered to a malnourished child for four to six months may prove to be too conservative. Without nutritional intervention and breast-fed only, the infant may be safer but stunted, inactive, and perhaps mentally affected, and the infant's future outcome bleak. A well-nourished infant is less susceptible to infection, so the dangers of early nutritional supplementation need to be weighed against the benefit of resistance to disease.[7]

During the early 1970s, Abbott Laboratories, American Home Products, and Nestlé participated in conferences on infant nutrition that were sponsored by the World Health Organization, UNICED, and the Protein Advisory Calories Group of the United Nations. Neither Borden's or Bristol-Myers took an active part in these conferences. In November 1975, several infant formula manufacturers formed the International Council of Infant Food Industries (ICIFI) and adopted a code of marketing ethics. Steven Bauer, President of ICIFI, described the code as a "mini-

[7]*Ibid.*, pp. 263–68.

mum standard" that "addresses itself to matters of ethics and professional standards but not to commercial matters [advertising or marketing policy], which remain the duties and obligations of individual member companies."[8] The ICIFI Code recognized the principle "that breast-milk is the preferred form of nutrition for infants not needing special diets" and that "breast-milk substitutes are intended to supplement breast-milk and [are] for use when mothers cannot, or elect not to, breast-feed for medical or other reasons." The code stated in part:

1. The members of ICIFI accept responsibility for the diffusion of information that supports sound infant feeding practices. . . .
2. Product information for the public will always recognize that breast-milk is the feeding of choice with the recommendation to seek professional advice when a supplement or alternative may be required.
3. Product labeling will affirm breast-feeding as the first choice for the nutrition of infants.
4. Product claims will reflect scientific integrity without implication that any product is superior to breast-milk.
5. Explicitly worded instructions and demonstrations for product use will be provided . . .
6. In cooperation with health authorities, professional communications and educational materials will be provided to caution against misuse . . .
7. Members' personnel will observe professional ethics . . . in medical/nursing centers, maternities, and physician's offices and all contacts.
8. Members will employ nurses, nutritionists, and midwives whenever possible to perform mothercraft services . . .
9. Individual contacts by mothercraft personnel and issuance of complimentary supplies of breast-milk substitutes will be in consultation with medical or nursing personnel . . .
10. Mothercraft personnel will support doctors . . . and will not discourage mothers from . . . breast-feeding.
11. Nurses' uniforms will be worn only by persons who are professionaly entitled to their use . . .
12. Compensation of mothercraft personnel will be on a basis of quality and level of services performed and without relationship to sales.
13. Adherence to this code will be obligatory on all members of ICIFI . . . [9]

Both Nestlé and American Home Products adopted the code. Abbott Laboratories, however, criticized the marketing code as too weak and subsequently withdrew from the ICIFI:

> Although supportive of the concept, [we] decided not to join the International Council of Infant Food Industries (ICIFI) because we felt that the use of mass-media campaigns for infant formula were inappropriate in third-world

---

[8] "Marketing Infant Foods," letter of E. Steven Bauer in *The Lancer*, 2 July 1977.
[9] *Hearings*, pp. 887–88.

settings, and the ICIFI code did not specifically exclude these practices. We subsequently published a printed code outlining our marketing policies. [Statement of Abbott Laboratories spokesperson] [10]

Unlike the ICIFI code, the Abbott Laboratories' own marketing code prohibited advertising directly to consumers. The Abbott Laboratories' code stated in part:

1. We believe that unsupervised, direct promotion of infant feeding products to mothers can unjustly impel them to make decisions concerning the care and nutrition of their babies for which they may lack adequate medical or nutritional knowledge. Therefore, we do not advertise our products through general circulation magazines, directories, newspapers, radio, television, billboards, and other public mass media.

2. We do not encourage use of our products where private purchase would impose a financial hardship on the family, or where inadequate facilities for preparation constitute a hazard to infant health.

3. If any contact with mothers is made . . . it must be with the explicit agreement of a health care professional. Samples are supplied only to professional health care personnel at their request.

4. Company representatives . . . are thoroughly taught the preference and value of breast-feeding . . . Deception and other unethical practices are expressly forbidden. Specifically, any inference that our employees are members of a hospital, clinic, or maternity center staff is contrary to company policy. Even in the case of female employees who are qualified nurses, nurses uniforms are not to be worn. Nurses are reimbursed through adequate salary, not sales commission.

5. Our product label and printed instruction, in addition to stressing the importance of breast-feeding, will emphasize the need for accurate, proper proportions in preparing the formula. Pictographs as well as the written word will be included in appropriate language.

6. We will direct additional company resources to: (a) encourage breast-feeding, (b) promote good overall nutritional practices, (c) improve infant and child care, (d) improve sanitation.

7. Unless proscribed by law, we will terminate any distributor who does not follow the code. The company has devised internal procedures and policy to maintain ongoing surveillance of our marketing practices. [11]

The surveillance system used by Abbott Laboratories consisted of asking all field managers to state in writing twice a year whether they were following the code, and of discussing the code with managers in different countries. Bristol-Myers and other drug companies in the infant formula industry also adopted codes similar to Abbott's.

These codes have not entirely satisfied critics. The ICIFI code, in particular, has been heavily criticized. The United Nations' Protein Advisory Group in a letter dated January 23, 1976, claimed that the ICIFI marketing code (1) implied that

[10] *Ibid.*, p. 270.
[11] *Ibid.*, pp. 206–7.

only "healthy" mothers should breast-feed their infants, (2) provided no way of ensuring that sales staffs in developing countries would communicate the superiority of breast-milk, (3) allowed marketing of formula among illiterate mothers who could not read the instructions for preparing the formula, (4) allowed company sales staff to "be visible in medical wards and maternity institutions," (5) failed to regulate promotional material, and (6) was subject to "several weaknesses, inadequacy, and vagueness."[12] In addition, INFACT critics claimed, the ICIFI code provided no surveillance or enforcement methods, it permitted mass advertising aimed at consumers to continue, it allowed nurses to promote the formula to mothers, and it allowed free samples for mothers of newborns. The code, they claimed, in effect "legitimized" these promotional practices. Doubts about the Abbott Laboratories code and others like it focused primarily on the effectiveness of the company's enforcement efforts, on the propriety of continuing to place their "nurses" in health and maternity institutions, and on doubts whether Abbott could control distribution of its products in the many third-world countries where even pharmaceutical drugs are legally sold over-the-counter without prescription.

1. Describe the marketing strategies of the companies involved in the case (distinguish the marketing methods used by the drug companies from those used by the food companies). Describe the strategies used by the critics of the infant formula companies. Explain the concerns of the critics of the formula companies.

2. Assess the promotional practices of the companies in terms of the moral standards that you think are appropriate for the sort of environment in which the companies are operating. Relate your assessment to the three theories of the manufacturer's duties discussed in the chapter. Are any of these three theories particularly appropriate or inappropriate for the third-world context within which the infant formula companies operate? Evaluate the advertisements used by the companies. Do companies have a duty to ensure that consumers do not misuse their products? Do the duties of the manufacturer end at the point of sale?

3. Compare and contrast the codes adopted by the ICIFI and by Abbott Laboratories. Assess the codes in terms of utilitarian criteria, in terms of their recognition of moral rights, and in terms of their adherence to standards of justice. What explanation can you give for the fact that the food companies tend to adopt the ICIFI code whereas the drug companies tend to adhere to a code like Abbott's?

4. In your judgment, are the infant formula companies morally responsible for the misuse of their products and for whatever infant malnutrition results from the use of infant formula in third-world countries? Are third-world governments responsible? Are third-world mothers responsible? Is the medical profession in the third-world responsible?

---

[12] Investor Responsibility Research Center, "Infant Nutrition, Breast Feeding, and Formula Promotion Practices," Analysis R, 6 April 1977, pp. R-13-R-14.

5.   Identify the probable costs and benefits that would result if the companies were to withdraw their products totally from third-world markets. In your judgment, would the benefits of such a withdrawal outweigh its costs? Suggest some practicable alternatives to total withdrawal.

6.   "By selling our formulas in the third-world we give the third-world mother a choice she did not have before; it is paternalistic to think we have a right to decide what is best for her. The third-world mother should be as free to decide whether to use the formula as her first-world counterpart is." Comment.

PART FOUR
BUSINESS AND ITS INTERNAL CONSTITUENCIES: EMPLOYEE ISSUES

The process of producing goods forces businesses not only to engage in external exchanges but also to coordinate the activities of the various internal constituencies who must be brought together and organized into the processes of production. Employees must be hired and organized; stockholders and creditors must be solicited; managerial talent must be tapped. Inevitably conflicts arise within and between these internal constituencies as they interact with each other and as they seek to distribute benefits among themselves. The next two chapters explore some of the ethical issues raised by these internal conflicts. Chapter Seven discusses the issue of job discrimination. Chapter Eight discusses the issue of conflicts between the individual and the organization.

CHAPTER SEVEN
THE ETHICS
OF JOB
DISCRIMINATION

INTRODUCTION

At a meeting held in 1974, the Social Democrats adopted the following resolution on "the controversy over quotas and preferential treatment":

> [The] quota principle is rapidly becoming embedded in American society . . . [because of] the attitude of some liberals, much of the news media, and a large segment of the business community towards white working people. . . . Although 70 percent of the poor are white, public attitudes and government policy implies that only some groups—minorities and women—merit the help of government . . . A society which apportions jobs and college admissions on the basis of race and sex will inevitably confront demand for even further compartmentalization . . . Quotas also have a profoundly destructive psychological impact on those who benefit from them. Quotas [imply] that minority groups must be given something in order to have something. We reject such a condescendingly racist notion as demonstrably absurd . . . [To] suggest, as some have, that quotas do not represent reverse discrimination, that quotas are simply "preferential inclusion" is simply semantic evasion. To include members of one group in order to fill a numerical goal is to exclude others. Quotas are quotas, whether they are called goals, preferential inclusion, affirmative action, or whatever.[1]

In 1976 Herbert Hill, national labor director of the NAACP, defended affirmative action programs against the attacks of the Social Democrats and others:

[1] Quoted in Lester A. Sobel, ed., *Job Bias* (New York: Facts on File, Inc., 1976), pp. 79–81.

A major manifestation of the sharp turning away from the goal of racial equality is to be found in the shrill and paranoid attacks against affirmative action programs . . . the diverse forces united in their intense opposition to affirmative action programs deliberately distort the issue by equating affirmative action based on numerical goals with a fiction called the "quota system" and "reverse discrimination." But there is a fundamental distinction between quotas and numerical goals. Quotas are used to exclude, while numerical goals are a means to include those workers who have been systematically excluded in the past . . . Those who attack the use of numerical goals often argue that affirmative action programs will penalize innocent whites who are not responsible for past discriminatory practices. This argumei t turns on the notion of individual rights and sounds very moral and high-minded indeed. But it ignores basic social reality. For example, black workers have not been denied jobs as individuals but as a class—no matter what their personal merits and qualifications. Women have not been denied training and jobs as individuals, but as a class, regardless of their individual talent or lack of it. Correspondingly, white males as a class have benefitted from this systematic discrimination. Wherever discriminatory employment patterns exist, hiring and promotion without affirmative action perpetuates injustice.[2]

The debates over discrimination and its remedies have been prolonged, acrimonious, and have continued to this day. Since the late 1950s, public concern has swirled around the plight of racial minorities, the inequality of women, and the "harm" that white males have suffered as a result of the preference shown to women and minorities. These continuing debates over racial and sexual equality have been focused largely on the work-place. This is inevitable: Racial and sexual discrimination have had a long history in employment, and it is in this area that discriminatory practices have the most substantial and long-lasting consequences.

Perhaps more than any other contemporary social issue, public discussions of discrimination have clearly approached the subject in ethical terms: The words "justice," "equality," "racism," "rights," and "discrimination" inevitably find their way into the debate. This chapter analyzes the various sides of this ethical issue. The chapter begins by examining the nature and extent of discrimination. It then turns to discussing the ethical aspects of discriminatory behavior in employment and ends with a discussion of affirmative action programs.

7.1 JOB DISCRIMINATION: ITS NATURE

I am twenty-three-years old, I have a B.A. in Spanish literature . . . During my interview for this job my interviewer kept looking at my legs and talking about how interesting he thought the job would be for me because I would be around men doing interesting work . . . "We usually don't hire married girls," he said. "We like to have young, pretty and available girls around the office." "You know," he added, "it cheers things up a lot." . . . I was hired and took the job because I was desperate. I was told I was awfully pretty and would

[2] Quoted in *Ibid.*, pp. 82–83.

most certainly be an asset to the office. . . . When I was hired I was told that two people constitute a team that would work on a specific project. . . . the "team" turned out to be a male, making around $15,000, and a female, making $6,000. Most "girls" have the same degrees as the men, or higher ones, but are still in the lower positions. The reason for this, I was told, was that most foreigners (whom the office deals with) don't "respect" women and would feel slighted if they had to deal with "one." (Wasn't that the reason given for not hiring blacks in offices and shops?—blacks would turn away customers!) . . . In my office all the men go out to eat together and all the women go out to eat together . . . the three blacks in the mailroom eat inside. They are not permitted to go out to eat. [Anonymous] [3]

To discriminate in employment is to make an adverse decision (or set of decisions) against employees (or prospective employees) based upon their membership in a certain class.[4] Discrimination in employment thus involves three basic elements. First, it is a decision against one or more employees (or prospective employees) based solely on the fact that they are *members of a certain group* and not on their ability to perform a given job. Secondly, the decision is based on the assumption that *the group is inferior* to other groups and therefore less worthy of equal treatment. Thirdly, the decision (or set of decisions) has a *harmful or negative effect* upon the interests of the employees, perhaps costing them jobs, higher positions, or better pay.

Discrimination in the United States has traditionally been aimed at two kinds of groups: racial groups and sexual groups. Today four main racial groups are recognized as having been subjected to discriminatory behavior: blacks, Hispanics, American Indians, and Orientals. Women and homosexuals are the two main sexually defined groups that have been subject to a tradition of discrimination.

Forms of Discrimination: Intentional and Institutional Aspects

A helpful framework for analyzing different forms of discrimination can be constructed by distinguishing the extent to which a discriminatory act is intentional and isolated (or noninstitutionalized) and the extent to which it is unintentional and institutionalized.[5] First, a discriminatory act may be part of the *isolated* (noninstitutionalized) behavior of a single individual who *intentionally* and knowingly discriminates out of personal prejudice. In the anonymous statement quoted above, for example, the attitudes that the male interviewer is described as having may not

[3] Anonymous, "We Usually Don't Hire Married Girls," quoted in *The Capitalist System* by Richard C. Edwards, Michael Reich, Thomas E. Weisskopf, 2nd ed. (Englewood Cliffs, NJ: Prentice-Hall, Inc., 1978), pp. 13–15.

[4] For a discussion of the meaning of discrimination see Barry R. Gross, *Discrimination in Reverse* (New York: New York University Press, 1978), pp. 6–28. I am relying here more on the notion of "invidious discrimination" developed, for example, in Ronald Dworkin, "Why Bakke Has No Case," *New York Review of Books,* 10 November 1977, p. 15.

[5] Joe R. Feagin and Clairece Booker Feagin, *Discrimination American Style* (Englewood Cliffs, NJ: Prentice-Hall, Inc., 1978), pp. 19–40.

be characteristic of other company interviewers: His behavior toward female job seekers may be an intentional but isolated instance of sexism in hiring. Secondly, a discriminatory act may be part of the routine behavior of an *institutionalized* group, which *intentionally* and knowingly discriminates out of the personal prejudices of its members. The Ku Klux Klan, for example, is an organization that intentionally institutionalizes discriminatory behavior. Thirdly, an act of discrimination may be part of the *isolated* (noninstitutionalized) behavior of a single individual who *unintentionally* and unknowingly discriminates against someone because he or she unthinkingly adopts the traditional practices and stereotypes of his or her society. If the interviewer quoted in the anonymous statement above, for example, acted unintentionally, then he would fall into this third category. Fourthly, a discriminatory act may be part of the systematic routine of a corporate organization or group that *unintentionally* incorporates into its formal *institutionalized* procedures practices that discriminate against women or minorities. The anonymous statement above, for example, describes an office in which the best-paying jobs are routinely assigned to men and the worst-paying jobs are routinely assigned to women, on the stereotypical assumption that customers will not do business with women. There may be no deliberate intent to discriminate, but the effect is the same: a racially or sexually based pattern of preference toward white males.

Historically, there has been a shift in emphasis from the discussion of discrimination as an intentional and individual matter, to its discussion as a systematic and not necessarily intentional feature of institutionalized corporate behavior. During the early sixties, employment discrimination was seen primarily as an intentional, calculated act performed by one individual upon another. Title VII of the Civil Rights Act of 1964, for example, seems to have had this notion of discrimination in mind when it stated:

> It shall be an unlawful employment practice for an employer (1) to fail or refuse to hire or to discharge any individual, or otherwise discriminate against any individual with respect to his compensation, terms, conditions, or privileges of employment because of such individual's race, color, religion, sex, or national origin; or (2) to limit, segregate, or classify his employees or applicants for employment in any way that would deprive or tend to deprive any individual of employment opportunities or otherwise adversely affect his status as an employee because of such individual's race, color, sex, or national origin.[6]

But in the late 1960s, the concept of discrimination was enlarged to include more than the traditionally recognized intentional forms of individual discrimination. By the early 1970s, the term "discrimination" was being used regularly to include also disparities of minority representation within the ranks of a firm, regardless of whether or not the disparity had been intentionally created. An organization was en-

---

[6]U.S. Congress, Senate, Subcommittee on Labor of the Committee on Labor and Public Welfare, *Compilation of Selected Labor Laws Pertaining to Labor Relations, Part II,* 93rd Congress, 2nd Session, 6 September 1974, p. 610.

gaged in discrimination if minority group representation within its ranks was not proportionate to the group's local availability. The discrimination would be remedied when the proportions of minorities within the organization were made to match their proportions in the available work force by the use of "affirmative action" programs. A Department of Labor guidebook for employers issued in February 1970, for example, stated:

> An acceptable affirmative action program must include an analysis of areas within which the contractor is deficient in the utilization of minority groups and women, and further, goals and timetables to which the contractor's good faith efforts must be directed to correct the deficiencies and thus to increase materially the utilization of minorities and women at all levels and in all segments of his work force where deficiencies exist. . . . "Underutilization" is defined as having fewer minorities or women in a particular job classification than would reasonably be expected by their availability.[7]

Many people have criticized the view that an institution is "discriminatory" if a minority group is underrepresented within its ranks. Discrimination is the act of individuals, these critics argue, and it is individual women and minorities whom it mistreats; consequently, we should not say discrimination exists until we know that a specific individual was discriminated against in a specific instance. The problem with this criticism is that it is generally impossible to know whether a specific individual was discriminated against. People compete with each other for jobs and promotions and whether a person wins a specific job or promotion depends to a large extent on chance factors such as who his competitors happened to be, what abilities his competitors happened to have, how interviewers happened to see him, and how he happened to perform at the crucial moments. Consequently, when a minority individual loses in this competitive process, there is generally no way of knowing whether that individual's loss was the result of chance factors or of systematic discrimination. The only way of knowing whether the process itself is systematically discriminating is by looking at what happens to minorities as a *group:* If minorities as a *group* regularly lose out in a competitive process in which their abilities as a *group* match those of non-minorities, then we may conclude that the process is discriminatory.

For purposes of analysis it is important to keep separate the ethical issues raised by policies that aim at preventing individuals from discriminating intentionally against other individuals, from those raised by "affirmative action" policies which aim at achieving a proportional representation of minorities within our business institutions. We will discuss each of these issues separately below. First, however, we must examine the extent to which our business institutions today are discriminatory. It is a commonly held belief that although business used to be discriminatory, this is no longer the case due to the great strides minorities and women

---

[7]U.S. Equal Employment Opportunity Commission, *Affirmative Action and Equal Employment: A Guidebook for Employers,* II (Washington, DC: Government Printing Office, 1974): D–28.

have made during the last few years. If this belief is correct then there is not much point in discussing the issue of discrimination. But is it?

7.2 DISCRIMINATION: ITS EXTENT

How do we estimate whether an institution is practicing discrimination against a certain group? By looking at statistical indicators of how the members of that group are distributed within the institution. A *prima facie* indication of discrimination exists when a disproportionate number of the members of a certain group hold the less desirable positions within the institution in spite of their preferences and abilities.[8] Three kinds of comparisons can provide evidence for such a distribution: (1) comparisons of the *average* benefits the institution bestows on the discriminated group with the average benefits the institution bestows on other groups; (2) comparisons of the proportion of the discriminated group found in the *lowest* levels of the institution with the proportions of other groups found at those levels; (3) comparisons of the proportions of that group that hold the *more advantageous* positions with the proportions of other groups that hold those same positions. If we look at American society in terms of these three kinds of comparisons, it becomes clear that some form of racial and sexual discrimination is being practiced in American society as a whole. And it also becomes clear that this discrimination has not abated during the last few years.

Average Income Comparisons

Income comparisons provide the most obvious indicators of discrimination. If we compare the average incomes of nonwhite American families, for example, with the average incomes of white American families, it turns out that white family incomes are substantially above those of nonwhites, as Table 7.1 indicates.

Table 7.1 also shows that, contrary to a commonly held belief, the income gap between whites and minorities has been *increasing* rather than decreasing. In fact, while real incomes of whites have been rising steadily, minority real incomes have been declining since 1973. In 1973 the median earnings of minorities were 80 percent of median white earnings; in 1978, they were still at the 80 percent level.[9]

Income comparisons also provide evidence of *sexual* discrimination. A comparison of median male earnings with median female earnings shows that women earn only a portion of what men earn, and, as Table 7.2 shows, this portion has remained fairly constant during the last decade.

[8]Walter B. Connolly, Jr., *A Practical Guide to Equal Employment Opportunity*, 2 vols. (New York: Law Journal Press, 1975), 1: 231–242; for a discussion of the relevance of statistics see Tom Beauchamp, "The Justification of Reverse Discrimination," in W.T. Blackstone and R. Heslep, *Social Justice and Preferential Treatment* (Athens, GA: The University of Georgia Press, 1977), pp. 84–110.

[9]*Facts on File World News Digest,* 38, no. 1981 (27 October 1978): 812.

TABLE 7.1 Average Family Incomes for Whites and Minorities

Year	White Median Family Income	Minority Median Family Income
	(In Constant 1977 Dollars)	
1950	$ 8,672	$ 4,704
1955	10,439	5,757
1960	11,940	6,610
1965	13,927	7,670
1970	15,975	10,169
1974	16,476	10,541
1975	16,065	10,495
1976	16,539	10,455
1977	16,740	10,142

Source: U.S. Bureau of the Census, STATISTICAL ABSTRACT OF THE UNITED STATES (Washington, D.C.: U.S. Government Printing Office, 1978), p. 452.

TABLE 7.2 Average Incomes for Men and Women

Year	Median Earnings		Women's Earnings As A Percent of Men's
	Women	Men	
1969	$4,977	$ 8,227	60.5%
1970	5,323	8,966	59.4
1971	5,593	8,966	59.5
1972	5,903	10,202	57.9
1973	6,335	11,186	56.6
1974	6,772	11,835	57.1
1975	7,504	12,758	58.8
1976	8,099	13,455	60.2
1977	8,618	14,626	58.9

Source: U.S. Department of Labor, THE EARNINGS GAP BETWEEN WOMEN AND MEN (Washington, D.C.: U.S. Government Printing Office, 1979), p. 6.

Contrary to a commonly held belief, the income gap between men and women has not improved. In 1955, women's earnings were 64 percent of men's earnings, but by 1977 their earnings had declined to 58.9 percent of men's earnings.[10] These disparities in earnings begin as soon as men and women leave school. For example, in 1976 (long after "affirmative action" was instituted), the average starting salary offered to women college graduates majoring in marketing was $9,768, while male graduates were offered average starting salaries of $10,236; women graduates majoring in humanities were offered $8,916, while men were offered $9,792; women social science graduates were offered $9,240, while men were offered $10,392.[11]

[10]U.S. Dept. of Labor, *The Earnings Gap Between Women and Men* (Washington, DC: U.S. Government Printing Office, 1979), p. 6.

[11]*Ibid.*, p. 17.

TABLE 7.3 Average Earnings for Men and Women in Different Occupations

Occupation	White Median Earnings		Black Median Earnings	
	Women	Men	Women	Men
Professional & Technical	$11,540	$18,626	$11,522	$16,217
Managers & Administrators	10,000	19,227	(n.a.)	13,591
Sales Workers	6,860	16,156	(n.a.)	(n.a.)
Clerical Workers	8,547	13,403	8,512	8,964
Craft Workers	8,882	15,135	(n.a.)	10,945
Operatives	7,505	13,010	6,504	10,612
Laborers	7,248	12,061	(n.a.)	8,320
Service Workers	6,104	9,420	5,880	7,420
Household Workers	1,887	(n.a.)*	3,788	(n.a.)

*"(n.a.)" indicates "not available."

Source: U.S. Department of Labor, THE EARNINGS GAP BETWEEN WOMEN AND MEN (Washington, D.C.: U.S. Government Printing Office, 1979), p. 14.

The median earnings disparities between men, women, and minorities cut across all occupations, as the summary of 1977 median earnings in Table 7.3 shows.

Lowest Income Group Comparisons

The lowest income group in the United States consists of those people whose annual income falls below the poverty level: For a family of four in 1977, the poverty level was set at $6,200. The poverty rate among minorities is substantially higher than among whites as the data in Table 7.4 show. This is not surprising in view of the fact that minorities have lower average incomes.

In view of the lower average incomes of women, it also comes as no surprise that families headed by single women fall below the poverty level much more often

TABLE 7.4 Percent of White and Minority Populations below Poverty Levels

Year	Percent of Whites Below Poverty Level	Percent of Minorities Below Poverty Level
1959	18.1%	56.2%
1966	11.3	39.8
1970	9.9	32.0
1972	9.0	31.9
1973	8.4	29.6
1974	8.6	28.3
1975	9.7	29.3
1976	9.1	29.4
1977	8.9	29.0

Source: U.S. Bureau of the Census, STATISTICAL ABSTRACT OF THE UNITED STATES (Washington, D.C.: U.S. Government Printing Office, 1978), p. 466.

271

TABLE 7.5 Male- and Female-Headed Families below Poverty Level

Year	Percent of Families with Male Head below Poverty Level	Percent of Families with Female Head below Poverty Level
1966	10.8%	41.0%
1970	8.2	38.2
1972	7.4	36.9
1973	6.6	34.9
1974	6.8	33.6
1975	7.8	34.6
1976	7.1	34.4
1977	6.9	32.8

Source: U.S. Bureau of the Census, STATISTICAL ABSTRACT OF THE UNITED STATES (Washington, D.C.: U.S. Government Printing Office, 1978), p. 466.

than families headed by single men. As Table 7.5 indicates, families headed by women are four times more likely to be impoverished than families headed by men.

The bottom income groups in the United States then, are statistically correlated with race and sex. In comparison to whites and to male-headed families, larger proportions of minorities and of female-headed families are poor.

Desirable Occupation Comparisons

The evidence of racial and sexual discrimination provided by the quantitative measures cited can be filled out qualitatively by examining the occupational distribution of racial and sexual minorities. As the figures for 1975 in Table 7.6 suggest, a larger percentage of whites move into the more desirable occupations, while minorities are channeled into those that are less desirable.

Just as the most desirable occupations are held by whites, while the less desirable are held by blacks, so also the most well-paying occupations tend to be reserved for men, and the others for women. Table 7.7 summarizes the disparities.

These statistics are not explainable in terms of the lower educational levels of minorities and women. In 1977, a white head of household with one to three years of high school earned more than a black head of household with one to three years of college.[12] In that same year, a male full-time worker with nothing more than a grammar school education earned, on the average, almost the equivalent of what a female full-time worker with a college degree earned.[13]

The three kinds of statistical comparisons cited indicate that American business institutions are discriminatory. Whether we compare average incomes, proportional representation in the highest economic positions, or proportional representation in the lowest economic positions, women and minorities are not equal to

[12] U.S. Bureau of the Census, *Statistical Abstract of the United States: 1978,* 99th ed. (Washington, DC: U.S. Government Printing Office), 1978, p. 457.

[13] *Ibid.,* p. 464.

TABLE 7.6 Whites and Minorities in Upper and Lower Income Occupations

Jobs & Median Earnings	% of Whites	% of Minorities
Managers & Administrators $15,425	11.2%	4.1%
Professional & Technical $14,873	14.8	10.4
Sales Workers $12,028	6.8	2.3
Craft Workers $12,028	13.8	9.4
Clerical Workers $11,176	17.8	15.2
Service Workers $ 8,638	10.8	20.1
Nonfarm Laborers $ 8,145	4.6	8.9
Farm Laborers $ 5,097	1.6	2.0

Source: THE U.S. FACT BOOK (New York: Grosset & Dunlap, Publishers, 1977), pp. 373 and 383.

TABLE 7.7 Women in Sexually Differentiated Occupations

Female Dominated Jobs	% of Jobs Held by Women	Male Dominated Jobs	% of Jobs Held by Women
PROFESSIONAL & TECHNICAL		*PROFESSIONAL & TECHNICAL*	
Librarians	82%	Lawyers	12%
Nurses	97	Doctors	11
Elementary Teachers	85		
SALESWORKERS		*SALESWORKERS*	
Demonstrators	91	Sales Representatives	10
Sales Clerks	71	Insurance Agents	23
CLERICAL		*CLERICAL*	
Secretaries	99	Mail Carriers	10
Bank Tellers	93	Shipping Clerks	21
OPERATIVES		*OPERATIVES*	
Dressmakers	95	Truck Drivers	2
Packers	64	Welders	5
SERVICE		*SERVICE*	
Waiters & Waitresses	89	Police	6

Source: U.S. Bureau of the Census, STATISTICAL ABSTRACT OF THE UNITED STATES (Washington, D.C.: U.S. Government Printing Office, 1980), pp. 418–420.

white males, nor have the last few years seen a narrowing of the racial and sexual gaps. It does not follow, of course, that any particular business is discriminatory. In order to find out whether a particular firm is discriminatory we would have to make the same sorts of comparisons among the various employment levels of the firm that we made above among the various economic and occupational levels of American society as a whole. To facilitate such comparisons within firms employers today are required to report to the government the numbers of minorities and women their firm employs in each of nine categories: officials and managers, professionals, technicians, sales workers, office and clerical workers, skilled craftworkers, semi-skilled operatives, unskilled laborers, and service workers.

7.3 DISCRIMINATION: UTILITY, RIGHTS, AND JUSTICE

Given the statistics on the comparative incomes and low-status positions of minorities and women in the United States, the question we must ask ourselves is this: Are these inequalities wrong, and if so, how should they be changed? To be sure, these inequalities directly contradict the fundamental principles on which the United States was founded: "We hold these truths to be self-evident: that all men are created equal and endowed by their creator with certain inalienable rights."[14] But historically we have often tolerated large discrepancies between these ideals and reality. The ancestors of most black Americans living today, for example, were brought to this country as slaves, treated like cattle, and lived out their lives in bondage, in spite of our ideals of "equality." As the personal property of a white owner, blacks prior to the Civil War were not recognized as people, and consequently had no legal powers, no claims on their bodies or their labors, and were regarded by the Supreme Court in one of its opinions, as "beings of an inferior order . . . and so far inferior that they had no rights that the white man was bound to respect."[15] Women were treated comparably. Through much of the nineteenth century, women could not hold office, could not vote, could not serve on juries, or bring suit in their own names; a married woman lost control over her property (which was acquired by her husband), she was considered incapable of making binding contracts, and, in a major opinion, she was declared by the Supreme Court to have "no legal existence, separate from her husband, who was regarded as her head and representative in the social state."[16] Why are these forms of inequality wrong? Why is it wrong to discriminate?

The arguments mustered against discrimination, generally fall into three groups: (1) utilitarian arguments, which claim that discrimination leads to an inef-

---

[14] Thomas Jefferson, *Declaration of Independence*.

[15] *Dred Scott* v. *Sanford*, 60 U.S. (19 How) (1857) at 407 and 421. See Don E. Fehrenbacher, *The Dred Scott Case* (New York: Oxford University Press, 1978).

[16] *Bradwell* v. *Illinois*, 83 U.S. (16 Wall) (1873). See Leo Kanowitz, *Women and the Law* (Albuquerque, NM: University of New Mexico Press, 1969), p. 36.

ficient use of human resources; (2) rights arguments, which claim that discrimination violates basic human rights; and (3) justice arguments, which claim that discrimination results in an unjust distribution of society's benefits and burdens.

Utility

The standard utilitarian argument against racial and sexual discrimination is based on the idea that a society's productivity will be optimized to the extent that jobs are awarded on the basis of competency (or "merit").[17] Different jobs, the argument goes, require different skills and personality traits if they are to be carried out in as productive a manner as possible. Furthermore, different people have different skills and personality traits. Consequently, in order to ensure that jobs are maximally productive, they must be assigned to those individuals whose skills and personality traits qualify them as the most competent for the job. Insofar as jobs are assigned to individuals on the basis of other criteria unrelated to competency, productivity must necessarily decline. Discriminating among job applicants on the basis of race, sex, religion, or other characteristics unrelated to job performance is necessarily inefficient and therefore contrary to utilitarian principles.[18]

Utilitarian arguments of this sort, however, have encountered two kinds of objections. First, if the argument is correct, then jobs should be assigned on the basis of job-related qualifications *only so long as such assignments will advance the public welfare.* If, in a certain situation, the public welfare would be advanced to a greater degree by assigning jobs on the basis of some factor not related to job performance, then the utilitarian would have to hold that in those situations jobs should *not* be assigned on the basis of job-related qualifications, but on the basis of that other factor. If, for example, society's welfare would be promoted more by assigning certain jobs on the basis of *need* (or sex or race) instead of on the basis of job qualifications, then the utilitarian would have to concede that *need* (or sex or race) and not job qualifications is the proper basis for assigning those jobs.[19]

Secondly, the utilitarian argument must also answer the charge of opponents who hold that society as a whole may benefit from some forms of sexual discrimination. Opponents might claim, for example, that society will function most efficiently if one sex is socialized into acquiring the personality traits required for raising a family (nonaggressive, cooperative, caring, submissive, etc.) and the other sex is socialized into acquiring the personality traits required for earning a living

---

[17]Norman Daniels, "Merit and Meritocracy," *Philosophy and Public Affairs,* 7, no. 3 (Spring 1978): 208-9.

[18]For economic analyses of the costs and benefits associated with discrimination, see Gary S. Becker, *The Economics of Discrimination,* 2nd ed. (Chicago: The University of Chicago Press, 1971); Janice Fanning Madden, *The Economics of Sex Discrimination* (Lexington, MA: D.C. Heath and Company, 1973). For a critical review of this literature see Annette M. LaMond, "Economic Theories of Employment Discrimination," in *Women, Minorities, and Employment Discrimination,* eds. Phyllis A. Wallace and Annette M. LaMond (Lexington, MA: D.C. Heath and Company, 1977), pp. 1-11.

[19]*Ibid.,* p. 214.

(aggressive, competitive, assertive, independent).[20] Or one might hold that one sex ends up with the traits suited for raising a family as a result of its inborn biological nature, while the other sex ends up with the traits suited for earning a living as a result of its own biology.[21] In either case, whether sexual differences are acquired or natural, one might argue that jobs that call for one set of sexually based traits rather than another, should be assigned on the basis of sex because placing people in jobs that suit their personality traits promotes society's welfare.[22]

The utilitarian argument against discrimination has been attacked on several fronts. None of these attacks, however, seem to have defeated its proponents. Utilitarians have countered that using factors other than job-related qualifications in fact never provides greater benefits than the use of job-related qualifications.[23] Moreover, they claim, studies have demonstrated that there are few, or no, morally significant differences between the sexes.[24]

Rights

Nonutilitarian arguments against racial and sexual discrimination may take the approach that discrimination is wrong because it violates a person's basic moral rights.[25] Kantian theory, for example, holds that human beings should be treated as "ends" and never used merely as "means." At a minimum, this principle means that each individual has a moral right to be treated as a free person equal to any other person and that all individuals have a correlative moral duty to treat each individual as a free and equal person. Discriminatory practices violate the principle in two ways. First, discrimination is based on the belief that one group is inferior to other groups: that blacks, for example, are less competent or less worthy of respect than whites or perhaps that women are less competent or worthy of respect than men.[26] Racial and sexual discrimination, for instance, may be based on stereotypes that see minorities as "lazy" or "shiftless" and see women as "emotional" and "weak." Such degrading stereotypes undermine the self-esteem of those groups against whom

[20] See the discussion of this view in Sharon Bishop Hill, "Self-Determination and Autonomy," in *Today's Moral Problems,* 2nd ed., Richard Wasserstrom, ed. (New York: Macmillan, Inc., 1979), pp. 118–33.

[21] See Steven Goldberg, *The Inevitability of Patriarchy* (New York: William Morrow & Co., Inc., 1973); and J.R. Lucas, "Because You Are a Woman," *Philosophy,* 48: 166–71.

[22] On this issue see Janet S. Chafetz, *Masculine, Feminine, or Human?: An Overview of the Sociology of Sex Roles* (Itasca, IL: Peacock, 1974); and Joyce Trebilcot, "Sex Roles: The Argument from Nature," *Ethics,* 85, no. 3 (April 1975): 249–55.

[23] See, for example, Thomas Nagel, "Equal Treatment and Compensatory Discrimination," *Philosophy and Public Affairs,* 2 (1973): 360; and Ronald Dworkin, *Taking Rights Seriously* (Cambridge: Harvard University Press, 1977), pp. 232–37.

[24] Susan Haack, "On the Moral Relevance of Sex," *Philosophy,* 49: 90–95: Jon J. Durkin, "The Potential of Women," in *Women in Management,* Bette Ann Stead, ed. (Englewood Cliffs, NJ: Prentice-Hall, Inc., 1978), pp. 42–46.

[25] Richard Wasserstrom, "Rights, Human Rights, and Racial Discrimination," *The Journal of Philosophy,* 61 (29 October 1964): 628–41.

[26] Richard Wasserstrom, "Racism, Sexism, and Preferential Treatment: An Approach to the Topics," *UCLA Law Review,* 24 (1977): 581–622.

the stereotypes are directed and thereby violate their right to be treated as equals. Secondly, discrimination places the members of groups which are discriminated against in lower social and economic positions: Women and minorities have fewer job opportunities and they are given lower salaries. Again, the right to be treated as a free and equal person is violated.[27]

A group of Kantian arguments, related to those above, hold that discrimination is wrong because the person who discriminates would not want to see his or her behavior universalized.[28] In particular, the person would not want to be discriminated against on the basis of characteristics that have nothing whatever to do with the person's own ability to perform a given job. Since the person who discriminates would not want to see his or her own behavior universalized, it is, according to Kant's first categorical imperative, morally wrong for that person to discriminate against others.

Justice

A second group of nonutilitarian arguments against discrimination views it as a violation of the principles of justice. John Rawls, for example, argues that among the principles of justice that the enlightened parties to the "original position" would choose for themselves is the principle of equal opportunity: "Social and economic inequalities are to be arranged so that they are attached to offices and positions open to all under conditions of fair equality of opportunity."[29] Discrimination violates this principle by arbitrarily closing off to minorities the more desirable offices and positions in an institution, thereby not giving them an opportunity equal to that of others. Arbitrarily giving some individuals less of an opportunity to compete for jobs than others is unjust, according to Rawls.

Another approach to the morality of discrimination that also views it as a form of injustice is based on the formal "principle of equality": Individuals who are equal in all respects relevant to the kind of treatment in question should be treated equally, even if they are dissimilar in other nonrelevant respects." To many people, as we indicated in Chapter Two, this principle is the defining feature of justice.[30] Discrimination in employment is wrong because it violates the basic principle of justice by differentiating between people on the basis of characteristics (race or sex) that are not relevant to the tasks they must perform. A major problem faced by this kind of argument against discrimination, however, is that of defining precisely what counts as a "relevant respect" for treating people differently and explaining why race and sex are not relevant, while something like intelligence or war service may be counted as relevant.

[27]This is, for example, the underlying view in John C. Livingston, *Fair Game?* (San Francisco: W.H. Freeman and Company, 1979), pp. 74–76.

[28]Richard M. Hare, *Freedom and Reason* (New York: Oxford University Press, 1963), pp. 217–19.

[29]John Rawls, *A Theory of Justice* (Cambridge: Harvard University Press, Belknap Press, 1971), pp. 83–90.

[30]Charles Perelman, *The Idea of Justice and the Problem of Argument* (London: Rutledge and Kegan Paul, 1963).

Discriminatory Practices

Regardless of the problems inherent in some of the arguments against discrimination, it is clear that there are strong reasons for holding that discrimination is wrong. It is consequently understandable that the law has gradually been changed to conform to these moral requirements and that there has been a growing recognition of the various ways in which discrimination in employment occurs. Among the practices now widely recognized as discriminatory are the following:[31]

Recruitment practices Firms that rely solely on the word-of-mouth referrals of present employees to recruit new workers tend to recruit only from those racial and sexual groups that are already represented in their labor force. When a firm's labor force is composed only of white males, this recruitment policy will tend to discriminate against minorities and women. Also, when desirable job positions are advertised only in media (or by job referral agencies) that are not used by minorities or women (such as, in English newspapers not read by Spanish-speaking minorities), or are classified as "for men only," recruitment will also tend to be discriminatory.

Screening practices Job qualifications are discriminatory when they are not relevant to the job to be performed, as, for example, requiring a high school diploma or a credential for an essentially manual task in places where minorities statistically have had high secondary-school drop-out rates. Aptitude or intelligence tests used to screen applicants become discriminatory when they serve to disqualify members from minority cultures who are unfamiliar with the language, concepts, and social situations used in the tests but who are in fact fully qualified for the job. Job interviews are discriminatory if the interviewer routinely disqualifies women and minorities by relying on sexual or racial stereotypes. These stereotypes may include assumptions about the sort of occupations "proper" for women, the sort of work and time burdens that may fittingly be "imposed" on women, the ability of a woman or a minority person to maintain "commitment" to a job, the propriety of putting women in "male" environments, the assumed effects women or minorities would have on employee morale or on customers, and the extent to which women or minorities are assumed to have personality and aptitude traits that make them unsuitable for a job. Such generalizations about women or minorities are not only discriminatory, they are also false.

Promotion practices Promotion, job progression, and transfer practices are discriminatory when employers place white males on job tracks separate from those open to women and minorities. Seniority systems will be discriminatory if past discrimination has eliminated minorities and women from the higher, more senior positions on the advancement ladder. To rectify the situation, individuals who have specifically suffered from discrimination in seniority systems should be given their rightful place in the seniority system and provided with whatever training is neces-

[31] Feagin and Feagin, *Discrimination American Style,* pp. 43–77.

sary for them. When promotions rely on the subjective recommendations of immediate supervisors, promotion policy will be discriminatory to the extent that supervisors rely on racial or sexual stereotypes.

Conditions of employment   Wages and salaries are discriminatory to the extent that equal wages and salaries are not given to people who are doing essentially the same work. If past discrimination or present cultural traditions result in some job classifications being disproportionately filled with women or minorities (such as, secretarial, clerical, or part-time positions), steps should be taken to make their compensation and benefits comparable to those of other classifications.

Discharge   Firing an employee on the basis of his or her race or sex is a clear form of discrimination. Less blatantly discriminatory are layoff policies that rely on a seniority system in which women and minorities have the lowest seniority because of past discrimination.

7.4 AFFIRMATIVE ACTION

All of the equal opportunity policies discussed above are ways of making employment decisions blind with respect to sex and race. These policies are all negative: They aim to prevent any further discrimination. They therefore ignore the fact that as a result of past discrimination women and minorities do not now have the same skills as their white male counterparts and that because of past discrimination women and minorities are now underrepresented in the more prestigious and desirable job positions. The policies discussed so far do not call for any positive steps to eliminate these effects of past discrimination.

In order to rectify the effects of past discrimination, many employers have instituted affirmative action programs designed to achieve a more representative distribution of minorities and women within the firm by giving preference to women and minorities. Affirmative action programs, in fact, are now legally required of all firms that hold a government contract. What does an affirmative action program involve? The heart of an affirmative action program is a detailed study (a "utilization analysis") of all the major job classifications in the firm.[32] The purpose of the study is to determine whether there are fewer minorities or women in a particular job classification than would be reasonably expected by their availability in the area from which the firm recruits. The utilization analysis will compare the percentage of women and minorities in each job classification with the percentage of those minority and female workers available in the area from which the firm recruits who have the requisite skills or who are capable of acquiring the requisite skills with training the firm could reasonably supply. If the utilization analysis shows

---

[32] On the requirements of affirmative action programs, see Connolly, Jr., *A Practical Guide to Equal Employment Opportunity*, 1: 359–73.

that women or minorities are underutilized in certain job classifications, the firm must then establish recruiting goals and timetables for correcting these deficiencies. Although the goals and timetables must not be rigid and inflexible quotas, they must nonetheless be specific, measurable, and designed in good faith to correct the deficiencies uncovered by the utilization analysis within a reasonable length of time. The firm appoints an officer to coordinate and administer the affirmative action program, and undertakes special efforts and programs to increase the recruitment of women and minorities so as to meet the goals and timetables it has established for itself.

Affirmative action programs like these have been attacked on the grounds that, in attempting to correct the effects of past discrimination, these programs themselves have become racially or sexually discriminatory.[33] By showing preference to minorities or women, the programs institute a form of "reverse discrimination" against white males.[34] A forty-five-year-old electrical worker at a Westinghouse plant, for example, is quoted as saying:

> What does bother me is the colored getting the preference *because* they're black. This I am against. I say, I don't care what his color is. If he has the ability to do the job, he should get the job—not *because* of his color. They shouldn't hire 20 percent just because they're black. This is discrimination in reverse as far as I'm concerned. . . . If they want it, they can earn it like I did. I am not saying deprive them of something—not at all.[35]

Affirmative action programs are said to discriminate against white males by using a nonrelevant characteristic—race or sex—to make employment decisions, and this violates justice by violating the principles of equality and of equal opportunity.

The arguments used to justify affirmative action programs in the face of these objections tend to fall into two main groups.[36] One group of arguments interprets the preferential treatment accorded to women and minorities as a form of *compensation* for past injuries they have suffered. A second set of arguments interprets preferential treatment as an *instrument* for achieving certain social goals. Whereas compensation arguments for affirmative action are backward looking insofar as they aim to rectify a past wrong, the instrumentalist arguments are forward looking insofar as they aim to achieve a future objective (and the presence or absence of

---

[33] See, for example, Barry R. Gross, *Discrimination in Reverse: Is Turnabout Fair Play?*; for a contrasting view see also Alan H. Goldman, *Justice and Reverse Discrimination* (Princeton: Princeton University Press, 1979).

[34] See, for example, the articles collected in Barry R. Gross, ed., *Reverse Discrimination* (Buffalo: Prometheus Books, 1977).

[35] Theodore V. Purcell and Gerald F. Cavanagh, *Blacks in the Industrial World* (New York: The Free Press, 1972), p. 164.

[36] See the essays collected in Marshall Cohen, Thomas Nagel, and Thomas Scanlon, eds., *Equality and Preferential Treatment* (Princeton: Princeton University Press, 1977); and William T. Blackstone and Robert D. Heslep, eds., *Social Justice & Preferential Treatment* (Athens, GA: The University of Georgia Press, 1977).

past harm is secondary).[37] We will begin by examining the compensation arguments and then turn to the instrumentalist arguments.

Affirmative Action as Compensation

Arguments that defend affirmative action as a form of compensation are based on the concept of compensatory justice.[38] Compensatory justice, as we noted in Chapter Two, implies that people have an obligation to compensate those whom they have intentionally and unjustly wronged. Affirmative action programs are then interpreted as a form of reparation by which white male majorities now compensate women and minorities for unjustly injuring them by discriminating against them in the past. One version of this argument holds, for example, that blacks were wronged in the past by American whites and that consequently blacks should now receive compensation from whites.[39] Programs of preferential treatment provide that compensation.

The difficulty with arguments that defend affirmative action on the basis of the principle of compensation is that the principle of compensation requires that compensation should come only from those specific individuals who intentionally inflicted a wrong, and it requires them to compensate only those specific individuals whom they wronged. For example, if five red-haired persons wrongfully injure five black-haired persons, then compensatory justice obligates only the five red-haired persons to give to only the five black-haired persons whatever the black-haired persons would have had if the five red-heads had not injured them. Compensatory justice, however, does not require that compensation should come from *all* the members of a group that contains some wrongdoers, nor does it require that compensation should go to *all* the members of a group that contains some injured parties. In the example above, although justice requires that the five red-haired persons must compensate the five black-haired persons, it does *not* require that all red-haired persons should compensate all black-haired persons. By analogy, only the specific individuals who discriminated against minorities or women in the past should now be forced to make reparation of some sort, and they should make reparation only to those specific individuals against whom they discriminated.[40] Since affirmative action programs usually benefit all the members of a racial or sexual group, regardless of whether they specifically were discriminated against in the past, and since these programs hinder every white male regardless of whether he himself specifically discriminated against someone in the past, it follows that such preferential programs

---

[37] George Sher, "Reverse Discrimination, the Future, and the Past," in *Ethics*, 90 (October 1979): 81–87.

[38] Paul W. Taylor, "Reverse Discrimination and Compensatory Justice," *Analysis*, 33 (1973): 177–82; see also, Anne C. Minas, "How Reverse Discrimination Compensates Women," *Ethics*, 88, no. 1 (October 1977): 74–79.

[39] Bernard Boxhill, "The Morality of Reparations," *Social Theory and Practice* 2, no. 1 (1972): 113–22.

[40] Alan H. Goldman, "Limits to the Justification of Reverse Discrimination," *Social Theory and Practice*, vol. 3, no. 3.

cannot be justified on the basis of compensatory justice.[41] In short, affirmative action programs are unfair because the beneficiaries of affirmative action are not the same individuals who were injured by past discrimination, and the people who must pay for their injuries are usually not the ones who inflicted those injuries.[42]

Various authors have tried to counter this objection to the "affirmative action as compensation" argument by claiming that actually *every* black person (or every woman) living today has been injured by discrimination and that *every* white person (or every male) has benefitted from those injuries. Judith Jarvis Thomson, for example writes:

> But it is absurd to suppose that the young blacks and women now of an age to apply for jobs have not been wronged . . . Even young blacks and women have lived through downgrading for being black or female . . . And even those who were not themselves downgraded for being black or female have suffered the consequences of the downgrading of other blacks and women: lack of self-confidence and lack of self-respect.[43]

And Martin Redish writes:

> It might also be argued that, whether or not the [white males] of this country have themselves participated in acts of discrimination, they have been the beneficiaries—conscious or unconscious—of a fundamentally racist society. They thus may be held independently "liable" to suppressed minorities for a form of unjust enrichment.[44]

It is unclear whether these arguments succeed in justifying affirmative action programs that benefit groups (all blacks and all women) instead of specific injured individuals and that penalize groups (white males) instead of specific wrongdoers.[45] Has every minority and woman really been injured as Thomson claims, and are all white

---

[41] See Karst and Horowitz, "Affirmative Action and Equal Protection," *Virginia Law Review,* 60 (1974).

[42] There are innumerable discussions of this objection to the compensation justification; see, for example, the series: Michael Bayles, "Reparations to Wronged Groups," *Analysis,* 33, no. 6 (1973); L.J. Cowan, "Inverse Discrimination," *Analysis,* 33, no. 10 (1972); Roger Shiner, "Individuals, Groups, and Inverse Discrimination," *Analysis,* 33 (June 1973); Paul Taylor, "Reverse Discrimination and Compensatory Justice," *Analysis,* 33 (June 1973); James Nickel, "Should Reparations Be to Individuals or Groups?," *Analysis,* 34, no. 9: 154–160; Alan H. Goldman, "Reparations to Individuals or Groups?," *Analysis,* 35, no. 5: 168–70.

[43] Judith Jarvis Thomson, "Preferential Hiring," *Philosophy and Public Affairs,* 2, no. 4 (Summer 1973): 381; for a similar claim with respect to blacks, see Graham Hughes, "Reparation for Blacks?," *New York University Law Review,* 43 (1968): 1072–73.

[44] Martin H. Redish, "Preferential Law School Admissions and the Equal Protection Clause: An Analysis of the Competing Arguments," *University of California at Los Angeles Review* (1974), p. 389; see also, Bernard R. Boxill, "The Morality of Preferential Hiring," *Philosophy and Public Affairs,* 7, no. 3 (Spring 1978): 246–68.

[45] Robert Simon, "Preferential Hiring: A Reply to Judith Jarvis Thomson," *Philosophy and Public Affairs,* 3, no. 3 (Spring 1974): 312–320; Gertrude Ezorsky, "It's Mine," *Philosophy and Public Affairs,* 3, no. 3 (Spring 1974): 321–330; Robert K. Fullinwider, "Preferential Hiring and Compensation," *Social Theory and Practice,* 3, no. 3 (Spring 1975): 307–20.

males really beneficiaries of discrimination as Redish implies? And even if a white male happens (through no fault of his own) to benefit from someone else's injury, does this make him "liable" for that injury?

Affirmative Action as an Instrument for Achieving Social Goals

A second set of justifications advanced in support of affirmative action programs is based on the idea that these programs are morally legitimate instruments for achieving morally legitimate ends. Utilitarians, for example, have claimed that affirmative action programs are justified because they promote the public welfare.[46] They have argued that past discrimination has produced a high degree of correlation between race and poverty.[47] As racial minorities were systematically excluded from better-paying, and more prestigious, jobs, their members have become impoverished. The kinds of statistics cited earlier in this chapter provide evidence of this inequality. Impoverishment in turn has led to unmet needs, lack of self-respect, resentment, social discontent, and crime. The public welfare, therefore, will be promoted if the position of these impoverished persons is improved by giving them special educational and employment opportunities. If opponents object that such affirmative action programs are unjust because they distribute benefits on the basis of an irrelevant criterion such as race, the utilitarian can answer that *need,* not race, is the criterion by which affirmative action programs distribute benefits. Race provides an inexpensive *indicator* of need because past discrimination has created a high correlation between race and need. Need, of course, is a just criterion of distribution.[48]

The major difficulties encountered by these utilitarian justifications of affirmative action have concerned, first, the question whether the social costs of affirmative action programs (such as, the frustrations felt by white males) outweigh their obvious benefits.[49] The utilitarian defender of affirmative action, of course, will reply that the benefits far outweigh the costs. Secondly, and more importantly, opponents of these utilitarian justifications of affirmative action have questioned the assumption that race is an appropriate indicator of need. It may be inconvenient and expensive to identify the needy directly, critics argue, but the costs might be small compared to the gains that would result from having a more accurate way of

---

[46] For examples of utilitarian arguments, see Thomas Nagel, "Equal Treatment and Compensatory Discrimination," *Philosophy and Public Affairs,* 2, no. 4 (Summer 1973): 348–363; James W. Nickel, "Preferential Policies in Hiring and Admissions, A Jurisprudential Approach," *Columbia Law Review,* 75: 534–558; Ronald Dworkin, "The De Funis Case: The Right to Go to Law School," *New York Review of Books,* 23, no. 1 (5 February 1976): 29–33.

[47] Owen M. Fiss, "Groups and the Equal Protection Clause," *Philosophy and Public Affairs,* 5, no. 2 (Winter 1976): 150–51.

[48] James W. Nickel, "Classification by Race in Compensatory Programs," *Ethics,* 84, no. 2 (1974): 146–50.

[49] Virginia Black, "The Erosion of Legal Principles in the Creation of Legal Policies," *Ethics,* vol. 84, no. 3 (1974); William T. Blackstone, "Reverse Discrimination and Compensatory Justice," in *Social Justice and Preferential Treatment,* eds. Blackstone and Heslep (Athens, GA: University of Georgia Press, 1977).

identifying the needy.[50] Utilitarians answer this criticism by arguing that *all* minorities (and women) have been impoverished and psychologically harmed by past discrimination. Consequently, race (and sex) provide accurate indicators of need.

Although utilitarian arguments in favor of affirmative action programs are quite convincing, the most elaborate and persuasive array of arguments advanced in support of affirmative action have proceeded in two steps: First, they have argued that the *end* envisioned by affirmative action programs is equal justice, and second, they argue that affirmative action programs are morally legitimate *means* for achieving this end.

The end that affirmative action programs are supposed to achieve is phrased in various ways: (1) In our present society, it is argued, jobs are not distributed justly because they are not distributed according to the relevant criteria of ability, effort, contribution, or need.[51] Statistics show that jobs are in fact still distributed according to race and sex. One end of affirmative action is to bring about a distribution of society's benefits and burdens that is consistent with the principles of distributive justice, and that eliminates the important position race and sex currently have in the assignment of jobs.[52] (2) In our present society, women and minorities do not have the equal opportunities that white males have and that justice demands. Statistics prove this. This lack of equal opportunity is due to subtle racist and sexist attitudes that bias the judgments of those (usually white males) who evaluate job applicants and that are so deeply entrenched that they are virtually ineradicable by good faith measures in any reasonable period of time.[53] A second end of affirmative action programs is to neutralize such conscious and unconscious bias in order to ensure equal opportunity to women and minorities. (3) The lack of equal opportunity under which women and minorities currently labor has also been attributed to the privations they suffered as children. Economic privation hindered minorities from acquiring the skills, experience, training, and education they needed to compete equally with white males.[54] Furthermore, since women and minorities have not been represented in society's prestigious positions, young men and women have had no role models to motivate them to compete for such positions as young white males have. Few black youths, for example, are motivated to enter the legal profession:

> Negro youth in the north, as well as the south, have been denied an inspiring image of the Negro lawyer, at least until recent years. On the contrary, they have been made sharply aware of the lack of respect and dignity accorded the

[50] Robert K. Fullinwider, "On Preferential Hiring," in *Feminism and Philosophy* Mary Vetterling-Braggin, Frederick A. Elliston, and Jane English, eds. (Totowa, NJ: Littlefield, Adams and Company, 1978), pp. 210–24.

[51] See Nickel, "Preferential Policies."

[52] Nagel, "Equal Treatment and Compensatory Discrimination."

[53] Lawrence Crocker, "Preferential Treatment," in *Feminism and Philosophy*, Vetterling-Braggin, and others, eds., pp. 190–204.

[54] George Sher, "Justifying Reverse Discrimination in Employment," *Philosophy and Public Affairs,* 4, no. 2 (Winter 1975): 159–70.

Negro lawyer . . . Negro youth also know in what lack of regard the Negro, if employed in law enforcement at all, is held. . . . Such knowledge does little to inspire Negroes to do anything but avoid involvement with the law whatever its form.[55]

A third end of affirmative action programs is to neutralize these competitive disadvantages with which women and minorities are currently burdened when they compete with white males, and thereby bring women and minorities to the same starting point in their competitive race with others. The aim is to ensure an equal ability to compete with white males.[56]

The basic *end* that affirmative action programs seek is a more just society, a society in which an individual's opportunities are not limited by his or her race or sex. This goal is morally legitimate insofar as it is morally legitimate to strive for a society with greater equality of opportunity. The *means* by which affirmative action programs attempt to achieve a just society is giving qualified minorities and females preference over qualified white males in hiring and promotion and instituting special training programs for minorities and females that will quality them for better jobs. By these means, it is hoped, the more just society outlined above will eventually be born. Without some form of affirmative action, it is argued, this end could not be achieved.[57] But is preferential treatment a morally legitimate *means* for attaining this end? Three reasons have been advanced to show that it is not.

First, it is often claimed that affirmative action programs "discriminate" against white males.[58] Supporters of affirmative action programs, however, have pointed out that there are crucial differences between the treatment accorded to whites by preferential treatment programs and immoral discriminatory behavior.[59] To discriminate, as we indicated earlier, is to make an adverse decision against the member of a group because members of that group are considered inferior or less worthy of respect. Preferential treatment programs, however, are not based on invidious contempt for white males. On the contrary, they are based on the judgment that white males are currently in an advantaged position and that others should have an equal opportunity to achieve the same advantages. Moreover, racist or sexist discrimination is aimed at destroying equal opportunity. Preferential treatment programs are aimed at restoring equal opportunity where it is absent. Thus, preferential treatment programs cannot accurately be described as "discriminatory" in the same immoral sense that racist or sexist behavior is discriminatory.

Secondly, it is sometimes claimed that preferential treatment violates the principle of equality itself ("Individuals who are equal in all respects relevant to the

[55] Carl and Callahan, "Negroes and the Law," *Journal of Legal Education*, 17 (1965): 254.

[56] Kaplan, "Equal Justice In an Unequal World," *N.W.U. Law Review*, 61 (1966): 365.

[57] Theodore V. Purcell and Gerald F. Cavanagh, *Blacks in the Industrial World* (New York: The Free Press, 1972), pp. 30–44.

[58] Carl Cohen, "Race and the Constitution," *The Nation*, 8 February 1975; Lisa H. Newton, "Reverse Discrimination as Unjustified," *Ethics*, 83 (1973): 308–12.

[59] Ronald Dworkin, "Why Bakke Has No Case."

kind of treatment in question should be treated equally") by allowing a nonrelevant characteristic (race and sex) to determine employment decisions.[60] But defenders of affirmative action programs have replied that sexual and racial differences are now relevant to making employment decisions. These differences are relevant because when society distributes a scarce resource (such as jobs) it may legitimately choose to allocate it to those groups that will best advance its legitimate ends. Since, in our present society, allocating scarce jobs to women and minorities will best achieve equality of opportunity, race and sex are now relevant characteristics to use for this purpose. Moreover, as we have seen, the reason that we hold that jobs should be allocated on the basis of job-related qualifications is that such an allocation will achieve a socially desirable (utilitarian) end: maximum productivity. When this end (productivity) conflicts with another socially desirable end (a just society), then it is legitimate to pursue the second end even if doing so means that the first end will not be as fully achieved.

Thirdly, some authors have objected that affirmative action programs actually harm women and minorities because such programs imply that women and minorities are so inferior to white males that they need special help to compete.[61] This objection may be met in several ways. First, the proponent of affirmative action may concede that the skills of many women and minorities are "inferior" to those of white males, but this disadvantage is due to the past discrimination of white males and not to any inferiority inherent in the natures of women or minorities. Secondly, the proponent of affirmative action programs may hold that these programs are based *not* on an assumption of minority or female inferiority but on a recognition of the fact that white males, consciously or unconsciously, will continue to bias their decisions in favor of other white males unless affirmative action programs lead them to counter this bias. As we have seen, statistics show that even when women and minorities are more qualified, white males are still granted higher salaries and positions by their white male counterparts. Thirdly, the proponent may argue that it is false that showing preference toward a group will make that group feel inferior: For centuries white males have been the beneficiaries of racial and sexual discrimination without apparent loss of their self-esteem.

Affirmative action programs, then, appear to be morally legitimate means for achieving just ends. The arguments for and against them, of course, continue.

Problems with Implementing Affirmative Action

Opponents of affirmative action programs have argued that other criteria besides race and sex have to be weighed when making job decisions in an affirmative action program. First, if sex and race are the only criteria used, this will result in the hiring of unqualified personnel and a consequent decline in productivity.[62] Secondly, many jobs have significant impacts on the lives of others. Consequently,

---

[60] *Ibid.*

[61] Alan Goldman, "Affirmative Action," *Philosophy and Public Affairs,* 5, no. 2 (Winter 1976): 187.

[62] Sidney Hook, "Discrimination Against the Qualified?," *The New York Times,* 1971.

if a job has significant impact on, say, the safety of others (such as the job of flight controller or surgeon), then criteria other than race or sex should have a prominent place and should override affirmative action.[63] And, thirdly, opponents have argued that affirmative action programs, if continued, will turn us into a more racially and sexually conscious nation.[64] Consequently, the programs should cease as soon as the defects they are meant to remedy are corrected.

The following guidelines have been suggested as a way of folding these sorts of considerations into an affirmative action program when minorities are under-represented in a firm:[65]

1. Both minorities and nonminorities should be hired or promoted only if they reach certain *minimum levels* of competency or are capable of reaching such levels in a reasonable time.
2. If the qualifications of the minority candidate are only *slightly less* (or equal to or higher) than those of the nonminority, then the minority should be given preference.
3. If both the minority and the nonminority candidates are adequately qualified for a position but the nonminority candidate is *much more* qualified, then:
   a. if performance in the job directly affects the lives and safety of people (such as a surgeon or an airline pilot), or if performance on the job has a substantial and critical effect on the entire firm's efficiency (such as, head comptroller), then the more qualified nonminority should be given preference; but
   b. if the position (like most positions in a firm) does not directly involve safety factors and does not have a substantial and highly critical effect on a firm's efficiency, then the minority person should be given preference.
4. Preference should be extended to minority candidates only so long as their representation throughout the various levels of the firm is not proportional to their availability.

The controversy over the moral propriety of affirmative action programs has not yet died. The Supreme Court has ruled that such programs do not violate the Civil Rights Act of 1964. It does not follow that these programs do not violate any moral principles. If the arguments examined above are correct, however, then affirmative action programs are at least consistent with moral principles. But the arguments themselves continue to be the subject of intense debate.

QUESTIONS FOR REVIEW AND DISCUSSION

1. Define the following concepts: job discrimination, institutionalized/isolated discrimination, intentional/nonintentional discrimination, statistical indicators of discrimination, utilitarian argument against discrimination, Kantian

---

[63] See Nickel, "Preferential Policies," p. 546.

[64] For example, Gross, *Discrimination in Reverse*, p. 108; for a reply to Gross see Boxill, "The Morality of Preferential Hiring."

[65] Theodore V. Purcell, "A Practical Way to use Ethics in Management Decisions," Paper for the Drew-Allied Chemical Workshop, June 26–27, 1980; and Nickel, "Preferential Policies."

arguments against discrimination, formal principle of "equality," discriminatory practices, affirmative action program, utilization analysis, "reverse discrimination," compensation argument for preferential treatment, instrumental argument for preferential treatment, utilitarian argument for preferential treatment, the end-goals of affirmative action programs, invidious contempt.

2. In your judgment, was the historical shift in emphasis from intentional/isolated discrimination to nonintentional/institutionalized discrimination good or bad? Justify your judgment.

3. Research your library for statistics published during the last year that tend to support or refute the statistical picture of racism and sexism developed in Section 7.2 of the text. In view of your research and the materials in the text, do you agree or disagree with the statement "the position of women and minorities relative to white males has changed considerably." Explain your position fully.

4. Compare and contrast the three main kinds of arguments against racial and sexual job discrimination. Which of these seem to you to be the strongest? The weakest? Can you think of different kinds of arguments not discussed in the text? Are there important differences between racial discrimination and sexual discrimination?

5. Compare and contrast the main arguments used to support affirmative action programs. Do you agree or disagree with these arguments? If you disagree with an argument, state clearly which part of the argument you think is wrong and explain why it is wrong. (It is not enough to say "I just don't think it is right.")

6. "If employers only want to hire [the best qualified] young white males, then they have a right to do so without interference, since these are their businesses." Comment on this statement.

CASES FOR DISCUSSION

Brian Weber[1]

The Kaiser Aluminum plant in Gramercy, Louisiana, opened in 1958. From the beginning, the Kaiser Gramercy plant had relatively few black workers. By 1965, although 39 percent of the local work force was black, Kaiser had hired only 4.7 percent blacks. In 1970, a federal review of Kaiser employment practices at the Gramercy plant found that of 50 professional employees, none were black; of 132 supervisors, only 1 was black; and of 246 skilled craftworkers, none were black. A 1973 federal review found that although Kaiser had allowed several whites with no prior craft experience to transfer into the skilled craft positions, blacks were not transferred unless they possessed at least five years of prior craft experience. Since blacks were largely excluded from the crafts unions, they were rarely able to acquire

---

[1] See Rick Harris and Jack Hartog, "The Catch-22 Case," *Civil Rights Digest*, 11, no. 2 (Winter 1979): 2–11.

such experience. As a result, only 2 percent of the skilled craftworkers at Gramercy were black. A third federal review in 1975 found that 2.2 percent of Kaiser Gramercy's 290 craftworkers were black; that of 72 professional employees, only 7 percent were black; and that of 11 draftsmen, none were black. Moreover, although the local labor market in 1975 was still 39 percent black, the Kaiser Gramercy plant's overall work force was only 13.3 percent black. Only the lowest paying category of jobs—unskilled laborers—included a large proportion (35.5 percent) of blacks, a proportion that was brought about by implementing a 1968 policy of hiring one black unskilled worker for every white unskilled worker.

By 1974, Kaiser was being pressured by federal agencies to increase the number of blacks in its better-paying skilled crafts positions. Moreover, the United Steelworkers Union was simultaneously pressing Kaiser to institute a program for training its own workers in the crafts, instead of hiring all its crafts workers from outside the company. As a response to both of these pressures, Kaiser agreed in 1974 to set up a training program that was intended to qualify its *own* workers (both white and black) for crafts positions, and that was also intended to eliminate the manifest racial imbalance in its crafts positions. According to the agreement with the union, Kaiser workers would be trained for crafts positions, in order of seniority, at Kaiser's own expense ($15–20,000 per year per trainee). One half of the slots in the crafts training program would be reserved for blacks until the percentage of black skilled craftworkers in the Gramercy plant approximated the percentage of blacks in the local labor force. Openings in the program would be filled by alternating between the most senior qualified white employee and the most senior qualified black employee.

During the first year of the program, thirteen workers were selected for the training program: seven blacks and six whites. Brian Weber, a young white worker who had applied to the program was not among those selected. Brian, a talkative, likeable southerner and father of three, had been working as a blue-collar lab analyst in the Gramercy plant. His position was rated as "semiskilled." He wanted very much to enter one of the skilled jobs. Upon investigation Weber found that he had several months more seniority than two of the black workers who had been admitted into the training program. Forty-three other white workers who were also rejected had even more seniority than he did. Junior black employees were thus receiving training in preference to more senior white employees. Weber later found that none of the black workers who had been admitted to the program had themselves been the subject of any prior employment discrimination by Kaiser.[2]

1. In your judgment, was the Kaiser plant practicing discrimination? If you believe it was discriminating, explain what kind of discrimination was involved and identify the evidence for your judgment; if you believe it was not discriminatory, prepare responses to the strongest objections to your own view.

[2]Weber subsequently sued Kaiser and the case was eventually heard by the U.S. Supreme Court. The Court ruled that Kaiser's affirmative action program was not in violation of the Civil Rights Act of 1964.

Was Kaiser management morally responsible for the situation in its plant? Why?

2. In your judgment, did the management of Kaiser act rightly when it implemented its preferential treatment program? Explain your judgment in terms of the ethical principles that you think are involved. Does the fact that none of the black workers had themselves been subject to any prior employment discrimination by Kaiser absolve Kaiser from any ethical duty to rectify the racial imbalance in its work force? What policies would you have recommended for Kaiser?

3. Was Brian Weber treated fairly or unfairly? Explain your judgment on the basis of the moral principles that you think are involved. What is the value of seniority relative to equality of opportunity? As a manager, how would you have dealt with Brian and others who felt as he did? Should seniority serve as a basis for deciding who gets trained for a job? What kinds of qualifications do you believe should be taken into account?

Affirmative Action at AT&T

On November 20, 1970, American Telephone and Telegraph (AT&T) routinely applied to the Federal Communications Commission (FCC) for permission to increase long-distance telephone rates in the operating companies under its control, an increase worth an annual $385 million to AT&T. With net earnings in 1970 of over $2 billion per year (making it the world's largest corporation), AT&T controlled 94 percent of all telephone operations within the United States. The actual provision of telephone services was accomplished through a network of twenty-two subsidiary "operating companies" (called the "Bell System") that AT&T controls and that are distributed throughout the United States. According to AT&T, increasing costs in its long-distance operations had made the rate increase necessary.

Three weeks later, on December 10, the FCC announced that it had received a petition from the Equal Employment Opportunity Commission (EEOC) to block the rate increase because AT&T was engaged in "pervasive, systemwide, and blatantly unlawful discrimination of women, blacks, Spanish-surnamed Americans, and other minorities."[1] The Equal Employment Opportunity Commission charged that AT&T was in violation of the Civil Rights Act of 1866, the Equal Pay Act of 1963, the Civil Rights Act of 1964, the Federal Communications Act of 1934, Presidential Executive Order 11246, the Fair Employment Acts of several states and the due process clause of the Fifth Amendment to the American Constitution. Specifically, the EEOC charged AT&T with the following practices: (1) using job classifications based on race and sex, (2) refusing to hire women and minorities because they lacked high school diplomas, had illegitimate children, or had arrest records, (3) maintaining sexually discriminatory retirement plans, (4) relying on sexually and racially discriminatory seniority systems, (5) denying promotional opportunities to women and minorities because of past discriminatory practices. These practices, the EEOC argued, had led to the high employee turnover rates that had plagued the company

[1] *New York Times*, 11 December 1970, p. 1.

since the early 1960s, and to an overall inefficient use of the available work force. These high turnover rates and inefficiencies, in turn, the EEOC suggested were the cause of AT&T's rising costs. The FCC should therefore refuse to grant AT&T the rate increase it had requested until it had eliminated the "callous indifference" evident in its alleged discriminatory practices.

AT&T responded quickly and vehemently. In a hastily convened press conference on December 11, Mr. H.I. Romnes, chairman of AT&T, denounced the EEOC charges as "completely distorted":

> What motivated this move we cannot surmise. Nor do we see how it can possibly advance the cause of equal opportunity. Rather, that cause can only be harmed if organizations sincerely committed to expanding minority employment and with a record of progress like our own can be singled out for public attack by a presumably responsible government agency. The EEOC's intervention in proceedings before the FCC on grounds of discriminatory practices by the Bell System is outrageous. We don't believe this is the place to resolve this kind of thing—in a rate case.
>
> In the field of equal employment we have been leaders, not followers. Total minority employment in the Bell System currently stands at 128,088 or 12.4 percent of our work force. In the past five years nonwhite employment in the Bell System has increased 152 percent. Since 1963, total employment in the Bell System has increased 37.5 percent, nonwhite employment 265 percent. Minorities currently represent some 2.9 percent of Bell System management and professional employees. Women account for 55.5 percent of Bell System employment; they account for 33.5 percent of management and professional employment. Women are actually employed in almost every job in the Bell System except climbing telephone poles, or working in a manhole, and things of that sort. No Bell company requires a diploma for any job.
>
> Some people think you should just reach down arbitrarily and name minority people as officers to achieve some sort of balance. We're just not going to do that. We only have one measure for promotion, and that's ability to perform. [Statement of H.I. Romnes, AT&T chairman] [2]

On January 21, 1971, the FCC announced that it would not allow the EEOC's charges to become part of the rate hearings because the EEOC had failed to demonstrate a relationship between the company's employment policies and rate levels. However, separate hearings would be held during 1971 and 1972 to examine the "serious questions" that the EEOC had raised. If the charges were substantiated, further legal action might then be in order.

The EEOC now began the long task of documenting the charges it had made. The EEOC worked on its presentation throughout the 1971 hearings and on December 1, 1971, it completed a 300 page report analyzing employment patterns in the Bell system. The report was supported by 5,000 pages of statistics and testimony and 25,000 pages of documents. The report studied in detail the thirty metro-

---

[2] See *New York Times,* 12 December 1970, p. 16, and *Wall Street Journal,* 14 December 1970, p. 6.

politan areas served by AT&T that had the largest numbers of minorities. Excerpts from the report follow:[3]

> The Bell System (with 732,450 employees) is the largest private employer in the world. There are four major types of nonmanagement jobs in the Bell system: craft workers, clerical workers, operators, and service representatives. The salary ranges for these and other jobs is as follows:

> **TABLE 7.8**
>
> | Job | Salary Range |
> | --- | --- |
> | Outside Sales | $10,000 – $14,000 |
> | Commercial Representative | $ 8,500 – $ 9,500 |
> | Crafts | $ 7,500 – $10,000 |
> | Service Representative | $ 6,000 – $ 7,000 |
> | Inside Sales | $ 6,000 |
> | Clerical Workers | $ 6,000 |
> | Operators | $ 5,000 – $ 6,000 |

> The operator's job is the least desirable major job in the system. The job is a "highly routine" structured and repetitive task; it is dull and uninteresting, highly regimented, [with] stringent rules governing dress, conversation at the switchboard, phraseology, and clerical accuracy, and the absence of any reasonable hope for future advancement.

> **Sex Segregation in the Bell System**

> A total sex segregation of jobs is reflected in virtually all Bell System documents. These documents unequivocally identify the following jobs as female: operator, clerical jobs, and first level management jobs. Craft jobs, outside sales jobs, and middle and upper management jobs are always identified as male jobs.

> *Major female nonmanagement jobs* Nationwide, eight out of ten female employees are in three major groups of jobs: operator (40 percent of all female employees), service representative (18 percent of all female employees), and clerical and stenographic (32 percent of all female employees). 99.9 percent of the operators are female; 99 percent of all service representatives are female; 93 percent of the low-paying clerical jobs are held by women. Of 1,369 *inside* sales workers, 95.2 percent are females, of 4,000 *outside* sales workers only 8.1 percent are females. In short, in 1971, almost every major low-paying job in the Bell System is a "female" job.

> *Major male nonmanagement jobs* One fourth of the operating company employees are in telephone craft positions. Except for the upper level manage-

---

[3]From *Congressional Record,* 118, part 4, February 15, 1972 to February 22, 1972 (Washington, D.C.: U.S. Government Printing Office, 1972): 4507–4531. For stylistic reasons I have deleted all indications of the innumerable ellipses involved. At some points I have rearranged the order of the excerpts to conserve space and to facilitate comprehension.

ment jobs, these classifications are the most desirable in the system. Not only is the pay a great deal higher and the opportunity for promotion much greater, the job itself is much more challenging and satisfying than the operator and clerical jobs. These more attractive craft jobs have never been open to females on the same basis as males. Of 190,000 telephone craft workers in the operating companies at the end of 1970, 99 percent were male. As noted before, males held 92 percent of the outside sales jobs.

Thus, all low-paying, high-turnover, dead-end jobs are female. High-paying, desirable jobs with substantial chances for promotion to middle and upper management are male.

Management jobs Management jobs are stratified into six levels. Levels one and two are primarily concerned with direct supervision of nonmanagement employees, and levels three and above with the formulation and implementation of company policy. *First level* management jobs include secretary ($8,900–$10,750), administrative clerk ($8,470), clerical supervisor ($8,470), chauffeur ($9,920), stenographer ($7,230), and supervisory assistant ($9,170). (Thus, many first level management positions pay less than craft jobs.)

There are few females in management jobs above the first level. Of all male managers in the thirty metropolitan areas studied, 45 percent are above management level one while a meager 6.3 percent of all female managers have progressed above this level. Of 2,650 employees above third level management, only 1.2 percent were female.

Moreover, within management levels, females find themselves confined to staff positions and not in the mainstream (line) positions of management. For instance, 91 percent of all females in "management" are secretaries. Of the 31 females above level three, all but three fill legal, medical, or other specialized (staff) support roles.

Wages In the thirty metropolitan areas studied, 80 percent of all female employees are in classifications whose maximum basic annual wage is less than $7,000; only 4 percent of all males are in such classifications. And while 34 percent of all males are in classifications with a maximum annual salary of at least $13,000, only 3 percent of all females are so situated. The average maximum wage for males in entry level jobs is $8,613; the average maximum wage for beginning females was $6,114 or only 71 percent of the male wage. A female in first level management averages $11,194; a male $14,170.

Recruitment methods (1) Employee referral has for some years been Bell's preferred method of attracting new employees. But female employees, traditionally confined to "female" jobs, will have limited familiarity with "male" jobs. They will be unaware of vacancies in craft jobs. Employee referral can have only one result: Females will continue to flow into "female" jobs and males into "male" jobs.

(2) The second major recruitment method is to attract graduating high school seniors. But high school counselors tend to counsel women away from "men's fields." Two major recruiting brochures used by every Bell system company picture only females as operator and service representatives, and both use only the feminine gender to describe these employees. "Male" brochures used in 1971 ask "Do you have jobs for young men?" Of the hundreds of brochures used, only one or two picture females or males in "opposite sex" jobs.

(3) The third major recruitment technique is classified advertising. In July, 1965, Illinois Bell's policy was that "ads for operators, stenographers, and typists would be classified under 'Help Wanted—Women,' as women generally fill these positions. Ads for sales trainees would be classified under 'Help Wanted—Men,' as sales people are more commonly thought of as men."

Hiring Bell companies force all applicants into one of two stereotyped molds. For instance, Northwestern Bell made these [assumptions] of applicants: "Men will probably be interested in outside construction, in skilled inside and outside plant occupations, truck driving, sales, and so forth. Most of them will think in terms of starting long-range career employment. Women will probably be interested principally in secretarial, stenographic, receptionist, clerical, switchboard operation, or in-plant selling types of work. Starting long-range careers will probably be secondary."

Nonmanagement promotion There are five basic obstacles to females' progress in Bell's promotion system. (1) Employees are not formally informed of vacancies or of the disposition of their promotion requests. Females, often confined to an isolated work area, would have little opportunity to learn of craft vacancies. (2) Company job descriptions, personnel manuals, and recruitment brochures describe lines of progression in nonmanagement jobs, but these are inevitably sex-segregated. (3) In eight Bell companies, seniority is on a department basis. When departmental seniority is imposed upon Bell's structure of sexually segregated departments, it becomes a substantial obstacle to females' progression. (4) Bell companies prefer to fill entry level craft jobs with new hires rather than with lower level (female) employees wishing to transfer. (5) Promotion qualifications (for crafts jobs) include (a) successful completion of the craft ("male") test battery, (b) craft experience, and (c) satisfactory or above average performance in one's present job. But the female preemployment test does not test capabilities for all the vocational jobs; females may not enter craft jobs, because they have no craft experience and they may not get craft experience, because they are excluded from the crafts; and operators, service representatives, and clerks, whose expectation for promotion is slim, become less interested in maintaining a high level of performance and therefore are deemed "unsatisfactory" by their supervisors. An additional factor that minimizes feminine interest in male jobs is the absence of role models in these jobs. Women (and men) are often quite reluctant to be the first pioneer in a new field.

Management promotion Approximately 50 percent of all middle and upper managers have been promoted primarily from craft jobs; the other prime source of middle and upper management personnel is college graduates. But women are restricted from doing craft work. Moreover, two "essential opportunity factors" needed for managerial promotion are denied to women: (1) special schools or training programs and (2) rotational assignments needed to gain experience that will be valuable in higher assignments. Finally, Bell managers have stereotypes of women's role in management, including: "Women in management are specialists," "The best women leave before a management job is available to them," "Women are not as mobile as men," "Women in management are a threat to men," "Women are not as competent as men," "In order to manage, a woman must have masculine characteristics," "Men cannot consider women as equals," "Women just don't want to manage," "Women cannot supervise men in the field," "Women prefer staff jobs,"

"Women are too emotional," "Men will not want management jobs that women hold," "Women should subscribe to a passive, domestic image," "Men and women should not work together too closely."

Black Segregation in the Bell System

By 1960, black employment in the telephone industry had inched up to 2.5 percent of the total industry employment. In that same year blacks comprised 10.5 percent of the national population. The increase in black employment was concentrated primarily in the job of operator. During the 1960s, black employment in the Bell System as a whole increased steadily, reaching 4 percent of the work force in 1963, 4.6 percent in 1966, and 9.8 percent in 1970. However, an overwhelming proportion of the black workers were still in one job, operator, and so a vastly disproportionate percentage of these black workers were female. In New York, for example, 92 percent of all black employees were female while only 50 percent of all whites were female. A 1969 report presented by AT&T vice-president Walter Straley explained the economic factors leading to the employment of blacks: "Most of our new hires go into entry level jobs, which means we must have access to an ample supply of people who will work at comparatively low rates of pay. That means lots of black people. There are not enough white, middle-class, success-oriented men and women to supply our requirements. It is therefore perfectly plain that we need nonwhite employees. Not because we are good citizens. Or because it is the law as well as a national goal to give them employment. We need them because we have so many jobs to fill and they will take them."

Black employment in 1970   At the end of 1970, the average wage of all Bell company employees in the thirty metropolitan areas was $9,080 per year, while the average wage for Bell's black employees in the thirty areas was only $6,817. In the thirty metropolitan areas studied, 52.4 percent of all black employees were in the Traffic Department (where operators are located), while only 23.4 percent of all Anglo employees held jobs in that department. Almost exactly the opposite pattern existed in the Plant Department (where craft jobs are located): 24.6 percent of all blacks were in plant jobs, while 44 percent of all Anglos were in these jobs. Although, nationwide, blacks comprised only 9.8 percent of all telephone employees in 1971, they made up 37.3 percent of all (lower paid) service workers. In the thirty metropolitan areas studied, only 11.3 percent of all blacks were in (higher paid) craft jobs, while 26.8 percent of all whites were in those jobs. No metropolitan area came even remotely close to employing blacks as craftworkers in proportion to the percentage of blacks in the population. Twenty-two areas employed blacks at rates less than 50 percent of their numbers in the relevant population. Not only are blacks generally underrepresented in the crafts jobs, they are almost totally excluded from the *top* craft jobs. Of approximately 82,000 white craft employees in the thirty metropolitan areas studied, 60.2 percent were in top craft jobs; of 6,450 black craft employees, only 34.9 percent were in top craft jobs. At the end of 1970, 78.7 percent of all black employees were in jobs paying a maximum basic annual wage of $7,000 or less; only 39.5 percent of all white employees were in jobs having such a low salary. While 28.2 percent of all whites are in jobs with a maximum basic annual salary of $10,000 or more, only 5.6 percent of all black employees had jobs with such wages. As of December 1970, blacks held 2.3 percent of management jobs, although they constituted 11.5 percent of the national population.

Moreover, only one in twenty black employees was in management while one in four white employees was a manager.

Black hiring   At least three Bell companies used recruiting brochures in 1971 that indicated that the requirement of a high school diploma still existed for craft jobs. Even those companies that no longer require a diploma to become a craftworker nevertheless grant a preference to high school graduates. Yet nationwide, while 77 percent of all whites between the ages of eighteen and twenty-four had completed high school, only 58.2 percent of blacks in the same age group were high school graduates. The Bell System has never undertaken any study, however, to validate its preference for a high school diploma. In 1971 virtually all companies continued to require at least a high school diploma for service representative and sales jobs, and most companies gave a preference to applicants with some college. Yet nationwide, while 31.6 percent of all whites in the eighteen to twenty-four age bracket had one or more years of college, only 20 percent of blacks of similar age had at least one year of college. The Bell System appears never to have undertaken any study to determine if college training is at all related to being a good service representative or sales worker.

Tests   Bell companies give two basic test batteries—one for craft jobs and another for operator, clerical, and service representative jobs. In one study, 40 percent of white applicants, but only 15 percent of black applicants, scored high enough on the craft tests to qualify for craft jobs. In another study, 58 percent of all white applicants qualified, but only 20 percent of all black applicants passed. Similarly, 70 percent of white applicants *passed* the operator/clerical/service representative tests, while 80 percent of the blacks *failed*. Although the Bell System has conducted at least twenty-seven studies of its test batteries, these studies contain virtually no evidence that the tests accurately predict job performance. However, the Bell system has responded to its desperate need to find enough operator applicants by eliminating the diploma requirements and test standards for operator applicants. The traditionally high requirements that screened out most blacks were maintained for craft jobs and service representatives; applicants failing to meet these high criteria, mostly blacks, were put in the operator job. Since operator has been cut off from the mainstream of movement upward within the system, most of the blacks in the Bell System will never have a real chance at a good job.

Management   The primary reason for the dearth of black managers in the Bell System are four: (1) Most black employees are females and, being women, their chances of promotion are slim; (2) most black females are operators in the Traffic Department, the department with the lowest percentage of managers; (3) few blacks have been hired as craft workers in the Plant Department, where the number of managers is large, and which provides middle and upper management personnel for all other departments; and (4) approximately 50 percent of all Bell System middle and upper level managers are college graduate hires, and black college graduates are in relatively short supply. The fact that it "takes time" to be promoted to management hardly explains the low number of black managers in the Bell System.

Segregation of Spanish-surnamed Americans

Twelve of the metropolitan areas surveyed have a substantial Spanish-surnamed American population and in none of these does Bell's total employment of Spanish-surnamed Americans approach their proportion in the population. In these twelve metropolitan areas, Spanish-surnamed Americans are employed by Bell companies at a rate only 40 percent of their proportion in the population. Bell would have to increase its current Spanish-surnamed employment by over 140 percent in order to achieve parity with the population. Moreover, in none of the twelve selected metropolitan areas does Bell's employment of Spanish-surnamed Americans even approach that of other employers in their area. The average Spanish-surnamed employee in the areas surveyed can expect to earn only 78 percent as much as her or his Anglo counterpart. Although only 45 percent of all employees (including blacks) are paid a rate of less than $7,000 a year, 64 percent of all Spanish-surnamed Americans are in this lowest bracket. Conversely, while over one-fourth of all employees earn more than $10,000 per year, only 8 percent of all Spanish-surnamed Americans have reached this level. As noted earlier, over one-fourth of Bell's Anglo employees are managers; yet only a paltry 6 percent of all Spanish-surnamed employees are managers. Almost all (90.5 percent) Spanish-surnamed managers are in the first level, while one-third of all Anglos have progressed to more responsible and more remunerative positions.

Recruitment   In 1971, none of the selected twelve metropolitan areas used any recruitment brochures that were printed in Spanish. In fact, in five of the areas surveyed there were no brochures that even contained pictures of Spanish-surnamed employees. Spanish-surnamed interviewers are a particular rarity in Bell's central employment office.

Hiring   The requirement of a high school or college diploma screens out a much greater proportion of the Spanish-surnamed than Anglos. While less than half of the Spanish-surnamed Americans in the country in the twenty-five to thirty-four-year old age bracket have completed high school, almost three-fourths of the non-Spanish-surnamed have. Only 15 percent of all Spanish-surnamed Americans have completed at least one year of college compared to 30 percent for all other national origins. Aside from one effort by New Jersey Bell, no attempt has been made to translate the current job tests into Spanish or to produce a culturally fair test for Spanish-surnamed applicants.

Special obstacles   There are two unique obstacles to Spanish-surnamed employment. First, the often extraneous requirement that almost perfect English be spoken is a substantial barrier. Only one company, New Jersey Bell, has made specific efforts to identify those jobs for which written or spoken English is not a requirement. No studies have been made to determine the level of English proficiency, if any, that is required for any job. Second is the height requirement for certain jobs. Because Spanish-surnamed Americans are significantly shorter than Anglos, fewer of their number will be able to meet these height standards.

Because they are denied employment at Bell and because they are confined to the lowest-paying jobs, Spanish-surnamed Americans lose over $137 million annually.

In August 1972, AT&T responded to the EEOC Report with an equally lengthy set of statistics and written testimony presented at the on-going hearings. John W. Kingsbury, assistant vice-president for human resource development at AT&T, argued that the primary duty of the Bell System is to provide communication services to Americans, and not to give jobs "to all comers, regardless of ability." If all employment qualifications were dropped, he pointed out, then the costs of training new recruits would "soar astronomically" and these costs in the end would have to be paid by consumers.[4] Moreover, Dr. Hugh Folk, a professor of economics and labor testifying at the hearings on behalf of AT&T, argued that the statistics used in the EEOC report did not prove that AT&T had discriminated against women. The traditional classification of some occupations as "women's jobs" and of others as "men's jobs" was of society's own making, he claimed. AT&T should not be punished for following the socially determined preferences of their workers, nor was it AT&T's responsibility to change them.

While the hearings progressed, settlement negotiations went on among AT&T, EEOC, and the various other government and labor groups that had by now become involved. With the threat of a government suit hanging over its head, AT&T finally reached an agreement with the government on December 28, 1972, and the agreement was ratified in a consent decree entered in the United States District Court of Pennsylvania.

Without admitting that it had discriminated in the past AT&T agreed in the Court's consent decree (1) not to discriminate in the future, (2) to set up goals and timetables for hiring more women and minorities into all nonmanagement job classifications where they are underrepresented, (3) to provide "delayed restitution" of $15 million in lost wages to 15,000 women and male minorities who "possibly" were discriminated against in the past because they did not try for promotions thinking they could not get them, and (4) to pay $23 million a year in "raises" to 36,000 workers who had previously been promoted but whose salaries had not increased to the new levels set under the agreement.[5] In turn, the EEOC agreed to withdraw all outstanding equal-employment actions against AT&T, and agreed that compliance with the terms of the decree would put AT&T in full compliance with the government's equal employment regulations.

The consent decree specified that AT&T would establish final six-year "goals" and annual "intermediate targets" designed to ensure that in six years the representation of minorities and women in each AT&T nonmanagement job classification would match their availability in the local labor market. Moreover, when needed to attain these "intermediate targets," the company was to show preference toward women and minorities. In particular, the company was required to promote the person who was "basically qualified" (that is, whose performance would be satisfactory), rather than the one who was "best qualified" or who was "most senior," if promoting the "basically qualified" person was necessary in order to reach the company's annual target.

At the end of 1973, the first year the decree was in effect, AT&T reached only 51 percent of its annual targets. The Government Coordinating Committee, a body charged with overseeing the consent decree, then threatened a contempt-of-

---

[4]"AT&T Fights Back," *U.S. News & World Report,* 14 August 1972, pp. 67–68.
[5]*Wall Street Journal,* 19 January 1973, p. 3.

court action against AT&T. Subsequently, however, AT&T signed a second consent decree agreeing to make up the 1973 shortfalls and to pay an additional $7 million in back pay awards. From that year on AT&T managed to achieve most of its annual targets: 90 percent in 1974, 97 percent in 1975, and 99 percent thereafter. Moreover, on April 22, 1977, the U.S. District Court for Eastern Pennsylvania ruled that the AT&T affirmative action requirement was legally permissible because it was "reasonably calculated" to remove the effects of past discrimination.

Not everyone was satisfied, however. On December 8, 1975, Dan McAleer, an AT&T service representative, sued AT&T, claiming that he had lost out on a promotion to a less qualified female employee as a result of AT&T's affirmative action program. McAleer had worked for AT&T for five years and had achieved a score of 34 out of 36 points on the company's performance ratings. Sharon Hulley, however, who had worked at AT&T for less than five years had only 30 points. Nonetheless, when McAleer and Hulley both applied for a promotion to staff assistant, the job went to Hulley. On June 9, 1976, the U.S. District Court in Washington, D.C., ruled that AT&T owed McAleer monetary compensation but did not owe him the promotion. AT&T owed McAleer monetary compensation for his losses, according to the court, because of "the need to share among the respective parties the burden of eradicating past discrimination and achieving equality of employment opportunities" and because of the need also "to protect innocent employees by placing this burden on the wrongdoing employer whenever possible."[6] However, AT&T did not owe McAleer the promotion because "such relief might well perpetuate and prolong the effects of the discrimination that the consent decree was designed to eliminate."[7] But the case was then appealed and before the Court could reach a final decision on the appeal, McAleer and AT&T settled out of court (for $14,000) and the case was dismissed.

On January 18, 1979, the consent decree expired. AT&T had reached 99.3 percent of the final goals it had set in 1973.

1. Compare Mr. H.I. Romnes's assessment of AT&T's employment record with the EEOC assessment expressed in its report. Could both be true?

2. In your judgment, if the allegations in the EEOC report are true, was AT&T practicing discrimination? Justify your answer fully. Identify the alleged discriminatory practices noted in the report. In your judgment, was the management of AT&T morally responsible for the way in which women and minorities had become distributed throughout the company? Explain your answer fully. Explain why you think AT&T management failed to change before the EEOC suit.

3. "This is [not] the place to resolve this kind of thing—in a rate case." "Jobs should not be given 'to all comers, regardless of ability'." "The [EEOC] statistics did not prove that AT&T had discriminated." "The traditional classi-

[6]*McAleer* v. *American Telephone & Telegraph Company,* 416 F. Supp. 435, 1976.
[7]*Ibid.*

fication of 'women's jobs' and 'men's jobs' was of society's own making.'' Comment on each of these claims used in AT&T's defense.

4. In your judgment, should AT&T have been required to implement the "delayed restitution," "raises," and preferential treatment policy specified in the consent decree of December 28, 1972? Explain your position fully in terms of the alleged situation described in the EEOC report and in terms of the moral principles involved. Should other companies follow AT&T?

5. In your judgment, was Dan McAleer treated fairly? Comment on the June 9, 1976 decision on the McAleer case. What should AT&T management do to deal with the dissatisfactions of other Dan McAleers?

CHAPTER EIGHT
THE INDIVIDUAL
IN THE
ORGANIZATION

INTRODUCTION

What are organizations like? Here are some descriptions of life inside organizations by three people positioned at different organizational levels:

Spot-welder at a Ford Assembly Plant:

I start the automobile, the first welds. . . . the welding gun's got a square handle, with a button on the top for high voltage and a button on the bottom for low. . . . We do about thirty-two jobs per car, per unit. Forty-eight units an hour, eight hours a day. Thirty-two times forty-eight times eight. Figure it out. That's how many times I push that button. . . . It don't stop. It just goes and goes and goes. . . . I don't like the pressure, the intimidation. How would you like to go up to someone and say, "I would like to go to the bathroom?" If the foreman doesn't like you, he'll make you hold it, just ignore you. . . . Oh, yeah, the foreman's got somebody knuckling down on him, putting the screws to him. But a foreman is still free to go the bathroom, go get a cup of coffee. He doesn't face the penalties. . . . When a man becomes a foreman, he has to forget about even being human, as far as feelings are concerned. You see a guy there bleeding to death. So what, buddy? That line's gotta keep goin'.[1]

Plant Manager at Ford Assembly Plant:

I'm usually here at seven o'clock. . . . Then I go out on the floor, tour the plant. . . . I'll change my tour so they can't tell every day I'm going to be in

[1] Studs Terkel, *Working: People Talk About What They Do All Day and How They Feel About What They Do* (New York: Pantheon Books, Inc., 1979), pp. 159, 160, 161.

the same place at the same time. The worst thing I could do is set a pattern where they'll always know where I'll be. I'm always stopping to talk to foremen or hourly fellas. . . . I may see a water leak, I say to the foreman, "Did you call maintenance?" Not do it myself, let him go do it. By the time I get back in the office, I have three or four calls, "Can you help me on this?" This is how you keep in contact. . . . The operating committee meets usually every other day: my assistant plant managers; an operations manager, he has two production managers; a controller; an engineering manager; a quality control manager; and a materials manager. That's the eight key figures in the plant. . . . You can't run a business sitting in the office 'cause you get divorced too much from the people. The people are the key to the whole thing. If you aren't in touch with the people they think he's too far aloof, he's distant. It doesn't work.[2]

Ex-president of conglomerate:

I don't know of any situation in the corporate world where an executive is completely free and sure of his job from moment to moment. . . . The danger starts as soon as you become a district manager. You have men working for you and you have a boss above. You're caught in a squeeze. The squeeze progresses from station to station. I'll tell you what a squeeze is. You have the guys working for you that are shooting for your job. The guy you're working for is scared stiff you're gonna shove him out of his job. . . . There's always the insecurity. You bungle a job. You're fearful of losing a big customer. You're fearful so many things will appear on your record, stand against you. You're always fearful of the big mistake. You've got to be careful when you go to corporation parties. Your wife, your children have to behave properly. You've got to fit in the mold. You've got to be on guard. When I was president of this big corporation . . . [the] corporation specified who you could socialize with, and on what level. . . . The executive is a lonely animal in the jungle who doesn't have a friend.[3]

Not everyone experiences organizations as these three people do. Nonetheless, these three descriptions of organizational life touch on many of the most problematic characteristics of business organizations: the alienation experienced by assembly line workers; the feelings of oppression created by the exercise of authority; the responsibilities heaped on the shoulders of managers; the power tactics employed by managers anxious to advance their career ambitions; the pressures felt by subordinates and superiors as they both try to get their jobs done. Other problems could be added to the list: health problems created by unsafe working conditions, conflicts of interest created by an employee's allegiance to other causes, the absence of due process for nonunionized employees; invasion of privacy by a management's legitimate concern to know its own workers. The list could go on.

This chapter explores these and other problems raised by life within business organizations. The chapter is divided into two main parts. The first part begins by describing the traditional model of the organization: the organization as a "rational"

---

[2]*Ibid.,* pp. 178, 179.
[3]*Ibid.,* pp. 405, 406.

structure. The following sections then discuss, first, the employee's duties to the firm as defined by this traditional model, and second, the employer's duties to the employee, again as defined by this model. The second main part of the chapter turns to describing a more recent view of the organization: the organization as a "political" structure. The last sections discuss the two main ethical issues raised by this more recent "political" analysis of the firm: employee rights and organizational politics.

8.1 THE RATIONAL ORGANIZATION

The more traditional "rational" model of a business organization defines the organization as a structure of formal (explicitly defined and openly employed) relationships designed to achieve some technical or economic goal with maximum efficiency.[4] E.H. Schein provides a compact definition of an organization from this perspective:

> An organization is the rational coordination of the activities of a number of people for the achievement of some common explicit purpose or goal, through division of labor and function and through a hierarchy of authority and responsibility.[5]

If the organization is looked at in this way, then the most fundamental realities of the organization are the formal hierarchies of authority identified in the "organizational chart" that represents the various official positions and lines of authority in the organization. Figure 8.1 provides a simplified example.

At the bottom of the organization is the "operating layer": those employees and their immediate supervisors who directly produce the goods and services that constitute the essential outputs of the organization. The work of the Ford spotwelder quoted at the beginning of this chapter was located at this level. Above the operating layer of laborers are ascending levels of "middle managers" who direct the units below them and who are in turn directed by those above them in ascending formal lines of authority. The plant manager quoted above worked within these middle levels of the organization. At the apex of the pyramid is "top management": the board of directors, the chief executive officer, and his or her staff. The expresident quoted earlier inhabited these upper levels of the organization.

The rational model of an organization supposes that most information is collected from the operating layers of the organization, rises through the various formal management levels, each of which aggregates the information, until it reaches top

---

[4]See James D. Thompson, *Organizations In Action* (New York: McGraw-Hill Book Company, 1967), pp. 4–6; see also, John Ladd, "Morality and the Ideal of Rationality in Formal Organizations," *Monist,* 54 (1970).

[5]E.H. Schein, *Organizational Psychology* (Englewood Cliffs, NJ: Prentice-Hall, Inc., 1965), p. 8.

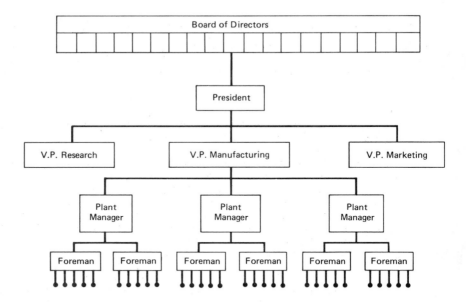

FIGURE 8-1

management levels. On the basis of this information the top managers make general policy decisions and issue general commands, which are then passed downward through the formal hierarchy where they are amplified at each managerial level until they reach the operating layer as detailed work instructions. These decisions of the top managers are assumed to be designed to achieve some known and common economic goal such as efficiency, productivity, profits, maximum return on investment, etc. The goal is defined by those at the top of the hierarchy of authority who are assumed to have a legitimate right to make this decision.

What is the glue that holds together the organization's many layers of employees and managers and that fixes these people onto the organization's goals and formal hierarchy? Contracts. The model conceives of the employee as an agent who freely and knowingly agreed to accept the organization's formal authority and to pursue its goals in exchange for support in the form of a wage and fair working conditions. These contractual agreements cement each employee into the organization by formally defining each employee's duties and scope of authority. By virtue of this contractual agreement, the employee has a moral responsibility to obey the employer in the course of pursuing the organization's goals, and the organization in turn has a moral responsibility to provide the employee with the economic supports it has promised. For, as we have already discussed at some length, when two persons knowingly and freely agree to exchange goods or services with each other, each party to the agreement acquires a moral obligation to fulfill the terms of the contract. Utilitarian theory provides additional support for the view that the employee has an obligation to loyally pursue the goals of the firm: Businesses could not function efficiently and productively if their employees were not single-mindedly devoted to pursuing their firm's goals. If each employee were free to use the resources of the firm to pursue his or her *own* ends, chaos would ensue and everyone's utility would decline.

The basic ethical responsibilities that emerge from these "rational" aspects of the organization focus on two reciprocal moral obligations: (1) the obligation of the *employee* to obey organizational superiors, to pursue the organization's goals, and to avoid any activities that might threaten that goal, and (2) the obligation of the *employer* to provide the employee with a fair wage and fair working conditions. These duties in turn are presumed to be defined through the organization's formal lines of authority and through the contracts that specify the employee's duties and working conditions. We will examine these two reciprocal duties in turn.

8.2 THE EMPLOYEE'S OBLIGATIONS TO THE FIRM

In the rational view of the firm, the employee's main moral duty is to work toward the goals of the firm and to avoid any activities which might harm those goals. To be unethical, basically, is to deviate from these goals in order to serve one's own interests in ways that, if illegal, are counted as a form of "white collar crime."[6]

As administrator of the company's finances, for example, the financial manager is entrusted with its funds and has the responsibility of managing those funds in a way that will minimize risk while ensuring a suitable rate of return for the company's shareholders. Financial managers have this contractual duty to the firm and its investors because they have contracted to provide the firm with their best judgment and to exercise their authority only in the pursuit of the goals of the firm and not for their own personal benefit. Financial managers fail in their contractual duty to the firm when they misappropriate funds, when they waste or squander funds, when they are negligent or fraudulent in the preparation of financial statements, when they issue false or misleading reports, and so on.

These traditional views of the employee's duties to the firm have, of course, made their way into the "law of agency," that is, the law that specifies the legal duties of "agents" (employees) toward their "principals."[7] The "restatement" of the law of agency, for example, states in section 385 that "an agent is subject to a

---

[6]The classic analysis of white collar crime is Edwin H. Sutherland, *White Collar Crime* (New York: Holt, Rinehart and Winston, Inc., 1949); see also U.S. Chamber of Commerce, "White Collar Crime: The Problem and Its Import," in Sir Leon Radzinowicz and Marvin E. Wolfgang, *Crime and Justice,* vol. I, *The Criminal In Society,* 2nd ed. (New York: Basic Books, Inc., 1977), pp. 314–55; and Donald R. Cressey, *Other People's Money* (Glencoe, IL: The Free Press, 1953). The most recent and most extensive analysis of white collar crime is Marshall B. Clinard, Peter C. Veager, Jeanne Brissette, David Petrashek, and Elizabeth Harries, *Illegal Corporate Behavior* (Washington, DC: U.S. Government Printing Office, 1979).

[7]See Phillip I. Blumberg, "Corporate Responsibility and the Employee's Duty of Loyalty and Obedience: A Preliminary Inquiry," in *The Corporate Dilemma,* Dow Votaw and S. Prakash Sethi, eds. (Englewood Cliffs, NJ: Prentice-Hall, Inc., 1973), pp. 82–113.

duty to his principal to act solely for the benefit of the principal in all matters connected with his agency"; and section 394 prohibits the agent from acting "for persons whose interests conflict with those of the principal in matters in which the agent is employed."[8] In short, the employee must pursue the goals of the firm and must do nothing that conflicts with those goals while he or she is working for the firm.

There are several ways in which the employee might fail to live up to the duty to pursue the goals of the firm: The employee might act on a "conflict of interest," the employee might steal from the firm, or the employee might use his or her position as leverage to force illicit benefits out of others through extortion or commercial bribery. We will turn now to examine the ethical issues raised by these tactics.

Conflicts of Interests

Conflicts of interest in business arise when an employee or an officer of a company is engaged in carrying out a transaction on behalf of the company and the employee has a private interest in the outcome of the transaction (a) that is possibly antagonistic to the best interests of the company, and (b) that is substantial enough that it does or reasonably might affect the independent judgment the company expects the employee to exercise on its behalf.[9] Or, more simply, conflicts of interest arise when the self-interest of employees in positions of trust leads them to discharge their offices in ways that may not be in the best interests of the firm. An official of a corporation, for example, is involved in a conflict of interest if he holds stock in one of the companies submitting bids for a construction contract. His interest in seeing the value of the stock improve may tempt him to give the contract to the building company in which he holds stock, even though it did not offer the best terms to the corporation for which he works.

Conflicts of interest need not be financial. For example, if my daughter-in-law is a saleswoman for a firm that manufactures the type of tools that my company purchases, I have an interest in seeing her succeed and may be motivated to give her my company's business even though other firms may offer better terms.

Conflicts of interest can also arise when officers or employees of one company hold another job or consulting position in an outside firm with which their own company deals or competes. An employee of one bank, for example, could be involved in a conflict of interest if the employee took a job serving a competing bank, or if the employee took a job serving an insurance company that leased the employee's own bank's equipment or facilities: At the very least the employee's loyalties would be divided between serving the interests of each competing firm. Similarly, a conflict of interest would be created if an accountant working for an insurance company also provides "independent" auditing services for some of the firms the

---

[8] Quoted in *ibid.*, pp. 87 and 88.

[9] Keith Davis and Robert L. Blomstrom, *Business and Society* (New York: McGraw-Hill Book Company, 1975), p. 182.

insurance company insures: The accountant might be tempted to pass on to the insurance company some of the private information gathered when auditing the books of those other firms.

Conflicts of interest may be actual or potential.[10] An *actual* conflict of interest occurs when a person actually discharges his or her duties in a way that is prejudicial to the firm and does it out of self-interest. A *potential* conflict of interest occurs when a person is merely motivated or tempted by self-interest to act in a way that is prejudicial to the firm. In the first case cited above, for example, the official of the corporation is involved in a merely *potential* conflict of interest, so long as his judgment is not biased by his stockholdings and he gives the contract to the construction company which offers his employer the best terms. The conflict of interest becomes *actual* if his judgment is biased toward the construction company in which he holds stock, and he acts on this bias.

If we accept the view (outlined in Chapter Two) that agreements impose moral duties, then *actual* conflicts of interest are unethical because they are contrary to the implied contract that a worker freely accepts when taking a job with a firm. The administrative personnel of a firm are hired to use their unbiased judgment to advance the goals of the firm. By accepting the position within the firm, the employee contracts to administer the assets of the firm in accordance with these goals and in return takes the salary connected with fulfilling this administrative task. To break this contractual relation violates the rights and duties created by the contract.

Potential conflicts of interest may or may not be ethical depending on the probability that the employee's judgment will be affected by the conflicting interest or will appear to be affected. Obviously, there are no general rules for determining whether or not an employee's private and conflicting interests are significant enough to affect his or her judgment: Much depends on the employee's personal psychology and intentions, on the employee's position in the firm and the nature of the employee's job, on how much he or she stands to gain from the transactions involved, and on the impact the employee's actions will have on others inside and outside the firm. To avoid problems many companies (a) specify the amount of stock that the company will allow employees to hold in supplier firms, (b) specify the relationships with competitors, buyers, or suppliers that the company prohibits employees from having, and (c) require key officers to disclose all their outside financial investments.

Conflicts of interest can be created by a variety of different kinds of situations and activities. Three kinds of situations and activities demand further attention: bribes, gifts, and insider information.

Commercial bribes and extortion A *commercial bribe* is a consideration given or offered to an employee by a person outside the firm with the understanding that when the employee transacts business for his or her own firm, the employee

---

[10]Thomas M. Garrett, *Business Ethics* (Englewood Cliffs, NJ: Prentice-Hall, Inc., 1966), p. 76.

will deal favorably with that person or with that person's firm. The consideration may consist of money, tangible goods, the "kickback" of part of an official payment, preferential treatment, or any other kind of benefit. A purchasing agent, for example, is accepting a bribe when he or she accepts money from a supplier who gives it to the agent in order to receive favored treatment in the agent's purchasing decisions. On the other hand, an employee is engaged in commercial *extortion* if the employee demands a consideration from persons outside the firm as a condition for dealing favorably with those persons when the employee transacts business for his or her firm. Purchasing agents, for example, who will buy only from those salespeople who give them certain goods or services are involved in extortion. Extortion and the acceptance of bribes obviously create a conflict of interest that violates the moral duty that the employee's work contract establishes, that is, the duty to use one's unbiased judgment in the pursuit of the employer's legitimately established goals.

Gifts Accepting gifts may or may not be ethical. The purchasing agent, for example, who accepts gifts from the salesperson with whom he or she deals without asking for the gifts and without making such gifts a condition of doing business with them, may be doing nothing unethical. If the agent does not give favored treatment to those from whom he or she accepts gifts and is not prejudiced against those who fail to give a "gift," no *actual* conflict of interest is created. A *potential* conflict of interest, however, may exist and the act may encourage a practice that in some instances becomes an actual conflict of interest or that may be subtly affecting the independence of a person's judgment. Vincent Barry suggests that the following factors should be considered when evaluating the morality of accepting a gift:[11]

1. What is the value of the gift? That is, is it substantial enough to influence one's decisions?
2. What is the purpose of the gift? That is, is the gift intended or accepted as a bribe?
3. What are the circumstances under which the gift was given? That is, was the gift given openly? Was it given to celebrate a special event (Christmas, a birthday, a store opening)?
4. What is the position of the recipient of the gift? That is, is the recipient in a position to influence his own firm's dealings with the giver of the gift?
5. What is the accepted business practice in the area? That is, is the gift part of an open and well-known industry practice?
6. What is the company's policy? That is, does the company forbid acceptance of such gifts?
7. What is the law? That is, is the gift forbidden by a law, such as a law prohibiting gifts in sports recruiting?

[11] Vincent Barry, *Moral Issues in Business* (Belmont, CA: Wadsworth Publishing Company, 1979), pp. 199–200.

Using insider information   Information about one's own company that is obtained in the course of one's employment, and that has not been publicly disclosed to those outside the company, is "insider information." Employees can sometimes profit from insider information. Employees may learn, for example, that their company is about to make a substantial contract with a certain firm and may use that information as a basis for making a private investment in that firm. Using insider information for one's own profit is wrong primarily because the resources and information put in the hands of an employee by investors are given to the employee with the agreement that the employee will use them solely to advance the firm's goals and not to advance his or her personal interests. But, in addition, insider information puts persons who are outside the firm at an unfair disadvantage when they unknowingly transact business with an insider who is using information that is not available to others and that actually belongs to the firm. Recent court decisions have held that for an employee to use material insider information when investing in securities is illegal.[12]

8.3 THE FIRM'S DUTIES TO THE EMPLOYEE

The basic moral obligation that the employer has toward employees, according to the rational view of the firm, is to provide them with the compensation they have freely and knowingly agreed to receive in exchange for their services. There are two main issues related to this obligation: the fairness of wages and the fairness of employee working conditions.[13] Both wages and working conditions are aspects of the compensation employees receive from their services, and both are related to the question of whether or not the employee contracted to take a job *freely* and *knowingly*. If an employee was "forced" to accept a job with inadequate wages or inadequate working conditions, then the work contract would be unfair.

Wages

From the employee's point of view, wages are the principal (perhaps the only) means for satisfying the basic economic needs of the worker and the worker's family. From the employer's point of view, wages are a cost of production that must be kept down lest the product be priced out of the market. Every employer, therefore, faces the dilemma of setting fair wages: How can a fair balance be struck between the employer's interests in minimizing costs and the workers' interest in providing a decent living for themselves and their families?

There is, unfortunately, no simple formula for determining a "fair wage." The

---

[12] For an analysis of the relevant court decisions see S. Prakash Sethi, *Up Against the Corporate Wall,* 3rd ed. (Englewood Cliffs, NJ: Prentice-Hall, Inc., 1977), pp. 281–315.

[13] The following analysis of wages and working conditions draws from Garrett, *Business Ethics,* pp. 53–62.

fairness of wages depends in part on the public supports that society provides the worker (social security, Medicare, unemployment compensation, public education, welfare, etc.), on the freedom of labor markets, on the contribution of the worker, on the needs of the worker, and on the competitive position of the firm.

Although there is no way of determining fair salaries with mathematical exactitude, we can at least identify a number of factors that should be taken into account in determining wages and salaries.[14]

1. The going wage in the industry and the area   Although labor markets in an industry or an area may be manipulated or distorted (by job shortages, for example), they generally provide at least rough indicators of fair wages if they are competitive and if we assume competitive markets are just. In addition, the cost of living in the area must be taken into account if employees are to be provided with an income adequate to their families' needs.

2. The firm's capabilities   In general, the higher the firm's profits the more it can and should pay its workers, while the smaller its profits the less it can afford. Taking advantage of cheap labor in captive markets when a company is perfectly capable of paying higher wages is exploitation.

3. The nature of the job   Jobs that involve greater health risks, that offer less security, that require more training or experience, that impose heavier physical or emotional burdens, or that take greater effort should carry higher levels of compensation.

4. Minimum wage laws   The minimum wages required by law set a floor for wages. In most circumstances, wages that fall beneath this floor are unfair.

5. Relation to other salaries   If the salary structure within an organization is to be fair, workers who do roughly similar work should receive roughly similar salaries.

6. The fairness of wage negotiations   Salaries and wages that result from "unfree" negotiations in which one side uses fraud, power, ignorance, deceit, or passion to get its way will rarely be fair. When the management of a company, for example, uses the threat of relocation to force wage concessions out of a wholly dependent community, or when a union "blackmails" a failing company with a strike that is certain to send the firm into bankruptcy, the resulting wages have little likelihood of being fair.

---

[14]See Henry J. Wirtenberger, *Morality and Business* (Chicago: Loyola University Press, 1962), pp. 186–89; Garrett, *Business Ethics*, pp. 53–58; and Barry; *Moral Issues in Business*, pp. 116–18.

Working Conditions:
Health and Safety

Each year more than 14,000 workers are killed and over 2,200,000 are disabled as a result of job accidents.[15] Occupational diseases resulting from exposure to chemical and physical hazards kill off an estimated additional 100,000 workers and disable at least 390,000 per year. Annual costs of work-related deaths and injuries are estimated to be $8 billion annually, while lost work time may reach 250 million person-working days per year.[16]

Work-place hazards include not only the more obvious categories of mechanical injury, electrocution, and burns, but also extreme heat and cold, noisy machinery, rock dust, textile fiber dust, chemical fumes, mercury, lead, beryllium, arsenic, corrosives, poisons, skin irritants, and radiation.[17] A government description of occupational injuries is dismaying:

> Three and a half million American workers exposed to asbestos face a dual threat: Not only are they subject to the lung-scarring pneumoconiosis of their trade, *asbestosis,* but they are endangered by *lung cancer* associated with inhalation of asbestos fibers. Recent studies of insulation workers in two states showed 1 in 5 deaths were from lung cancer, seven times the expected rate; half of those with twenty years or more in the trade had x-ray evidence of asbestosis; 1 in 10 deaths were caused by *mesothelioma,* a rare malignancy of the lung or pleura which strikes only 1 in 10,000 in the general working population. Of 6,000 men who have been uranium miners, an estimated 600 to 1,100 will die during the next twenty years as a result of *radiation exposure,* principally from lung cancer. Fifty percent of the machines in industry generate *noise* levels potentially harmful to hearing. Hundreds of thousands of workers each year suffer skin diseases from contact with materials used in their work. The *dermatoses* are the most common of all occupational illnesses. Even the old, well-known industrial poisons, such as mercury, arsenic, and lead, still cause trouble.[18]

In 1970 Congress passed the Occupational Safety and Health Act and created the Occupational Safety and Health Administration (OSHA) "to assure as far as possible every working man and woman in the nation safe and healthful working conditions."[19] Unfortunately, from the beginning OSHA found itself embroiled in

[15] *President's Report on Occupational Safety and Health, 1972* (Washington, DC: U.S. Government Printing Office, 1972), p. 111.

[16] Rollin H. Simonds, "OSHA Compliance: Safety is Good Business," *Personnel,* July–August 1973.

[17] William W. Lowrance, *Of Acceptable Risk* (Los Altos, CA: William Kaufmann, Inc., 1976), p. 147.

[18] U.S. Department of Health, Education and Welfare, "Occupational Disease . . . The Silent Enemy," quoted in *ibid.,* p. 147.

[19] *Occupational Safety and Health Act of 1970,* Public Law, 91–596.

controversy. But in spite of the severe criticism it has received,[20] an inadequate number of field inspectors (800), and often inefficient forms of regulation, the existence of OSHA has led many firms to institute their own safety programs. A 1975 poll revealed that 36 percent of the firms surveyed had implemented safety programs as a result of OSHA, while 72 percent said that the existence of OSHA had influenced them in their safety efforts.[21]

Although more attention is now being paid to worker safety, occupational accident rates have not necessarily been declining. Between 1961 and 1970, the number of injuries per million working hours in manufacturing industries rose by almost 30 percent: from 11.8 injuries per million, to 15.2 per million.[22] By 1973, the rate had moved up to 15.3 per million, and by the late 1970s, the incidence of disabling injuries continued to be 20 percent higher than in 1958.[23]

Risk is, of course, an unavoidable part of many occupations. A race-car driver, a circus performer, a rodeo cowboy, all accept certain hazards as part of their jobs. And, so long as they (a) are fully compensated for assuming these risks and (b) freely and knowingly choose to accept the risk in exchange for the added compensation, then we may assume that their employer has acted ethically.[24]

The basic problem, however, is that in many hazardous occupations, these conditions do not obtain:

1. Wages will fail to provide a level of compensation proportional to the risks of a job when labor markets in an industry are not competitive, or when markets do not register risks because the risks are not yet known. In some rural mining areas, for example, a single mining company may have a monopoly on jobs. And the health risks involved in mining a certain mineral (such as uranium) may not be known until many years afterwards. In such cases, wages will not fully compensate for risks.

2. Workers might accept risks unknowingly because they do not have adequate access to information concerning those risks. Collecting information on the risks of handling certain chemicals, for example, takes up a great deal of time, effort, and money. Workers acting individually may find it too costly, therefore, to collect the information needed to assess the risks of the jobs they accept.

3. Workers might accept known risks out of desperation because they lack the mobility to enter other less risky industries or because they lack information on the alternatives available to them. Low-income coal miners, for example, may know the hazards inherent in coal mining, but since they lack the resources needed to travel elsewhere, they may be forced to either take a job in a coal mine or starve.

---

[20] See, for example, Robert D. Moran, "Our Job Safety Law Should Say What It Means," *Nation's Business*, April 1974, p. 23.

[21] Peter J. Sheridan, "1970–1976: America in Transition—Which Way Will the Pendulum Swing?," *Occupational Hazards* (September 1975), p. 97.

[22] *President's Report*, p. 71.

[23] Barry, *Moral Issues in Business*, p. 121.

[24] See Russell F. Settle and Burton A. Weisbrod, "Occupational Safety and Health and the Public Interest," in *Public Interest Law*, eds. Burton Weisbrod, Joel F. Handler, and Neil K. Komesar (Berkeley: University of California Press, 1978), pp. 285–312.

When any of the three conditions above obtain, then the contract between employer and employee is no longer fair; the employer has a duty, in such cases, to take steps to ensure that the worker is not being unfairly manipulated into accepting a risk unknowingly, unwillingly, or without due compensation. In particular:

1. Employers should offer wages that reflect the risk-premium prevalent in other similar but competitive labor markets.
2. To insure their workers against unknown hazards the employer should provide them with suitable health insurance programs.
3. Employers should (singly or together with other firms) collect information on the health hazards that accompany a given job and make all such information available to workers.

Working Conditions: Job Satisfaction

The rational parts of the organization put a high value on efficiency: All jobs, all tasks, are to be designed so as to achieve the organization's goals as efficiently as possible. And since efficiency is achieved through specialization, the rational aspects of organizations tend to incorporate highly specialized jobs.[25]

Jobs can be specialized along two dimensions.[26] Jobs can be specialized *horizontally* by restricting the range of different tasks contained in the job and increasing the repetition of this narrow range of tasks. The spot-welder quoted in the introduction to this chapter, for example, does nothing but apply welds to car bodies, "thirty-two jobs per car, forty-eight (cars) an hour, eight hours a day." Jobs can also be specialized *vertically* by restricting the range of control and decision making over the activity that the job involves. Whereas the job of the spot-welder is highly specialized vertically, the job of the plant manager is much less vertically specialized.

Job specialization is most obvious at the operating levels of organizations. Assembly-line work usually consists of closely supervised, repetitive, and simple tasks. Low level clerical jobs also tend to be fragmented, repetitive, dull, and closely monitored as this example shows:

> I worked for a while at the Fair Plan Insurance Company, where hundreds of women sat typing up and breaking down sextuplicate insurance forms. My job was in endorsements: *First, third, and fourth copies staple together/place the pink sheet in back of the yellow/If the endorsement shows a new mortgagee/stamp the fifth copy "certificate needed . . . "* Other sections, like coding, checks, filing, and endorsement typing, did similar subdivided parts of the paperwork. The women in the other sections sat at steel desks like mine, each working separately on a stack of forms or cards. Every section had a supervisor who counted and checked the work. She recorded the number of pieces we completed, and the number of errors we made, on our individual production

---

[25] Thompson, *Organizations in Action,* pp. 51–82.

[26] Henry Mintzberg, *The Structuring of Organizations* (Englewood Cliffs, NJ: Prentice-Hall, Inc., 1979), pp. 69–72.

sheets. These production sheets were the basis for our periodic merit raises. Aside from counting and checking, the supervisor also tried to curtail talking and eating at desks.[27]

The debilitating effects that job specialization can have on workers were first noted over two hundred years ago by Adam Smith when he wrote:

In the progress of the division of labor, the employment of the far greater part of those who live by labor, that is, of the great body of the people, comes to be confined to a few very simple operations, frequently to one or two. But the understandings of the greater part of men are necessarily formed by their ordinary employments. The man whose whole life is spent in performing a few simple operations has no occasion to exert his understanding. . . . He naturally loses, therefore, the habit of such exertion and generally becomes as stupid and ignorant as it is possible for a human creature to become. . . . It corrupts even the activity of his body, and renders him incapable of exerting his strength with vigor and perseverance, in any other employment than that to which he has been bred.[28]

More recent research on the mental health of assembly-line workers has tended to corroborate Smith's early suspicions. In a study of auto workers, for example, A.W. Kornhauser found that about 40 percent suffered some sort of mental health problem and that only 18 percent could be considered to have "good mental health."[29] A later study in 1972 found that many American workers suffered from ulcers, lack of self-esteem, anxiety, and other psychological and psychosomatic diseases.[30] In a survey of fifteen years of research on job satisfaction, Stanislav Kasl found that, among other factors, low job satisfaction was related to "lack of control over work; inability to use skills and abilities; highly fractionated, repetitive tasks involving few diverse operations; no participation in decision-making," and that poor mental health was related to similar factors.[31]

Not all workers are equally affected by job specialization. Older workers and workers in large urban areas seem to show more tolerance for routine monotonous jobs, apparently because older workers scale down their expectations over the years, while urban workers reject the Puritan work ethic and so prefer not to become involved in their work.[32] Nonetheless, only 24 percent of all blue-collar workers would choose the same type of work if they could start all over again, an

[27] Barbara Garson, *All The Livelong Day: The Meaning and Demeaning of Routine Work* (Garden City, NY: Doubleday & Co., Inc., 1975) p. 157. Reprinted by permission of Doubleday & Co.

[28] Adam Smith, *The Wealth of Nations* (New York: Modern Library, 1937), p. 734.

[29] A.W. Kornhauser, *Mental Health of the Industrial Worker: A Detroit Study* (Huntington, NY: R.E. Krieger, 1965).

[30] H. Sheppard and N. Herrick, *Where Have All the Robots Gone?* (New York: The Free Press, 1972).

[31] Stanislav Kasl, "Work and Mental Health," in *A Matter of Dignity*, eds. W.J. Heisler and John W. Houck (Notre Dame, IN: University of Notre Dame Press, 1977).

[32] See J.L. Pierce and R.B. Dunham, "Task Design: A Literature Review," *Academy of Management Review*, October 1976, pp. 83–97.

indication that a substantial portion of workers do not find their jobs intrinsically satisfying.[33]

The injuries that highly specialized work has upon the well-being of workers poses an important problem of justice for employees. The most narrowly specialized forms of work are those that require the least skills (since one of the functions of specialization is to dispense of the need for training). And unskilled labor, of course, commands the lowest levels of compensation. As a consequence, the psychological costs of dull, meaningless, and repetitive work tend to be borne by the group of workers that is paid least: unskilled laborers.

Not only may the injuries of specialization be inequitable, they are often also related to a lack of freedom. Unskilled workers often have no real freedom of choice: They must either accept work that is meaningless and debilitating or else not work at all. The freedom that is essential to a fair work contract is therefore often absent.

How should these problems of job dissatisfaction and mental injury be dealt with? A few years ago, Hackman, Oldman, Jansen, and Purdy argued that there are three determinants of job satisfaction:

> *Experienced Meaningfulness.* The individual must perceive his work as worthwhile or important by some system of values he accepts.
> *Experienced Responsibility.* He must believe that he personally is accountable for the outcome of his efforts.
> *Knowledge of Results.* He must be able to determine, on some regular basis, whether or not the outcomes of his work are satisfactory.[34]

To influence these three determinants, the authors claim, jobs must be expanded along five dimensions:

1. *Skill Variety* the degree to which a job requires the worker to perform activities that challenge his skills and abilities.
2. *Task Identity* the degree to which the job requires a completion of a whole and identifiable piece of work—doing a job from beginning to end with a visible outcome.
3. *Task Significance* the degree to which the job has a substantial and perceivable impact on lives of other people, whether in the immediate organization or the world at large.
4. *Autonomy* the degree to which the job gives the worker freedom, independence, and discretion in scheduling work and determining how he will carry it out.
5. *Feedback* the degree to which a worker, in carrying out the work activities required by the job, gets information about the effectiveness of his efforts.[35]

[33] *Work in America: Report of a Special Task Force to the Secretary of Health, Education, and Welfare* (Washington, DC: Congressional Quarterly, Inc., 1973), p. 15.

[34] Richard Hackman, Grey Oldham, Robert Jansen, and Kenneth Purdy, "A New Strategy for Job Enrichment," *California Management Review*, 17, no. 4 (Summer 1975): 58.

[35] *Ibid.*, p. 59.

In short, the solution to job dissatisfaction is perceivable enlargement of the narrowly specialized jobs that give rise to dissatisfaction: broadening the job "horizontally" by giving the employee a wider variety of tasks, and deepening the job "vertically" by allowing the employee more perceivable control over these tasks. Jobs can be horizontally enlarged, for example, by replacing single workers performing single repetitive tasks with teams of three or four who are jointly responsible for the complete assembly of a certain number of machines.[36] And such team jobs can be vertically enlarged by delegating to the team the responsibility of determining their own work assignments, work breaks, and inspection procedures.

8.4 THE POLITICAL
ORGANIZATION

To anyone who has ever worked within a large organization, the goal-directed and efficient structure that the rational model of the organization attributes to business firms will seem a bit incomplete if not altogether unreal. Although much of the behavior within organizations accords with the orderly picture drawn by the rational model, a great deal of organizational behavior is neither goal-directed nor efficient nor even rational. Employees within organizations often find themselves embroiled in intrigues, in on-going battles for organization resources, in feuding between cliques, in arbitrary treatment by superiors, in scrambles for career advancement, in controversies over what the organization's "real" goals are or should be, and in disagreements over strategies for pursuing goals. Such behaviors do not seem to fit within the orderly pattern of the rational pursuit of organizational goals.[37] To understand these behaviors and the ethical issues they raise we must turn to a second model of the firm, one that focuses less on its rational aspects and more on its political features: The "political model of the organization."[38]

The political analysis of the organization that we shall now sketch is a more recently developed view of organizations than the rational analysis. Unlike the rational model, the political model of the organization does not look merely at the formal lines of authority and communication within an organization nor does it presume that all organizational behavior is rationally designed to achieve an objec-

---

[36] Lars E. Björk, "An Experiment in Work Satisfaction," *Scientific American* (March 1975), pp. 17–23.

[37] For a compact contrast of rational and political behaviors, see Robert Miles, *Macro Organizational Behavior* (Santa Monica, CA: Good Year Publishing, 1980), pp. 156–61.

[38] For some recent analyses of the firm based on the "political" model see James G. March, "The Business Firm as a Political Coalition," *Journal of Politics,* 24 (1962): 662–68; Tom Burns, "Micropolitics: Mechanisms of Institutional Change," *Administrative Science Quarterly,* VI (1962–62): 255–81; Michael L. Tushman "A Political Approach to Organizations: A Review and Rationale," *Academy of Management Review* (April 1977), pp. 206–16; Jeffrey Pfeffer, "The Micropolitics of Organizations," in *Environments and Organizations,* Marshall W. Meyer, and others, eds. (San Francisco: Jossey-Bass, Inc., Publishers, 1978), pp. 29–50.

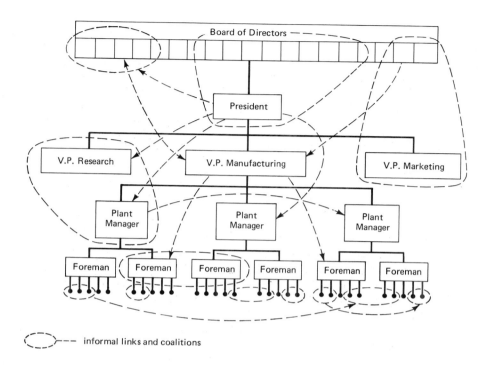

 informal links and coalitions

FIGURE 8-2

tive and given economic goal such as profitability or productivity. Instead the political model of the organization sees the organization as a system of competing power
coalitions and of formal and informal lines of influence and communication that
radiate from these coalitions.[39] In place of the neat hierarchy of the rational model,
the political model postulates a messier and more complex network of clustered
power relationships and crisscrossing communication channels (see Figure 8.2).

In the political model of the organization, individuals are seen as grouping together to form coalitions that then compete with each other for resources, benefits,
and influence. Consequently, the "goals" of the organization are those established
by the historically most powerful or dominant coalition.[40] Goals are not given by
"rightful" authority, but are bargained for among more or less powerful coalitions.
The fundamental organizational reality, according to this model, is not formal
authority or contractual relationships, but *power:* the ability of the individual (or
group of individuals) to modify the conduct of others in a desired way without hav-

---

[39] See R.M. Cyert and J.G. March, *A Behavioral Theory of the Firm* (Englewood Cliffs,
NJ: Prentice-Hall, Inc., 1963); H. Kaufman, "Organization Theory and Political Theory," *The
American Political Science Review,* 58, no. 1 (1964): 5–14.

[40] Walter R. Nord, "Dreams of Humanization and the Realities of Power," *Academy of
Management Review* (July 1978), pp. 674–79.

317

ing one's own conduct modified in undesired ways.[41] An example of an organizational coalition and the nonformal power it can exert even over formal authorities is provided by this account of life in a government agency:

> We had this boss come in from Internal Revenue [to run this OEO department]. He wanted to be very, very strict. He used to have meetings every Friday— about people comin' in late, people leavin' early, people abusin' lunch time. . . . Every Friday, everyone would sit there and listen to this man. And we'd all go out and do the same thing again. Next Friday he'd have another meeting and he would tell us the same thing. (Laughs.) We'd all go out and do the same thing again. (Laughs.) He would try to talk to one and see what they'd say about the other. But we'd been working all together for quite awhile. You know how the game is played. Tomorrow you might need a favor. So nobody would say anything. If he'd want to find out what time someone came in, who's gonna tell 'em? He'd want to find out where someone was, we'd always say, "They're at the Xerox." Just anywhere. He couldn't get through.[42]

As this example shows, behavior within an organization may *not* be aimed at rational organizational goals such as efficiency or productivity, and both power and information may travel completely outside (even contrary to) formal lines of authority and communication. Nonetheless, formal managerial authority and formal communication networks provide rich sources of power. The spot-welder quoted earlier was referring to the power of formal authority when he said, "I don't like the pressure. . . . If the foreman doesn't like you, he'll make you hold it. . . . Oh, yeah, the foreman's got somebody knuckling down on him, putting the screws to him." And the ex-president of the conglomerate whom we also quoted earlier was in part referring to the power of formal authority when he said, "You have men working for you and you have a boss above. You're caught in a squeeze. The squeeze progresses from station to station." The formal authority and sanctions put in the hands of superiors, then, are a basic source of the power they wield over subordinates.

If we focus on power as the basic organizational reality, then the main ethical problems we will see when we look at an organization are problems connected with the acquisition and exercise of power. The central ethical issues will focus not on the contractual obligations of employers and employees (as the rational model would focus them), but on the moral constraints to which the use of power within organizations must be subjected. The ethics of organizational behavior as seen from the perspective of the political model, then, will focus on this question: What are the moral limits, if any, to the exercise of power within organizations? In the sections that follow we will discuss two aspects of this question: (1) What, if any, are the

---

[41] On the primacy of power in organizations, see Abraham Zaleznik, "Power and Politics in Organizational Life," *Harvard Business Review* (May–June 1970), pp. 47–60. The definition of "power" in the text is derived from Virginia E. Schein, "Individual Power and Political Behaviors in Organizations: An Inadequately Explored Reality," *Academy of Management Review* (January 1977), pp. 64–72. Definitions of power are, of course, controversial.

[42] Terkel, *Working,* p. 349.

moral limits to the power managers acquire and exercise over their subordinates? (2) What, if any, are the moral limits to the power employees acquire and exercise on each other?

8.5 EMPLOYEE RIGHTS

Observers of corporations have repeatedly pointed out that the power of modern corporate management is much like that of a government.[43] Governments are defined in terms of four features: (1) a centralized decision-making body of officials who (2) have the power and recognized authority to enforce their decisions upon subordinates ("citizens"); these officials (3) make decisions that determine the public distribution of social resources, benefits, and burdens among their subordinates and (4) they have a monopoly on the power to which their subordinates are subject. These same four features, observers have argued, also characterize the managerial hierarchies that run large corporations: (1) Like a city, state, or federal government, the top managers of a corporation constitute a centralized decision-making body; (2) these managers wield power and legally recognized authority over their employees, a power that is based on their ability to fire, demote, or promote employees and an authority that is based on the law of agency that stands ready to recognize and enforce managerial decisions; (3) the decisions of managers determine the distribution of income, status, and freedom among the corporation's constituencies; and (4) through the law of agency and contract, through their access to government agencies, and through the economic leverage they possess, managers of large corporations effectively share in the monopoly on power that political governments possess.[44]

These analogies between governments and managements, several observers have held, show that the power managers have over their employees is fully comparable to the power government officials have over their citizens. Consequently, if there are moral limits to the power government officials may legitimately exercise over citizens, then there are similar moral limits that should constrain the power of managers.[45] In particular, these authors argue, just as the power of government should respect the civil rights of citizens, so the power of managers must respect the moral rights of employees. What are these employee rights? The moral rights of employees would be similar to the civil rights of citizens: the right to privacy, the right to consent, the right to freedom of speech, and so on.[46]

[43] For example: Richard Eells, *The Government of Corporations* (New York: The Free Press of Glencoe, 1962); and Arthur Selwyn Miller, *The Modern Corporate State* (Westport, CN: Greenwood Press, 1976).

[44] See Earl Latham, "The Body Politic of the Corporation," in *The Corporation in Modern Society,* ed. Edward S. Mason (Cambridge: Harvard University Press, 1960).

[45] See, for example, David W. Ewing, *Freedom Inside the Organization* (New York: McGraw-Hill Book Company, 1977), pp. 3–24; Garrett, *Business Ethics,* pp. 27–30.

[46] David W. Ewing, "Civil Liberties in the Corporation," *New York State Bar Journal,* (April 1978), pp. 188–229.

The major objection to this view of employee rights is that there are a number of important differences between the power of corporate managers and the power of government officials and these differences undercut the argument that the power of managers should be limited by employee rights comparable to the civil rights that limit the power of government. First, the power of government officials (in theory at least) is based on *consent,* whereas the power of corporate managers is (in theory again) based on *ownership:* Government officials rule because they have been elected or because they have been appointed by someone who has been elected; corporate managers "rule" (if that is the right word) because they own the firm for which workers freely choose to work, or because they have been appointed by the owners of the firm. Consequently, since the power of government rests on the consent of the governed, that power can legitimately be limited when the governed choose to limit it. On the other hand, since the power of managers rests on ownership of the firm, they themselves have the right to impose whatever conditions they choose to impose on employees who freely and knowingly contracted to work on their firm's premises.[47] Second, the power of corporate managers, unlike that of most government officials, is effectively limited by unions: Most blue-collar workers and some white-collar workers belong to a union that provides them with a degree of countervailing power that limits the power of management. Accordingly, moral rights need not be invoked to protect the interests of employees.[48] Third, whereas a citizen can escape the power of a particular government only at great cost (by changing citizenship), an employee can escape the owner of a particular management with considerable ease (by changing jobs). Because of the relatively high costs of changing citizenship, citizens need civil rights which can insulate them from the inescapable power of government. They do not need similar employee rights to protect them from the power of a corporation whose influence is easily escaped.[49]

Advocates of employee rights have responded to these three objections in a number of ways: First, they claim, corporate assets are no longer controlled by private owners; they are now held by a dispersed and almost powerless group of stockholders. This kind of dispersed ownership implies that managers no longer function as agents of the firm's owners, and, consequently, that their power no longer rests on property rights.[50] Secondly, although some workers are unionized, many are not and these nonunionized workers have moral rights which managers do not always

---

[47]This ownership and contract argument is the basis of traditional legal views on the employee's duty to obey and be loyal to his employer. See Blumberg, "Corporate Responsibility," pp. 82–113.

[48]Donald L. Martin, "Is an Employee Bill of Rights Needed?" in *The Attack on Corporate America,* ed., M. Bruce Johnson (New York: McGraw-Hill Book Company, 1978).

[49]*Ibid.*

[50]The classic exposition of this view is Adolf Berle and Gardner Means, *The Modern Corporation and Private Property,* 1932; a more recent exposition of similar themes is Adolf Berle, *Power without Property* (New York: Harcourt Brace Jovanovich, Inc., 1959); see also John Kenneth Galbraith, "On the Economic Image of Corporate Enterprise," in *Corporate Power in America,* eds., Ralph Nader and Mark J. Green (Middlesex, England: Penguin Books, 1977); and John J. Flynn, "Corporate Democracy: Nice Work if You Can Get It," in *ibid.*

respect.[51] Thirdly, changing jobs is sometimes as difficult and as traumatic as changing citizenship, especially for the employee who has acquired specialized skills that can be used only within a specific organization.[52]

There is, then, a continuing controversy over the adequacy of the *general* argument that, since managements are like governments, the same civil rights that protect citizens must also protect employees. Whether this general argument is accepted or not, however, a number of independent arguments have been advanced to show that employees have certain *particular* rights that managers should respect. We will look at these arguments next.

The Right to Privacy

Speaking broadly, the right to privacy is the right to be left alone. We will not discuss this broad characterization of the right to privacy, however, but will concentrate on privacy as the right of a person not to have others spy on his or her private life. In this more narrow sense, the right to privacy can be defined as the right of persons to determine the type and extent of disclosure of information about themselves.[53]

The employee's right to privacy has become particularly vulnerable with the development of recent technology.[54] Electronic spy devices, polygraph or "lie detector" machines, and computerized methods of storing, retrieving, and communicating information are some of the new devices that have made invasions of privacy a simple affair. In addition, advances in personality inventory tests have made it possible to uncover personal characteristics and tendencies that a person would rather keep private.

Not only have these innovations made a person's privacy more vulnerable, but they have come at a time when managers are particularly anxious to learn more about their employees. Advances in industrial psychology have demonstrated relationships between an employee's private home life or personality traits, and on-the-job performance and productivity.

There are two basic types of privacy: psychological privacy and physical privacy.[55] *Psychological privacy* is privacy with respect to a person's inner life. This includes the person's thoughts and plans, personal beliefs and values, feelings and wants. These inner aspects of a person are so intimately connected with the person

---

[51] Jack Stierber, "Protection Against Unfair Dismissal," in *Individual Rights in the Corporation*, eds., Alan F. Westin and Stephen Salisbury (New York: Pantheon Books, Inc., 1980).

[52] David W. Ewing, *Freedom Inside the Organization* (New York: McGraw-Hill Book Company, 1977), pp. 36–41.

[53] See Charles Fried, *An Anatomy of Values: Problems of Personal and Social Choice* (Cambridge: Harvard University Press, 1970), p. 141.

[54] Arthur R. Miller, *The Assault on Privacy: Computers, Data Banks and Dossiers* (Ann Arbor: University of Michigan Press, 1971).

[55] See Garrett, *Business Ethics*, pp. 65–67, who distinguishes these two types of privacy (as well as a third kind, "social" privacy).

that to invade them is almost an invasion of the very person. *Physical privacy* is privacy with respect to a person's physical activities. Since people's inner lives are revealed by their physical activities and expressions, physical privacy is important in part because it is a means for protecting psychological privacy. But many of our physical activities are considered "private" apart from their connection to our inner life. A person normally feels degraded, for example, if forced to disrobe publicly or to perform biological or sexual functions in public. Physical privacy, therefore, is also valued for its own sake.

The purpose of rights, as analyzed in Chapter Two, is to enable the individual to pursue his or her significant interests and to protect these interests from the intrusions of other individuals. To say that persons have a moral right to something is to say at least that they have a vital interest in that "something." Why is privacy considered important enough to surround it with the protection of a right?[56] To begin with, privacy has several *protective* functions. First, privacy ensures that others do not acquire information about us that, if revealed, would expose us to shame, ridicule, embarrassment, blackmail, or other harm. Secondly, privacy also prevents others from interfering in our plans simply because they do not hold the same values we hold. Our private plans may involve activities that, although harming no one, might be viewed with distaste by other people. Privacy protects us against their intrusions and thereby allows us the freedom to behave in unconventional ways. Thirdly, privacy protects those whom we love from being injured by having their beliefs about us shaken. There may be things about ourselves that, if revealed, might hurt those whom we love. Privacy ensures that such matters are not made public. Fourthly, privacy also protects individuals from being led to incriminate themselves. By protecting their privacy, people are protected against involuntarily harming their own reputations.

Privacy is also important because it has several *enabling* functions. First, privacy enables a person to develop ties of friendship, love, and trust. Without intimacy these relationships could not flourish. Intimacy, however, requires both sharing information about oneself that is not shared with everyone and engaging in special activities with others that are not publicly performed. Without privacy, therefore, intimacy would be impossible and relationships of friendship, love, and trust could not exist. Secondly, privacy enables certain professional relationships to exist. Insofar as the relationships between doctor and patient, lawyer and client, psychiatrist and patient all require trust and confidentiality, they could not exist without privacy. Thirdly, privacy also enables a person to sustain distinct social roles. The executive of a corporation, for example, may want, as a private citizen, to support a cause that is unpopular with his or her firm. Privacy enables the executive to do so without fear of reprisal. Fourthly, privacy enables people to determine who they are by giving them control of the way they present themselves to society

[56] The analyses in this paragraph and the following are drawn from Fried, *Anatomy of Values,* pp. 137–52; Richard A. Wasserstrom, "Privacy" in *Today's Moral Problems,* 2nd ed., Richard A. Wasserstrom, ed. (New York: Macmillan, Inc., 1979); Jeffrey H. Reiman, "Privacy, Intimacy and Personhood," *Philosophy and Public Affairs,* 6, no. 1 (1976): 26–44; and James Rachels, "Why Privacy is Important," *Philosophy and Public Affairs,* 4, no. 4 (1975): 295–333.

in general and of the way that society in general looks upon them. At the same time, privacy enables people to present themselves in a special way to those whom they select. In both cases, this self-determination is secured by the right of the individual to determine the nature and extent of disclosure of information about oneself.

It is clear, then, that our interest in privacy is important enough to recognize it as a right. However, this right must be balanced against other individuals' rights and needs. Employers in particular sometimes have a legitimate right to inquire into the activities of employees or prospective employees. The employer is justified in wanting to know, for example, what a job candidate's past work experience has been and whether the candidate has performed satisfactorily on previous jobs. An employer may also be justified in wanting to identify the culprits when the firm finds itself the subject of pilferage or employee theft, and of subjecting employees to on-the-job surveillance in order to discover the source of thefts. How are these rights to be balanced against the right to privacy? Three elements must be considered when collecting information that may threaten the employee's right to privacy: relevance, consent, and method.[57]

Relevance   The employer must limit inquiry into the employee's affairs to those areas that are directly relevant to the issue at hand. Although employers have a right to know the person they are employing and to know how the employee is performing, employers are not justified in inquiring into any areas of the employee's life that do not affect the employee's work performance in a direct and serious manner. To investigate an employee's political beliefs or the employee's social life, for example, is an invasion of privacy. Moreover, if a firm acquires information about an employee's personal life in the course of a legitimate investigation, it has an obligation to destroy the information, especially when such data would embarrass or otherwise injure the employee if it were leaked. The dividing lines between justified and unjustified investigation are fairly clear with respect to lower level employees: There is clearly little justification for investigating the marital problems, political activities, or emotional characteristics of clerical workers, sales workers, or factory laborers. The dividing line between what is and what is not relevant, however, becomes less clear as one moves higher in the firm's management hierarchy. Managers are called on to represent their company before others and the company's reputation can be significantly damaged by a manager's private activities or emotional instability. A vice-president's drinking problem or membership in a disreputable association, for example, will affect the vice-president's ability to adequately represent the firm. The firm in such cases may be justified in inquiring into an officer's personal life or psychological characteristics.

Consent   Employees must be given the opportunity to give or withhold their consent before the private aspects of their lives are investigated. The firm is justified in inquiring into the employee's life only if the employee has a clear understanding

---

[57]The remarks that follow are based in part on Garrett, *Business Ethics,* pp. 67–72.

that the inquiry is being made and clearly consents to this as part of the job or can freely choose to refuse the job. The same principle holds when an employer undertakes some type of surveillance of employees for the purpose, say, of uncovering or preventing pilferage. Employees should be informed of such surveillance so they can ensure they will not inadvertently reveal their personal lives while under surveillance.

Methods   The employer must distinguish between methods of investigation that are both ordinary and reasonable, and methods that are neither. Ordinary methods include the supervisory activities that are normally used to oversee employees' work. Extraordinary methods include devices like hidden microphones, secret cameras, wiretaps, lie detector tests, personality inventory tests, and spies. Extraordinary methods are unreasonable and unjustified unless the circumstances themselves are extraordinary. Extraordinary methods of investigation might be justified if a firm is suffering heavy losses from employee theft that ordinary supervision has failed to stop. Extraordinary devices, however, are not justified merely because the employer hopes to be able to pick up some interesting tidbits about employee loyalties. In general, the use of extraordinary devices is justified only when the following conditions have been met: (1) The firm has a problem that can be solved in no other manner than by employing such extraordinary means; (2) the problem is serious and the firm has well-founded grounds for thinking that the use of extraordinary means will identify the culprits or put an end to the problem; (3) the use of the extraordinary devices is not prolonged beyond the time needed to identify the wrongdoers or after it becomes clear that the devices will not work; (4) all information that is uncovered but that is not directly relevant to the purposes for which the investigation was conducted is disregarded and destroyed.

Freedom of Conscience
and Whistleblowing

In the course of performing a job, an employee may discover that a corporation is doing something that he or she believes is injurious to society. Indeed, individuals inside a corporation are usually the first to learn that the corporation is marketing unsafe products, polluting the environment, suppressing health information, or violating the law.

Employees with a sense of moral responsibility who find that their company is injuring society in some way will normally feel an obligation to get the company to stop its harmful activities and consequently will often bring the matter to the attention of their superiors. Unfortunately, if the internal management of the company refuses to do anything about the matter, the employee today has few other legal options available. If, after being rebuffed by the company, the employee has the temerity to take the matter to a government agency outside the firm, or worse, to disclose the company's activities to a public medium, the company has the legal right to punish the employee by firing him or her. Furthermore, if the matter is serious enough, the company can reinforce this punishment by putting the matter on the employee's record and, in extreme cases, seeing to it that the employee is black-balled by other companies in the industry.[58]

Several authors have argued that this is in effect a violation of an individual's right to freedom of conscience.[59] It is a violation of the right to freedom of con-science because the individual is forced to cooperate with an activity that violates the individual's personal moral beliefs. What is the basis of this right? The right to freedom of conscience derives from the interest that individuals have in being able to adhere to their religious or moral convictions.[60] Individuals who have religious or moral convictions commonly see them as absolutely binding and can transgress them only at great psychological cost. The right to freedom of conscience protects this interest by requiring that individuals may not be forced to cooperate in activities that they conscientiously believe are wrong.

These arguments, however, have not yet had a substantial effect on the law, which still by and large reinforces the employee's duty of maintaining loyalty and confidentiality toward the employer's business.[61] In the absence of legal protections of the employee's right to freedom of conscience, some authors have supported the practice of "whistleblowing."[62] An employee "blows the whistle" on a company when, knowing that the company is engaged in serious unethical activity and having made reasonable but unsuccessful efforts to get the company to desist by working from within, the employee chooses to disclose the information to the public.

Whistleblowing is, obviously, a serious act. If the information the whistle-blower discloses to the public is mistaken, self-serving, false, biased, or distorted, the employee may grieviously and unjustly harm an innocent company. Or if the company is already prepared to deal with the problem, the whistleblower's public disclosure may serve only to make the company defensive and recalcitrant about doing anything more about it. And, of course, the whistleblower may find that blowing the whistle brings with it nothing more than a great deal of personal grief and injury. Various authors have suggested, therefore, that before blowing the whistle, individuals should consider the following factors:[63]

1. How comprehensive is the worker's knowledge of the situation? Is the work-er's information accurate and substantiated?
2. What, exactly, are the unethical practices involved? Why are these unethical? What public values do these practices harm?

[58] For examples see Ralph Nader, Peter J. Petkas, and Kate Blackwell, *Whistle Blowing* (New York: Grossman Publishers, 1972).

[59] For example, Ewing, *Freedom Inside the Organization,* pp. 115–27.

[60] See John Rawls, *A Theory of Justice* (Cambridge: Harvard University Press, 1971), pp. 205–11.

[61] See, Blumberg, "Corporate Responsibility."

[62] E.g., Nader, Petkas, and Blackwell, *Whistle Blowing;* and Charles Peters and Taylor Branch, *Blowing the Whistle: Dissent in the Public Interest* (New York: Praeger Publishers, Inc., 1972).

[63] See Nader, Petkas, and Blackwell, *Whistle Blowing,* p. 6; Sissela Bok, "Whistleblowing and Professional Responsibilities," draft prepared for the Hastings Institute Project on the Teaching of Ethics, April 1979; W.L. LaCroix, *Principles for Ethics in Business* (Washington, DC: University Press of America, 1976), p. 110.

3. How substantial and irreversible are the effects of these practices? Are there any compensating public benefits that justify the practices?
4. What is the employee's obligation to bring such practices to an end? Can the employee do more to end the practices by working within the organization or by going outside? What probable effects will either alternative have on the company's practices? On society? On the firm? On other organizations? On the employee?

In addition, proponents of the practice of whistleblowing have suggested that employers and labor unions should develop reasonable protections for conscientious employees so that they are not forced to choose between going outside the firm or compromising their ethics by participating in what they believe are immoral or illegal activities. One possibility, for example, is the appointment of an internal "ombudsman" who is authorized to receive and communicate employee doubt and criticisms to superiors and who would have the authority to make public outside the corporation any complaints that did not receive a proper managerial response. But most important is ensuring that the organization is structured in ways that will reduce or entirely eliminate the employee's need to blow the whistle.[64]

The Right to Participate

A democratic political tradition has long held that government should be subject to the consent of the governed because individuals have a right to liberty and this right implies that they have a right to participate in the political decisions which affect them. Within a democracy, therefore, decision-making usually has two characteristics: (1) Decisions that affect the group are made by a majority of its members, (2) decisions are made after full, free, and open discussion.[65] Either all the members of the group participate in these decision-making processes or they do so through elected representatives.

A number of authors have proposed that these ideals of democracy should be embodied in the corporation.[66] The individual employee within the organization should be permitted to participate in the decision-making processes of the organization. As a first step toward such democracy, some have suggested that, although decisions affecting workers should not be made *by* workers, they should, nonetheless, be made only after full, free, and open discussion *with* workers. This would mean open communication between workers and their supervisors, and the establishment of an environment that encourages consultation with workers. Employees would be allowed to freely express criticism, to receive accurate information about decisions that will affect them, to make suggestions, and protest decisions.

A second further step toward "organizational democracy" would give individual employees not only the right to consultation but also the right to make decisions about their own immediate work activities. These decisions might include

---

[64] Kenneth D. Walters, "Your Employee's Right to Blow the Whistle," *Harvard Business Review,* vol. 53, no. 4 (1975).

[65] Robert G. Olson, *Ethics* (New York: Random House, Inc., 1978), pp. 83–84.

matters such as working hours, rest periods, the organization of work tasks, and the scope of responsibility of workers and supervisors.

A third step toward extending the ideals of democracy into the work-place would allow workers to participate in the major policy decisions that affect the general operations of the firm. European firms, for example, particularly in West Germany, have adopted the concept of "codetermination."[67] Starting in 1951, German law required that each firm in the basic industries (coal, iron, and steel) should be administered by an eleven-member board of directors composed of five directors elected by stockholders, five directors elected by employees, and one director elected by the other ten. Further extension of the law to firms with more than twenty workers required such firms to have twelve-member boards composed of eight directors elected by stockholders and four directors elected by employees. These "Works Councils" decide issues such as plant shut-down or relocation, mergers with other firms, substantial product diversification, or the introduction of fundamentally new labor methods.

Full organizational democracy has not been particularly popular in the United States. Part of the reason, perhaps, is that employees have not shown a great deal of interest in participating in the firm's broader policy decisions. A more important reason, however, is that American ideology distinguishes sharply between the power exercised in political organizations and the power exercised within economic organizations: Whereas power in political organizations should be democratic, power in economic organizations should be left in the private hands of managers and owners.[68] Whether this ideological distinction is valid is something the reader must decide. Many authors continue to argue that, given the large and dominant role that business organizations are now playing in our daily lives, democracy will soon touch only the peripheral areas of our lives if it continues to be restricted to political organizations.[69]

The Right to Due Process

For many people, the most critical right of employees is the right to due process. For our purposes, "due process" refers to the fairness of the process by which decision-makers impose sanctions on their subordinates. An ideal system of due process would be one in which individuals were given clear antecedent notice of the rules they were to follow, which gave a fair and impartial hearing to those who are

[66] Warren G. Bennis and Philip E. Slater, *The Temporary Society* (New York: Harper & Row, Publishers, Inc., 1968); Vincent P. Mainelli, "Democracy in the Workplace," *America*, (15 January 1977), pp. 28–30; see also the essays in *Self-Management: New Dimensions to Democracy*, eds., Ichak Adizes and Elizabeth Mann Borgese (Santa Barbara, CA: Clio Books, 1975).

[67] Frederick D. Sturdivant, *Business and Society* (Homewood, IL: Richard D. Irwin, Inc., 1977), pp. 347–49.

[68] See Robert A. Dahl, *After the Revolution? Authority in a Good Society* (New Haven: Yale University Press, 1970), pp. 117–18.

[69] C. Pateman, "A Contribution to the Political Theory of Organizational Democracy," *Administration and Society*, 7 (1975): 5–26.

believed to have violated the rules, which administered all rules consistently and without favoritism or discrimination, which was designed to ascertain the truth as objectively as possible, and which did not hold people responsible for matters over which they had no control.

It is obvious why the right to due process is seen by many people as the most critical right of employees: If this right is not respected, employees stand little chance of seeing their other rights respected. Due process ensures that individuals are not treated arbitrarily, capriciously, or maliciously by their superiors in the administration of the firm's rules, and sets a moral limit on the exercise of the superior's power.[70] If the right to due process were not operative in the firm, then even if the rules of the firm protect the employee's other rights, these protections might be enforced sporadically and arbitrarily.

The most important area in which due process must play a role is in the hearing of grievances. By carefully spelling out a fair procedure for hearing and processing employee grievances, a firm can ensure that due process becomes an institutionalized reality. Here is an example of one company's fairly simple set of procedures for ensuring due process in grievances:

> All problems should be taken up initially with the employee's immediate supervisor. Most of the problems will be settled at this point to the satisfaction of the employee. There may be times, however, when the nature of the problem is such that the supervisor may not be able to give an immediate answer. In those instances where the immediate supervisor is unable to solve the problem within two working days following the date of presentation by the employee, the employee may review the problem with his departmental manager or superintendent. In situations where, after having discussed his problem with his immediate supervisor and departmental manager or superintendent, an employee still has questions, he may take the problem to the personnel manager for disposition.[71]

Trotta and Gudenberg identify the following features as the essential components of an effective grievance procedure:

1. Three to five steps of appeal, depending upon the size of the organization. Three steps usually will suffice.
2. A written account of the grievance when it goes past the first level. This facilitates communication and defines the issues.
3. Alternate routes of appeal so that the employee can bypass his supervisor if he desires. The personnel department may be the most logical alternate route.
4. A time limit for each step of the appeal so that the employee has some idea of when to expect an answer.

[70] See T.M. Scanlon, "Due Process," in *Due Process*, eds., J. Roland Pennock and John W. Chapman (New York: New York University Press, 1977), pp. 93-125.

[71] Quoted in Maurice S. Trotta and Harry R. Gudenberg, "Resolving Personnel Problems in Nonunion Plants," in Westin and Salisbury, *Individual Rights*, p. 306.

5. Permission for the employee to have one or two co-workers accompany him at each interview or hearing. This helps overcome fear of reprisal.[72]

8.6 ORGANIZATIONAL POLITICS

The discussion so far has focused primarily on formal power relationships within organizations: that is, the ethical issues raised by the power that the formal structure of the organization allows managers to exercise over their subordinates. These power relations are sanctioned and overt: They are spelled out in the firm's "organizational chart," inscribed in the contracts and job descriptions that define the employee's duties to the firm, recognized by the law (of agency), openly employed by superiors, and largely accepted as legitimate by subordinates.

The ethical constraints on the use of this formal power that we reviewed above have also been approached from a largely formal perspective. The rights to privacy, to due process, to freedom of conscience, and to consent can all be formalized within the organization (by formulating and enforcing rules, codes, and procedures) just as the power relationships they constrain are formalized.

But as we have already seen, organizations also contain informal pockets and channels of power: sources of power that do not appear on organizational charts and uses of power that are covert and perhaps not recognized as legitimate. We must turn now to look at this underbelly of the organization: organizational politics.

Political Tactics in Organizations

There is no settled definition of "organizational politics." For our purposes, however, we can adopt the following definition: "Organizational politics" are the processes in which individuals or groups within an organization use nonformally sanctioned power tactics to advance their own aims; such tactics we shall call "political tactics."[73]

A word of caution is necessary, lest the reader interpret "their own aims" to mean "aims in conflict with the best interests of the organization." Although the aims of a coalition in a firm may conflict with the best interests of the firm (a problem we will examine), such conflict is neither inevitable nor even, perhaps, frequent. Two factors tend to suppress such conflicts: (1) the careers of individuals often depend on the health of their organizations and (2) long-time association with an organization tends to generate bonds of loyalty to the organization. Often, therefore, what one person *perceives* as a conflict between a certain group's aims and the best interests of the organization is in fact a conflict between the beliefs of that person and the beliefs of the group concerning what the "best interests" of the

---

[72]*Ibid.*, pp. 307–8.

[73]This definition is from Bronston T. Mayes and Robert W. Allen, "Toward A Definition of Organizational Politics," *Academy of Management Review* (October 1977), pp. 672–78.

organization are: The group may genuinely believe that X is in the best interests of *both* the organization and itself, while the person may genuinely believe instead that Y, which conflicts with X, is what is in the best interests of the organization.

Because organizational politics aim at advancing the interests of one individual or group (such as, acquiring promotions, salary or budget increases, status, or even more power) by exerting nonformally sanctioned power over other individuals or groups, political individuals tend to be *covert* about their underlying intents or methods.[74] Virginia E. Schein, for example, gives this illustration of a department head intent on strengthening her position in an organization:

> The head of a research unit requests permission to review another research group's proposal in case she can add information to improve the project. Her covert intent is to maintain her current power, which will be endangered if the other research group carries out the project. Using her informational power base, her covert means are to introduce irrelevant information and pose further questions. If she sufficiently confuses the issues, she can discredit the research group and prevent the project from being carried out. She covers these covert intents and means with the overt ones of improving the project and reviewing its content.[75]

The fact that political tactics are usually covert means that they can easily become deceptive or manipulative. This is evident if we examine more examples of organizational political tactics. In a recent study of managerial personnel, respondents were asked to describe the political tactics they had experienced most frequently in the organizations in which they had worked.[76] The following kinds of tactics were reported:

Blaming or attacking others Minimizing one's association with an outcome that is failing or has failed by blaming one's rivals for the failure or "denigrating their accomplishments as unimportant, poorly timed, self-serving, or lucky."

Controlling information Withholding information detrimental to one's aims or distorting information "to create an impression by selective disclosure, innuendo," or overwhelming the subject with "objective" data (graphs, formulas, tables, summations) designed to create an impression of rationality or logic and to obscure important details harmful to one's interests.

Developing a base of support for one's ideas Getting others to understand and support one's ideas before a meeting is called.

Image building Creating the appearance of being thoughtful, honest, sensitive, on the inside of important activities, well-liked, confident.

---

[74] Miles, *Macro Organizational Behavior,* pp. 161–64.

[75] Schein, "Individual Power and Political Behaviors," p. 67.

[76] Robert W. Allen, Dan L. Madison, Lyman W. Porter, Patricia A. Renwick, Bronston T. Mayes, "Organizational Politics," *California Management Review,* 22, no. 1 (Fall 1979): 77–83.

Ingratiation   Praising superiors and developing good rapport.

Associating with the influential

Forming power coalitions and developing strong allies

Creating obligations   Making others feel obligated to oneself by performing services or favors for them.

Some researchers have argued that the basic source of power is the creation of dependency: A acquires power over B by making B dependent upon A for something. Some authors identify the following political tactics by which such dependencies can be created:[77]

Getting control over scarce resources desired by others   Controlling employees, buildings, access to influential persons, equipment, useful information.

Establishing favorable relationships   Getting others to feel obligated to oneself; making others think one is a friend; building a reputation as an expert; encouraging others to believe that one has power and that they are dependent on that power.

Anyone who has ever worked within organizations can undoubtedly think of many examples of the use of political tactics in organizational life. Here is a former executive's description of the use of some "ploys" he encountered during his corporate career:

> [This is] a ploy for many minor executives to gain some information: I heard that the district manager of California is being transferred to Seattle. He knows there's been talk going on about changing district managers. By using this ploy—"I know something"— he's making it clear to the person he's talking to that he's been in on it all along. So it's all right to tell him. Gossip is another way of building up importance within a person who starts the rumor. He's in, he's part of the inner circle . . . When a top executive is let go. . . . suddenly everybody in the organization walks away and shuns him because they don't want to be associated with him. In corporations, if you back the wrong guy, you're in his corner and he's fired, you're guilty by association. . . . A guy in a key position, everybody wants to talk to him. All his subordinates are trying to get an audience with him to build up their own positions.[78]

The Ethics of Political Tactics

Obviously, political behavior in an organization can easily become abusive: Political tactics can be used to advance private interests at the expense of organizational and group interests; they can be manipulative and deceptive; and they can

---

[77]These are culled from the pages of John P. Kotter, *Power in Management* (New York: American Management Associations, 1979), a book which argues that "skillfully executed power-oriented behavior" is the mark of the "successful manager."

[78]Terkel, *Working*, pp. 407, 409, 410.

seriously injure those who themselves have little or no political power or expertise. On the other hand, political tactics can also be put at the service of organizational and social goals, they may sometimes be necessary to protect the powerless, and they are sometimes the only defense a person has against the manipulative and deceptive tactics of others. The dilemma for the individual in an organization is knowing where the line lies that separates morally legitimate and necessary political tactics from those that are unethical.

Very few authors have examined this dilemma.[79] This is unfortunate because, although few organizations are totally pervaded by political behavior, it is also the case that no organization is free of it: We are all political animals even if our political campaigns are largely confined to the office. We shall here only be able to make a start at analyzing the many complex ethical issues raised by the political maneuvering that inevitably goes on within organizations. The issues can best be approached by addressing three questions that can focus our attention on the morally relevant features of using political tactics. (1) The *utilitarian* question: Are the goals one intends to achieve by the use of the tactics socially beneficial or socially harmful? (2) The *rights* question: Do the political tactics used as means to these goals treat others in a manner consistent with their moral rights? (3) The *justice* question: Will the political tactics lead to an equitable distribution of benefits and burdens?[80]

The utility of goals   Utilitarian principles require that managers pursue those goals that will produce the greatest social benefits and the least social harm. If we assume that business organizations generally perform a socially beneficial function and that activities that harm the organization will probably diminish these social benefits, then utilitarianism implies that the individual manager should avoid harming the organization and that the manager should work to ensure that the organization carries out its beneficial social functions as efficiently as possible. The basic function of most businesses, for example, is to produce goods and services for consumers. Insofar as a business organization is serving this function in a socially beneficial and nonharmful way, the employee should avoid harming the business and should strive to ensure that the business carries on its productive function with a minimum of waste. Two kinds of political tactics directly contradict this norm and are therefore typically judged unethical: Political tactics that involve the pursuit of personal goals at the expense of the organization's productive goals, and political tactics that knowingly involve inefficiency and waste. Suppose, for example, that the head of a research unit secretly withholds critical information from other research units in the same company so that his own unit will look better than the others. As a result, his career ambitions are advanced and his unit gets a larger budget allocation the following year. Was his tactic of withholding information to

[79] See John R.S. Wilso, "In One Another's Power," *Ethics,* 88, no. 4 (July 1978): 299–315; L. Blum, "Deceiving, Hurting, and Using," in *Philosophy and Personal Relations,* A. Montefiore, ed. (London: Routledge and Kegan Paul, 1973).

[80] See Gerald Cavanagh, Dennis Moberg, and Manuel Velasquez, "The Ethics of Organizational Politics"; paper presented to meeting of the Academy of Management, Detroit (August 1980), forthcoming in *Academy of Management Review.*

gain an edge on others morally legitimate? No: The tactic was clearly inconsistent with the efficient pursuit of the company's productive functions.

Of course, businesses do not always have socially beneficial and nonharmful goals. Pollution, planned obsolescence, price-fixing, and the manufacture of hazardous products are some obvious organizational goals that utilitarianism would condemn. To the extent that a business pursues such goals, the employee has a duty not to cooperate (unless, perhaps, the employee is threatened with personal losses of such magnitude that he or she is in effect coerced to comply). Utilitarian principles imply that to voluntarily pursue goals that are socially harmful or to voluntarily cooperate in such a pursuit is immoral, regardless of what kinds of political tactics one uses.

Unfortunately, organizational goals are not always clear because there may be no consensus over what the organization's goals actually are. This is especially the case, for example, when a company is in the process of undergoing a change in management or a change in organization and more or less widespread bargaining erupts over what the new goals should be. When organizational goals are in the process of being redefined in this way, the various coalitions and individuals within the organization will usually attempt to use political tactics to install the goals that each wants, either through a unilateral exercise of power (a new management, for example, may try to get rid of all the old staff and to hire its own "team") or through political compromise (the new management may try to persuade the old staff to accept new goals). In such fluid situations the individual has no choice but to examine the goals being proposed by the various coalitions, and to make a conscientious attempt to determine which goals are in the long run the most socially beneficial. Whereas the use of political tactics to install illegitimate organizational goals would be unethical, political tactics may be used to ensure the installation of morally legitimate goals *provided that the tactics meet the two criteria here following:*

The consistency of political means with moral rights   Some political tactics are obviously deceptive, as when a person creates the impression that he or she has an expertise that the person does not in fact have. Other tactics are manipulative. It is manipulative, for example, to feign love in order to extract favors from a person. Deception and manipulation are both attempts to get a person to do (or believe) something that that person would not do (or believe) if he or she knew what was going on. These sorts of political tactics are unethical to the extent that they fail to respect a person's right to be treated not merely as a means but also as an end; that is, they fail to respect a person's right to be treated only as he or she has freely and knowingly consented to be treated. Such moral disrespect is exhibited in many of those political tactics that take advantage of our emotional dependencies and vulnerabilities, both of which provide others with the cheapest and most reliable levers for acquiring power over us. A skilled administrator, for example, can become adept at pretending friendship and concern, and adept at getting others to look upon him or her with affection, respect, loyalty, indebtedness, trust, gratitude, and so on. The administrator can then exploit these feelings to get subordinates to do things for him or her that they ordinarily would not do, especially if they knew the deception involved and knew the covert motives on which the administrator acted. A skillful administrator might also learn to take advantage of particular individuals' personal vulnerabilities such as vanity, generosity, sense of responsibility, susceptibility to flattery, gullibility, naiveté or any of the other traits that can lead a person to unwittingly put himself or herself at the mercy of others. By covertly taking advantage of these vulnerabilities, the manager can get employees to serve the manager's aims, even though they would not do so if they knew the covert motives on which the manager acted.

But are deceptive and manipulative political tactics always wrong? What if I am forced to work in an organization in which others insist on using deceptive and manipulative tactics against me? Must I remain defenseless? Not necessarily. If the members of an organization know that certain kinds of covert political tactics are in common use within an organization, and if, nonetheless, they freely choose to remain within the organization and become skillful in using and defending themselves against these tactics, then one can presume that these organizational members have tacitly consented to having those kinds of covert political tactics used against themselves. They have freely agreed to play an organizational game, as it were, in which everyone knows that fooling the other players and maneuvering them out of winning positions is all part of the game. Dealing with them on the basis of this tacit consent would not violate their right to be treated as they have freely and knowingly chosen to be treated.

However, the use of deceptive or manipulative political tactics is clearly unethical when: (1) they are used against persons who do not know, or do not expect, that these kinds of tactics will be used against themselves or (2) they are used against persons who are not free to leave the organization in which these tactics are being used or (3) they are used against persons who are not skilled at defending themselves against these tactics. Using a deceptive or manipulative tactic in any of these instances violates the moral respect due to persons, especially if the tactic injures a person by maneuvering the person into unknowingly acting against his or her own best interests.

The equity of the consequences   Political tactics can create injustices by distorting the equality of treatment that justice demands. An individual who controls an organization's budget or information system, for example, may covertly administer that system unjustly by showing favoritism to those persons or groups who can advance the individual's career. Such political tactics blatantly violate the basic principle of distributive justice discussed earlier: Individuals who are similar in all relevant respects should be treated similarly, and individuals who are dissimilar in relevant respects should be treated dissimilarly in proportion to their dissimilarity.

Political tactics can also create injustices among those employees who have few or no political skills. Those without political skills are easily maneuvered into accepting a smaller share of the organization's benefits than their abilities or needs may merit in comparison to others. Benefits are then no longer distributed to these people on the basis of their relevant characteristics: An injustice is committed against them.

Not only can political tactics leave others better or worse off than they deserve, but politics can also be used to gain unjust advantages for oneself. An engineer who is competing with another engineer for promotion to department head, for example, may cultivate and flatter her superiors, while simultaneously using innuendo to discredit her rival. As a result she may get the promotion, even though the other engineer was more qualified. Using political tactics in this way to acquire advantages on the basis of nonrelevant characteristics is also unjust.

In addition to these immediate inequities, the prolonged prevalence of political tactics within an organization can generate long-term and debilitating organizational effects. Several researchers have found that the use of power in organizations tends to routinize the dehumanized treatment of less powerful individuals. David Kipnis, for example, found that individuals who exercise power find themselves increasingly tempted to "(a) increase their attempts to influence the behavior of the less powerful, (b) devalue the worth of the performance of the less powerful, (c) attribute the cause of the less powerful's efforts to power controlled by themselves rather than to the less powerful's motivations to do well, (d) view the less powerful as objects of manipulation, and (e) express a preference for the maintenance of psychological distance from the less powerful."[81] Power, in short, corrupts.

Chris Argyris and others have maintained, on the other hand, that those who are controlled by the powerful, "tend to feel frustration, conflict, and feelings of failure," that they "adapt" by leaving the organization, by trying to climb the organization's ladder, by retreating to aggression, daydreaming, regression, or simple apathy; and that the organization itself becomes characterized by competition, rivalry, and hostility.[82] In deciding whether to use political tactics, the individual should seriously consider, therefore, the long-range consequences that the exercise of power implied by these tactics can have on oneself and on others.

QUESTIONS FOR REVIEW AND DISCUSSION

1. Define the following concepts: the rational model of the organization, employee's obligations to the firm, law of agency, conflict of interest, actual/potential conflicts of interest, commercial bribe, commercial extortion, morality of accepting gifts, insider information, theft, fair wage, OSHA, unfairly imposed employee risk, horizontal/vertical job specialization, job satisfaction, the political model of the organization, power, government-management analogy, right to privacy, physical/psychological privacy, relevance, consent, extraordinary methods, right to freedom of conscience, whistleblowing, right to participate, right to due process, organizational politics, political tactics.

2. Relate the theory of the employee's obligations to the firm in this chapter to the discussion on contractual rights and duties in Chapter Two. Relate the

---

[81] David Kipnis, "Does Power Corrupt?," *Journal of Personality and Social Psychology*, 24, no. 1 (1972): 33.

[82] Chris Argyris, *Personality and Organization* (New York: Harper & Brothers, 1957), pp. 232–37.

six criteria for just wages in this chapter to the various standards of justice developed in Chapter Two. Relate the problems of job satisfaction described in this chapter to the discussion of alienation in Chapter Three. Relate the discussions of employee rights in this chapter to the theory of moral rights developed in Chapter Two.

3. Compare and contrast the rational model of the organization with the political model of the organization. Would you agree with the following statement: "The rational model of the organization implies that the corporation is based on consent, while the political model implies that the corporation is based on force"? Which of the two models do you think provides the more adequate view of the university? Of the company you work for? Explain your answers.

4. In view of the contractual agreement that every employee makes to be loyal to the employer, do you think whistleblowing is ever morally justified? Explain your answer.

5. Do you agree or disagree with the claim that corporate managements are so similar to governments that employees should be recognized as having the same "civil rights" as citizens have?

CASES FOR DISCUSSION

DBCP

For over a year, rumors had been circulating among the workers of the Occidental Chemical Plant in Lathrop, California that the men working in their Agricultural Chemical Division were unable to have children. In June of 1977, the union asked some of their men to volunteer for semen analysis. Seven people volunteered. All had abnormally low sperm counts. Follow-up studies on five of the men on July 22 showed that they were functionally sterile. All had been involved in the production of Dibromochloropropane (DBCP).[1] News of the sterility among the workers in the Occidental plant sent shock waves through the industry. The two major producers of DBCP, Dow Chemical and Shell Chemical, were especially concerned about their workers. Subsequent tests of 432 DBCP workers in California, Colorado and Arkansas revealed that one third had been rendered infertile by DBCP.[2]

DBCP is a widely used pesticide. In 1951 Dow discovered that DBCP was a highly effective soil fumigant capable of eliminating small worms that attack the root systems of corn, soybeans, grapes, citrus, peaches, figs, walnuts, pineapples, and other crops. After carrying out initial toxicology tests from 1952 to 1954, Dow concluded that, although DBCP produced slight skin irritations and was highly toxic when taken orally or when its vapors were inhaled, it could be used safely when

[1] U.S. Congress, Senate, *Worker Safety in Pesticide Production: Hearings before the Subcommittee on Agricultural Research and General Legislation of the Committee on Agriculture, Nutrition, and Forestry,* 95th Congress, 1st session, 13 and 14 December 1977, pp. 3–5.

[2] Ronald B. Taylor, "Pesticides," *San Jose Mercury,* 1 July 1979, p. 1F.

handled carefully in well-ventilated areas. By 1957 Dow was manufacturing and selling DBCP. The labels included the following warnings:

> Warning. Harmful liquid and vapor; causes skin irritation and blisters on prolonged contact; avoid breathing vapor; avoid contact with eyes, skin, and clothing; do not take internally; and use only with adequate ventilation.[3]

Shell started its production of DBCP in 1955 after commissioning several research studies by the University of California to determine the toxicologic properties of DBCP. These tests also showed DBCP was toxic when taken orally or inhaled but revealed "no indications of testicular effect."[4]

In 1958 Shell received a "confidential report" from a University of California researcher, Dr. Charles Hine, describing the results that inhaling DBCP had on rats. The rats were exposed to DBCP fumes in concentrations of 5, 10, 20, and 40 ppm (parts per million) five days a week for ten weeks. No rats survived 40 ppm. Subsequent autopsy showed damage to the liver, lung, kidney, brain, adrenals, and testes of the rats. "Testes decreased in size at 5 ppm, but the difference was not significant until 10 ppm."[5] Since Shell had partially funded the study, the information was considered the confidential property of Shell.

In 1961 the results of the Shell study were combined with the results of a similar study of the effects of DBCP on rats, guinea pigs, rabbits, and monkeys that Dr. T. Torkelson had carried out for Dow. The combined study was published in 1961 in the *Journal of Toxicology and Applied Pharmacology*. The joint study concluded in part:

> The most striking observation at autopsy [of the animal] was severe atrophy and degeneration of the testes of all species. In the rats this was characterized by degenerative changes in the seminiferous tubules, an increase in sertoli's cells, a reduction in the numbers of sperm cells, development of abnormal forms of sperm cells . . . Until further experience is obtained, close observation of the health of the people exposed to this compound should be maintained.[6]

The Torkelson-Hine study recommended that occupational exposure to DBCP be controlled to less than 1 ppm in air.

Dow and Shell submitted the results of the Torkelson study to the federal government in 1961 to obtain registration of DBCP in accordance with a new law that had been passed in 1959. After submitting the study to the federal government, Dow asked that the information be treated as a confidential trade secret and that it not be revealed to competing companies seeking to register their products.[7] Al-

---

[3] *Worker Safety in Pesticide Production*, p. 120.
[4] *Ibid.*, p. 126.
[5] *Ibid.*, p. 126.
[6] *Ibid.*, pp. 24, 25.
[7] *Ibid.*, p. 28.

though the study had already been published in a public journal, Dow now held that, since Dow had paid for the study, the information was proprietary and that competing companies should pay for their own registration studies.

> One of the primary reasons for our efforts to protect our health and safety data as trade secret is the major competitive harm that would result from its release. We cannot afford to continue to spend millions of dollars each year on pesticides research if our data are to be made publicly available. Such release would permit our competitors, both here and abroad, to enter the market in competition with us for a fraction of the cost and with very little of the risk. . . . therefore, in order to protect our own business interests and proprietary rights, as well as the viability of the free enterprise system, we are compelled to seek judicial relief for the protection of our valuable scientific data . . . [T]he cost of registration of pesticides has become so immense that some protection of our competitive position is essential if the pesticide industry in this country is to continue its investment in the research necessary to develop safer and more effective pesticides. [Statement of Dow representative] [8]

In spite of the recommendation in the Torkelson study that workers exposed to DBCP be kept under "close observation," and in spite of the evidence of testicular damage caused by DBCP, neither Dow Chemical nor Shell Chemical carried out sperm tests on those workers involved in the production of DBCP between 1955 and 1977.

> In 1961, we weren't in the habit of thinking in terms of sperm and getting these kinds of tests. In fact, even today this is a difficult problem. It is a difficult problem because of social difficulties that people may have, because of church attitudes. In no way have we been able to get a 100 percent response for sperm. [Statement of Dow representative] [9]

But why weren't the workers made aware of the results of the studies and informed that sperm tests were available to them? Couldn't workers then decide for themselves (as they did after the revelations of sterility among Occidental workers) whether to take the sperm tests or to refrain because of "church," "social," or other reasons? When asked these questions, a Dow spokesman replied as follows:

> I can only surmise that in the early 1960s and late 1950s, chlorinated and brominated compounds were known to have caused a big impact on kidney and liver. This is what the doctors were monitoring for . . . But the feeling was, when . . . you look at liver, and you look at spleen, and you look at heart, these, too, are organs of concern. . . . If one was to look at the medical information and go back to the historical observations of people you will find that most of the studies were done on kidney, on liver, on passage of urine, on feces, on many of these kinds of observational studies. Blood sampl-

[8]*Ibid.*, p. 28.
[9]*Ibid.*, p. 24.

ing and sperm tests were just not part of a routine physical examination. [Statement of Dow representative] [10]

The position of Shell Chemical was similar:

[Until] the recent past, industrial physicians did not consider the testes as a primary target organ, concern was for such organs as the liver, kidney, and lungs . . . Significantly, neither the 1958 nor the 1961 reports recommended explicitly doing fertility testing or measuring sperm density. They did indicate an apparent less dense sperm concentration in those animals which showed significant, discernible testicular degeneration . . . The logical conclusion was that the decreased sperm counts were secondary to the atrophy [reduction in size] of the testes. And so, the conclusion at that time by practitioners in occupational health was that if the DBCP concentration was kept within the limits recommended and that if the testicular integrity was maintained, there was no reason, given the state-of-the-art at that time, to do sperm testing on workers. [Statement of Shell Chemical representative] [11]

The National Cancer Institute undertook studies of the possible carcinogenic effect of DBCP on rats in 1972. A large number of the rats developed stomach tumors after DBCP was orally administered. This result was published in summary abstract form in 1975 and in final form in 1977. In 1979 Hazelton Laboratories completed a study of the effects on rats of inhaling DBCP at the low-dose levels encountered in plants manufacturing DBCP. After reading a preliminary draft of the study, a scientist is reported as saying "those rats had tumors all the way up to their brains. We're going to have an outbreak of similar problems in workers, I'm pretty sure."[12]

After being informed of the sterility found among DBCP workers in the Occidental plant, Dow and Shell suspended production of DBCP in August 1977. Officials of the two companies held that the cost of protecting workers against DBCP were greater than the slim profits that could be made from its sales.[13] First Dow (on August 25, 1977) and then Shell (August 26) announced a recall of all DBCP.

Although the federal EPA had banned all uses of DBCP shortly after the sterile workers were discovered in 1977, pressures from agricultural interests led EPA assistant director, Steven D. Jellinek, to lift the ban partially on September 19, 1978. DBCP remained illegal for use on most vegetables, but it could be manufactured and used on gardens (home gardens, golf courses, public parks), pineapples, tree fruit, grapes, and ornamental flowers so long as EPA label restrictions were followed and so long as manufacturers allowed work-place concentrations of no more than one-part-per-billion. Dow and Shell declined to resume production of DBCP,

[10]*Ibid.*, pp. 24, 25, 26.
[11]*Ibid.*, p. 32.
[12]Taylor, "Pesticides."
[13]*Ibid.*

but Amvac Chemical Corporation of Los Angeles was soon producing some 2,500 gallons per day.[14]

The Environmental Protection Agency has pointed out that if the pesticide were completely banned, farmers would suffer a $400 million loss from crop damages in the first three years of the ban.[15] A citrus grower in California has reported that, since 1977 when he stopped using DBCP in his 25-acre lemon grove in California, "production has gone from 1,400 boxes to 800 boxes, to less than 300 boxes."

1. In your judgment, did Dow and Shell before 1977 do all they should have done for workers involved in the manufacture of DBCP? Explain your answer in terms of the ethical principles that you believe are involved.

2. In your judgment, did Dow and Shell do all they should have done for workers who might use their products? Explain.

3. In your judgment, were Dow and Shell morally responsible for the sterility of the DBCP workers?

4. Do you agree with Dow's arguments for classifying health studies as "trade secrets"?

5. In view of the potential crop losses predicted by the EPA, do you think it would be morally permissible to manufacture DBCP so long as potential employees were informed of the risks involved?

Bendix Politics

On September 24, 1980, William Agee, chairman of Bendix Corporation was scheduled to address a special meeting of 600 company staff members at Bendix headquarters in Southfield, Michigan. There was plenty to talk about since under Agee's leadership the company was undergoing a major change in direction and a controversial major internal reorganization. Not only were employees concerned that theirs might be one of the dozens of jobs that would be cut from the new organization, there was also some residual uneasiness over Agee's firing of William Panny, the former president, and the simultaneous resignation of Jerome Jacobson, the former executive vice-president for strategic planning. At the meeting Agee planned to announce his choice for Jacobson's replacement: Mary Cunningham, a young (twenty-nine year old) Harvard Business School Graduate who had been with Bendix for fifteen months. There was a problem, however.

As he usually did when preparing a meeting, Agee solicited reports from his senior executives concerning what they felt were the most significant issues on the minds of Bendix employees. One of the items that appeared was a concern over the nature of the relationship between Agee and Cunningham and the rising rumors over what was termed "this whole female thing." Since Mary Cunningham's arrival at Bendix she had been working closely with Bill Agee, and he had quickly promoted her from his executive assistant to vice-president for corporate and public affairs.

[14] *Ibid.*, p. 2F.
[15] *Ibid.*, p. 1F.

Both handsome people, the two necessarily worked and traveled together and gossip started when first Cunningham and then Agee separated from their spouses. As one Bendix staff member put it:

> There were rumors for a long time, and they just grew and grew. The two of them were seen together at the GOP convention [in July 1980]. The TV camera panned in on them, with Agee on one side of Gerald Ford and Mary on [Agee's] other [side], and people thought it was really stupid of them to be seen like that. But they acted like they didn't care. And with her being his top business aide, they traveled all over the country together. That got tongues to wagging. It was almost inevitable.[1]

Agee decided to deal with the rumors. At the September 24th meeting with 600 employees present, he announced Mary Cunningham's promotion to vice-president for strategic planning, and then made the following statement:

> I know it has been buzzing around that Mary Cunningham's rise in this company is very unusual and that it has something to do with a personal relationship we have. Sure it's unusual. Her rise in this company is unusual because she's a very unusual and very talented individual. It is true that we are very close friends and she's a very close friend of my family. But that has nothing to do with the way that I and others in this company evaluate performance. Her rapid promotions are totally justified.[2]

If the announcement was intended to lay "the female issue" to rest, it failed. Prior to the meeting, William Agee had received a telephone call from a newspaper reporter who indicated that some Bendix people who were unhappy with Agee had gotten in touch with him. They were planning to "leak" Agee's statement to the press. It might be better, the reporter had suggested, if Agee allowed him to be present at the meeting. Agee had acquiesced. The day after the meeting the reporter printed the story, rumors and all, on the front page of a Detroit newspaper. By evening, the story had hit the news wires, and over the next few days it became national news.

The event focused national attention on Bendix at the very time the organization was undergoing substantial changes. Some of the changes dated back to 1976 when William Agee took over the chairmanship of Bendix after W. Michael Blumenthal left the job to become secretary of the treasury under President Jimmy Carter. William Agee introduced a new, more open style of management into Bendix. The year after he took over as chairman he installed a special telephone line through which employees could contact him directly with complaints. He got rid of the large meeting table in the center of the headquarters' meeting room and replaced it with large comfortable chairs. He discarded the policy of reserving the best company

---

[1] *The Detroit News,* 5 October 1980, p. 4C.

[2] See *Newsweek,* 6 October 1980, p. 79; and *Wall Street Journal,* 26 September 1980, p. 33.

parking space for himself, saying that it was deserved by the person who arrived first at work each day.

The most important changes, however, grew out of a need to reevaluate the company's major operations. Ranked as the 88th largest industrial company in the United States, Bendix sales had been steadily growing. In 1979 sales were $3.8 billion, up from $2.6 billion in 1975, and profits were $162.6 million, up from 1975 profits of $79.8 million. Bendix had large operations, however, in the automotive industry and in the forest products industry, and neither of these industries was doing well. DBA, its largest foreign automotive subsidiary, in fact, had a long history of deficits. And its forest products plants had been unable to develop more efficient technologies. As a consequence, Bendix earnings from these operations had started to slide and only its income from other investments had kept Bendix's overall income high. One obvious solution was to dispose of its holdings in these industries and to buy into other more profitable businesses.

When William Agee took over the helm of Bendix, he hired William P. Panny as president (formerly a vice-president of Rockwell International) to assist him in these changes. It was widely thought that eventually Panny would succeed Agee. Together, the two of them sold off a large part of the ailing DBA automotive subsidiary, reduced its work force, and closed some of its plants. By 1980, a much reduced DBA would once again be operating in the black. Moreover, by 1979 Agee had begun work on selling off the Bendix forest products business. In September of 1980, he announced the completion of negotiations to sell off the forest products operations for $435 million. Other divestitures and further diversifications were in the offing.

During these major change-overs, disagreements had begun to emerge between Agee and Panny. In 1978, William Agee felt that Bendix should purchase ASARCO, a mining company which had lost $30 million in 1977. Agee believed that ASARCO would be worth much more in the future than the then depressed price of its stock indicated. But Panny argued against the purchase as unreasonable and held that at most Bendix should purchase 20 percent of the company. Panny carried the day with the Bendix management team and only 20 percent of ASARCO was purchased. The next year ASARCO's profits climbed to $259 million and the price of its stock doubled.

More important, however, was a disagreement over whether Bendix should abandon the automotive business altogether. Agee's publicly stated view was that the automobile industry was "in the winter of its life."[3] Panny, however, disagreed. Bendix had been in the automotive industry for decades and the company had acquired great familiarity and experience with its workings. It would be unwise, Panny felt, to turn from a well-known business to others in which the company had little experience and with which its employees were not familiar.

In June of 1979 Agee hired Mary Cunningham to serve as his executive assistant. Mary Cunningham was described as an "unusually brilliant," "uncommonly

[3]Peter W. Bernstein, "Upheaval at Bendix," *Fortune,* 3 November 1980, p. 52.

ambitious," "politically astute," "beautiful," "sophisticated," "poised" woman with "high ideals." Almost immediately after arriving from the Harvard Business School, she was assigned to put her extensive financial analytical skills to work on some major Bendix investment projects. One of her largest projects was an analysis of the possible acquisition of the Warner and Swasey Company, a machine-tool business. The investment looked good. Bendix already had a machine-tool business that, together with the acquisition of Warner and Swasey, would make Bendix the second largest U.S. machine-tool builder. Relying on the analysis, Agee purchased Warner and Swasey in April 1980 for $300 million. The buy paid off: Warner and Swasey was holding $65 million in liquid assets and $40 million in stock, which, when disposed of, made their real purchase price $195 million.

In June of 1980, Bill Agee promoted Mary Cunningham, then only twenty-nine, to vice-president for corporate and public affairs. (The move was not unusual for Agee; in 1979 he had promoted Bernard B. Winograd, who was then twenty-eight, to corporate treasurer.) By now the two were working closely together. A company staff person described her with the words: "She's his key advisor; she counsels him on the most important things in the company."[4] But some insiders sensed trouble. Later, a Bendix executive commented, "She is very smart and she knows how corporations work—that's how she's done so well—but when it came to her relationship with Bill Agee, she didn't act smart, she didn't use her political sense."[5]

Several Bendix managers now began to complain that Cunningham had too much access to Agee and that he was becoming increasingly inaccessible to others. Said one official:

> People don't like the way she conducts herself. She's not as careful as she should be. She's always invoking the chairman's authority for everything she does. Mary has so clearly identified herself with him that people don't feel they can question her or contradict her.[6]

The feelings of the managers were further ruffled when Agee had Cunningham carry out an in-depth analysis of Bendix's automotive business in June 1980. Mary Cunningham angered several managers when she inspected the floors of the automotive plants without first telling the plant managers that she was going to do so. Bendix managers (including Mr. Panny) afterwards harshly criticized the three-volume analysis that Mary Cunningham and her seven-person staff (derisively referred to as "Snow White and the Seven Dwarfs") had produced. The Cunningham report, according to the managers, was unenlightening and did not contain anything they did not already know.[7]

[4] *Wall Street Journal,* 26 September 1980, p. 33.

[5] *San Jose Mercury,* 10 October 1980, p. 20A.

[6] S. Freedberg, G. Storch, and C. Teegartin, "Two At the Top," *The Detroit News,* 5 October 1980, p. 5C.

[7] Bernstein, "Upheaval at Bendix," p. 52.

Agee's reorganization of the company had now started to move into its internal affairs. In early 1980 Agee announced that the company would be internally reorganized. Up to this time Bendix had been highly centralized: Most company divisions were run out of corporate headquarters in Southfield near Detroit. Agee intended to make the divisions much more autonomous. Panny, however, strongly opposed the reorganization, arguing that the company was not ready to be decentralized and that the employees did not want it.

In September 1980, Agee fired Panny. According to *Fortune Magazine* it was rumored in Detroit that several Bendix executives had earlier gone to Panny to "complain" about Cunningham's relationship to Agee.[8] Panny, according to the *Fortune* rumor, was "planning" to bring the matter to the Bendix board of directors, but Agee fired him before he had the chance. A few hours later, Jerome Jacobson, a Bendix executive, resigned from his position as vice-president for strategic planning.

Matters then became more heated. According to author Gail Sheehy, who interviewed both Cunningham and Agee, "anonymous letters" now began to be sent to Bendix board members, making "malicious references" to the conduct of the pair.[9] The letters, according to Sheehy, urged board members, to "investigate their relationship" at once.

Agee acted quickly. First he arranged meetings with Bendix's top managers and with the board's executive committee. To each group he said the same thing: The rumors going around were utterly false; he and Cunningham had "no romantic involvement."[10] Then he moved to promote Mary Cunningham to the vacated position of vice-president for strategic planning. At the fateful company meeting of September 24, he announced her promotion, and simultaneously attempted to lay "the female issue" to rest. The next day, however, the story was reported in the nation's newspapers along with the rumors suggesting that Mary Cunningham's rapid promotions were due to her "romantic involvement" with Bill Agee.

The day the news broke in the papers, Mary Cunningham decided she had to move quickly if she was to out maneuver "them." (She did not know who had sent the anonymous letters.) Her first instinct was to resign, since this would prevent the board from firing her first and would ensure that Bill Agee would not be compromised by her continuing presence in the company. But by the next day she had instead decided to request a temporary leave of absence from the company. This tactic would leave her with a palatable option should the board want her to leave, but at the same time it would pressure the board to take the option of retaining her. Since the board had publicly approved her promotion only a few days earlier, it would probably not be willing to reverse itself publicly so soon afterwards. Conse-

[8]*Ibid.*, p. 53.
[9]Gail Sheehy, "Cunningham Encounters the Mildew of Envy," *Detroit Free Press,* 13 October 1980, p. 4B.
[10]Bernstein, "Upheaval at Bendix,", p. 54.

quently, on September 28, she submitted to the board a letter requesting an "immediate but temporary" leave which "should not be construed in any sense as tantamount to resignation." The letter continued by explaining that a resignation would set "a dangerous precedent" because it would enable "female executives to be forced out of a company through malicious gossip" and would also "tend to confirm the most base and erroneous assumptions suggested by the media."[11]

The next afternoon a committee comprised of a few members of the Bendix board of directors met and decided to announce in the name of the board that they had "complete confidence" in Mary Cunningham and that "it would be unjust for a corporation to respond to speculation in the media by accepting her request."[12] After the meeting, one of the board members gave her a bit of advice: She should be careful because she was being used by others to get at Bill Agee and if the thing went on for much longer Agee's position would be in danger.[13]

The drama was not yet over. Mary Cunningham was still unsure whether it might not be better for her to resign. When the full board met a few days later and the members discussed the issue among themselves, a large number felt that she should not continue on at Bendix. Too many difficulties would confront her if she continued in her present role, they felt. This was made known to Cunningham. Subsequently, on October 9, she issued another statement:

> I have submitted my resignation, effective today, as an officer of the Bendix Corporation . . . I am convinced that the unusual convergence of events beyond my control has substantially impaired my ability to carry out my responsibilities as a corporate officer of Bendix . . . I am grateful for the many supportive communications from the business community and others concerned with the right to be judged on merit alone.[14]

1. List all the political tactics that you think were used by the various parties involved in the case. Explain why you classify these as "political tactics."

2. In your judgment, were any of these political tactics morally legitimate? Were any morally illegitimate? Explain your answer in terms of the relevant moral principles involved.

3. Was William Panny treated fairly? Was Mary Cunningham treated fairly? Explain your answer fully.

4. Is it possible to eliminate from an organization the kinds of political tactics that you think were being used in Bendix? If you do not think it is possible, explain why; if you think it is possible, describe the methods by which such tactics can be eliminated.

[11] *San Jose Mercury,* 1 October 1980, p. 12A.

[12] *Ibid.*

[13] Gail Sheehy, "Cunningham's Idealism Gets Lost in Corporate Jungle," *Detroit Free Press,* 14 October 1980, p. 3B.

[14] *Detroit Free Press,* 10 October 1980, p. 15A.

The Coors Polygraph Test

On April 5, 1977, the members of Brewery Workers Local No. 366 walked off the job at the Adolf Coors Brewery Plant in Golden, Colorado.[1] The wildcat strike was motivated in part by Coors's use of lie detector tests in a preemployment examination required of prospective employees. Said an officer of the union: "When you get through being grilled on that lie detector, you feel dirty."[2]

To support their case the union collected several notarized affidavits in which striking employees alleged that the company had asked them improper questions during the lie detector test. Two of the notarized affidavits read in part as follows:[3]

> In April of 1973, I, John A. K _____ , had to submit to a polygraph test for employment at the Adolph Coors Company in Golden, Colorado. Of the many personal questions asked, the two listed below were particularly aggravating.
> 1. Are you a homosexual?
> 2. Do you know of any reason that you could be blackmailed?

> I, Oliver A. D._____ , was hired by the Adolph Coors Company on October 23, 1972. Below are listed some of the questions I was asked on the lie detector while going through my screening for a job.
>> Do you get along with your wife?
>> What is your sex preference?
>> Are you a communist?
>> Do you have money in the bank?
>> Have you ever stolen anything and was [sic] not caught at it?
> I feel that these questions were degrading and an invasion of my privacy. I also feel these questions are unnecessary for the Coors Company to ask of anyone seeking a job with them.

Coors executives responded to these allegations by saying that they did not know these alleged questions were being asked of their prospective employees. The polygraph questionnaires, they said, were administered by an outside agency which Coors had hired before 1975.[4]

However, Coors was unwilling to give up using polygraph tests altogether. In 1960, a member of the Coors family had been kidnapped and killed. In August 1977, a bomb was planted in a Coors recycling plant. Chairman William Coors and his brother, Joseph Coors, both said they wanted to ensure that they did not hire someone who might again endanger their families or their employees. In addition, the Coors brothers felt that the polygraph tests would reveal some information that the company should have:

[1] "Bitter Beercott," *Time,* 26 December 1977, p. 15.

[2] *Ibid.*

[3] Copies of these affidavits were obtained from Brewery Bottling, Can and Allied Industrial Union-Local No. 366; 4510 Indiana Street, Golden, Colorado.

[4] "Bitter Beercott."

[The tests reveal] whether the applicant may be hiding some health problem ... [and ensure that] the applicant does not want the job for some subversive reason such as sabotaging our operation. [Statement of William Coors]

Coors therefore continued to use the polygraph test but formulated a standard questionnaire that the polygraph agency was to use in the preemployment examination. The new questionnaire consisted of seven question areas. Before a job applicant even made an appointment with the polygraph agency, the applicant was given a copy of the questions and was asked to review the questions carefully. If he had any hesitations about answering the questions on a lie detector, he was invited to discuss his problems with the employment staff. The seven questions were as follows:

1. Did you tell the complete truth on the employment application?
2. Have you ever used any form of illegal drug or narcotic on the job?
3. Has the use of alcohol frequently impaired your ability to perform on the job?
4. Are you concealing any information about subversive, revolutionary, or communistic activity?
5. Are you applying for a job with this company so you can do it or any of its employees harm?
6. Are you presently wanted by the authorities for a felony?
7. Have you ever stolen any kind of merchandise, material, or money from an employer?[5]

Coors assured each applicant that these were the only questions that he or she had to answer. The polygraph agency was to adhere to the questionnaire.

1. Would Coors have been justified in using a polygraph and in asking the questions alleged in the notarized affidavits? Explain your answer fully in terms of the ethical principles involved.
2. Was Coors justified in using a polygraph to gather responses to any or all of the seven questions in its revised questionnaire? Explain your answer fully.
3. Could Coors have protected its interests by using any other methods? Explain your answer fully.

---

[5]A copy of the questionnaire was also obtained from Brewery Bottling, Can, and Allied Industrial Union-Local No. 366.

INDEX